ASPECTS OF LOUISBOURG

The Louisbourg Institute

ASPECTS OF LOUISBOURG

Edited by
Eric Krause
Carol Corbin
William O'Shea

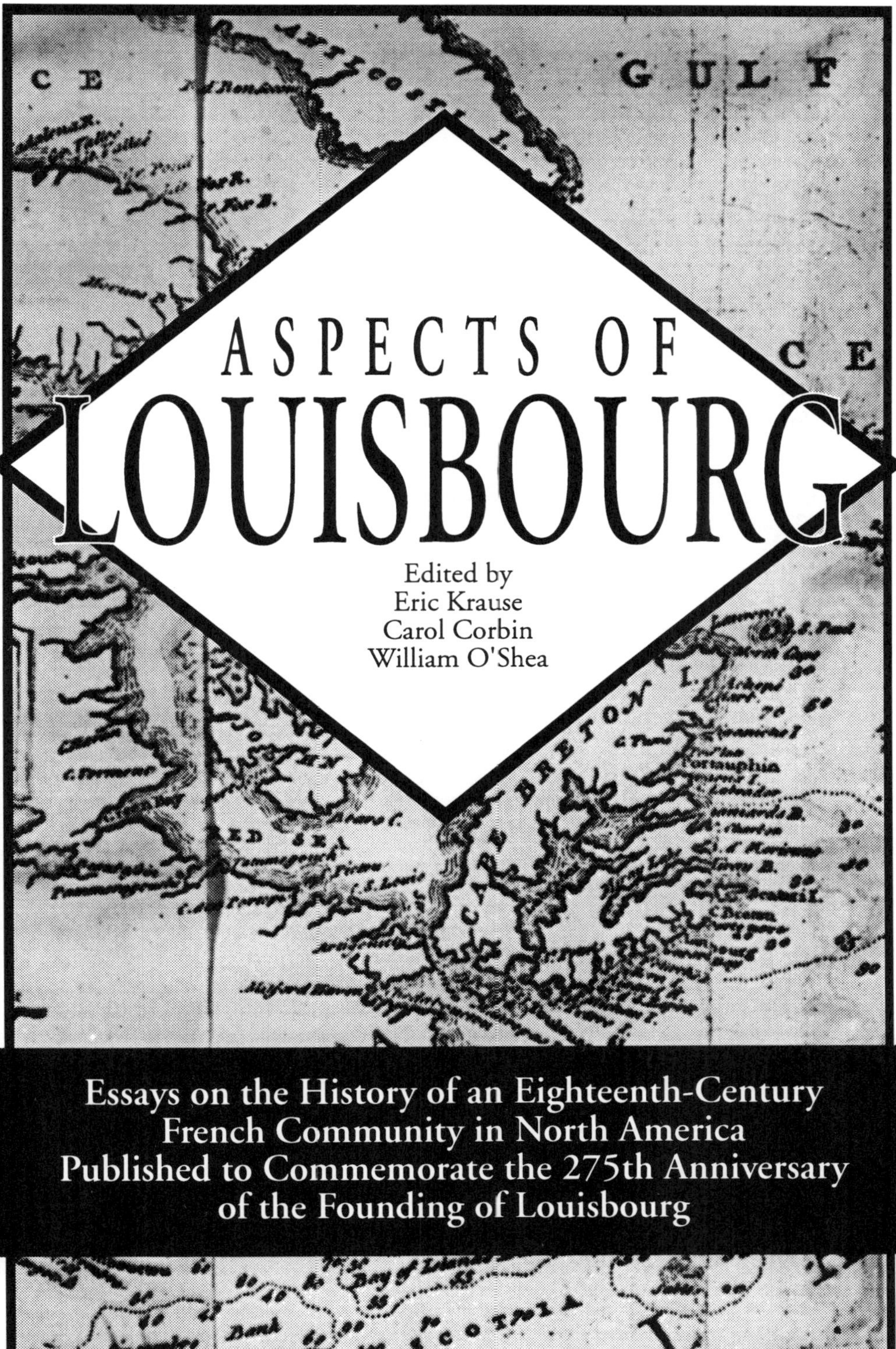

Map: McCord Museum U/A Gentleman's Magazine, January 1746, opposite page 72

Essays on the History of an Eighteenth-Century
French Community in North America
Published to Commemorate the 275th Anniversary
of the Founding of Louisbourg

The University College of Cape Breton Press
University College of Cape Breton
P.O. Box 5300
Sydney, Nova Scotia B1P 6L2 Canada

© Copyright 1995 by The Louisbourg Institute
All rights reserved, First Published 1995
Printed in Canada.

Canadian Cataloguing-in-Publication Data

Main entry under title:

"Published to commemorate the 275th anniversary of the founding of Louisbourg"
Includes bibliographical references.
ISBN 0-92033-676-0

1. Louisbourg (N.S.) -- History. 2. Louisbourg (N.S.) -- Antiquities. I. Krause, Eric, 1943- II. Corbin, Carol. III. O'Shea, William A.

FC2349.L6A86 1995   971.695501   C95-950215-7
F1039.5.L8A86 1995

Aspects of Louisbourg

Articles previously published in *Proceedings of The Seventeenth Meeting of the French Colonial Historical Society, "An Appearance of Strength": The Fortifications of Louisbourg, Histoire Sociale-Social History, Acadiensis, Material History Bulletin/Bulletin d'histoire de la culture matérialle, Nova Scotia Historical Review, Journal of Garden History, The Cod Fishery of Isle Royale, Publications of the Colonial Society of Massachusetts, The Northern Mariner/Le Marin du Nord,* and *Archivaria.*

Illustrations:
Front cover: (photograph) the reconstructed King's Bastion, courtesy of the Fortress of Louisbourg National Historic Site; 18th-century map photo courtesy of the McCord Museum of Canadian History, Montreal, M3577, 1746. *A New Chart of the Coast of New England, Nova Scotia, New France or Canada, with the Islands of Newfoundld. Cape Breton St. John's &'c...,* Nicholas Bellin, Etching, Ink laid on paper.
Back cover: Fortress of Louisbourg interpreter, photograph courtesy of the Fortress of Louisbourg National Historic Site; 18th century map photo courtesy of the Bibliothèque Nationale de France, Paris, Cabinet des Estampes, VD-20a-44, 1729. *CARTE DES ENVIRONS DE LOUISBOURG en l'Jsle Royale 1729.*
Military title page: Photo courtesy of the Anne S. K. Brown Military Collection, Brown University Library, Providence, Rhode Island, 1725.

CONTENTS

Foreword
William A. O'Shea
iii

List of Abbrevations
vii

INTRODUCTION
From port de pêche to ville fortifiée:
The Evolution of Urban Louisbourg, 1713-1758
A.J.B. Johnston
3

MILITARY
"An appearance of strength":
The Fortifications of Louisbourg
Bruce W. Fry
19

Mutiny at Louisbourg, December 1744
Allan Greer
70

Another Soldiers' Revolt in Ile Royale, June 1750
Allan Greer
110

SOCIAL
Communities and Families: Family Life and
Living Conditions in Eighteenth-Century Louisbourg
Kenneth Donovan
117

The People of Eighteenth-Century Louisbourg
A.J.B. Johnston
150

The Gardens of 18th-Century Louisbourg
Anne O'Neill
162

ECONOMICS

The Cod Fishery of Isle Royale, 1713-1758
B.A. Balcom
169

The Fishermen of Eighteenth-Century Cape Breton:
Numbers and Origins
A.J.B. Johnston
198

The Price and Profits of Accommodation:
Massachusetts - Louisbourg Trade, 1713-1744
Donald F. Chard
209

The Other Louisbourg: Trade and Merchant Enterprise
in Ile Royale, 1713-1758
Christopher Moore
228

PRESERVATION CONSERVATION RESEARCH

Preserving History: The Commemoration
of 18th-Century Louisbourg, 1895-1940
A.J.B. Johnston
253

Commemorating Louisbourg, c.1767
A.J.B. Johnston
286

The Concept of the Louisbourg Underwater Museum
Robert Grenier
289

The Fortress of Louisbourg Archives:
The First Twenty-Five Years
Eric Krause
296

Illustrations

Foreword

The eighteenth-century French community of Louisbourg, located on Cape Breton Island at the entrance to the Gulf of St. Lawrence, flourished from 1713 to 1758. Established as a base for the cod fishery, its strategically-located and relatively ice-free harbour made it an important port and trading centre. The French government fortified the town and the harbour with a complex of bastioned walls and detached batteries and installed a garrison to protect the town and the civilian population. Each summer the harbour was filled with ships from France, the West Indies, Québec and New England.

The economic success of Louisbourg, a desire to control the North Atlantic fishery, and a convenient European war between France and England provided the impetus for an attack in 1745 organized by New England mercantile interests and supported by an English naval squadron. Garrisoned by English troops during four years, Louisbourg was returned to France by treaty in 1749 and came to life again, more successfully than before. In 1758, as part of a worldwide effort by England to destroy the French empire, Louisbourg was again besieged and defeated. The fortress walls were systematically levelled in 1760 and the town garrisoned by British troops for another decade.

By the last quarter of the 18th century the garrison was gone, and the majority of the inhabitants moved on to Halifax or the new capital at Sydney. Those buildings which had not fallen into ruin were mined for brick, cut stone and iron hardware. Louisbourg slowly disappeared under mounds of grass. Its population throughout most of the 19th century consisted of a small number of families of Irish farmers and fishers — some of whom traced their ancestry to soldiers in the Louisbourg garrison after 1758.

But the colonial town was never forgotten, and in 1895 the Society of Colonial Wars erected a monument on the occasion of the 150th anniversary of the siege of 1745. In the early part of the century there were attempts to acquire the land and stabilize the casemates. Louisbourg was declared a National Historic Site in 1926 and a

National Historic Park in 1940. In the mid-1930s a modest museum was constructed and major building foundations stabilized as part of Depression make-work programmes.

The collapse of the coal industry on Cape Breton in the late 1950s led to a Royal Commission report that suggested a diversified economy for the area. One recommendation was a major project to rebuild a portion of the original fortified town of Louisbourg. The generation-long undertaking called on the skills of archaeologists, historians, conservators, curators, artisans, and interpreters. One product of this effort is a major interpretive model of Canada's past with sound academic underpinnings. Canada's premier living history interpretive programme is reflected in the physical reconstruction of buildings and fortifications, in exhibits, furnishings and costumes. Another, perhaps more signicficant, product is a unique databank of information about 18th-century French construction and military and civilian experiences.

These essays are a sampling of the historical and interpretive writing inspired by the reconstruction since 1980. All the works have been published previously in books or academic journals. They provide a window on life in this part of the world during the early 18th century as well as a documentation of the archival and commemorative activities of the present. But there is much more to be learned about Louisbourg. Archival holdings of 750,000 pages of historical records and an archaeological collection of more than 5 million artefacts provide the opportunity to study in detail an early 18th-century French experiment at transplanting a culture and a sense of order to Atlantic Canada.

The impetus to develop this collection of essays is tied directly to the 1995 commemorative activities taking place at the Fortress and in the Town of Louisbourg this summer. The year 1995 marks the 275th anniversary of the official founding and fortification of the 18th-century French community and the 250th anniversary of the New England-led siege of Louisbourg.

This is the first of a *Louisbourg Series* planned by the Louisbourg Institute, a cooperative undertaking uniting the interests of the Fortress of Louisbourg National Historic Site and the University College of Cape Breton. Future volumes will provide access to more of the vast amount of historical, archaeological, curatorial, and cultural resource conservation information that is available about Louisbourg, and they will become source books for both amateur and professional interests.

Partners in this enterprise with the Louisbourg Institute include Dr. Robert Morgan and the Beaton Institute, University College of Cape Breton, Penny Marshall and the UCCB Press and the staff of the Fortress of Louisbourg National Historic Site.

An earlier version of each essay in this collection first appeared elsewhere. Without the kind permission of those noted below, this issue would not have been possible:

(1) A.J.B. Johnston, "From port de pêche to ville fortifiée: The Evolution of Urban Louisbourg, 1713-1758," *Proceedings of The Seventeenth Meeting of the French Colonial Historical Society* (May, 1991), pp. 24-43, by permission of the French Colonial Historical Society.
(2) Bruce W. Fry, *"An appearance of strength": The Fortifications of Louisbourg*, Vol. 1 (Ottawa, 1984), pp. 47-59, 147-161, 185-187, 194-196, by permission of the Minister of Public Works and Government Services, copyright holder, 1984.
(3) Allan Greer, "Mutiny at Louisbourg, December 1744," *Histoire Sociale-Social History*, Vol. 10, No. 20 (novembre/November, 1977), pp. 305-336, by permission of Éditions de l'Université d'Ottawa.
(4) Allan Greer, "Another Soldiers' Revolt in Ile Royale, June 1750," *Acadiensis*, Vol. 12, No. 2 (Spring/printemps, 1983), pp. 106-109, by permission of *Acadiensis*.
(5) Kenneth Donovan, "Communities and Families: Family Life and Living Conditions in Eighteenth Century Louisbourg," *Material History Bulletin/Bulletin d'histoire de la culture matérielle*, Vol. 15, (Summer/été, 1982), pp. 34-47, by permission of the National Museum of Science and Technology, Ottawa.
(6) A.J.B. Johnston, "The People of Eighteenth-Century Louisbourg," *Nova Scotia Historical Review*, Vol. 11, No. 2 (1991), pp. 75-86, by permission of the Public Archives of Nova Scotia.
(7) Anne O'Neill, "The Gardens of 18th-Century Louisbourg," *Journal of Garden History*, Vol. 3, No. 3 (July-September, 1983), pp. 176-178, by permission of Taylor & Francis, publishers of the *Journal of Garden History* in which this material was first published.
(8) B.A. Balcom, *The Cod Fishery of Isle Royale, 1713-58* (Ottawa, 1984), pp. 3-19, 66, 80-81, by permission of the Minister of Public Works and Government Services, copyright holder, 1984.
(9) A.J.B. Johnston, "The Fishermen of Eighteenth-Century Cape Breton: Numbers and Origins," *Nova Scotia Historical Review*, Vol. 9, No. 1, (1989), pp. 63-72, by permission of the Public Archives of

Nova Scotia.
(10) Donald F. Chard, "The Price and Profits of Accommodation: Massachusetts-Louisbourg Trade, 1713-1744," in "Seafaring in Colonial Massachusetts," *Publications of the Colonial Society of Massachusetts*, Vol. 51 (1980), pp. 131-151, by permission of the Society.
(11) Christopher Moore, "The Other Louisbourg: Trade and Merchant Enterprise in Ile Royalle 1713-58," *Histoire Sociale-Social History*, Vol. 12, No. 23 (mai/(May, 1979), pp. 79-96, by permission of Éditions de l'Université d'Ottawa.
(12) A.J.B. Johnston, "Preserving History: The Commemoration of 18th Century Louisbourg, 1895-1940," *Acadiensis*, Vol. 12, No. 2 (Spring/printemps, 1983), pp. 53-80, by permission of *Acadiensis*.
(13) A.J.B. Johnston, "Commemorating Louisbourg c.1767," *Acadiensis*, Vol. 13, No. 2 (Spring/printemps, 1984), pp. 147-149, by permission of *Acadiensis*.
(14) Robert Grenier, "The Concept of the Louisbourg Underwater Museum," *The Northern Mariner/Le Marin du Nord*, Vol. 4, No. 2 (April 1994), pp. 3-10, by permission of The Canadian Nautical Research Society.
(15) Eric Krause, "The Fortress of Louisbourg Archives: The First Twenty-Five Years," *Archivaria*, No. 26 (Summer, 1988), pp. 137-148, by permission of the editors, *Archivaria*.

In addition, the editors would like to thank the Fortress of Louisbourg National Historic Site, for its financial and photographic support and for obtaining the permission to use illustrative materials. We also thank the University College of Cape Breton; as well as B.A. Balcom, Margie Cameron, Ken Donovan, Heather Gillis, Isabel Levy, A.J.B. Johnston, Sandra Larade, and Jacqueline Mac Donald.

LIST OF ABBREVIATIONS

AFL	Canada. Louisbourg. Archives of the Fortress of Louisbourg
AG	France. Archives du Génie
AM	France. Archives de la Marine
AN	France. Archives Nationales
ASHA	France. Archives de la Guerre, Archives du Service Historique de l'Armée
ASQ	Canada. Quebec. Archives du Séminaire de Quebec
BG	France. Ministère de la Défense, Bibliothèque du Génie
BN	France. Bibliothèque Nationale
CO	Great Britain. Colonial Office
Col.	France. Archives des Colonies
CTG	France. Comité Technique du Génie
DFC	France. Dépôt des Fortifications
FL	Canada. Fortress of Louisbourg
FLNHP	Canada. Louisbourg. Fortress of Louisbourg National Historic Park
NAC	Canada. National Archives of Canada
NBM	Canada. New Brunswick Museum
PAC	Canada. Public Archives of Canada
PCO	Canada. Parks Canada (Ottawa)
Port de Rochefort	France. Archives Maritimes, Port de Rochefort
PRO	Great Britain. Public Record Office

INTRODUCTION

From *port de pêche* to *ville fortifiée*: The Evolution of Urban Louisbourg, 1713-1758[1]

A.J.B. Johnston

For four decades in the eighteenth century France had an overseas colony of significance on Cape Breton Island. That colony was designated Ile Royale, and its principal settlement was a seaport stronghold called Louisbourg. Known in military history as the site of two major sieges (captured by the New Englanders in 1745 and by the British in 1758), Louisbourg has attracted surprisingly little attention in the context of urban history. Yet it was a populous civilian settlement in its own right, with several thousand inhabitants.[2] For far too long and by far too many, the settlement at Louisbourg has been regarded as but yet another of the many forts erected by the French in defence of their empire in North America (like Chambly, de Chartres or Carillon). In reality Louisbourg was not a fort. It was a town (smaller than but similar to Québec and Montréal), a town which began as a humble fishing port but which evolved into a European-style fortified town.

When the French came ashore for a formal *prise de possession* of Louisbourg on 2 September 1713 they had no intention at the time of erecting a major fortress there. The mandate of the settlement party relocating from Placentia (the Newfoundland colony which had been ceded to Great Britain by the terms of the Treaty of Utrecht) was first and foremost to re-establish and safeguard the French cod fishery.

That the fishery figured so prominently in French colonial thinking comes as no great surprise. The overall North Atlantic fishery employed tens of thousands of people and was widely regarded as a "nursery for seamen." Moreover, the cod fishery generated great wealth for France, more than the fur trade of the interior of the North American continent. France was therefore eager to retain its share of the ocean harvest.[3] The Minister of the Marine, the Comte de Pontchartrain, instructed the contingent heading for Ile Royale to select the most suitable harbor in the new colony as their principal settlement.[4] Military and strategic considerations for the region were not to be disregarded, but they were second to concerns about re-establishing the fishery and creating a port for future trade and commerce.[5]

The harbor selected as the principal settlement for Ile Royale was Louisbourg. In the document formalizing the *prise de possession* the signators declared that "after having visited all the ports in the said island of Cape Breton ... we believed and decided that we could not make a better choice" than Louisbourg. At the time of its settlement Louisbourg was known as Havre à l'Anglois. The leaders of the 1713 expedition renamed the harbor Port St-Louis, a designation which was later changed in France to Louisbourg.[6]

While the settlement party from Placentia (116 men, 10 women, and 23 children) thought Louisbourg would be France's best choice on Ile Royale, their selection was not definitive. The final decision would come in France, and it would be a decision made by officials within the Ministry of the Marine. Besides Louisbourg, two other harbors on Ile Royale would receive serious consideration: Port Toulouse (St. Peters) and Port Dauphin (Englishtown). Each location had its supporters among the engineers, officers, and officials in the new colony. Some argued on behalf of Louisbourg, citing its excellent harbor and its potential for fishery and commerce. Louisbourg's drawback -- which everyone admitted -- would be the difficulty and expense of fortifying a place surrounded by rows of low-lying hills. A few preferred Port Toulouse because it too had a good harbor yet would cost much less than Louisbourg to fortify. Moreover, putting Ile Royale's capital at Port Toulouse was thought likely to attract more Acadians from British-held Nova Scotia than any other location. Others wrote enthusiastically about Port Dauphin, describing its arable land, its stands of forest, and the relative ease of making it defensible. One French officer wrote that more could be achieved at Port Dauphin for 10,000 *livres* than by spending 200,000 at Louisbourg. On the other hand, few fishermen judged Port Dauphin to be a good location for their livelihood: it was too long a sail to the rich fishing banks.

In the end, however, ease of defensibility and pecuniary considerations seemed to make the difference. In 1715, with the Regency period just beginning, the newly-created Conseil de Marine announced its decision: Port Dauphin, not Louisbourg, would be the administrative center of the new colony of Ile Royale.[7] Soon, most royal officials and a large contingent of soldiers left Louisbourg for Port Dauphin. The civilian population of Louisbourg dropped from well over 700 in 1715 to between 500 and 600 in 1716.[8]

As it turned out, the Conseil de Marine's preference for Port Dauphin did not last long. By 1717 Louisbourg was once again emerging as the best choice for the capital of Ile Royale. Its population rebounded because it was simply the best choice on the island for fishery and trade. In 1720 Louisbourg's pre-eminent position within the colony was confirmed when officials in France moved the center of royal government back to the town, away from Port Dauphin. Shortly thereafter, work began on the town's fortifications. There were even medals struck in France to commemorate the official founding of Louisbourg in 1720.

Short-lived though Port Dauphin's time was as the capital of Ile Royale, that period did have a definite impact on Louisbourg, particularly with regard to town planning. The 1715 decision not to make Louisbourg the seat of royal administration had meant that construction in the town went on from 1713 in a largely uncontrolled manner. Until 1717, and even afterward, urban development in Louisbourg took place more or less where and how the first residents wanted it. Fishermen and merchants grabbed the prime waterfront land for their fish flakes, wharves, and warehouses. Builders erected whatever structures they wanted, using whatever materials they preferred. A few lots were set aside for military purposes or king's buildings, but the rest of the construction just happened, with no particular concern for street alignments, town blocks, property lines, or building codes (other than the sections dealing with buildings in the *Coutume de Paris*,[9] which applied on Ile Royale as it did elsewhere in New France). In other words, during the first few years of the settlement at Louisbourg, town planning was largely conspicuous by its absence. The place was simply a *port de pêche*, like others along the Atlantic coast. The initial haphazard location of buildings at Louisbourg is apparent on the early maps and plans of the settlement.

The first person to attempt to give the settlement at Louisbourg the look of a planned town was Jean-François de Verville, the engineer who held responsibility for the construction of fortifications on Ile Royale during the early years of the colony. Acting on orders from France, Verville came up in 1717 with what mounted to a conceptual development scheme for Louisbourg, which was being described as *"le poste le plus important"* on Ile Royale.[10] The engineer drew (or had drawn) a cartographic plan of where the fortifications should go and where the townsite development should be. Though necessarily sketchy on details, and despite the fact that there would be many modifications to the original trace in the years that followed, the 1717 plan basically set the parameters for how Louisbourg was to evolve over the next four decades.

The 1717 plan revealed first of all that the future town of Louisbourg and its defences were going to be concentrated on the peninsula at the southern end of the harbor. The defences, as Verville initially conceived them, were to consist of two full bastions, two half-bastions, and three connecting curtain walls placed on what high ground there was. They would form a classic bastioned trace and close off the landward end of the peninsula.[11] As of 1717 there was no indication that the walls would be extended across the tip of the peninsula and then continue along the waterfront to form a completely enclosed *enceinte*. Those developments would come later.

In dealing with the space inside the proposed walls, Verville's plan offered only an indication of how the urban area might eventually look. He depicted a simple grid pattern for about a third of the *intra muros*, a grid which showed about a dozen rectangular or square town blocks. The tentative street system was to consist of a broad quay along the waterfront and then a long thoroughfare running east to west, intersected by a half-dozen short streets running north to south. Several of the blocks and a couple of the streets were projected as going through a large pond; Verville was not going to let the symmetry of his proposal be undone by a little water. Similarly, the engineer was not bothered by the existence of standing buildings. His 1717 plan shows proposed streets and block boundary lines going right through existing homes and warehouses. Rather than adapt his plan to the settlement that had evolved, Verville was intent on reshaping the young town according to his vision of what a New World fortified town should be.

It was predictable that Verville would have taken such an

THE EVOLUTION OF URBAN LOUISBOURG

approach.[12] As a military engineer his over-riding priority was to make Louisbourg defensible and orderly. Everything else came second. If buildings had to be torn down, if property lines had to shifted to fit his imagined layout, then so it would be. A geometrical look to the settlement was considered important to satisfy the dominant aesthetic of the era. Moreover, from the military point of view, straight streets that led directly to gates, bastions, or the *place d'armes* allowed for the greatest ease in moving troops and equipment around in the event of an attack. Verville's initial plan for the layout of Louisbourg virtually pretended that the engineer had an unsettled site with which to deal.

While Verville was producing his trace, the governor and commissaire-ordonnateur of Ile Royale were working to sort out the formal ownership of property in the colony, beginning with Louisbourg. In the fall of 1717 they issued a list of official concessions.[13] The document spelled out who owned what as best could be done, given that there were no surveyed lots and the town was not yet laid out in a grid. Instead, references were made to adjacent properties and to the stepped-off distances from the shoreline or some other natural feature.

That same year, 1717, also witnessed the first written restrictions on construction in Louisbourg. The regulations came in the form of ordinances issued either in France or in the colony itself. The earliest ordinances restricted residents on where they could build in relation to the planned fortifications and informed them that they were henceforth to mark their property boundaries. Other regulations quickly followed. By 1723 no fewer than 14 different measures had been issued dealing with a variety of Louisbourg urban questions. Some dealt with very general matters; others with details such as minimum height to which buildings had to be erected and a prohibition on using bark as a roofing material.[14]

One imagines that the residents of Louisbourg might have felt some resentment over the restrictions that were imposed on them beginning in 1717. The freedom of the first few years of the settlement had definitely disappeared. Henceforth all construction would have to follow new rules. Worse still for some homeowners, it seemed from Verville's plans that a good many of them would have to tear down their existing homes and rebuild where the engineer's geometry placed them, on set lots within laid-out blocks.

If Louisbourg's residents were hoping that the initiatives to control the town's development were passing fancies, they were to be disappointed. The move toward planning and symmetry, once begun, was not to be turned aside. Additional regulations and more comprehensive versions of Verville's trace were soon developed. Land that was to serve a particular purpose -- be it as a king's building, quay, market, fortification, cemetery, or simply open terrain -- was identified. Among the townspeople whose property holdings were thereby called into questions there was predictable confusion, confrontation, and calls for compensation.[15] Yet the push for town planning continued. Indeed, so strong was the inclination among some local officials to exercise their power and see the town reorganized that there was even a suggestion from commissaire-ordonnateur de Mézy that the inhabitants of the colony be forced to have a house and storehouse within the walls of Louisbourg. All outlying -- and thus unprotected -- buildings could thus be destroyed. Happily for the hundreds of fishermen of Ile Royale, located around the harbor at Louisbourg and in over a dozen smaller outports on the island, de Mézy's recommendation was rejected as impractical by the Conseil de Marine in France.[16]

By the early 1720s Louisbourg's streets, blocks and lots were being defined in considerable detail. On paper -- the paper of the maps and plans of the various *ingénieurs du roi* who served on Ile Royale -- Louisbourg was emerging as a fairly symmetrical settlement, complete with more than a dozen intersecting streets and more than forty town blocks.[17] In reality, however, there were still many buildings standing here and there, not in any particular alignment one with another. This was particularly true along the waterfront, the area first settled and which remained the commercial heart of the busy port. In 1726 Louisbourg welcomed 39 trading vessels from France and 57 from Canada, the West Indies, and New England. The town's resident civilian population that year stood at 951, with an additional 450 soldiers in the garrison.[18]

While Verville wanted to give order to Louisbourg's urban face, he did not always help his own cause. The engineer continued to tinker with his plans, altering block, lot and street lines. One inhabitant, who chose to remain anonymous, sent a memoir to the Minister of the Marine, complaining bitterly of Verville's ever-changing plans. The inhabitant wrote that *"les allignements que M. L'ingenieur a prix et qu'il a change tous les ans, causent un Tort Considerable ... Malgre les concessions qu'ils ont en forme, les Terrains marques*

THE EVOLUTION OF URBAN LOUISBOURG

par le d. Ingenieur, sur lesquels ils ce sont Batir de Bonne Foy ... ils voyent que par un nouveau plan, tous leurs travaux tombent ...."[19]

Bitterness and frustration over changing plans was certainly understandable. Nonetheless, from Verville's point of view progress was being made. With each passing year more and more old structures were replaced, and the new construction generally took place within the approved grid, with the buildings erected at the front of their lots facing the street. Homeowners who wished to have a yard -- for a kitchen garden and perhaps a fenced--in area for a few chickens, pigs and goats -- had ample space behind their building. Speaking of animals, as part of the overall tightening up of urban life at Louisbourg, commissaire-ordonnateur de Mézy issued an ordinance in June 1724 that forbade the free roaming of pigs through the streets of the town. The *cochons* were ruining gardens and fish catches and represented a danger to the growing population of children.[20]

While most Louisbourg builders and homeowners gradually accommodated themselves to the range of controls and town planning measures introduced from 1717 on, there were exceptions. Along the busy waterfront, in front of what Verville designated Blocks 3 and 4, there were clusters of buildings, many of them merchant warehouses, that did not fit into the planned grid. Either by force of argument or through the influence of their owners, these structures continued to stand. Indeed, by 1722 Verville's plans were showing an acceptance of the buildings and their unsymmetrical orientation. The waterfront buildings were not given block numbers, but they did receive formal concessions and became known as the Ile du Quay, Presqu'Ile du Quay, and Place du Port.

Yet another exception to the general trend toward symmetry was provided by prominent Louisbourg resident Joseph Lartigue. Fishing proprietor, merchant, and (as of 1734) judge of the Bailliage, Lartigue occupied land right from the founding of Louisbourg in the area which Verville wanted to become Block 1, a block which was to be reserved for king's buildings. In compensation for terrain given up to the king for the construction of an artillery warehouse in that area, Lartigue was given a triangular wedge of land directly across from Block 1. It became his official concession, one entirely outside the approved grid.[21]

As the 1730s dawned Louisbourg looked much different than it had 17 years earlier at its founding. A 1731 view painted by the engineer Verrier *fils* reveals both a busy port and a community of solid-looking buildings. Indeed, the town even had a skyline, thanks to the presence of two massive buildings, the King's Bastion barracks and the *Hôpital du Roi*. Monumental by New World standards -- the barracks was the larger of the two at well over 300 feet long and between 44 and 52 feet wide -- these two huge king's buildings, with their elegant spires, came to dominate all subsequent painted views of the town.[22]

One should pause at this juncture to compare the overall layout of Louisbourg to that of contemporaneous New Orleans. Setting aside the impact of topography, it is interesting to note that Louisbourg's layout was similar to New Orleans' in that the plans for both communities called for the placement of a church in the center of the streetscape along the waterfront. It turned out in Louisbourg that no such church was ever constructed, but the intention was clearly there on the plans and on the ground, in an emplacement that was forever left for the *église paroissiale*.[23]

Throughout the 1730s the urban face of Louisbourg continued to evolve. Sustained growth in the economy led to a steady increase in population. There were 1116 civilian residents in 1734 and 1463 in 1737; totals which when added to the garrison (about 550 men at the time) gave the community a population of over 2000.[24] Increasingly, much of the construction took place on previously undeveloped lots, away from the waterfront. Meanwhile, in 1734, every property concession in the town was formally measured and recorded for the first time by a professional surveyor (François Vallée). The resulting survey and plan, consisting of 45 numbered blocks plus a few others that were not given an official number, was approved and signed by the king.[25]

While the blocks, lots, and streets were being finalized, so too were the fortifications surrounding them. The original idea of erecting a bastioned trace system only on the landward side was reconsidered. Instead, colonial officials in the Marine offices in France decided to extend the defences across the tip of the peninsula (*Pointe à Rochefort*), then along the waterfront to link up with the already constructed defences of the Dauphin Demi-Bastion. That meant that the eastern end of Louisbourg, which faced out to sea, would not be developed into the seven town blocks that Verville had envisioned. Rather, the area would become a defensive stronghold, with two new bastions, an elaborate gate, and North America's only loop-holed wall. The re-orientation of that part of the town to a military rather than an urban role necessarily brought about a relocation of the parish and hospital cemeteries in Block 40 (through which the projected fortifications were slated to pass). The burial grounds for the community had already been shifted twice before, and this third move would take the graveyards entirely outside the walls of the town.[26]

Throughout the 1730s and on into the 1740s large sums of money were spent on Louisbourg's fortifications, slowly bringing the *enceinte* to completion. By the mid-1740s Louisbourg had become a fully enclosed *ville fortifiée*.[27] On the eve of the town's first assault, which came in the spring of 1745, Louisbourg's civilians probably numbered about 2000, its garrison around 700, and its non-resident fishing and mariner population several hundred. During the siege itself -- a six-week assault on the town -- parts of the community were severely damaged. The French inhabitants were deported to France soon after, and over the next four years of non-French control, the New England and British occupiers repaired what they deemed necessary and constructed what they felt they required (for instance, a new barracks and a brewery). Streets and gates were renamed accordingly (for example, rues Royalle and Toulouse became Dukes and Frederick Streets) but these and other changes did nothing to alter the basic shape of urban Louisbourg.

The war that had led to the conquest of Louisbourg -- the War of the Austrian Succession (King George's War) -- ended officially in 1748 with the signing of the Treaty of Aix-la-Chapelle. One of the clauses of the treaty stipulated that Great Britain return Ile Royale to France. Accordingly, during the summer of 1749 just under 2000 men, women, and children as well as a garrison of more than 1000 men set sail from France for Louisbourg.[28] For many of the civilians it was a return to their place of birth, or at least a place they had begun to call home. As the British withdrew, the Louisbourgeois once again took possession of the fortified town. Repairs and modifications commenced at once, beginning a second period of French occupation at Louisbourg, a period that was to last only a decade.[29]

This second period differed little from the first with regard to urban questions. There were more buildings erected, but such construction took place within the existing grid. There were additional local ordinances passed -- dealing with topics such as property-owners being threatened to develop their land or else lose it, citizens being compelled to remove the ice in front of their homes, and people being told to remove wood and other debris from along the quay -- but none of the regulations were significantly different from those issued during the first period.[30] The only aspect of Louisbourg urban life that represented a noteworthy change was an increased concentration of people inside the walls of the town. Where in the 1720s and 1730s between twenty and thirty per cent of Louisbourg's total population (civilian plus military) had lived outside the fortifications -- typically on fishing properties that ringed the harbor -- that percentage stood at thirteen per cent in 1752. The wholesale destruction of fishing properties during the 1745 siege had led many colonists to seek the security of living inside the walls of the town when the reoccupation of Louisbourg began. For the same basic reason -- a feeling of vulnerability -- there were also dramatic reductions in the population of Ile Royale's many fishing outports during the 1750s.[31] At Louisbourg, however, rightly or wrongly, the citizens seemed to feel relatively safe, living as they did both in proximity to a large garrison (increased to about 2100 in 1755, and to about 3500 in 1758) and behind the European-style fortifications of the town.

The outer works of Louisbourg's defences were modified somewhat during the 1750s, but not to the degree proposed by the colony's latest engineer, Louis Franquet. Where Franquet proposed the construction of elaborate redoubts and other features beyond the *enceinte* of the place, the Ministry of the Marine could find only enough money to authorize modest earthworks.[32] So when a second assault on Louisbourg came during the summer of 1758, the *ville fortifiée* looked much as it had at the time of the first siege (except that its garrison was now five times larger). A combined army and naval force of 27,000 British blockaded, besieged, and bombarded Louisbourg for seven weeks. Once again the French colonial town capitulated, and once again its inhabitants were deported to France.[33]

The 1758 capture of Louisbourg meant the end of French regime on Cape Breton. It also led ultimately to the disappearance of the walled town itself. A British occupying force took over the town and garrisoned it for another ten years, until 1768. With each passing year following Louisbourg's conquest, however, the town looked less and less like the one the French had built and lived in for over four decades. First there was the unrepaired destruction from the 1758 siege. Then in 1760, acting on the orders of Prime Minister William Pitt, the British blew up the walls surrounding the settlement. Two years later fire swept through part of the town and more than a dozen buildings were pulled down to contain the flames. The final blow was the British garrison's withdrawal in 1768. More than half of the 500 inhabitants living in Louisbourg the year before departed when the soldiers left. The once significant *ville fortifiée* had become, in the words of the new British Governor of Nova Scotia, Lord William Campbell, a "decayed city ... going to ruin." The town that according to one historian had begun *"à présenter un aspect de cité forte et offrait quelque resemblance avec la ville de Saint-Malo"* was no more.[34]

The years that followed saw Louisbourg evolve as a place of scattered houses, grazing animals, and ruins. Much of the brick, stone and lumber of the French period was taken and reused elsewhere. By 1770 Louisbourg was not an urban area at all. Much as it had started out, it was again a *port de pêche*, though this time it was a port of scattered families of English and Irish descent. Unfortunately for them, and in contrast to their 18th-century French predecessors, there was no likelihood this time that an imperial power would be prepared to make their harbor settlement an administrative center or a strategic stronghold. Within the context of the now British colony of Nova Scotia that role now belonged to Halifax, founded in 1749 as a counterbalance to Louisbourg.

Notes

1. The author would like to acknowledge the assistance provided him in the preparation of this paper by Eric Krause, Historical Records Supervisor at the Fortress of Louisbourg National Historic Site.
2. There is a paragraph on Louisbourg in John W. Reps, *The Making of Urban America. A History of City Planning in the United States* (Princeton: Princeton University Press, 1965), p. 68; and a longer discussion of the place in André Charbonneau, Yvon Desloges, et Marc Lafrance, *Québec the Fortified City: From the 17th to the 19th Century* (Ottawa: Parks Canada, 1982), pp. 348-49. Jean-Eric Labignette wrote an entire chapter on "Urbanisme" in his unpublished study "Louisbourg en L'Isle Royale, 1713-1761" (manuscript on file, Fortress of Louisbourg). Though never published, Labignette's study has been revised and presented by Etienne Taillemite and René Baudry, and is still worth reading.
3. B.A. Balcom writes: "The per capita value of total exports for Isle Royale in 1737 was approximately eight times greater than that of Canada for the years 1735-39." *The Cod Fishery of Isle Royale, 1713-58* (Ottawa: Parks Canada, 1984), p. 5. Add the figures from the rest of the French fisheries in North American waters and the

value to France is tremendous.
4. J.S. McLennan, *Louisbourg from its foundation to its fall, 1713-1758* (Sydney, N.S.: Fortress Press, 1969), p. 10.
5. Bruce W. Fry, "*An appearance of strength*": *The Fortifications of Louisbourg*, 2 Vols. (Ottawa: Parks Canada, 1984), Vol. 1, p. 53; and Frederick J. Thorpe, *Remparts lointains: La politique française des travaux publics à Terre-Neuve et à l'île Royale, 1695-1758* (Ottawa: Université d'Ottawa, 1980), pp. 21, 29, 31. As for French hopes about commerce flourishing in Ile Royale, in 1706, seven years before the relocation from Placentia, Antoine-Denis Raudot, the intendant of New France, envisioned Cape Breton becoming the center of a prosperous inter-colonial and international trade. See Christopher Moore, "The Other Louisbourg: Trade and Merchant Enterprise in Ile Royale, 1713-58," *Histoire sociale/Social History*, Vol. 12 (23 mai/May 1979), pp. 79-96.
6. McLennan, *Louisbourg from its foundation*, p. 12.
7. *Ibid*, pp. 32-34.
8. Barbara Schmeisser, "The Population of Louisbourg, 1713-1758," *Manuscript Report Series*, Vol. 303 (Ottawa: Parks Canada, 1976), pp. 5-7. For a look at how large a component the fishing population was in the total Ile Royale population see A.J.B. Johnston, "The Fishermen of Eighteenth-Century Cape Breton: Numbers and Origins," *Nova Scotia Historical Review*, Vol. 9, No.1 (1989), pp. 62-72.
9. M. Desgodets and M. Goupy, *Des Bâtiments, suivant La coutume de Paris, Traîtant de ce qui concerne des Servitudes réelles, les Rapports des Jurés-Experts, les Reparations locataires, douairières, usufruitières, bénéficiales, &c* (Rouen: chez la Veuve de Pierre Dumesnil, 1787). The sections on buildings date back to the 1500s.
10. "*Mémoire du Roy aux Mrs de Costebelle et de Soubras*," AN, Col., B, Vol. 39, f. 270v, June 25, 1717.
11. The construction of Louisbourg's defences is discussed at length in Fry, "*An appearance of strength*." Much of what follows in this paragraph is based on a study of Verville's 1717 plan, referred to in the Louisbourg archives as 1717-2. AN, Outre-Mer, DFC, IV-145, 1717.
12. Verville's career and background are outlined by F.J. Thorpe in "Jean-François de Verville," pp. 648-50 of Vol. 2 of the *Dictionary of Canadian Biography* (Toronto: University of Toronto Press, 1969). Anne Blanchard provides additional information about Verville (whom she identifies as Jean-François du Verger, Sieur de Verville) in *Dictionnaire des ingénieurs militaires, 1691-1791* (Montpellier: [Centre d'histoire militaire et d'études de défense nationale] Université Paul-Valéry, 1981), p. 750, and in *Les ingénieurs du "Roy" du Louis XIV à Louis XVI. Etude du corps des fortifications* (Montpellier: Université Paul-Valéry, 1979).
13. "*Toisé des Graves et Concessions accordées ...*," AN, Col., C^{11}B, Vol. 2, ff. 151-61, November 10, 1717.
14. Gilles Proulx, "Tribunaux et loix de Louisbourg, 1713-1758," *Travail Inédit*, Tome 303 (Ottawa: Parks Canada, 1975), pp. 54-56.
15. For an example of the confusion surrounding expropriation questions, see the Comte de Maurepas' comments about the Antoine Paris case. AN, Col., B, Vol. 27, ff. 1236-38, Maurepas aux Srs. St-Ovide et de Mézy, March 28, 1724.
16. AN, Col., C^{11}B, Vol. 5, ff. 119-24v, Lettre of de Mézy, June 17, 1720, Conseil (August 13, 1720).
17. There are hundreds of maps and plans of eighteenth-century Louisbourg, located in archives in France, Great Britain, Canada and the United States. For a sampling of the range of maps and plans that exist see *Bulletin of the Association for*

Preservation Technology, Vol. 4, Nos. 1-2 (1972). For an overview of the mapping efforts of the French engineers on Ile Royale, see Joan Dawson, "Beyond the Bastions: French Mapping of Cape Breton Island, 1713-1758," *Nova Scotia Historical Review*, Vol. 10, No. 2 (1990), pp. 6-30.

18. Population and vessel figures are from McLennan, *Louisbourg from its foundation*, pp. 71-72; garrison figure is from Allan Greer, "The Soldiers of Isle Royale, 1720-45," *History and Archaeology*, Vol. 28 (Ottawa: Parks Canada, 1979), p. 93.

19. AN, Col., C^{11}B, Vol. 7, ff. 158-159v, Mémoire à Monseigneur, le Comte de Maurepas, December 12, 1724.

20. AN, Col., C^{11}B, Vol. 10, f. 7, Ordonnance sur la Circulation des Cochons dans Louisbourg, de Mézy, June 5, 1724.

21. There are unpublished historical reports on all the blocks of 18th-century Louisbourg which were reconstructed during the 1960s and 1970s. Particularly useful for this paragraph were Christian Pouyez et Gilles Proulx, "L'île du quai de Louisbourg," *Travail Inédit*, Tome 149 (Ottawa: Parks Canada, 1972), and Selma Barkham, "A Summary of Information Concerning Lartigue's Houses Near the Petit Etang, 1714-1758" (manuscript on file; Fortress of Louisbourg, 1967).

22. The history of the King's Bastion barracks is found in Blaine Adams, "The Construction and Occupation of the Barracks of the King's Bastion at Louisbourg," *Canadian Historic Sites: Occasional Papers in Archaeology and History*, Vol. 18 (Ottawa: Parks Canada, 1978).

23. A.J.B. Johnston, *Religion in Life at Louisbourg, 1713-1758* (Montréal and Kingston: McGill-Queen's University Press, 1984), pp. 34-38; and Samuel Wilson, *Bienville's New Orleans, A French Colonial Capital, 1718-1768* (New Orleans: Friends of the Cabildo, 1968). For a layout of other French towns of the same period see also Pierre Lavedan, *Histoire de l'urbanisme, Renaissance et Temps modernes* (Paris: Henri Laurens, 1959), p. 478 for New Orleans, p. 518 for Detroit.

24. Schmeisser, "The Population of Louisbourg," p. 56; Greer, "The Soldier," p. 93.

25. Vallée's 1734 plan is reproduced as Fig. 7 of the *Bulletin of the Association for Preservation Technology*, Vol. 4, Nos. 1-2 (1972). Rue Toulouse, the main thoroughfare leading from the harbor, was 30 *pieds* wide (or about 32 feet or 9.72 meters). Most of the rest of the streets were 24 *pieds* wide (or 25.58 feet or 7.78 meters). One street was as narrow as 12 *pieds*. Rodrigue Lavoie, "Etude sur les propriété de Louisbourg, Rapport No. II- Les Rues" (manuscript on file, Fortress of Louisbourg, 1965). To see generally how Louisbourg's layout changed in the late 1730s, compare Figures 7 through 10 in the *Bulletin of the Association for Preservation Technology*.

26. On the various locations of Louisbourg's cemeteries see Johnston, *Religion in Life*, pp. 146-47.

27. Fry, "*An appearance of strength*," Vol. 1, p. 163.

28. There were 1966 men, women, and children listed on the Louisbourg census for 1749 (AN, Outre-Mer, G^1, Vol. 466, pièce 76), plus another 21 people described as "*habitans de L'Isle Royalle residente à Rochefort le 17 aout 1749.*" (Archives Maritimes, Port de Rochefort, Série IR, Vol. 47).

29. Two examples of changes made by the French are their removal of the galleries, seats, and pews the English had put in the *Chapelle St-Louis* and their extensive renovations to the hospital, which the English had used as a barracks. Johnston, *Religion in Life*, pp. 55, 80.

30. Proulx, "Tribunaux et loix de Louisbourg," pp. 55-56.

31. Schmeisser, "The Population," p. 56.

32. Fry, "*An appearance of strength,*" Vol. 1, pp. 125-34.
33. The latest account of the 1758 siege is Julian Gwyn's "French and British Naval Power at the Two Sieges of Louisbourg, 1745 and 1758," *Nova Scotia Historical Review*, Vol. 1, No. 2 (1990), pp. 63-93.
34. Wayne Foster, "The Post-Occupational History of the Old French Town of Louisbourg, 1760-1930" (manuscript on file, Fortress of Louisbourg, 1965); A.J.B. Johnston, "Preserving History: The Commemoration of 18th Century Louisbourg, 1895-1940," *Acadiensis*, Vol. 12, No. 2 (Spring 1983), pp. 53-80; and Labignette, "Louisbourg en L'Isle Royalle ...," p. 79.

MILITARY

"An appearance of strength" The Fortifications Of Louisbourg

Bruce W. Fry

Louisbourg: A Historical Introduction

The economic and political condition of France after a half-century of virtually continuous warfare, combined with lack of initiative in military engineering following Vauban's death, resulted in stasis as far as the development of fortifications and the construction of new frontier defences were concerned. The terms of peace ratified by the series of agreements referred to as the Treaty of Utrecht salvaged what was possible from the wreckage of Louis XIV's dynastic and territorial ambitions; it was also the turning point in the fortunes of New France.[1]

Drawn by the apparently limitless wealth of fish and fur, the French had been exploring deeper into the North American continent since the early part of the 16th century. By the beginning of the following century, Quebec and Montreal had become the starting points of expeditions reaching out across the Great Lakes into the prairies and down the Mississippi waterway to the Gulf of Mexico. At the same time, expanding English settlements along the eastern seaboard gradually denied the French access to the Atlantic coast except in the area of the Gulf of St. Lawrence, and armed conflict became inevitable. European military technology thus followed closely on the heels of exploration and colonization, but the essential ingredient of 18th-century warfare as practised in Europe -- a network of strongly fortified towns -- was missing. New France was sparsely populated and its few towns were only lightly defended. For the most part, New France could be characterized as a wilderness with isolated garrisons guarding natural routes leading to the hinterland.

At a time when the potential of New France could have been realized, Louis XIV's priorities remained firmly European, yet the insistence of Chancellor Pontchartrain in retaining fishing rights on the Atlantic coast and ensuring that the islands of Cape Breton and St. Jean (Prince Edward Island) remained French reveals an unexpected, vigorous appreciation of the potential value of the fishing trade. More surprising was the commitment of the French government to strengthen existing fortifications in Canada (at Quebec and Montreal primarily) and to fortify strategic locations on Cape Breton -- a commitment that, despite many complaints and queries over costs, and the vicissitudes of Regency government, was respected until the final collapse of New France in 1759.

The decision to safeguard French fishing interests by formally establishing a colony on Cape Breton followed immediately upon the ratification of the Treaty of Utrecht, and the island, in recognition of its enhanced status, thereafter became known as Isle Royale.[2] Choice of the location of its capital took somewhat longer, and not until 1719 was *Havre à l'Anglois*, by then renamed Louisbourg, given preference over the two other ports under consideration.[3] A brief summary of the town's history will aid an understanding of the way in which the defences were laid out and modified.[4]

The director of fortifications appointed to the colony was Jean-François du Verger de Verville, a member of the Corps of Engineers. His proposals for the three ports had all been quite similar in approach: a simple line of fortifications linking bastioned redoubts to isolate a piece of land overlooking the harbour. It is clear that already by 1717 Verville had a firm idea of the way in which he would defend Louisbourg, and the instructions he received were in effect an official sanctioning of his project, for which he was then given a free hand. The harbour itself, by virtue of its narrow channel, could be well defended against hostile ships, and in the unlikely event that any did force an entrance, the navigable waters would be completely exposed to artillery fire. Four batteries, one on an islet beside the channel mouth, another opposite the channel on the north shore, and the others on the promontory overlooking the southwest arm, were to ensure the necessary cross-fire. Verville was also concerned about the landward approaches, and to guard against

THE FORTIFICATIONS OF LOUISBOURG

an attack from the west he proposed to isolate the promontory by a defensive line *"en forme d'ouvrage à double couronne"*: a partial *enceinte* consisting of three fronts, two full bastions occupying the centre and a half-bastion at each extremity, one on the harbour shore, the other on the open coast, forming a double-crown work. The bastion built on the highest point of ground and constructed as an independent masonry redoubt was to be the first priority. The other bastions and curtains were initially to be thrown up as *fortifications de campagne* in earth; only later were the plans modified to include masonry escarps in all sectors. The town was to develop behind the line and the governor's quarters and garrison barracks were to be incorporated in a building extending across the gorge of the principal bastion -- the Bastion du Roy. Thus closed on all sides, the bastion could be held against an attack from an enemy who had broken into the town, and was therefore regarded from its conception as the citadel of the town. Work proceeded slowly, Verville concentrating on the citadel at the expense of the harbour defences until 1723, when he received specific instructions to begin the batteries. Friction between Verville and the governor, St. Ovide de Brouillan, over priorities and authority culminated in Verville's recall in 1725; the engineer who had been sent out the year before to serve as his lieutenant at Louisbourg, Etienne Verrier, now became chief engineer of the town. For the next five years, construction was begun or continued at various locations, so that the citadel remained unfinished for the time. The Island Battery and the shore battery (Royal Battery) were begun, as was the half-bastion on the harbour shore (the Dauphin Half-Bastion). The gorge of this work was closed off by a curved battery, the guns of which complemented the harbour defences.

The town itself was not neglected. As the population grew and a systematic town plan was implemented, government buildings were added: a hospital occupying an entire town block, a storehouse (*magazin général*), and a bakery with an armoury on its upper floor. Residences for the chief engineer and other king's officials were also provided by the Crown. Not until 1733 was Verrier able to turn his attention once more to the King's Bastion, completing the gun platforms and parapets. He had also been extending the defences southwards to the Princess Bastion which completed the original *enceinte*. Between the Princess Bastion and the King's Bastion was the other full bastion of the "double crown," the Queen's

Bastion. Construction on this work and the connecting curtains continued with some delays until 1735. The last section of the landward *enceinte*, the curtain wall between the King's Bastion and the Dauphin Half-Bastion, was not undertaken until 1736-37. But before the *enceinte* could be considered properly finished, another major project was initiated by the governor's concerns for the town, undefended to the seaward or east side of the promontory. A new *enceinte* was therefore proposed, one which would be ultimately connected to the original one by defensive works along the shore to north and south, enclosing the town completely. Like the westward-facing defences, the eastward-facing ones were to consist of three fronts with full bastions located in the centre. To the north was to be a simple communication on pilings across the large pond behind a gravel strand near the extremity of the promontory. On the strand itself was to be another artillery battery, adding yet more fire-power to the harbour defences. This battery (*Pièce de la Grave*) was to be connected with a quay wall following the harbour until it joined the earlier *enceinte* beneath the semicircular battery of the Dauphin Half-Bastion. The quay itself, while primarily designed as a facility for off-loading goods and materials arriving by ship, was laid out as a tenaille front. A long, straight curtain was flanked at each extremity, a parapet surmounted the wall along its entire length, and gun embrasures were let into the flanks. Further fire-power was provided by a spur battery in the shallows beneath the battery of the Dauphin Half-Bastion.

To the south, overlooking the rocky shoals of the coast, the old *enceinte*, terminating with the Princess Bastion, was linked to the new by a crenellated curtain running parallel to the beach and into the right flank and the face of the new, southerly bastion, named for the town's governor, Brouillan. The other full bastion was named in honour of the Minister of the Marine, Maurepas. The possibility of an approach by small boats being made through the shoals was obviously a cause of concern, since a cavalier was added to the rear of the Princess Bastion, thereby commanding the inward-curving beach. A covered gallery with loopholes for swivel guns made up the left face of the half-bastion.

By 1743, more than 20 years after work had first begun, the defences of the town and the harbour were substantially complete. All land or sea approaches were well flanked, and powerful artillery batteries commanded the most vulnerable sectors. The ramparts were fronted by a ditch, covered way and glacis. Incorporating natural ponds, a considerable part of the ditch was either water-filled or at least marshy. In front of the Dauphin Half-Bastion and for some way along the curtain was a large expanse of water, the level of which could be controlled to some extent by the operation at high or low tide of a sluice in a small dam (*batardeau*) which sealed off the harbour end of the ditch. Because the King's Bastion was located on relatively high ground, with bedrock close to the surface, the ditch in front of it was dry, but drainage patterns, influenced by the excavation of the ditch, produced a marshy area that extended southwards to the coast. In front of the easterly defences the ditch was completely flooded, and the Maurepas Bastion was located in a pond which surrounded the ramparts.

Wherever the terrain permitted, the outer edge of the ditch was delimited by a counterscarp, beyond which were a covered way and glacis. The covered way was enlarged at several points to form *places d'armes*, but no other outworks were included. The main road into the town followed the harbour shore past the Royal Battery, around the shallows of the southwest arm, and entered by way of the Dauphin Gate. The gate was designed in the grandiose style common to European fortifications, with classical columns surmounted by military trophies flanking the royal coat of arms. Guardhouses stood alongside the road immediately behind the gate. The security of the entrance was ensured by the multiplicity of barriers. Approaching from the country, the road led through a passageway in the glacis, which could be closed off, crossed the covered way, and then came to a wooden bridge over the flooded ditch. The final section of bridge was formed by a drawbridge.

Although the Dauphin Gate was the only practical access to the town by land under normal, peacetime circumstances, two other elaborate, guarded gateways were built: the Queen's Gate, in the curtain between the Princess and Queen's Bastions, and the Maurepas Gate, between the Maurepas and Brouillan bastions. Three postern tunnels (sally-ports) were incorporated in the defences, one in the left re-entrant angle of the Dauphin Half-Bastion, another in the right re-entrant angle of the King's Bastion, and the third in the curtain between the King's and Queen's bastions. Finally, the Frederick Gate, an ornamental gate of timber with a slate roof, spanned the principal wharf on the quay.

The prosperous community which grew up within the walls

and along the harbour, where a *fauxbourg* of dwellings, fishing shacks and inns developed, owed its existence to trade based primarily on the fishing industry.[5] The predominant position that Louisbourg came to command in the Atlantic trading system led inevitably to rivalry with the New England colonies. As the political climate in Europe degenerated into war, the French colonies in North America were encouraged to go on the offensive; privateers based at Louisbourg began to harass New England shipping, provoking reciprocal action in which the British navy was quick to participate.[6] Expeditions from Louisbourg captured the English fishing establishment at Canso on the northeastern mainland of Nova Scotia in May 1744, and in September unsuccessfully attacked Annapolis Royal, the English town and fort overlooking the Bay of Fundy. These acts focussed attention on Louisbourg and provided further incentives to New England factions pushing for an expedition against the French stronghold. Their motives were inspired more by profit than by fear, as McLennan has pointed out:

> When the British colonies sent out about ten times as many privateers as the French, the latter being vastly less effective, it is not reasonable to believe that New England was seriously dismayed by French privateering or failed, in irritation at her small losses, to calculate her surpassing gains.
>
> These considerations led to the conclusion that ... New England had no real fear of invasion but that the monopoly of the fisheries meant such prospective wealth, the sound business insight in the leaders of her people led to their grasping an opportunity to benumb French competition in the markets of the world. This opportunity presented itself when war existed: Louisbourg was short of provisions, its fortifications weak, its garrison small and mutinous.[7]

These forces, put in motion by William Shirley, Governor of Massachusetts, resulted in an expedition that contained all the ingredients of a Hollywood swashbuckling epic: Commodore Warren, bringing a Royal Navy squadron from the West Indies to assume command of the combined British and Provincial fleet, in contrast with the amateur soldiers of the Provincial Army led by a New England merchant, William Pepperrell, landing through the surf on the beaches to the southwest of the town under French fire; the abandonment of the Royal Battery without a shot being fired and its subsequent occupation by New Englanders who turned the guns on the town; cannon and mortar batteries being set up to batter the walls and bombard the town after tremendous exertions in dragging the ordnance across miles of swamp; a party of Provincials killed and scalped by Indians; a naval blockade and chase as a French supply ship attempted to bring relief to the town but was fought to a standstill and captured; a daring night assault on the Island Battery, repulsed with considerable loss to the attackers; siege batteries advancing ever closer despite spirited fire from the defenders and the exploding of guns caused by the New Englanders' over-enthusiastic "double-shotting"; the bombarding of the Island Battery from heights above the lighthouse; and the systematic destruction of embrasures on the Dauphin and King's bastions. The only element lacking was an all-out assault, carrying the place by storm. With the Island Battery effectively out of action, the New Englanders were in fact preparing for a combined assault. Warren was to force the harbour at the same time as a landward assault was launched on the breach established in the Dauphin Half-Bastion, but the French realized the hopelessness of their situation and surrendered. They had held out for 43 days of siege since the first battery was established; the Provincial Army took possession of the town on 28 June, 47 days after their landing.

Euphoria quickly gave way to disillusionment. Throughout the entire siege only 101 New Englanders had been killed, the majority in the abortive attempt on the Island Battery; in the months that followed, some 1200 died of disease in the overcrowded, unsanitary conditions they had to endure during the winter of 1745-46.[8] More concerned with the political equilibrium in Europe than the potential of a North American empire, the British government conceded Cape Breton at the negotiating table. By the summer of 1749 the French were back in Louisbourg.

Not surprisingly, little had been done to the fortifications during the occupation. In an effort to reduce the danger from the nearby high ground which had proved so beneficial to the besiegers, a makeshift cavalier had been raised on the ramparts of the Dauphin Half-Bastion, making use of the rubble from the ruined Circular Battery. The right flank of the King's Bastion, which, next to the Dauphin Half-Bastion, had sustained the worst damage, had been repaired sufficiently to be able to serve as an effective battery. The New Englanders appear to have carried out few other major repairs.

Reverting to the *status quo ante bellum* accentuated the obvious: conflict between England and France for control of North America was inevitable, and Nova Scotia was the battleground. The British, deprived of a ready-made fortified naval base, established Halifax as a counterbalance to Louisbourg. The French, alarmed by the implications of a gradual encirclement, incited their Indian allies to harass the settlers and strengthened the garrison and fortifications of Louisbourg. Troop build-ups began on both sides, and British naval squadrons began to patrol the coast and seize French ships.[9]

The value of Cape Breton had been realized belatedly by the French government, as their expensive and ill-fated attempt to recapture Louisbourg from the New Englanders in 1746 had shown.[10] Now its importance as a centre of commerce and a strategic outpost to New France was reflected in the appointment of an experienced engineer, Louis Franquet, in 1750. Initially responsible for recommending improvements to Louisbourg, he became in 1754 director general of fortifications for the whole of New France as well as Isle Royale. It is therefore ironic that, with the ever-increasing threat of war, so little was done to improve the town's defences. Franquet's report offered two options; the first was based upon correcting faults in the existing *enceinte*, while the second, more expensive, alternative emphasized defence in depth by modifying and supplementing the outworks. The former was adopted, but there were delays in appointing a contractor to carry out the work. In Louisbourg the issue was clouded by that chronic malaise of colonial management, conflicting lines of authority, while at Versailles the indecision caused by the divergent recommendations from governor and engineer was heightened by frequent ministerial changes. Work on the fortifications was to a great extent paralysed.[11] Improvements were essentially limited to strengthening the Dauphin Half-Bastion and gate area, rebuilding the right flank of the King's Bastion, enlarging the ditch in front of the curtain between the Princess and the Queen's bastions, transforming the *place d'armes* there into a *demilune*, and adding a counterguard in front of the Princess Bastion. War was declared between the two powers in the spring of 1756, by which time Franquet, fearing an attack at any moment, concentrated on raising field fortifications along the coastline at the most likely landing places.

The second siege was in many respects a re-enactment of

the first, albeit on a larger scale and with a professional cast. An audacious landing under heavy fire was again effected on the beaches west of the fortress (8 June 1758); siege batteries were established, often on the same vantage points as earlier ones, and the systematic, ruthless pounding of the place into submission began.[12] A spectacular climax to the events was reached with the burning of all but two French men-of-war in the harbour. Demoralized and in desperate straits, the French surrendered 49 days after the landing and following 37 days of heavy bombardment.

There was to be no repetition of the events following the Treaty of Aix-la-Chapelle. Regardless of any possible exchanges of territory at a future peace conference, Pitt was determined that the French were to have no stronghold on the North American coast: "The King is come to a Resolution, that the said Fortress, together with all the works, and Defences of the Harbour, be most effectually and most entirely demolished ...."[13] The work was carried out that year.

The fortified towns of Canada continued to expand as urban centres after the British conquest, and the original structures suffered in consequence. No trace of the fortification walls of Montreal now remain, while those of Quebec City, repaired, modified and maintained by the British army for over a century and then stabilized as a promenade around the town once their military function had ceased, bear little resemblance to the original. Louisbourg, by contrast, was abandoned except for the occasional dwelling, and the small fishing community of English and Scottish settlers that became the modern town grew up along the north shore of the harbour, away from the French town. The site, falling gradually into ruin and growing over with grass, was largely undisturbed by subsequent development and became an archaeological time-capsule reflecting a short but intense occupational span.

Recognizing the historical significance of the place, the Canadian government designated it a historic site in 1928 and created the Fortress of Louisbourg National Historic Park in 1940. In 1960 the ambitious concept of "restoring" the town was put forward and approval was given by Parliament to initiate a modified version of the project; the aim was to "restore" a major portion of the town and its fortifications to a state representing their appearance during the French régime.[14] A full assessment of the present programme would be as fascinating as the study of the original French achievements, and an objective evaluation a worthwhile contribution towards an appreciation of the difficulties and responsibilities entailed in preserving our cultural heritage.

Such analysis is outside the scope of the present work, but inasmuch as the course of modern events has had a direct impact on the research process and its results, as expressed in construction or exhibits, reference will be made to particular cases. Despite escalating costs and ever-extending deadlines, the Canadian government stood by its commitment, very much as its 18th-century French counterpart had done, and provided the funds that enable the reconstruction programme to continue. Despite the constraints inherent in the requirement to sustain a largely construction-oriented endeavour, the historical and archaeological research carried out during this period would not have been possible without this commitment.

Louisbourg: The Setting
Choice of Site

The reasons for choosing Louisbourg, as opposed to other harbours on Cape Breton, once it became clear that Placentia (Newfoundland) could no longer remain a French colony, are not self-evident. That the French authorities were concerned primarily about safeguarding the fishing industry was stated in the original instructions from Pontchartrain to L'Hermitte in 1713; the Placentia inhabitants were to be relocated in a port that could be defended, was within easy reach of the fishing grounds, and suitable for landing and drying the catch.[15] Of the three most propitious areas -- Port Toulouse (modern-day St. Peters), Louisbourg and Port Dauphin (modern-day Englishtown) -- initial reports favoured Port Dauphin, and the official position was made clear to Verville when he was instructed to prepare estimates for fortifying all three locations:

> [Louisbourg] would have been made the principal establishment if the port could have been easily fortified, and if there had been a large enough gravel strand on which to dry the catch from the fishing vessels, but the meagre strand there, together with the enormous costs required to fortify this port safely, made the late king, in response to requests from the officers of Isle Royale and merchants of the kingdom, decide upon Port Dauphin as the principal establishment ....

THE FORTIFICATIONS OF LOUISBOURG

the Council wishes to make the Sieur de Verville aware that as far as his fortification designs are concerned, it is not acceptable to fortify in the colonies to the same extent as in Europe because of the great cost ....[16] (Author's translation).

By the following year the members of the council had reconsidered and declared Louisbourg to have priority. Verville was to proceed upon the lines he had already recommended for fortifying the harbour there. In a letter to Costebelle and Soubras, governor and *commissaire* of the new colony, it was stated that

His Majesty has decided to begin the fortifying of this island at the port of Louisbourg, it being the most important port in terms of its advantages over the others for the fishery and because of its location.[17] (Author's translation).

The decision was influenced by commercial rather than military considerations, but Verville can scarcely be held responsible on the basis of his report of the year before.[18] The engineer was careful to adhere to his instructions and draw up proposals for the three sites, even finding time to consider a fourth possibility, Baye Royalle, just south of Port Dauphin. While noting that the harbour at Louisbourg "according to the feeling of the merchants and fishermen appears in this respect the best on the island,"[19] his overall recommendation for Port Toulouse appears to have been more favourable:

Because of the lie of the land, well suited to being fortified, by the difficulty of forcing an entry into the port once the channel markers have been removed, because of the fertility of the land and because it is close to Acadia with its fishing grounds, this port is one of the best locations on the island.[20] (Author's translation).

The fortifications proposed for all locations were similar, consisting of masonry *redoutes bastionnées* and field fortifications combined to isolate a small section of coastline. Comparative costs showed that Louisbourg would be the most expensive to establish, followed by Port Toulouse and then Port Dauphin.[21] In opting for Louisbourg, the council was committing the government to the most expensive choice, one which their subsequent decision to improve the field fortifications by revetting them in masonry was to render even more costly.[22]

If Verville cannot be criticized for encouraging the selection of the Louisbourg site, his report may be questioned for what he did not say. His comments on Port Toulouse reveal that a tenable defensive position was something to which he attached importance, but at Louisbourg his main preoccupation was the harbour: the Royal and Island batteries originated with his initial proposals. He felt that the landward side was relatively safe as no landings were possible and sufficient command of the nearby knolls could be achieved by the construction of *"une forte Redoute Bastionnée exécutée en maçonnerie ...."* By the following year he revised his ideas of coastal security:

> I was assured that an assault landing on the beach at Louisbourg was impossible at any time and that there would be no need to fortify it.
>
> We came ashore at five places in a single morning, it is wise to examine closely what one is told in America.[23] (Author's translation).

Curiously, there is little evidence that he initially considered the terrain from an attacker's point of view. Once alive to the possibilities of an attack overland, and given the authority to proceed with the fortifications, he concentrated on the landward fronts to the exclusion of the harbour defences until specifically ordered to remedy his oversight,[24] but his original choice of ground was poor. Superficially, the proposed *enceinte* looks reasonable: the main redoubt is located on the highest point of land, the other redoubt, initially to be a fascined earthwork, occupies another hillock, and the extremities rest on the coastline and harbour shore respectively. The partial polygon enclosing these works was large and not quite regular, each angle being obtuse and not identical. The two regular bastions were wide and well proportioned, but the plan of the promontory on which the three fronts were laid out indicates the engineer's dilemma. To the south, beyond the point where the *enceinte* joins the coast, is Cap Noir, itself dominated by a rocky eminence with a dangerous command of the Princess-Queen's front. More serious is the rising, broken ground to the northwest. There a series of low knolls overlooks the Dauphin Half-Bastion -- where the fortifications join the harbour-front and the main entrance to the town was located. Not only did this provide an ideal location for gun batteries to fire against the King's-Dauphin front and the whole town, but it also provided a considerable expanse of dead ground, seriously reducing the effectiveness of defensive fire from the King's Bastion.

To have advanced the line of fortifications to incorporate these dangerous sectors would have created more problems. The two knolls chosen as the foremost points of the double-crown work[25] were well to the rear of the high land at each extremity: to abandon them in order to base the extremities on the heights at Cap Noir and in front of the Dauphin Bastion would mean setting a major portion of the defences in low-lying, swampy ground and greatly expanding the total area. To maintain the two central knolls but to swing the extremities forward would create an unacceptable re-entrant in the *enceinte*, with long curtains exposed to enfilading fire. Excluding the possibility of relocating the entire alignment, the alternatives would have been along the lines of Franquet's 1751 proposal to establish detached works on the commanding ground, but would have been a solution confined to the immediate environs.

What surprisingly few of the site plans indicate -- and none with any real accuracy -- is the extent to which the ground rises from the shore. Verville does not appear to have attached any importance to this serious shortcoming nor to have reflected on the dangerous degree to which his plan left the town exposed. The very fact of locating the King's Bastion on the highest point of the *enceinte* meant that the fortifications would have to slope away on each side, particularly so in the sector of the King's-Dauphin front. Viewed from across the harbour, the town, its streets rising towards the King's Bastion, lies completely unprotected, the King's-Dauphin curtain is vulnerable to enfilade, and the right flank of the King's Bastion is not screened by its glacis. Perhaps with the advantage of hindsight, Jean-Pierre Roma, evaluating Louisbourg's role as a fortress after it was returned to France in 1748, succinctly outlined its weaknesses:

> It is a place shaped like an amphitheatre commanded by several heights from which it can be raked with cannonballs and musketry so effectively that no one is safe there, either in the houses or in the streets.[26] (Author's translation).

Capping this unfavourable situation was the Royal Battery. Located at the water's edge midway along the north shore of the harbour, it was designed to complement the harbour defences by commanding the channel should any hostile ships successfully run the gauntlet of the Island Battery's cannon. For this function it was theoretically well located. Equally, however, it was superbly located to fire directly into the town, albeit at extreme range and not with all of its guns. It was itself commanded by a nearby ridge of high ground and had little effective defence to the rear.

By concentrating on the immediate vicinity of the town site and the landward defences, and by not bringing out the problems caused by the downward slope to the Dauphin Half-Bastion, Verville conveyed an impression of a better defensive position than was actually the case. The Council of Marine and the Corps of Engineer's committee were probably not even aware of the dangers of Roma's "amphitheatre" effect.

This effect is most pronounced from the ridges which surround the harbour and command the fortress from a distance of some two miles. The elevations entailed are relatively low; at the highest point the ground is not more than 61 m above sea level, and drops in a series of terraces until the harbour shore is reached. To the southwest the ground levels off into an extended marshy plain (*Plaine de Gabarus*) of which the peninsula of Louisbourg is a part. The ground here is only 0.35-4.5 m above sea level except where glacial activity or outcrops of bedrock have resulted in small knolls. The knoll chosen for the site of the King's Bastion was no more than 13.7 m above sea level, while the hillock on which the Queen's Bastion was built was 12.2 m above sea level.[27] Several high points ranging between 9.1 and 13.7 m above sea level are within close range of the fortifications.[28]

Choice of the ground was less than propitious. While it is true that for Franquet a choice of location no longer existed, he appears to have had an unjustifiable confidence in the capacity of the ground to discourage would-be attackers, even when he knew of the events of the first siege:

> The ground in front consists mainly of rock of a kind which creates almost insurmountable problems to an approach by way of trenching, from which I conclude that, by carrying out the proposed improvements [raising the glacis, placing more traverses on the covered way, and enlarging the[*places d'armes*], any enemy will only be able to advance an attack on the above-mentioned three fronts [those facing landward] with great difficulty and with all the preparation and procedures of a formal siege.[29] (Author's translation).

The location of the town was thus not given the fullest attention by the engineers responsible for its defences, both at the beginning and, more incredibly, after the ground had proved unsafe. In fact, if not hopeless, the whole position was, to say the least, a challenge to a military engineer. Because of the amphitheatre effect, construction of detached works on the nearby knolls would not have entirely solved the problem of commanding fire: the encircling ridges would have been ideal locations from which to cannonade such redoubts as well as the main *enceinte*. Moreover, other circumstances militated against the choice of Louisbourg. Verville had revised his opinions concerning the possibility of landings along the coast. Had he given more time and thought to local conditions, he might also have recognized the problems of building on a low spit of land jutting out into the Atlantic. Destructive gale-force winds can sweep across the exposed site, lifting roofs and smashing boats; heavy seas can tear out huge sections of the shoreline and flood the low-lying land; coastal fog can create a chilly, damp micro-climate in which the drying of mortar becomes difficult. The next 20 years were to reveal the extent to which climate combined with poor materials to cause continual frustration and misery to the builders. While access to the fishing grounds was of prime importance to the French, Louisbourg was not necessarily the only logical choice, Port Toulouse being much closer to the rich Canso banks. We are left to conclude that if Verville did not actively recommend Louisbourg over other possibilities, he did not prepare his report with the thoroughness his training should have demanded. Beyond this lies the question of his judgement as an engineer, which was constantly questioned by the governor to the extent that he was eventually recalled. He had proposed lines of fortification similar to Louisbourg's for Ports Toulouse and Dauphin, which he felt were naturally defensible, but which were also commanded by higher ground. Granted that the likelihood of a serious attack was considered remote at the time, there is little justification for ignoring such a basic concept of fortification.

Yet in essence Verville's proposals for defending Louisbourg went unaltered. The only major modification was the addition of the front comprising the Brouillan and Maurepas bastions and its communications to the original defences, but this did not entail the alteration of any of the works Verville had proposed. The weakness of its defensive position being unsuspected or ignored, Louisbourg was judged more than adequate to fulfil its role as a base for the fishing industry.

Physical Environment

Initially, the terrain must have looked very much like the undisturbed coastal zone of present-day Nova Scotia: low hills covered for the most part with scraggly, stunted fir or spruce trees rising above innumerable lakes and streams, or open patches of swampy ground upon which heather, pitcher-plants and other vegetation capable of flourishing in the acidic, poorly drained soil grow in profusion. The earliest known view of Louisbourg Harbour[30] depicts just such a scene, with the forest almost to the shore in most areas. The area to be occupied by the town and fortifications is shown as being already partially cleared: the displaced settlers from Placentia had begun establishing themselves there, as evidenced by the numerous habitations and fishing wharves all along the harbour shore. The defences Verville proposed were already under consideration, at least in the eyes of the artist, who showed the hills which were to be the sites of the bastions clear of trees and marked by tall poles. Subsequent activity on the site necessarily altered the ground considerably as the ditch was dug and the original hillsides were modified to accept the ramparts, but in the course of archaeological excavation, natural soil horizons and old land surfaces were exposed enabling a comprehensive picture of the pre-occupation landscape to be formed.

In the immediate area of Louisbourg, underlying bedrock is predominantly Proterozoic (Pre-Cambrian) -- metamorphosed sedimentary rocks classified in the Forchu Group and comprised of volcanic tuff and acidic lava, breccia, shale and sandstone. Later inclusions of softer strata deposited in basins in the older rock have largely been eroded away, causing lakes to form and creating coastal indentations such as Louisbourg Harbour.[31] Weathering and glacial activity have produced a stony parent material of glacial till from which, in turn, the local soils have developed. Deposited by the retreating ice-fields of the last glaciation, the cover varies from a few centimeters in depth to some 6 or 7 m in moraines or hollows in the bedrock. While the basically unaltered parent material is colloquially referred to as "pink clay," it is far too coarse to be classified as such, and deposits of true clay which can be fired are rare in the area, the nearest ones being on the Mira River. The subsoil is more correctly a sandy loam, as are the soils that develop from it, but poor drainage and high rainfall cause it to be heavy and sticky when excavated, whence the popular designation. In its undisturbed condition, it is hard and compact when dry because of the pressure exerted by the ice, but once excavated and redeposited, it lacks cohesion. Moreover, the quantity of inclusions is high, apart from the basic sand constituent: particles range from gravel (particles 2-7.5 mm in diameter) to cobbles (7.5-25 mm) to stones (over 25 mm) and huge glacial erratics. Bedrock close to the surface is affected by weathering and disintegrates rapidly into shaly fragments. Excavating in such material is no easy task and the resultant fill is less than ideal for constructing earthworks.

It is scarcely surprising that the topsoil is of poor quality. Podzolization occurs to varying extents throughout the area, the majority of soils being classified as gleyed podzols of the Mira Series, formed by imperfect drainage of constantly moist soils.[32] The leaching of minerals from just below the surface by the steady percolation of rainwater and their redistribution lower down give the soils of the area a colourful and highly distinctive profile. The surface or L-H horizon (fresh litter and decomposed organic material) formed beneath the vegetation cover is dark brown to almost black and peat-like in texture. Rainwater turns acidic as it percolates through this horizon so that the underlying Ae horizon is almost totally leached out and presents a light grey to almost chalk-white appearance. The top of the B horizon is stained yellowish brown by redeposited iron. Present intermittently in this horizon at Louisbourg is a true iron-pan: a hard, brittle band only a few millimeters thick and so dark as to appear almost black, as opposed to the more diffuse iron-enriched zone which is sometimes referred to erroneously as an iron-pan. As the effects of weathering and percolation become less apparent, the colours of the B horizon become a more muted pinkish or greyish brown and merge into the C horizon, essentially unaltered parent material.[33] Where a complete soil profile has been buried intact, the original surface is thus readily identifiable, given a basic understanding of the soil horizon. Discovery of the dark L-H horizon immediately on top of the greyish-white Ae horizon did cause confusion during the initial archaeological investigations of 1962 and 1963, leading to interpretation of these layers as evidence of extensive fire (charcoal and ash) or as layers of lime-rich mortar.[34] More prevalent has been the practice of describing a buried L-H horizon as an old sod or turf-line; this term should be applied only when a turf existed originally, but ground cover locally contains very little grass to produce a true turf except in once-cultivated areas. Hence the term should be confined to sectors where grass had been introduced, such as on the glacis, terrepleins or parapets, and pre-occupation buried surfaces referred to as buried organic layers.

There is little reason to assume any radical change in flora since the 18th century. Pollen analysis from buried surfaces within the King's Bastion reveals a ground cover typical of the coastal plain today: a predominance of heath (*Ericaceae*) and ferns (*Polypodiaceae*) with small shrubs (*Viburnum*) and moss (*Sphagnum*). Also present was a tree cover showing a preponderance of species common today, such as balsam fir (*Abies balsamae* [L.] Mill.), alder (*Alnus*) and spruce (*Picea*) with high proportions also of birch (*Betula*). Pine (*Pinus*) and hemlock (*Tsuga*) were then, as now, not common, but a surprising range of hardwoods no longer found in the immediate vicinity -- such as hickory (*Carya*) and oak (*Quercus*) -- was present, albeit in very small proportions. Maple (*Acer*) and willow (*Salix*) still abound at some distance from the site.[35] Louisbourg was not noted for an abundance of good construction lumber, as St. Ovide and L'Hermitte had pointed out as early as 1713,[36] and the best hardwood stands must have been rapidly exhausted. Significantly, samples of wood surviving in buried surfaces are identified as fir and spruce, while samples of beams and flooring are pine and hemlock. The few traces of hardwood that have been identified are either oak or maple.[37]

Post-Demolition History to 1960

Following the demolition of the fortifications and the eventual abandonment of the town, the site did not, as so often happens in the forest zone of Eastern Canada, revert to its original vegetation. Intensive occupation of a relatively small area (ca. 57 acres) radically changed the soil of the site with the cultivation of gardens and the accumulation of earth fill for the defences. Organic waste and the large amounts of lime used in mortar for the defences and dwellings greatly enriched the otherwise acid soil and a thick turf rapidly developed with the result that the whole area, ruined ramparts and house foundations alike, took on the appearance of open meadowland with low knolls. One species of grass has been identified as being European in origin and is known within the province only in

THE FORTIFICATIONS OF LOUISBOURG

the Louisbourg area,[38] raising the possibility that the French imported grass seed for the purpose of stabilising the ramparts and parapets; however, the grass, while of the strong, tenaciously rooted variety preferred for this purpose,[39] is found around the town but less commonly on the glacis.

While the defences had been systematically demolished and most of the houses destroyed during the siege or subsequently allowed to fall into ruin, the site was not completely deserted.[40] The French were gone, but a British garrison remained in occupation until 1768. By 1784 only four of the old French buildings remained standing and the residual British population was limited to a few families. Throughout the 19th century, settlement was equally limited, settlers of Irish, Scottish or English descent living in shacks along the shore or in wooden houses among the ruins. Animals grazed freely across the site and were penned in those casemates of the King's Bastion that had withstood demolition and the ravages of the climate. Visitors attracted by the romantic allure of history compared the once-thriving town with the desolate heath it had become and sought for ghosts -- or treasure -- in the ruins. On a more practical level, the site became a good source of building material, and many dressed sandstone blocks were removed to Halifax for use in public buildings or taken as foundation stones by settlers occupying the harbour shore outside the fortress. Removal of the entire "east gate," presumably the Maurepas, for this purpose is recorded. Bricks were a valuable commodity too, quarried and sold by lots of a thousand at a time. Where houses were constructed within the limits of the French town, foundations, cellars, wells and latrines left their mark on the site, as did attempts at field clearance and the establishment of property lines. Maps and photographs from the early years of the 20th century clearly indicate the density and type of occupations at the time. Yet the effect on the archaeological record was mitigated by the size of the site, only the most readily accessible areas being picked over.

Ironically, the worse damage has been the result of sporadic attempts to stabilize or "restore" the ruins. Interest in the site as an historic monument was first expressed at the turn of the century by Captain D.J. Kennelly, Royal Indian Navy (retired), the superintendent and co-owner of the *Sydney and Louisburg Coal and Railway Company*, when the company began buying up the old town with a view to extending the railway there and building a coal dock. These plans never materialized and the railway never progressed beyond the northeast end of the harbour, but Kennelly developed an interest in the site and determined to preserve it. He was successful in bringing about legislation declaring the place a national historic monument and establishing a memorial trust in 1903. Over the next three years he concentrated his efforts on the still-standing casemates of the King's Bastion: three on the left flank and four on the right had survived with their stone arches and the rampart above them intact. All loose masonry and protective earth fill over the arches were removed, the intact masonry supported with wooden cribbing and planks, and a cement pad poured on the roofs. Considerable amounts of rampart material must have survived more or less *in situ*, since a 1906 report noted that "about twelve hundred cubic yards" were removed from the roofs and around the casemates, sufficient to build a roadway 700 ft. long and 20 ft. wide across the King's Bastion to the contemporary access road. His activities were confined to structures which had survived above ground, and little excavation below the existing surface was carried out. On the inside of the casemates, a layer of broken stones was deposited on the surface, which was level with the terreplein of the bastion, before the cementing took place. On the left flank the escarp had survived, albeit in poor condition, providing a rear wall to the casemates, and enough excavation was carried out to permit stabilization of the escarp wall down to the level of the casemate floors and the terreplein of the bastion. A drystone drain was installed to allow water in the casemates to run off through the rubble accumulated at the left re-entrant angle.

Kennelly's enthusiasm and energy led to the gradual acquisition by the federal government of all properties within and immediately adjacent to the ruins of the town, and to the eventual declaration, in 1928, of the area as a historic site. Ambitious, if somewhat vague, proposals for the reconstruction of major elements of the fortifications were put forward, along with expressions of concern for the condition of the casemates.[41] Work carried out then was mercifully more modest in scope, although inevitably some of the most interesting areas of the town were objects of attention. In 1935-36 a museum and caretaker's house were built in what was Block 34 of the French town, thereby destroying house foundations. In the following decade, the casemates were again subjected to maladroit attempts to stabilize them, the facade of the left flank interior was

THE FORTIFICATIONS OF LOUISBOURG

extensively rebuilt, and repointing in cement was carried out on all exposed surfaces. The fill was entirely removed from the two *pavillons* or wings of the barracks and the walls were refaced from the foundation up to terreplein height; the rest of the building was stabilized by extensive repointing, but excavation did not extend much below terreplein level. The ditch on the town side was completely cleared, and the basement wall repointed or rebuilt on its outer surface, and the piers of the bridge across the ditch were reconstructed. Doorways, fireplaces and vents were rebuilt with dubious accuracy, and the bakery ovens in the basement of the north half of the building similarly disturbed. On the townside *place d'armes* the guardhouse foundations were stabilized.

After the war further attempts at stabilization were made under the auspices of the federal Engineering Service. Use of heavy equipment in archaeologically delicate areas ensured that this programme was an unmitigated disaster. The hospital, which occupied an entire town block, suffered the worst damage.[42] The house of the *commissaire-ordonnateur* was similarly treated, and a roadway bulldozed through the ramparts at the site of the Queen's Gate, destroying all traces of the original structure.

Of the work of the 1930s and 1940s, few records remain.[43] Most were apparently destroyed as "dead file" material in the late 1950s, although several photographs of these and earlier periods have survived.

Prior to the present programme, the last major intervention on the site was archaeological testing in various sectors throughout the park in an attempt to determine the feasibility of restoring the surviving remains.[44] The majority of the work consisted of locating the corners of structures and giving a brief description of the condition of the masonry, although the fortifications of the town were not examined apart from the guardhouse at the Queen's Gate and the powder magazine in the Brouillan Bastion. Considering the time and resources available, the programme encompassed a remarkably wide range, even including some test-trenching in the Island and Royal batteries. Unfortunately, there was no subsequent backfilling, with the result that trenches continued to erode and exposed structures to deteriorate. While objects of pottery, glass and metal were recovered, dressed stone doorway and window surrounds of architectural significance were left in the field to be shattered by winter frosts and displaced by work crews.

The various interventions recorded since the fall of Louisbourg all left their mark, but in overall terms, if we except the hospital, the barracks and *commissaire-ordonnateur's* house, the effect on the site was not too serious. In archaeological terms, the town and its defences had been extremely well preserved and offered a rare opportunity for the excavation of a fortress relatively undisturbed since its demise. In 1961 the site appeared as open, grass-covered fields in which the outlines of buildings and streets could be clearly traced; the fortifications were a series of grass-covered mounds and moss-covered rubble in which the demolition craters were clearly visible. Only the casemates and the cemented remains of a few buildings hinted at the extent of the material that lay beneath the surface.

The Sieges

A detailed account of the 1745 and 1758 sieges is beyond the scope of this report (reference may be made to several published sources[45]), but an analysis of tactics and an attempt to identify siegeworks positions are necessary prerequisites to an assessment of the degree to which the fortifications met expectations.

The 1745 Siege

The two sieges were remarkably similar. The first siege has been characterized, more in admiration than in criticism, as "a campaign of amateurs."[46] Certainly there were many irregular and even bizarre aspects to the campaign, which appears to have depended as much upon luck, audacity and Divine Providence as upon proper planning. In overall terms, however, there is no doubt that the organizers' strategy was sound. A direct assault on the harbour by naval vessels being rightly considered impractical, the expedition set ashore at the nearest safe landing place in Gabarus Bay, then moved overland to positions around the harbour and in front of the fortifications. Taking the harbour batteries was essential prior to any attempt to force the entrance to the harbour, and at the same time, siege batteries would attempt to destroy the landward fortifications.

Thus a two-pronged attack developed, the first major move being against the Royal Battery. No assault of this strategic work was necessary as the French precipitately abandoned it and the New Englanders walked in without firing a shot. The structure had not been disabled by the departing garrison and its guns had been inadequately spiked; consequently, the besiegers used the battery as a base and opened fire almost immediately with the four 36-*livre* cannon whose embrasures allowed them to be trained on the town.

At the same time, the beginning of the land approach to the town was signalled by the opening of the Green Hill Battery. The location of this battery has caused some confusion to historians, but the confusion is more apparent than real and stems from attempts to locate it by correlating various documentary sources rather than examining the ground. Pinpointing Green Hill on the several plans of the siege cannot be done accurately because the plans themselves are not sufficiently accurate. Various prominent landmarks such as ponds, White Point and Flat Point are all sufficiently displaced, when compared to modern topographic sheets, that Green Hill may be any of several hills in the area. But it was selected, even before the expedition set sail, as the one hill that commanded both the town and all other heights in the immediate vicinity,[47] and only one hill meets this requirement.

Green Hill was nonetheless too far away for effective artillery bombardment; shots fell randomly with little apparent effect on the defences. Batteries closer to the town had to be established. Again, the lie of the land dictated the obvious route: moving down the slopes of Green Hill in a northeasterly direction, one comes to a series of lower hills between the Barachois and the King's-Dauphin front. The area, known as the *fauxbourg* of the Dauphin Gate,[48] was divided into properties, one of which, belonging to Jacques Rabasse, was chosen as the location for a battery of Coehorn mortars. Although no surviving maps or plans indicate exactly where this property was, the description of a *hauteur* on the edge of the Barachois near the *rue du fauxbourg* makes the high ground overlooking the pond a logical choice, as the plans showing the siegeworks suggest, imprecise though they are, and the hill may be identified with some confidence. Located on a ridge parallel to and some 460 m from the right face of the King's Bastion, the Rabasse Battery's field of fire was depicted as concentrating on that area of defences, although lines of fire were also drawn between the battery and the right flank of the Queen's Bastion. It is not clear whether the fire is incoming, outgoing, or both.

The weak point of the *enceinte* was the Dauphin Bastion, and it was there that the major efforts of the land attack were concentrated. Taking advantage of the cover offered by the ridge extending from the Rabasse height toward the Dauphin Bastion, the New Englanders dug a trench in which two additional batteries could be erected. One, some 400 m from the Dauphin Gate, was used primarily to neutralize the guns of the right flank of the King's Bastion, which effectively flanked the Dauphin Bastion and vicinity, delaying the advance. The other, on the *"hauteur de Francoeur,"* was almost at the foot of the glacis, the distance to the gate being estimated at a mere 250 yards (222 m). Other descriptions make it clear that this hill was the one which had been a cause of concern to St. Ovide in the 1730s and which Franquet lowered by 7 *pieds* in the 1750s; at this time, because of a lime kiln built there for the repair work to the Dauphin Bastion, it was referred to as the *"hauteur du four à chaux."*

From such an advanced position, the tenaille front incorporating the gate was at point-blank range. The battery was within musket-shot of the ramparts, and much small-arms fire was exchanged. All efforts now concentrated on opening a breach in the wall. The task was not without danger: the battery was exposed to the fire from the bastion it was attacking and from the right flank of the King's Bastion. The area in front of the Dauphin was also exposed to fire coming over the water from the *Pièce de la Grave*, to the great discomfort of the gunners in the advance batteries.[49]

The Royal Battery had been aligned so that only a few of its guns could be used directly against the town, but the New Englanders promptly removed the remainder from their embrasures and set them up in field batteries. Some were used to supplement the Coehorn mortars of the Rabasse Battery and others were destined for a battery being constructed on a bluff overlooking the harbour and directly opposite the Dauphin Bastion. Known to the French as the *"hauteur de Martissan"* after the owner of the property, to the English it was Titcomb's Battery, named after its commander, Major Moses Titcomb.[50] Although farther from the bastion than the Rabasse Battery (670 m as opposed to 460 m), the guns in the new position could fire over the water at the exposed and unprotected masonry of the Dauphin Gate and Circular Battery. No intervening ground or glacis would deflect the shot. The effect of 36-*livre* (the equivalent of British 42-pounder) cannonballs under such conditions was devastating.

The siege was progressing well as far as the attackers were concerned and it seemed that events would soon culminate in a successful assault, but there was one drawback. Ideally, an assault should combine the army, storming a breach, and the navy, forcing the harbour, but while the land advance had established a breach and was ready to launch an assault by the end of May, the harbour batteries had yet to be silenced. Commodore Warren of the British squadron would not risk his ships until the Island Battery no longer constituted a threat.

Rather than carry out the logical, if more painstaking, steps of encircling the harbour and bombarding the Island Battery from a height, the New Englanders attempted a direct assault on the island, but were repulsed with the heaviest losses they were to endure throughout the whole campaign. Only then were guns taken around the harbour to Lighthouse Point and the Island Battery reduced. The way into the harbour was now clear and an assault imminent; the town surrendered.

The 1758 Siege

A landing in force on the same beaches as before was the prelude to the siege of 1758, although this time the French had endeavoured to forestall such an eventuality. Entrenched positions for troops armed with muskets and even small cannon were established around the shores of the most suitable landing places to both the north and the south of the town, but in the face of resistance, the British troops landed and began to encircle the harbour. As before, silencing the Royal and Island batteries was considered a priority, and as before, the French had abandoned Royal Battery without a struggle, but lest it be used against the town, they had removed its guns and partially demolished its defences. Thereafter, the Royal Battery had no importance in the sequence of events.

The experience of the first siege -- and perhaps common sense --indicated that the best way to deal with the Island Battery was from the commanding heights of Lighthouse Point and the campaign again took the form of a two-pronged attack. Wolfe struck north along the harbour shore, then pushed east and south to the lighthouse, while the other forces took position on Green Hill and began establishing a wide arc of batteries.

Once the Island Battery had been put out of action, Wolfe returned to take up an advanced position on the north of the land attack, with the intention of pushing forward to "two Eminences not far from the West Gate."[51] The most detailed and demonstrably accurate plans of the siege establish that these hills were the *"hauteur de la justice"* and the *"hauteur du four à chaux"*; the latter position was never operational as the town surrendered before the battery was fully established.

Apart from the much larger, professional British force in 1758, the major new dimension as compared to the earlier siege was the presence of a French naval squadron in the harbour. McLennan lists ten ships with armament ranging from 16 to 74 guns,[52] a force to be reckoned with in terms not only of sheer fire-power but also of the number of men capable of augmenting the defence of the town. Much effort therefore went into building siege batteries directed at the ships rather than the town, and earthworks intended to screen troop movements and encampments from the fire of the potentially lethal floating batteries. This in part explains the numerous siegeworks ringing the northeastern sector of the harbour beyond the Royal Battery. In fact, only one French ship, the 36-gun frigate *Aréthuse*, was ever used to any effect, and the French failure to exploit to the full the aggressive potential of the other ships has been severely criticized. The culmination of the siege was the destruction by fire of all but two ships. (One of the two was captured by a hotly contested cutting-out expedition and the other, the *Aréthuse*, escaped).[53] The demoralized French surrendered.

Although this siege was carried out by a professional force, it gives little impression of the ordered symmetry of a classic siege such as might be expected in a European context. No extended parallels are apparent and only in the direction of the Dauphin Bastion was there a systematic advance. The attack developed to the south of Green Hill consisted of a line of batteries extending away from, rather than parallel to or approaching the *enceinte*, the positions being dictated not by principles of geometry but by the lie of the land. A low, broken line of hills and knolls stretches across the peninsula on a roughly north-south alignment, and the trace of the defences is such that, except for the proximity of the Princess Bastion to the isolated point of Black Rock, the Dauphin Bastion is nearest to any high ground. The expanse of open bog is greatest in the south-westerly quarter; the high ground is the only choice for siege artillery.

The impracticality of an assault over this terrain does not justify McLennan's criticism that extending the attack southward from Green Hill was futile.[54] The issue of the ships in the harbour had not been resolved at the time the southerly advance was made, and it made good sense to keep the siege trains out of reach of the harm that the *Aréthuse* had demonstrated could be inflicted. Moreover, the weakness of the Princess Bastion was appreciated by those familiar with the town from the 1745-49 occupation, and the opportunity existed for extending an attack along the coastline to the vantage point of Black Rock. Franquet had been fully aware of this danger, recommending a detached redoubt in the area or at least razing the rock. Failing to accomplish either, he made do with an entrenched line from the glacis to Black Rock and small cannon mounted in field positions on the only high points along the coast. Any advance following the coastal plain would be contested directly and would also be subject to flanking fire from the ramparts. Under such circumstances, long-range batteries to destroy the flank embrasures are almost mandatory as a prelude to an advance; there is no need to assume that they would be attempting to breach the walls. Even if no advance were contemplated, sound siege tactics consisted of harassing the defenders over as wide an area as possible. Constantly on the alert, uncertain as to where the main attack would develop, unable to concentrate their strength in one sector, obliged to use more ammunition than they could afford, they would be forced all the more quickly to surrender.[55]

Whether or not, as part of the long-range bombardment, conscious attempts were made to damage the town and to terrorize the inhabitants is open to dispute. Certainly the French believed the worst of their enemies[56] and McLennan cites Amherst's orders to aim at the fortifications and not the town as if his gunners had to be instructed to desist from conduct unbecoming the rules of siege warfare.[57] Taking into account the compact layout of the town behind the walls and the inaccuracy of 18th-century artillery, it seems inevitable that a high proportion of projectiles would land within the town whatever the gunners' intentions might have been. In the siege of Quebec the following year, there was no doubt: Wolfe, desperate to force a surrender, resorted to the deliberate bombardment of civilian targets.[58]

As topographical detail is more accurately depicted on some of the plans of the second siege than on those of the first, identification of positions may be made more confidently. Central to both sieges is Green Hill. Wolfe appears to have bypassed the Rabasse position and set up a battery on the *"hauteur de la justice,"* which had not been exploited in the first siege. His next move, toward the lime-kiln hill, was common to both sieges. Similarly, across the Barachois, the *"hauteur de Martissan"* (Titcomb's Battery of the first siege) was again a logical choice; however, the batteries were now located farther from the shore, probably on the ridge above the present-day road, and considerably more guns were deployed. While the exact location of the batteries on the far side of the harbour may be debated, the terrain leaves little room for many alternatives.

Fieldworks

Positive identification of actual remains in the field is far more problematical. The terrain itself is a large factor. In a region where topsoil is at best a thin, stony litter over bedrock or waterlogged peat bog, the survival rate of temporary earthworks can scarcely be expected to be very high. Dense forest cover since the end of the French occupation has obscured many of the positions and made field investigation an arduous, frustrating task in which aerial surveys have been of only limited help. Nor has subsequent settlement contributed to preservation of the works around the harbour or closest to the town. On the Rabasse, Francoeur and Martissan heights no discernible traces of batteries or trenches survive, all three areas having been cleared for farming from the 18th century until the early 1960s, and the majority of works clustered around the northeast arm of the harbour have been effaced by the growth of the present-day town.

During the first siege only five batteries (not counting the Royal Battery) were established, and all the areas except Green Hill are devoid of any vestiges from either siege. The identification of Green Hill topographically is further confirmed by the numerous trenches, depressions and remains of breastworks on the crest and slopes, scarcely recognizable though most of them are. It was used as a starting point for the extensive works employed in the second siege and therefore the basic assumption is that any earthworks located there are attributable exclusively to the second siege. Certainly there was no way of distinguishing works of the earlier period.

Some of the best-preserved and most readily identifiable

THE FORTIFICATIONS OF LOUISBOURG

fieldworks are those constructed by the French. Franquet's Black Rock entrenchment has already been mentioned. Of the several V-shaped positions forward of this area, three are still clearly visible on knolls at the edge of the shore. The extensive lines of trenches in the Flat Point landing area and across the White Point peninsula have all survived virtually intact. At the main landing place of Kennington Cove (*L'Anse à Cormorandière*), trenches along the east end of the bay may still be seen, but coastal erosion and land clearance have destroyed everything else. North of the lighthouse, substantial traces of trenches are still visible at Gun Landing Cove (*L'Anse à Gauthier*) although coastal erosion is accelerating there.

The 1758 siege was characterized not only by the number of batteries and trenches established, but also by the many redoubts and defenced encampments flung up by the British. In part necessitated by the threat of the French ships' guns, they were required as a standard precaution against sorties by the besieged and any relief forces that might come to the aid of the town.

A British plan of the campaign shows the troop dispositions in detail. The main encampment is well to the west of the town, strung out along the ridges overlooking the Flat Point (Landing Cove) Brook. Turning thence in a northeasterly direction, various camps and redoubts occupy the high ground overlooking the harbour itself but out of effective cannon range. In the hills above the Royal Battery are still more encampments, together with batteries firing on the ships. A final encampment, established by Wolfe's brigade, is situated on the ridge above *L'Anse à Gauthier*, northeast of the lighthouse. On the lower ridges immediately behind Green Hill and dominating the Barachois and southwest arm of the harbour are advance posts and siege batteries. Across the open ground leading to Green Hill is an *épaulement* to protect troops from the fire of the *Aréthuse*.

Rectangular earthworks and depressions are still to be found on the wooded slopes along Flat Point Brook. To the south of the modern road to Kennington Cove, the remains follow the ridge to the west of the brook. North of the road, similar remains may be traced until their alignment intersects the brook, but beyond that, no positive identifications have been made.

In the area of Green Hill, the *épaulement* has vanished but the square redoubt on the knoll immediately to the northwest is still visible. Closer to the Barachois, trenches and redoubts clustered around the stream may still be seen, although the area has been disturbed by the construction of Marconi's towers in 1901, other buildings in the early 1900s, and a recent picnic ground.

Above the Royal Battery, the most prominent feature still to be seen is a large, rectangular enclosure comprising a ditch and raised earthwork -- the remains of a large troop camp. Vague trench outlines may still be detected on the slopes behind the camp, but any traces of the emplacements on the forward slopes have been obliterated by the construction of the modern visitor reception centre.

On the far side of the harbour are well-preserved remains of a double-crown redoubt of earth, occupying twin knolls overlooking what is today known as Havenside. From the way the work is positioned, it was designed not to fire on the ships, but to thwart any surprise attacks against the various batteries set up in the Lighthouse Point area.

For the most part, what has survived of the various siegeworks is badly degraded and barely recognizable. The best-preserved features are the square encampment above the Royal Battery, the double-crown redoubt at the northeast end of the harbour, and the French entrenchments around Flat Point Cove.

Conclusions

Twice besieged, Louisbourg was twice taken. From its inception, the place was criticized by a succession of governors for the inadequacy of its defences and faults in its construction which were attributed to the shortcomings of the engineers and contractors. The litany of complaints about the climate and the poor quality of the masonry which is such an integral part of the official correspondence certainly support the view that the place was in constant, abysmal disrepair, a helpless prey to any enemy who chose to attack it. Two statements, one from a French source, the other from a British, illustrate the prevailing attitude:

> The walls have to be recoated with roughcast mortar every three years, the harshness of the climate causing the roughcasting to fall away, which causes the joints [in the masonry] to deteriorate, the stones, being extremely irregular, cannot be laid in regular courses with proper joints as is done everywhere else ... the climate of Ile Royale is so hard, ... the weather there changes easily several times a day, for it can

happen that it is snowing heavily, the next moment it is raining down by the bucketful and within the same hour it freezes so hard as to shatter stones; these freezing temperatures following the heavy rain are what distort the walls and make them work apart so that they can no longer stand ....[59] (Author's translation).

More disparaging was the opinion of the British during the 1745-49 occupation:

Upon the whole the General design of the Fortifications is Exceeding Bad and the Workmanship worse executed and so Disadvantageously Situated that almost every rising Ground or little Eminence Commands one part or other, that either a Vast Sum of mony must be laid out to Fortify it properly or it will never answer the Charge or Trouble.[60]

The vulnerability of the low-lying site was of concern to the French also. The problems with masonry, particularly the parapets and embrasures, which caused Verrier so much trouble in every sector, need no further elaboration. Franquet's detailed reports on the dilapidated condition of the escarps and the major repairs needed to restore them to their proper state clearly demonstrate that the problems were, if anything, worse in the years immediately preceding the second siege.[61] The outspoken criticisms heaped upon Franquet by the military commanders, who held him chiefly responsible for the inadequacies of the defences,[62] together with statements made during the siege to the effect that the masonry could not withstand the concussion of the guns on the ramparts as they were fired,[63] reinforce the overall impression of decrepitude and vulnerability.

Was Louisbourg an expensive failure as a fortress? The very use of the term "fortress" conjures up an image of grand military strategy not entirely appropriate to the context of Louisbourg and should be applied with reservation. While it would be fatuous to contend that a town surrounded by ramparts and with a population comprised in large part of troops was not a fortress, the town was not conceived of as performing the same role as the strategic frontier places such as Neuf Brisach or Briançon; it was not placed on Isle Royale as part of a grand territorial design. Louisbourg's origins were commercial rather than military.[64] French usage sheds some light on the issue. While the word *"forteresse"* exists in the language, it is rarely applied to fortified towns, *"place forte"* or *"ville fortifiée"* being the more usual terms; *"forteresse"* is used poetically, rather than technically, or sometimes to refer to prisons.[65] The term *"forteresse"* was never applied to Louisbourg, and the alternatives appear to have been used rarely, if at all. On the many maps and plans and in the official correspondence such phrases as *"la ville de Louisbourg," "la ville de Louisbourg et ses fortifications,"* occasionally *"le port de Louisbourg,"* and often simply just *"Louisbourg"* are common currency. This is natural both in the European context in which towns, almost by definition, were walled, and in the context of a town whose *raison d'être* was fishing and commerce, not frontier defence. The same argument may be applied to numerous examples: we speak of Quebec City and the City of Montreal, but never think of them as fortresses, and in spite of its extensive defences, Portsmouth is a harbour town, not a fortress.

Why does Louisbourg emerge from history as a fortress rather than a town? Despite the interest and patriotic fervour briefly aroused by the two successful sieges, Louisbourg was never the focal point of British colonial policy in North America and has consequently become little more than an historical footnote, a stepping stone in the path of conquest. Historians treating of the grand themes -- the epic of empire, the struggle for dominance of a continent, the birth of a nation -- consider Louisbourg primarily in the context of Anglo-French rivalry. The place flits briefly across the stage as a nest of privateers and a stronghold threatening the expansion of New England and hence as the proving ground for the arms of a nation not yet born; later it is the obstacle barring the route to Quebec and Canada.[66]

While a case may be made for these points of view, to regard Louisbourg exclusively in such an historical context is to overemphasize its military and strategic aspect. The very term "fortress" has powerful military connotations which distort our perceptions. To anyone unfamiliar with the detailed studies of the town and its commerce undertaken over the last two decades, the realization that there was more than a military presence comes as a surprise. The site was not chosen as a strategic frontier location controlling access to a hinterland in the manner in which, for example, Mont Louis was established in the Pyrenees.[67] The population was not conscripted to maintain the fortifications; the fortifications were constructed to defend the town and harbour. Thus, in relation to the European background, Louisbourg was a fortified town and isolated place vulnerable to attack and therefore, in accordance with

French custom, furnished with a defensive perimeter. By any European standards, this perimeter was modest.

As first conceived, the *enceinte* of Louisbourg was little more than a basic horn-work like that used to cover a *faubourg* of a large town such as Besançon or Verdun. Smaller towns of roughly the same size as Louisbourg -- or even less -- were, because of their strategic locations, much more strongly defended. Montmédy in the Ardennes, Le Quesnoy on the northeast frontier of France, and Neuf Brisach in Alsace may be cited among numerous other examples. It is only when we consider even smaller places, located some distance to the rear of the principal frontier barriers, that anything comparable to Louisbourg may be found. In terms of the actual trace of fortifications, it most closely resembles Mont Dauphin, located on a narrow, rocky outcrop commanding the valleys leading to the Italian passes guarded by the mountain stronghold of Briançon, and the port of Antibes on the Côte d'Azur. The latter in particular invites direct comparison with Louisbourg because of its sheltered port and the defences which cut off a promontory of land enclosing the port. The headland on the other side of the port entrance commands the approaches with a square, four-bastioned fort (*Le Fort Carré*) of early 16th-century origin.[68] Yet even in the most simple fortifications, more extensive use of outworks is evident in the European examples than was ever the case at Louisbourg.

In a strictly North American context, Louisbourg's preeminence is perhaps more readily understandable, Parkman claiming it to be "reputed the strongest fortress," French or British, in North America, with the possible exception of Quebec.[69] If we are to take "fortress" to apply in a general sense to any fortified work, this was undoubtedly true, but in the sense of fortified towns, we may legitimately ask what others existed at that time. The French holdings in North America were vast, extending up the St. Lawrence to the Great Lakes, westward to the foothills of the Rockies, and south along the Ohio and Mississippi river systems through Louisiana to the Gulf of Mexico. But the area could scarcely be considered overpopulated, 90 percent of the inhabitants clustering in a small region along the St. Lawrence on each side of Quebec City; any claim to the rest was "an illusion of territorial power."[70] Towns were few and far between and, in essence, numbered only five: Louisbourg on the Atlantic coast, Quebec, Trois-Rivières and Montreal on the St. Lawrence, and New Orleans on the Gulf of Mexico. Of these, only three --

Louisbourg, Quebec and Montreal -- were furnished with bastioned masonry fortifications. The defences proposed for New Orleans in 1722 were never realized.[71]

Elsewhere, strategic routes were guarded by isolated posts whose function was essentially military. Controlling access to the Acadian peninsula, for instance, were Forts Beauséjour and Gaspareau; south of Montreal along the valley of the Richelieu, leading to Lake Champlain, were Forts Chambly, St. Thérèse, St. Jean and Isle aux Noix; on Lake Champlain were Forts St. Frédéric and Carillon (Ticonderoga); further west on the upper St. Lawrence and Lake Ontario were Forts La Présentation, Frontenac and Niagara; Fort Presqu'ile guarded the portages from Lake Erie to the Ohio River at the headwaters of which was situated Fort Duquesne (Pittsburg). Between Lakes Erie and Huron, Detroit was at once a frontier fort and an important trading post, as was Michilimackinac on Lake Michigan, while a string of lesser posts extended across the prairies as far as the Saskatchewan River. Fort Chartres guarded the southerly route toward the Mississippi. Although New Orleans was never fortified, several forts were constructed around the bay from time to time. Only a few forts -- Niagara, Chartres, Chambly, St. Frédéric and Carillon -- made extensive use of masonry; the rest were enclosed by simple wooden palisades or earthen ramparts, or a combination of both, and for the most part, the traces consisted of four bastions based on a square figure. Beauséjour, with five bastions, was an ambitious exception. Used as strategic bases in the French and Indian War (1754-63), the forts played the role reserved for fortresses in the European theatres of war, although no regular artillery sieges were conducted against them. Only against the essentially European fortifications of Louisbourg and Quebec were European methods employed (in both cases made possible by sufficient command of the sea to permit the transportation of siege artillery). Viewed in this context, Louisbourg may be seen not as one of the great fortresses, but as one of the very few places only remotely deserving of the description.

Mighty fortress or no, Louisbourg certainly absorbed a disproportionate amount of funds compared to what was spent on fortifications elsewhere in New France, and Thorpe has demonstrated that expenses actually exceeded those on Quebec.[72] Given the construction problems that plagued the place and loom so large in the official correspondence, were the fortifications an unjustifiable extravagance, an attempt by European engineers and contractors to impose European concepts on a North American context to which they were ill-suited?

There did not seem to be anything over-ambitious in the simple line of redoubts and retrenchments Verville initially proposed for the three possible locations he had in mind. Nor was the concept of *redoubts bastionnées* without precedent. A more ambitious series of redoubts had already been envisaged for Quebec by Beaucours and Chaussegros de Léry before the decision was made to defend the town with a continuous *enceinte*;[73] the substantially intact foundations and parts of the escarp of the bastion or *éperon* in front of the *redoute Dauphine* demonstrate that, in its intended form, it would have looked quite similar to the originally free-standing King's Bastion at Louisbourg. In the case of Quebec, a line of independent redoubts was abandoned in favour of a regular, bastioned *enceinte* constructed in advance of the original alignment, whereas at Louisbourg the communications between the redoubts were strengthened and revetted in masonry. How this decision came about and who took it is not clear. Thorpe would have it that in spite of instructions to keep the defences simple in accordance with the size of the colony, Verville exceeded his mandate and committed the government to an extensive, ambitious construction programme.[74] Little justifies this assertion since the engineer's first proposals were in line with his instructions and only later was he authorized to use masonry for anything other than the King's Bastion.[75]

It has further been asserted that the decision to use masonry was a grave error, the more rudimentary colonial techniques, using earth and timber, as proposed by engineers with colonial experience, such as l'Hermitte, being far more suited to the conditions.[76] While a commitment to masonry was indisputably costly in terms of time, effort and money, once the original choice of site and the decision to fortify it had been made there was little alternative. A masonry escarp was a means to an end, not an aesthetic whim; its function was to retain the earthen mass of the rampart and to present to an enemy a steep, unscaleable surface. The undesirable characteristics of masonry in the face of artillery bombardment were fully appreciated by the French engineers, but earthworks alone would erode too quickly, filling the ditches and forming gentle slopes that would present less of an obstacle; this was a criticism levelled at the earlier Dutch style of fortifications built in much less severe climates.

At Louisbourg, conditions were poor. The builders experienced difficulties in excavating the ditches in all sectors of the fortifications, encountering bog, boulders, high water tables and bedrock. The ditches did not produce enough earth; when the new *enceinte* at Rochefort Point was constructed, topsoil had to be stripped from within the town, even from the cemetery, to add to the rampart fill. Even so, Franquet's general criticism of the fortifications was that they were too low and their parapets not thick enough. The earth that could be found was of poor quality: stony, glacial till that is heavy and sticky when wet but lacks consistency when dry. The French complained of its poor quality during construction, as did the British when they tried to tunnel into the ramparts to place their demolition charges, and the recent archaeological excavations have borne out these complaints all too well, extensive shoring being the only remedy to frequent trench collapse. Wherever a soft cover of earth was desirable to absorb enemy fire, as on the glacis, a distinctive feature of the fill was the quantity of stones at the bottom, the better earth, in such scarce supply, being carefully reserved for the upper layers.

Lacking consistency, the earth finds its natural angle of repose on a fairly gentle slope: approximately 35 degrees to the horizontal as opposed to the 45 degrees theoretically attainable. While a steep slope could be achieved with careful terracing, a distinct difference existed between what was originally proposed and what was revealed in archaeological sections across the slope of the curtain ramparts. Both Verrier's original specifications and Franquet's recommended revisions called for a 45-degree slope, but neither of them achieved this, the slopes being much gentler. Thus, even if there had been sufficient supplies of earth to raise the ramparts entirely in that material, the steepest slopes attainable would still have been far too easily assailed. Some form of retaining wall was therefore necessary. The French were largely unsuccessful, in their quest for durable palisade posts, and the posts installed rotted very quickly; wood could never have been a reliable means of retaining the ramparts. Masonry was the only solution available.

The error lay less in choice of technique than in choice of site. An essential prerequisite to any construction is a good source of materials, but Louisbourg and its environs are not blessed with a wealth of natural resources. While supplies of sandstone, gypsum

THE FORTIFICATIONS OF LOUISBOURG

for plaster and limestone for mortar are all to be found elsewhere on the island, the French added to their difficulties by locating their principal establishment just about as far away from such sources as they could. Lumber, too, was constantly in short supply, good stands of timber being rare and hardwood virtually non-existent. Because of easy access to the sea, the builders of Louisbourg came to rely more and more on materials imported from other centres for their requirements: bricks and lumber from New England, sandstone, ornamental limestone and building hardware from France.[77]

Choice of site was thus less than ideal from a purely construction point of view. The inadequacies of the site in military terms have already been discussed. In light of our assessment of the defences and the main events of the two sieges, are we able, with the advantage of hindsight, to identify fundamental errors or omissions in the design of the fortifications? The application of a polygonal figure -- and hence a bastioned trace -- to the contours of the terrain made the low hills that were incorporated as bastions a logical choice, assuming that the decision to settle Louisbourg was irrevocable. It has been suggested that the other side of the harbour on the high ground above Lighthouse Point would have been a better military choice since there was no commanding ground in the immediate area,[78] but such a position is not tenable. Viewed from the harbour shore or from the road, the high ground appears to offer a secure location, but in fact the approaches from the north are furrowed with high ridges and gullies providing natural trenches along which whole armies could advance under perfect cover. Moreover, there is no easy communication with the shore or the hinterland; anyone attempting to defend it would be easily cut off and starved into surrender. Nor, from the commercial aspect, could an adequate quay front be established.

Commanding ground is not necessarily fatal if it can be controlled. Vauban characteristically took advantage of undefended ground when besieging a place, but was always careful to control the same ground with detached works when improving the defences of the captured town, which could never be taken by the same tactics he had used. The sieges and subsequent additions to the defences of Besançon and Luxembourg are classic examples. No attempt to remedy the problem of the commanding hills around Louisbourg ever got beyond the proposal stage.

There was, perhaps, some justification for this prior to the first siege: an approach overland by siege artillery was considered impractical. Ironically, such an opinion seems to have been encouraged by St. Ovide, who in his obsessive concern to ensure the complete protection of the harbour, felt that the landward defences could look after themselves. Complaining to the minister that Verville was wasting his time on the *enceinte* rather than concentrating on the harbour batteries, he successfully brought about a revision of priorities. His assessment of the landward defences is worth citing:

> Up to the present, work has concentrated on building a bastion to defend against a landward attack, which could only come about once an enemy had landed in the harbour, and this would be impossible today if construction of the harbour batteries had been begun first ...;

these batteries would oblige an army to land down the coast in Gabarus Bay and from there

> he would be absolutely incapable of carrying out [an attack on the town] because the only access is by way of mountainous slopes; over rocks; and through swampy forests which are almost impassable even to the local inhabitants, who can only get through with difficulty.[79] (Author's translations).

To what extent Verville concurred with St. Ovide's evaluation of the situation is not known, but he certainly never recommended any detached works, nor did he express any concern over the potential danger from the nearby hills. Verrier, responsible primarily for carrying out the construction of the fortifications according to his predecessor's designs, was similarly unconcerned with any problems beyond the foot of the glacis. We have already encountered his condescending tone in finally preparing plans to build, if the minister should so order it, a simple *lunette* in front of the Dauphin Gate "to relieve the governor's fears."

While the fears in question were expressed by Governor Duquesnel, the issue had been raised previously, probably by the obsessively cautious St. Ovide:

> A counterguard must be built in front of the Dauphin Gate, this gate being completely exposed ... this counterguard will besides augment the harbour defences and prevent an enemy setting up a position in the area of Martisan's property.[80] (Author's translation).

The accuracy of the prediction requires little comment. In view of the damage inflicted on the gate, the Circular Battery and even the right flank of the King's Bastion by Titcomb's Battery, established on the *"hauteur des Martissan"* in 1745, it is interesting to speculate on the outcome had the counterguard been built. Aggressive fire could have kept the besiegers from establishing both Titcomb's and the advanced batteries, while the structure would have screened the gate area from the worst bombardment.

Perhaps the most caustic criticisms of Verrier's capabilities came from the *commissaire-ordonnateur*, Bigot, following the first siege. The gate, he said, was no stronger than that of a country house and Verrier's only justification that

> he only made [the walls on either side of the gate] and the Dauphin Gate itself strong enough to resist musketry fire; I wouldn't have believed that it was acceptable to incur such expenses in the name of the king to protect merely against musket shots.[81] (Author's translation).

If Bigot reported Verrier's statement accurately, we must conclude that the attitude expressed as early as 1723 by St. Ovide prevailed, and that there was a general air of confidence shared by engineers and governors alike that no artillery attack need be expected from overland. It is scarcely likely that Bigot was unaware of this, although he was careful to disclaim all knowledge after the event.

Concerned above all with the security of the harbour, St. Ovide was by extension concerned with the security of the Royal Battery. It appears that he foresaw the potential threat from the rear, where the defences were light and, again, nearby, commanding hills offered an advantageous position to an attacker: the same prescient memorandum in which a counterguard was deemed necessary for the Dauphin Gate indicated the need of a redoubt on the hill above the Royal Battery.[82]

Control of the battery was an essential element of the 1745 siege. The French failure to defend it and the consequences of their precipitate retreat have already been discussed. Strategically, the error lay in the design, which concentrated the defences to seaward. That the engineers failed to take sufficient heed of the problem, even after it had been pointed out, proved to be a serious miscalculation. Muller seized upon the contemporary event to illustrate theories:

> There is generally another fault committed, which is, that if these forts or batteries are left open behind, or are very little fortified towards the land; the enemy may land men in the

dark and surprise them ....The same thing happened last year at Cape Breton, where the French had a battery of 15 large pieces of canon which the English surprised in the dark, and turned the canon against the place, whereby they became soon masters of it.[83]

What is surprising is the degree to which the French were unable to benefit from the lessons of the first siege. Most of Franquet's efforts were expended on the ramparts of the landward *enceinte*, and his project for improving control of the approaches and commanding heights were not authorized. More seriously, little was done to improve the situation at the Royal Battery, with the result that the work was again more of a liability than a vital element of the defence once a landing had been effected.

Franquet's project for establishing redoubts in front of the Dauphin Bastion and on Black Rock was not unduly ambitious, consisting as it did of extending the existing line of fortifications no further than the range of musketry, with well-protected communications connecting directly to the main works. The shortcoming of the redoubts, especially the one in front of the Dauphin Bastion, would have been that, anchored to the *enceinte*, they would not achieve command of more than the immediate environs and would have been subject to the same bombardment as the bastion behind them. The redoubts would have come into their own if an enemy attempted a direct approach, but would have been no deterrent to the establishment of siege batteries. In describing the various fronts of fortification, Franquet frequently mentioned the ground immediately beyond the glacis and the natural defence of the bog; with the flanking fire from the redoubts, he felt, an attack would be unlikely to succeed.[84]

The mine gallery under the glacis, Verrier's lack of concern for any additional outworks, and Franquet's confidence that no effective siege trenches could be dug in the boggy terrain all point to the conclusion that the engineers felt themselves well prepared to resist a *"siege en reglue"* and its precisely laid-out parallels and saps systematically drawing closer to the foot of the glacis. They seem almost to have fallen victim to the efficiency of their own training. To the Corps of Engineers, siegecraft had become a highly refined art practised with surgical precision according to well-defined rules and timetables derived from estimates originally prepared by Vauban. Only a regular siege conducted according to their rules could succeed and the terrain would not permit one: therefore the fortifications could withstand an attack even in the unlikely event that an enemy could bring artillery into action on the landward side.

If that was their reasoning, the outcome of the first siege should have disabused them. True, Franquet wished to command the nearest heights, but even so, he gave no consideration to the hills around the Barachois and to Green Hill, which was well within range. The poor results obtained by the New Englanders' battery on Green Hill in 1745 should not be taken as a general indication of the effective range of siege artillery; it reflected rather on the quality of that particular artillery and the gunners. Fire from the King's Bastion actually dismounted one of the Green Hill guns -- no mean feat considering that the besiegers were having difficulty hitting the walls at that range (ca. 1500 m).[85] The ring of British batteries in 1758 is more indicative of effective range.

In retrospect, Green Hill appears to have been the key. In both sieges it was a most effective assembly point and location for opening the artillery bombardment. From there an advance to left or right could be made, bringing artillery into forward positions, making optimum use of natural cover and hence digging the minimum of trenches. How would things have gone had the French themselves controlled Green Hill? Although it is itself commanded by the ridges to the northwest, the range is extreme. More important, it was one thing to land artillery on the beaches and drag them over the low swampy ground to the Green Hill position, but would have been quite another to manoeuvre them up into the higher ground beyond. Green Hill is at a natural crossroads. The low, open ground extending towards the coast curves around the hill, running in one direction along the harbour shore and in the other to Black Rock. In the second siege the frigate *Arthéuse*, anchored in the Barachois, effectively held up the British advance by commanding these approaches; from a position on Green Hill, the command is superb. Rising above the *"Plaine de Gabory,"* the hill's slopes provide a natural glacis for any fortification on its crest. Had the French invested less in the Royal Battery and instead built a powerful little fort on Green Hill, the whole land attack might well have been thwarted.

Such a fort would have been in the true Vauban tradition. One thinks of Mont Chaudane above Besançon, or, more appropriately, of the forts on the heights on either side of the small Mediterranean port of Collioure, near the Spanish border. However, prior to the first siege, the necessity did not appear to exist, and afterward, considering the fate of Franquet's projects, it seems unlikely that such a proposal would have been accepted even if it had been made. As the withdrawals from the Royal Battery and the coastal defences around Kennington Cove demonstrated, the troops' ability to conduct a spirited resistance in a detached position was limited. Perhaps this justified the early rejection of Franquet's redoubts: "the troops which at all times have been garrisoned here can never be compared with the old-established infantry of France as far as defending a place is concerned ...." (author's translation) wrote Rouillé in his letter rejecting any advanced works.[86]

Much has been made of the condition of the masonry as a contributory factor to the fall of Louisbourg. Was this, too, a reflection on the engineers' capabilities? The design of the fortifications and many of the buildings clearly did not take sufficient account of the climate, but to maintain that there was no construction season and the walls fell down as soon as they had been built[87] is oversimplification. Normally, construction can be carried out from mid-May to mid-October, while the problems of maintenance first began to manifest themselves with the parapets and embrasures a few years after construction. Use of beach sand still retaining a high salt content has been blamed for the failure of the mortar to set, largely perhaps on the basis of Franquet's speculations,[88] but the need for properly preparing sand for mortar was well known, as several treatises note and as Verville was careful to specify in his original *devis*.[89] The source of the trouble seems to have been in the small, irregular stones used for most of the construction, combined with the length of time required for lime mortar to set in a region of constant fogs, high humidity and driving rain. Once moisture has penetrated the joints -- or has never left them -- the effects of freezing temperatures are devastating. Naturally these first became evident on the most exposed areas, the parapets.

Archaeological excavation of the fortifications has demonstrated that under certain conditions the masonry was solidly built and able to withstand the combined ravages of climate, time and man, the most striking examples being the casemates of the King's Bastion, the powder magazine of the Dauphin Bastion, and the quay wall. The casemates and the escarps to which they were attached owed their survival primarily to the massive interior partition walls

THE FORTIFICATIONS OF LOUISBOURG

which acted as buttresses. If Verville had been allowed to continue with his idea of placing casemates behind all the escarps of the King's Bastion, all the walls would have been better preserved. As it was, the lack of interior buttresses caused the escarps of the faces to deteriorate badly, a problem Franquet recognized but was unable to rectify.

Approaching the problem from another direction, Verrier and Boucher were fully conscious of the shortcomings of the mortar and were able to devise the thoroughly practical, if unconventional, solution of encasing the walls in planks which acted as forms behind which the masonry could set firm. Franquet recognized the virtue of this technique, as his rebuilding of the right flank escarp of the King's Bastion testified. The extensive use of turf on the parapets and merlons was another inelegant but workable solution. It was never their intent or hope to build maintenance-free walls; a regular maintenance schedule was an essential prerequisite of sound defence. In using Medusa cement rather than lime mortar, the engineers responsible for the modern reconstruction of Louisbourg have reduced, rather than eliminated, the problem. Less than 20 years after construction, large cracks have appeared in the masonry and embrasures are being forced by frost action away from the parapets in which they are set. Climactic conditions caused and are causing unending maintenance problems.

In siege warfare as it had come to be practised in Europe in the 17th and 18th centuries, no place was expected to last indefinitely against an enemy. Fortresses presented a series of barriers to invading armies and served as bases for friendly armies. The ability to wage war successfully depended on the tactical disposal of armies in relation to fortified places: the campaigns of Marlborough (1702-10) are the classic examples. Vauban himself was a strong advocate of *camps retranchés*, large fortified enclosures in the lee of a fortified place permitting an army to rest and renew its supplies in safety while retaining the flexibility of movement that was lost once the army moved into the place itself. Once an enemy had committed himself to the siege of one place or to advance along a particular route, forces from other places could be regrouped to relieve the siege and to attack in their turn. Fortresses and armies were thus interdependent.

In this form of warfare, Louisbourg could not participate. It had no neighbours and no friendly armies were within reasonable distance. The nearest and only equivalent was the French navy, and relief by sea was a forlorn hope. Given sufficient determination on the part of an enemy who managed to control the sea and set an army ashore, no real chance existed of help arriving from the outside or even of getting a message through to ask for that help.

Nevertheless, the fall of Louisbourg in either siege was not a foregone conclusion. In spite of the disadvantages of the location and the disrepair of the fortifications, resistance was spirited. In both sieges the effects of prolonged bombardment on the town and civilian population were as much a factor in bringing about a surrender as anything else. In the first siege the New England troops were becoming disenchanted, especially after the Island Battery fiasco, and could well have decamped in the face of another setback. The only practicable breach established was in the Dauphin Bastion. Although the King's Bastion, its right face and flank in particular, suffered badly, no assault on it was ever contemplated. Both in 1745 and 1758, Louisbourg held out unaided for more than six weeks after the enemy had landed, and even in comparison with the length of sieges in the European theatres of war, such resistance was creditable by any standards.[90]

War games may be devised to replay the events of both sieges, to speculate on the great "ifs" of history, in attempts to identify the crucial points in the campaigns. Could the defence have been more inspired? Should there have been more sorties, should the landings have been resisted more vigorously? Could the harbour shore have been held by better placement of redoubts and intelligent use of the ships available? On the other side, what steps could the besiegers have taken to achieve quicker results with less risk? Such speculations are irrelevant: the events speak for themselves. Forced into the historical limelight as a reluctant fortress, Louisbourg fell to besieging armies after resisting, alone and unaided, for much longer than could have been expected considering its many defects. More could not be asked.

In establishing a fortified town on a remote island in the Atlantic off the North American mainland, the French were extending into the New World the fortification concepts of the Old. Engineers, contractors, administrators and soldiers came with those concepts to reinforce the conceit that here was another corner of France. Inevitably, the search to understand Louisbourg's fortifications has led back along that route to the European origins of the bastioned

THE FORTIFICATIONS OF LOUISBOURG

system.

Louisbourg's defences, albeit simple and inadequate by European standards, were squarely in line with methods and theories dating back to Vauban and beyond him to the Italian engineers who served under Francis I. The bastioned system had dominated European military architecture for well over a century prior to Louisbourg's founding and was beginning to show signs of obsolescence. Conceived as a response to a medieval form of warfare, bastions provided the defence with an overwhelming superiority against an enemy attempting to break through the walls of a place by main force. Geometrically calculated flanking fire ensured that no area of the *enceinte* could be assaulted openly with impunity and no blind spots existed to be used as a refuge for miners attempting to topple the walls. But the very success of such a defence stimulated progressive improvements in siege tactics. An enemy, forced by the protruding configuration of the bastions and an impenetrable curtain of fire from the flank batteries to begin his attack from a considerable distance away from the walls, had to approach gradually, under cover, until such time as he could hope to establish a breach. In bringing siegecraft to its highest form, Vauban above all eliminated the advantage bestowed upon the defence by the system he himself had been at such pains to improve. In its original form the bastioned system depended for its success on a poorly armed, inadequately protected force coming into its fields of fire. It was an inherently supine, nonagressive, form of defence that was no match for an enemy pushing forward well-protected trenches and siege batteries, especially with the improvements in artillery that occurred in the 17th century. In order to be effective, the passive defence of solid walls had to be combined with mobile forces on the outside. Toward the end of his career, Vauban stressed this repeatedly and began experimenting with different forms of fortifications, realizing the shortcomings of the basic bastioned design. Yet the medieval traditions died hard and Vauban's inventive curiosity was not perpetuated. Thus at Louisbourg the traditional, simple *enceinte* emerged, its defences essentially designed to deal with an enemy at close quarters. It is almost as if the engineers, so familiar with the rites of siege warfare, felt that no attack was to be considered seriously until it approached the foot of the glacis.

The short life span of the town and the lack of development subsequent to its destruction and abandonment offered a unique opportunity to examine a bastioned system unmodified by the changing military requirements of later generations. The initial research objective -- to provide sufficient architectural detail of the fortifications to allow convincing reconstruction -- could not have been accomplished without first understanding the methods and theories that were the common currency of the French military engineers who built Louisbourg, then assessing in detail what their intentions were and what they claimed to have accomplished. Scrupulous though the engineers' records were and graphically impressive though their many plans and drawings are, no real dimension could be given to the emerging image of bastioned work without visiting and studying numerous existing sites in Europe. To study Louisbourg's defences, archaeological excavation was the sole means of grasping reality. Thus the three strands of documentary research, analogues in military architecture, and analysis of the excavated remains are inextricably interwoven.

The exercise of participating in a major reconstruction programme, far from being a limiting factor, resulted in more exacting research, detail for detail, than would have been the case had no requirement existed that structures should actually arise. In dealing with an archaeological site of an 18th-century European culture, an adequate understanding of the site can only come about through an examination of the architectural, documentary and material evidence of that culture as a whole and of the site in particular. This paper is offered as a contribution towards such an understanding.

Notes

1. Pierre Goubert, *Louis XIV and Twenty Million Frenchmen* (New York, 1970), pp. 264-65.
2. J.S. McLennan, *Louisbourg from its foundation to its fall* (Sydney, N.S.: Fortress Press, 1969), p. 12.
3. J.S. McLennan, *op. cit.*, Chapters 2 & 3, *passim*.
4. Directly as a result of the massive reconstruction project now reaching its final phases, much pertinent material has been acquired and much has been written although relatively little has been published to date. For an overall appreciation, J.S. McLennan, *op. cit.*, thus remains an authoritative source. More recently, an assessment of French construction in the area has furnished a useful outline of pertinent events at Louisbourg among other places: F.J. Thorpe, "The Politics of French Public Construction in the Islands of the Gulf of St. Lawrence, 1695-1758" (Ph.D. thesis, University of Ottawa, 1973). The historical summary is based on this

THE FORTIFICATIONS OF LOUISBOURG

work unless explicit reference to the contrary is made.

5. For a detailed examination of the economics of trade and its significance for the colony, see Christopher Moore, "Merchant Trade in Louisbourg, Isle Royale" (M.A. thesis, University of Ottawa, 1977).
6. The incidents leading up to the first siege of Louisbourg and an account of the siege itself are described in J.S. McLennan, *op. cit.*, Chapters 8-10, *passim*.
7. *Ibid.*, p. 134.
8. G.A. Rawlyk, *Yankees at Louisbourg* (Orono, Maine: University of Maine Press, 1967), pp. 152, 157.
9. For background to the acts of hostility on both sides, see J.S. McLennan, *op. cit.*, Chapter 11 *passim*.
10. The expedition led by the Duc d'Anville, broken by Atlantic storms off the Nova Scotia Coast. See *ibid.*, p. 174; also G.A. Rawlyk, *op. cit.*, pp. 157-58.
11. McLennan cites documentary evidence from the "*Journal du siege de Louisbourg, 1758*" to the effect that Franquet was seriously ill all this time, which would have reduced his effectiveness when considerable energy was required. J.S. McLennan, *op. cit.*, p. 198.
12. Again, McLennan's account is valuable in its detail. *Ibid.*, Chapters 13, 14, *passim*.
13. Part of Pitt's instructions to Amherst, February 1760, cited in *ibid.*, p. 290.
14. For a discussion on the concepts of restoration vs. reconstruction, see Bruce W. Fry, "Restoration and Archaeology," *Historical Archaeology*, Vol. 3 (1969), pp. 49-65.
15. AN, Col., B, Vol. 35, ff. 248v-51v, cited in J.S. McLennan, *op. cit.*, p. 10; also F.J. Thorpe, *op. cit.*, p. 22.
16. "*On y [at Louisbourg] auroit fait le principal Etablissement si ce port avoit pu estre aisement fortifiée, et s'il y avoit eu assés de grave pour y faire secher le poisson des Vaisseaux de pescheurs, mais le peu de grave qu'il y a et la depense immense qu'il en auroit couté pour mettre ce port entièrement hors d'insulte determina le feu Roy sur la demande des officiers de l'Isle Royalle et des Negocians du Royaume a faire partir le principal Etablissement au Port Dauphin ... Le Conseil fera observer au Sr. de Verville au sujet de ses fortifications qu'il ne convient point par raport aux grandes depenses que cela cause, de fortifier aussi en grand dans les colonies que l'on fait en Europe ....*" AN, Col., F^3, Vol. 51, pp. 2-9, Instructions to Verville from the Council of Marine, 23 June 1716.
17. "*Elle [sa Majesté] s'est déterminée a commencer les fortifications de cette Isle par le Port de Louisbourg comme le Port le plus important tant par raport aux avantages qu'il a sur les autres pour la pesche par sa situation.*" AN, Marine, A^1, Article 54, p. 61, Mémoire du Roy au Sieur de Costebelle et au Sieur Soubras, 26 juin 1717.
18. As suggested in F.J. Thorpe, *op. cit.*, p. 28.
19. "*Suivant le sentiment de tous les marchands et pescheurs paroist a ce sujet le meilleur de l'Isle.*" AN, Col., F^3, Vol. 51, p. 23.
20. "*Par l'heureuse disposition du Terrain pour la fortification, par la difficulté de l'Entrée du port en ôtant les balises, par la bonté du terrain et par la proximité de l'Acadie avex les avantages de la pesche, ce port est un des meilleurs postes de l'isle.*" *Ibid.*, p. 27.
21. *Ibid.*, pp. 74, 54, 85, 93-94. A summary of comparative costs is given by Verville as follows: Louisbourg: 121 244 l.; Port Dauphin: 85 468 l.; Port Toulouse: 106 783 l.; and defensive works at Baye Royalle: 16 082 l.
22. *Ibid.*, pp. 95-96, "*Mémoires du Conseil de marine au Sieur de Verville, Brigadier d'Ingenieurs.*"
23. "*On avoit assuré que la plage de Louisbourg ne pouvoit estre abordée en aucune Saison et qu'il seroit inutile de la fortifier .... On a debarqué a cinq endroits dans une seule matinée,*

il est bon d'examiner de pres ce que l'on dit en Amerique." Ibid., p. 172.

24. F.J. Thorpe, *op. cit.*, p. 36.

25. Cf. AN, Col., F³, Vol. 51, pp. 193-94, Instruction to Verville, 10 June 1718 (also cited in F.J. Thorpe, *op. cit.*, p. 33).

26. *"C'est une place en amphitheatre commandée par diverses hauteurs de façon que le Boulet & la bale l'enfilent au point, que l'on n'y peut estre en sureté nulle part, ny dans les maisons ny dans les rues."* AN, Col., C¹¹B, Vol. 29, f. 366, *"Mémoire sur l'Isle Royale"* par M. Roma, officier, 1750. Roma was not, in fact, a military man, but had authorization to found a fisheries venture on Ile St. Jean (Prince Edward Island).

27. Recent studies have shown that the sea level is rising at a rapid rate. Along the Cape Breton coastline it is approximately 80 cm (2.43 ft.) higher than during the French régime. D.R. Grant, "Recent Coastal Submergence of the Maritime Provinces," *Canadian Journal of Earth Science*, Vol. 11 (1970), pp. 70-79.

28. Precise figures on the range of muzzle-loading cannon in the 18th century cannot be given with any accuracy as too many variables existed; however, at the time of the first siege of Louisbourg one authority records point-blank range "of different pieces of cannon" as "about 300 fathom," while extreme range of "random shot" varies between 2,250 fathoms for a 24-pounder to 1,520 for a 4-pounder.

Based on an English fathom, an average point-blank would be 1,800 ft. or 548.64 m; based on the French *toise*, we would have 1,918.8 ft. or 584.85 m. "Point-blank" range is obtained by firing the gun with the barrel horizontal. "Random shot" with the barrel elevated to 45 degrees would vary between over 4,000 m and 2,900 m.

Guillaume Leblond, *A Treatise of Artillery* (Ottawa: Museum Restoration Service, 1970), p. 42.

29. *"Le terrain qui est en avant, est un composé de roc, et d'une nature a former de difficultés quasi insurmontables au cheminement d'une tranchée, d'ou je conclus qu'au moyen des augmentations projettées* [raising the glacis, placing more traverses on the covered way, and enlarging the place d'armes] *l'on n'approchera des dits trois fronts* [those facing landward] *que difficilement, et avec les formalités d'un siege en regle."* BG, Ms 205b, à Mgr. Rouillé Ministre et Secrétaire d'État de la Marine, Louisbourg, 13 octobre 1750, p. 12.

30. BN, Dépot des Cartes et Plans de la Marine, Service Hydrographique, Portefeuille 131, *"Veue du Port de Louis-bourg dans L'Isle Royalle,* printed in 1716 or 1717, artist unknown, published in John Fortier, comp., "The Fortress of Louisbourg: Cartographic Evidence," *APT*, Vol. 4, Nos. 1-2 (1972), Fig. 1.

31. Canada. Department of Mines and Technical Surveys. Geological Survey of Canada. Geological Series, Maps 1056A, Sheet 11 G/13 (Louisbourg).

32. Information concerning soil formation and local soil types has been provided by the Nova Scotia Soil Survey Station of the Government of Canada Department of Agriculture Research Branch, Truro, Nova Scotia. The author is particularly indebted to James I. McDougall, and to pedologist John L. Nowland, who worked closely with Louisbourg staff for several years, examined archaeological sections, prepared soil profiles and gave many invaluable lectures on the subject.

33. For a more complete description of typical soil horizons, see National Soil Survey Committee of Canada, *Proceedings of the Sixth Meeting of the National Soil Survey Committee of Canada*, (Laval University, Quebec, October 1965), pp. 18-22.

34. Cf. Iain C. Walker, "Preliminary Report: Excavations at King's Bastion, Fortress of Louisbourg, September to December 1962" (manuscript on file, Fortress of Louisbourg, 1963), p. 28; Peter D. Harrison, "Report on the Right Face Casemates,

THE FORTIFICATIONS OF LOUISBOURG

King's Bastion, Fortress of Louisbourg" (manuscript on file, Fortress of Louisbourg, 1964), Fig. 17.

35. Pollen analysis supplied by the Pleistocene Palynology Laboratory, Geological Survey of Canada, Dept. of Mines and Technical Surveys.

36. Cf. F.J. Thorpe, *op cit.*, p. 292.

37. Based on identification of 50 wood samples located in the King's Bastion. Analysis supplied by the Department of Forestry, Forest Products Research Branch, Ottawa Laboratory.

38. Identified as purple heath-grass (*Molinia caerulea*). W.G. Dore and A.E. Roland, "The Grasses of Nova Scotia," *Proceedings of the Nova Scotian Institute of Science*, Vol. 4 (1942), p. 212.

39. Cf. "*dent de chien*" recommended by de Ville, *op. cit.*, p. 275.

40. Details on the history of the Louisbourg area subsequent to 1760 are based on Wayne Foster, "Post-Occupational History of the Old French Town of Louisbourg 1760-1930" (manuscript on file, Fortress of Louisbourg, 1965).

41. "Memo re Louisbourg Historic Park" draft prepared for approval of the Historic Sites and Monuments Board of Canada by Judge W. Crowe, 23 March 1929; copies to Major Pinard, Secretary to the Board, and Senator J.S. McLennan, documents on file, FLNHP.

42. J. Russel Harper, "The Fortress of Louisbourg: A report of preliminary archaeological investigations carried out in the summer of 1959 under contract with Department of Northern Affairs and National Resources" (manuscript on file, Fortress of Louisbourg and Historic Sites Service, Ottawa, 1962).

43. Labour and material costs; copies on file, FLNHP.

44. J. Russel Harper, *op. cit.*

45. For the first siege: Raymond F. Baker, "A Campaign of Amateurs: The Siege of Louisbourg, 1745," *Canadian Historic Sites: Occasional Papers in History and Archaeology*, Vol. 18 (Ottawa: Parks Canada, 1978); J.S. McLennan, *op. cit.*, pp. 128-65; and G.A. Rawlyk, *op. cit.* For the second siege: J.S. McLennan, *op. cit.*, pp. 236-89. For a detailed discussion of the landing, see J. Mckay Hitsman and C.C.J. Bond, "The Assault Landing at Louisbourg, 1758," *Canadian Historical Review*, Vol. 35, No. 4 (December 1954), pp. 314-30.

46. Raymond F. Baker, *op. cit.*, pp. 7-13.

47. *Ibid.*, p. 24.

48. "*Fauxbourg de la Porte Dauphine*" appears on several plans of the town and harbour; hence, although correct usage in modern French would be *faubourg*, the archaic form is retained for the purposes of this report.

49. Raymond F. Baker, *op. cit.*, p. 30.

50. *Ibid.*

51. J.S. McLennan, *op. cit.*, p. 263.

52. Wolfe's Orders, 30 June 1758, as cited in J.S. McLennan, *op. cit.*, p. 269.

53. *Ibid.*, pp. 267-68, 271-72, 274-75, 278, 280-84.

54. *Ibid.*, pp. 276-78.

55. Obviously, there is a nice balance to be maintained between keeping the defenders on the *qui vive* and in overextending the manpower and supplies available to conduct an effective siege. Thus Vauban warned against opening fire from siege batteries too soon and too far away, or of wasting ammunition unnecessarily where no attack would develop. Sebastien Le Prestre de Vauban, *Traité de l'attaque et de la défense des places* (La Haye: P. de Hondt, 1737), p. 89.

56. AN, Col., C^{11}B, vol. 38, ff. 79-81, Drucour's Siege Journal (includes copies of

letters to and replies from the British commanders, 6-8 July 1758).

57. J.S. McLennan, *op. cit.*, p. 276.

58. C.P. Stacey, *Quebec, 1759: The Siege and the Battle* (Toronto: MacMillan, 1959), pp. 64-65.

59. "*Il faut crespir les Murs tous les trois ans, la dureté du climat faisant tomber les crespissages ce qui dégrade les joints, les parements, le Moillon etant très baroque, ne pouvant faire les joints ni les lits aussi quarrés qu'ils se font par tout ailleurs ... le climat de l'Isle Royale est très dur, ... le temps y change facilement plusieurs fois par jour, car il arrive souvent qu'il neige abondamment, le moment d'après il pleut à verse et dans la même heure il gèle à pierre fendre; ce sont ces gelées qui viennent après les pluyes qui gonflent les murs, et qui les écartent à ne pouvoir se soutenir.*" AN, Col., C¹¹B, Vol. 21, ff. 271-79, "*Memoire pour les ouvrages faits et à faire pour les fortifications de Louisbourg et pour sa deffence,*" anon., n.d. (1739). This document is classified with Verrier's correspondence, but it seems highly unlikely that he was the author, as many of the recommendations were specifically contrary to his point of view. Cross-reference to other correspondence suggests that the author was in fact the departing governor, St. Ovide, summarizing a list of priorities and problems for his successor, Forant.

60. PAC, MG 11, CO 217, Vol. 28, Knowles and Bastide, "State of the Fortifications," 8 July 1746.

61. AN, Col., C¹¹B, Vol. 36, ff. 263-67, Franquet to Minister, 6 December 1756.

62. AN, Col., C¹¹C, Vol. 16-2, ff. 221-240, St. Julhien to Minister, 20 September 1757.

63. AN, Col., C¹¹B, Vol. 38, f. 91, Drucour's Siege Journal; BG, Ms. in ff. 66, 75v, Grillot de Poilly's Siege Journal.

64. F.J. Thorpe, *op. cit., passim*. Chapters 1 and 8 in particular develop this argument.

65. Larousse du XXᵉ Siècle: "*Le mot 'forteresse' est longtemps peu usité dans le langage militaire français, où l'on employait et où l'on emploie encore de préférence le terms de 'place forte' pour désigner une ville entourée de fortifications, et celui de 'fort' pour indiquer un ouvrage établi à l'écart de tout centre de population. C'est surtout après la guerre franco-allemande de 1870 qu'on s'est servi en France, du terms de 'forteresse', plutôt pour qualifier les troupes ou les armes qui servent à l'attaque ou à la défense des places fortes, que pour désigner les places mêmes ...*"

66. Francis Parkman, *A Half Century of Conflict* (New York: Collier Books, 1962), pp. 290-96, 310-26; *ibid., Montcalm and Wolfe* (New York: Collier Books, 1962), pp. 385-407; and W.J. Eccles, *The Canadian Frontier, 1534-1760* (New York: Holt, Rinehart and Winston, 1969), pp. 151, 154, 177-78.

67. Lt. Col. Cornet, "Mont Louis, création de Vauban," *Revue Historique de L'Armée* (Ministère de la Défense Nationale), No. 2 (1971), pp. 21-37.

68. Today little survives of the fortifications: the sea-wall, frequently indented to provide flanking fire as it follows the outline of the coast and the mole around the harbour are still preserved, as is the Fort Carré, but the landward defences have disappeared.

69. Parkman, *A Half-Century of Conflict, op. cit.*, p. 293.

70. Marcel Trudel, *Introduction to New France* (Toronto: Holt, Rinehart and Winston, 1968), p. 128.

71. Samuel Wilson, Jr., *Bienville's New Orleans* (New Orleans: Friends of the Cabildo, 1968), p. 15 and plan opposite.

72. F.J. Thorpe, *op. cit.*, pp. 15, 146, 150.

73. A detailed history of the Quebec fortifications, co-authored by André Charbonneau, Yvon Deloges and Marc Lafrance, has recently been published. *Quebec the Fortified City: from the 17th to the 19th Century* (Ottawa: Parks Canada,

THE FORTIFICATIONS OF LOUISBOURG

1982). The present writer was responsible for the 1973-78 excavations of the Redoute Dauphine and the ramparts of existing Quebec City.

74. F.J. Thorpe, *op. cit.*, p. 28.

75. AN, Col., F³, Vol. 51, pp. 95-96, Mémoire du Conseil, 3 July 1717.

76. This theme is first propounded by J.S. McLennan, *op. cit.*, p. 51, who uses the well-preserved entrenchments around Flat Point to support his argument. It is taken up by F.J. Thorpe, *op. cit.*, pp. 10-11.

77. F.J. Thorpe, *op. cit.*, pp. 316-17.

78. Margaret Fortier, "The development of the fortifications at Louisbourg," *Canada: An Historical Magazine*, Vol. 1, No. 4 (June 1974), p. 19.

79. "*L'on est Jusqu'à attaché à faire un bastion pour deffandre la terre qui ne peut être attaquée, quaprés que L'ennemy ce sera emparé du port, ce qui luy seroit impossible aujourdhui, sy l'on avoit commancé de faire des Batteries en dedans du havre ... il ne scauroit absolumment Executé ce dessein* [an attack on the town] *par les difficultés des chemins qui ne sont que des montagnes escarpées; des Rochers; des fondrières de sapinages presque impracticables mesme par le gens du pays, qui ne scauroient sen tirer quavec peine.*" AN, Col., C¹¹B, Vol. 6, ff. 178-180v, St. Ovide to Minister, 22 November 1723.

80. "*Il faut faire une contregarde devant la Porte Dauphine, cette Porte etant entièrement découverte ... cette contrearde serviroit d'ailleurs a la deffense du Port et à empêcher que les Ennemis puissent s'établir aux environs du Martisens.*" AN, Col., C¹¹B, Vol. 21, f. 276, "*Mémoire pour les ouvrages faits et à faire*," anon., n.d. (1739), probably written by St. Ovide.

81. "*qu'il ne les* [the walls on either side of the gate] *avoit fait, ainsi que la porte dauphine, que pour resister a la mousqueterie; je n'aurois pas cru qu'il fut convenu de faire au roy une dépense pareille à celle quil a fait, pour mettre cette ille à l'abri seulement du coup de fusil.*" AN, Col., F³, Vol. 50, pp. 374-75, Bigot, 1 August 1745.

82. AN, Col., C¹¹B, Vol. 21, f. 278, "*Mémoire pour les ouvrages faits et à faire.*"

83. John Muller, *A Treatise Containing the Elementary Part of Fortification, Regular and Irregular* (1746; Ottawa: Museum Restoration Service, 1968), pp. 201-02.

84. AG, CTG, 14-1-32, "*Mémoire sur le front de fortification*," Franquet, 20 November 1751.

85. Raymond Baker, *op. cit.*, p. 25.

86. AG, CTG, 14-1-45, Minister to Franquet, 15 March 1752.

87. Christopher Duffy, *Fire and Stone. The Science of Fortress Warfare 1660-1860* (London: David and Charles, 1975), p. 38.

88. AG, CTG, 14-1-43, "*Mémoire ... sur les materiaux ...,*" Franquet, 20 November 1751.

89. AN, Col., F³, Vol. 51, f. 60.

90. For a listing of various sieges and their duration, see David Chandler, *The Art of Warfare in the Age of Marlborough* (London: Barsford, 1976), App. 3, pp. 308-10.

Mutiny at Louisbourg, December 1744

Allan Greer

I

Late in December, 1744, a mutiny erupted in the fortress of Louisbourg, capital of the French colony of Isle Royale. With only a few exceptions, all the soldiers in the garrison turned on their officers, threatening to kill them and ransack the town. Faced with such complete rebellion, the local authorities could only give into the insurgents' demands. As a result, no blood was spilled and the openly violent confrontation was short-lived. Nevertheless, this episode seems to be a noteworthy event in the military history of the eighteenth-century French empire. Unlike other contemporary mutinies, it occurred in wartime and involved the nearly unanimous participation of the soldiery. Certainly the French authorities in the Marine ministry considered it a serious matter and, as a result, some mutineers were severely punished at Rochefort where the garrison was quartered after Louisbourg surrendered to the English in June 1745. The purpose of this essay will be, first of all, to reconstruct the events of the mutiny, not a simple task since the only useable sources, court-martial transcripts and the reports of officers and colonial officials, are all the special pleas of men anxious to save their lives or their careers. Secondly, an attempt will be made to outline the long-term and immediate causes of the revolt. This involves an examination of some of the peculiar characteristics of military life in Louisbourg in the decades preceding the outbreak.

The colony of Isle Royale was established in 1713, although Louisbourg had only been its capital for 25 years by 1744. Administrative hub and centre of the fisheries that were the mainstay of the island's economy, Louisbourg was also a military stronghold. Its massive stone fortifications were designed to protect the colony and guard the maritime approaches to Canada. In the year of the mutiny, the Isle Royale garrison was made up of nine companies of *troupes de la marine*, or *compagnies franches de la marine*, one of them a special artillery company, together with 150 men from the Swiss Karrer regiment. There were about 600-650 men in all and the majority (perhaps 525-575) were concentrated in the capital, leaving 75 soldiers to man the colony's isolated outposts. Soldiers -- that is, military personnel excluding officers -- made up about one quarter of Louisbourg's population when a census was taken in 1737. The most important organizational unit in the garrison was the company. Each *compagnie franche* was commanded and administered by a captain who was fairly autonomous, although subordinate to the *état-major*. This body included the town major and his assistants and the commanding officer, who also generally acted as governor of the colony.

The Swiss contingent with its peculiar organization and special privileges was a complicating element in the garrison. It apparently operated as a large company with three subaltern officers and almost 150 men all under the command of a *capitaine-lieutenant*. The latter, usually referred to as the "Swiss commandant," owed allegiance to his colonel who resided at the regiment's base in France, but he was also subject to the control of the colonial *état-major*. Colonel Karrer was bound by contract to maintain his regiment in the service of the Marine ministry in return for a monthly payment of 16 *livres* per man.[1] In principle, he was responsible for recruiting, equipping, and paying his officers and men. However, in practice, part of the 16 *livres* per man-month owed to Karrer was remitted directly to his officers stationed at Isle Royale for distribution as wages to the troops. The French authorities at Louisbourg gave rations to the Swiss soldiers like those issued to the men of the *troupes de la marine*. The cost of this food was retained in the colonial treasury. In effect, the Swiss soldiers paid for their rations through wage deductions exactly as the French did, even though Colonel Karrer was theoretically responsible for their upkeep and pay. Karrer's contract guaranteed his regiment certain special privileges, notably judicial autonomy. Most of these were common to all Swiss regiments in the French service. The special status of the Karrer contingent at Louisbourg was often a source of annoyance to the military and civilian administrators of the colony. Bitter disputes occasionally arose when the Swiss officers felt their rights were threatened.[2]

II

Isle Royale had been at peace with its neighbours during the two decades and more that the fortifications of Louisbourg were under construction but, in the spring of 1744, war broke out between France and England. In the North American possessions of the two belligerents, privateers were soon equipped to prey on enemy shipping and consequently one of the first effects that the war produced in Louisbourg was a shortage of provisions and other supplies. The colony was heavily dependent on imported commodities but French traders hesitated to send their ships across the Atlantic where they might be captured. In Canada, another major supplier of foodstuffs, harvests were poor. To make matters worse in Louisbourg, hundreds of British prisoners captured by the colony's raiders had to be fed in the summer and autumn. More than most other groups however, the soldiers of the garrison, both French and Swiss, were sheltered from the effects of shortages of this kind. In return for a constant deduction from their pay that was unaffected by market fluctuations, the men received rations from the larger stocks of flour, salt pork and other staples that the government maintained for their consumption. Occasionally, in time of food shortages, they would be given reduced rations or biscuit instead of bread so that the authorities could distribute supplies from the king's storehouse to needy civilians. Often the problem was one of food quality rather than quantity and soldiers frequently complained when their bread was made of rotten flour mixed with good.[3] Thus, it was not an unprecedented development when late in 1744 the *commissaire-ordonnateur* François Bigot, the colony's highest ranking civilian official, ordered the public sale of foodstuffs from the government storehouse and the soldiers, whose rations were still not reduced, received inferior provisions as a result.

The event that pushed the garrison to revolt occurred about one week before Christmas when the troops received their fortnightly issue of "vegetables." These were the dried peas and beans which were the major ingredient of the soup that formed the soldiers' evening meal. In this case, they were rotten and completely inedible. Some men apparently became ill from eating them but those who simply did without and ate only their bread ration and their spruce beer were in no danger of starving.[4] What infuriated the troops was the knowledge that there were good vegetables in the storehouse but that these were being sold to the townspeople; meanwhile, they received swills which they were obliged to pay for through wage deductions. A deputation of Swiss soldiers therefore attempted to return the bad vegetables in exchange for good ones but was rebuffed by the keeper of the royal storehouse.[5] Complaints were made to the commander of the Karrer detachment, Gabriel Schönherr, but they were unavailing.[6]

About 22 or 23 December, a petition addressed to Louis Dupont Duchambon, the acting garrison commanding officer, was drawn up. Some Swiss soldiers visited the barrack-rooms of the *troupes de la marine* and secured the support of some of the French troops.[7] Thus the petition read: "A large number of French and Swiss soldiers very respectfully beg you ...," although it seems that only the Swiss, and especially Abraham Dupâquier, Joseph Renard and Laurent Soly, played an active role at this stage. Soly, of unknown nationality, had previously served in the Spanish army and elsewhere. He was killed or captured early in the siege of 1745 and therefore was never brought to trial.[8] Renard was 33 years old, a Catholic and was born in German Lorraine.[9] Most active of the three, it seems, was Dupâquier, a 25-year old native of Neuchatel. His family's social standing cannot have been humble as his father was previously lieutenant-colonel in a Swiss regiment in the service of the king of Sardinia.[10] It was apparently he who was chiefly responsible for composing the petition. Fortunately a copy has been preserved and a reading of it makes it evident that rotten vegetables was not the only issue that annoyed the soldiers. In a deferential yet somewhat menacing tone, this document begins with complaints about the vegetables and then proceeds to allude to a number of other grievances after the general observation, " ... *vous sçavez Monsieur que l'Injustice regne a touttes mains en ce pays ....*"[11]

This petition was not handed over the commandant immediately, no doubt because the soldiers did not expect it would have any more effect than the complaints to Schönherr if it were submitted in the regular way. Instead, plans were made for a peaceful assembly where it would be presented and the authorities forced to take notice. Joseph Renard testified at his court-martial that there was no question of assembling at the time the petition was drawn up and he and Dupâquier insisted that the idea of bringing the troops out in a mass only occurred to them on the evening before the mutiny. Their testimony seems suspect however. They had every reason to portray their actions as a relatively sudden outburst (all the less culpable since they had been drinking the night of the twenty-sixth) rather than as a premeditated plot. However, the Swiss sergeant Christophe Jout admitted that Soly and Renard had spoken to him the day before Christmas of plans for a peaceful protest gathering.[12] The judges who later tried these men did not, in fact, consider it necessary to establish the existence of a plot before December 26 in order to convict them and showed no interest in pursuing this question. The sources therefore give no indication as to how elaborate the plot was in the day or two before and after Christmas, how many soldiers were privy to it, whether the French were involved or whether a decision was made to bear arms at the projected assembly.

    Whenever the plot was hatched, it was the evening of 26 December that Soly, Renard and Dupâquier went from room to room in the Swiss section of the barracks asking the men to join them, *"pour s'assembler le landemain afin de demander a leurs off.^{rs} de leur procurer Justice sur les Vivres qui leurs Etoient dus ...."*[13] Some of the men were sleeping but Renard made a list of the names of those who agreed to participate. Afterwards, Renard and Dupâquier were nominated to go to speak with the French soldiers who occupied adjoining rooms.[14] Dupâquier was sent because he "knew the French," apparently a rare quality for a member of the Karrer detachment. He admitted to having communicated with only a few men in two of the eight French companies and he claims that he merely informed them of the Swiss plans for an assembly. The three leaders then returned to their room and remained awake for the rest of the night.

    Next morning, the twenty-seventh, at about six o'clock, the Swiss began assembling behind the barracks building in the courtyard enclosed by the King's Bastion. Although this gathering was completely unauthorized and illegal, it was effected through the use of normal military procedures and routine discipline. The sergeants did not appear as most of them had their own dwellings in the town. However, a corporal named du Croix, who had apparently not been involved in the plans, took charge and arranged the men in their ranks, ordered the drummers to beat out the signal for the assembly and returned to the barracks to order those who had not yet appeared to fall in.[15] He even overruled one of the leading organizers, Joseph Renard, and ordered him to return to his place when the latter began to take some initiative. Dupâquier and Renard later declared at the court-martial that they had not intended to carry arms but had changed their minds when all the others went for their guns after a voice in the crowd had urged them to "give more weight to their just demands." They may well have been lying. In any case, the officer who was eventually fetched by the first sergeant found himself facing almost the entire Karrer detachment, armed and in battle formation.

Schönherr was sick at the time and it was Ensign Rasser, the second Swiss officer, who first met the rebellious troops.[16] When the drumming ceased Rasser asked for an explanation and was handed a note which outlined the men's grievances.[17] He examined this and then spoke with a few individual soldiers, one by one, about their complaints. When the ensign recalled the scene eight months later, he remembered the troops' orderly and respectful behaviour and their assurances that they had no intention of committing violent actions or of neglecting their duties to their superiors; they wished only *"de Reclamer leur Justice des Vexations qu'on leur Faisoit Journellement...."*[18] Rasser mentioned three specific grievances in this affidavit and prominent among them was the problem of the rotten vegetables. There was also a complaint about work the soldiers were forced to perform without wages for the king's service and for private individuals. Lastly, the men asked for compensation for work they had done on an expedition against Canso earlier in the year and for the pillage they had been promised but had never received.[19]

The complaint about unpaid labour was not a new one for the Swiss. In 1727 they had contested the custom of *"piquoit"* duty by which the *état-major* made soldiers coming off guard duty spend a few hours cleaning the barracks or doing chores in the government storehouse.[20] The practice persisted however and Joseph Renard complained of having to fetch wood and clean the governor's latrine.[21] Men were often obliged to work without remuneration for their own officers as well.[22] Both Renard and Dupâquier declared at their court-martials that such *"ouvrages extraordinaires"* were a major source of dissatisfaction.

The treatment of the soldiers who took part in the Canso raid was a specific case that aroused the anger of both French and Swiss troops. Soon after war broke out in March 1744, plans had been made to capture this nearby English fishing post. In its aims and its organization, the Canso expedition bore more resemblance to a privateering venture than to a normal military campaign.[23] It was largely financed by merchants and government officials and was composed of soldiers from the Louisbourg garrison as well as over 200 sailors all under the command of Dupont Duvivier, an influential officer of the *troupes de la marine*. Duquesnel, the colony's governor, convinced 80 French soldiers and 37 Swiss to volunteer for the mission with the promise that they would have a share of the booty.[24] A small fleet left Louisbourg the twentieth of May and quickly captured Canso and a British naval sloop after a short exchange of cannon fire.[25] The soldiers saw no action until they landed and were ordered to load quantities of codfish, government stores and the private effects of the British inhabitants into the boats. When some hesitated they were roughly treated by their officers. "*Le moindre des Miserables seroit mieux traitté parmi des barbares*," wrote the men who served on board one of the boats.[26] As soon as the victorious party returned to Louisbourg, the ships' officers and sailors and the garrison officers who had accompanied them made off with most of the plunder before anything was turned over to the courts to be distributed as lawful prize. In the end, the soldiers received nothing for their trouble. Governor Duquesnel, who had guaranteed them a share of the spoils, died on 9 October and, although one group of soldiers addressed a petition to the *ordonnateur* in November, they received no satisfaction.[27]

Rasser listened to these grievances in the courtyard of the citadel. He promised only to communicate them to his superior, Schönherr. Then, warning the men not to repeat their demonstration, he made them present arms and ordered them to return to the barracks and stay there. This done, the ensign rushed to Schönherr's bedside and reported the disturbance. The senior officer told Rasser to ask de la Perelle, the town major, to order the replacement of the bad vegetables. But already it was too late. As he emerged from Schönherr's house, the drums were beating again. This time it was the French sounding the general alarm. After their officer had left, it seems, some Swiss soldiers had gone to the other side of the barracks and reproached the French as cowards for not joining in the demonstration. The men of the *troupes de la marine* may have been slow to act but once they took up the challenge they were far less restrained than the others. With their intervention the relatively mild protest was transformed into a serious revolt.

Soldiers, both French and Swiss, poured out into the courtyard equipped for battle. The drummers continued to beat the *générale* and, as their comrades assembled, they marched out of the citadel[28] surrounded by an escort with bayonets fixed. As this body passed through the streets of the town, the garrison officers, who for the most part lived in private houses, were roused by what must have sounded like a signal that the fortress was under attack. Coming to the citadel to investigate, they found themselves facing the muskets of men who threatened to "blow their heads off" if they entered the enclosure.[29] These were the ten soldiers, French and Swiss, who had spent the night on routine guard duty at the entrance to the citadel under the command of the Swiss sergeant, Christophe Jout. Soly and Renard had spoken with him three days earlier about their plans for a demonstration and, the morning of the mutiny, Jout ordered his sentries not to allow any officers or civilians to pass. As the party of drummers marched by the guard post, he was heard to say, "*Les françois commencent a s'animer et ils font mieux les choses que les notres Etant armés Bayonnette au Bout fusil.*"[30]

Eventually a number of Officers managed to elude the sentries and gain entry to the courtyard. Among them was Ensign Rasser who described the scene inside as one of tumult and disorder. The soldiers talked openly of killing all the officers and burning the town. The officers present tried desperately with bravado and cajoling to regain control of their companies. According to Rasser, he brought the Karrer contingent to obedience first while the French were still pointing guns at their officers and threatening to shoot if their demands were not met.[31] Meanwhile, Major de la Perelle was following the drummers and their escort through the town vainly ordering them to halt. At one point, he attempted to stand in their path but he was picked up roughly and carried thirty paces.[32] Giving up at length, he went to the citadel where by now the atmosphere had cooled somewhat. The officers had apparently agreed to accept all the rebels' demands and the men showed their willingness to recognize de la Perelle's authority by following, more or less, his parade-ground commands.

Before the major's arrival, acting Governor Duchambon, the supreme military authority in the colony, had appeared at the citadel and surrendered to the troops' demands. Duchambon had no alternative but capitulation. His garrison, almost to a man, was in open revolt.[33] At the best of times, help from France or Canada would take months to arrive but, given the war and British command of the seas, the colony was particularly isolated in 1744. Moreover, there was no alternative force within the colony that could dream of opposing the rebels, as the Isle Royale militia, unlike its Canadian counterpart, was small and ineffective. The promise to redress all grievances quelled the violence, but the soldiers remained uneasy. Duchambon and Bigot, writing to the Minister of Marine four days later, declared that the complaints of the French and the Swiss were identical but the specific demands they mentioned as having come from the French troops were not the same as those presented to Rasser by the Swiss. The situation was confused and a great variety of demands were apparently put forward. The governor and *ordonnateur* recorded three of them: (1) an increase in the issue of firewood and the return to the soldiers of five cords of wood confiscated for theft; (2) the immediate distribution of the rations that some of the men had missed because they were away participating in the Canso attack and in a later expedition against Port Royal, and (3) the reimbursement of the clothing deduction that had been taken from the wages of more than 100 French recruits who had arrived in 1741 but never received the uniforms it was supposed to have paid for.[34]

The second demand in Duchambon's and Bigot's list was not repeated in any other document. It is possible that, in reporting to the minister, they may have misinterpreted or misrepresented much more serious complaints about the treatment of volunteers during and after the Canso raid. At any rate, the only contemporary account of the mutiny not written by an observer directly involved in the events considered injustices committed against the Canso volunteers to be the major grievance of all the soldiers.[35] The complaint about the missing uniforms was a uniquely French affair but it had much in common with the rotten vegetables problem which aroused the anger of both French and Swiss troops. The soldiers had often endured with patience delays and shortages in the issue of military supplies and allowances but they were annoyed that wage deductions were not adjusted when items they paid for were not delivered.

The soldiers' demand for more firewood cannot have come as a surprise to the local authorities as they had long been aware that fuel supplies were inadequate. Within a few years of the founding of Louisbourg the scrubby spruce forest had been stripped from all the country within three miles. The minister in France was eventually persuaded to allow wood to be purchased for the garrison but only at the rate of one half cord per man even though about twice that quantity was required to last through the long Cape Breton winter.[36] The men were therefore obliged to cut and transport half their fuel and each year several of them contracted frostbite and injured themselves scrambling over the brush and stumps in order to fetch a few logs of what was in fact inferior firewood. The exceptionally cold winter that had arrived earlier than usual in 1744 must have made the mutineers' demand for an adequate fuel supply especially emphatic.[37] As for the confiscation before Christmas of five cords of "stolen" wood, the soldiers petition to Duchambon alluded to this event in rather different terms. It seems that a group of soldiers returning to the town with a load of firewood were met by some officers claiming to own the land where it had been cut. The officers ordered them to turn over the wood and then broke the sledge they had used to carry it.[38]

Military discipline and punishment, wages, the routine hardships of service and the dangers of war do not seem to have been issues for the mutinous soldiers. Instead, their objectives were extremely modest. They showed no desire in their words or actions to modify the military system or to subvert the hierarchical structure of the garrison except as a temporary emergency measure. All the recorded grievances that were brought up by the French and the Swiss were essentially complaints about material losses and the redress the men sought was monetary compensation.

Consequently, one of the rebels' first acts was to make use of the established sentry posts in the town to secure control of the government storehouses and the house of François Bigot, the man in charge of finances and guardian of the colonial treasury.[39] The governor and officers had promised to give in to the soldiers' demands but it was up to Bigot to make the actual payments. Of course, they had wished, the mutineers could simply have seized what they wanted but, despite repeated threats to do so, they never undertook such bold action. Apparently interpreting Duchambon's surrender as implicit recognition that their demands were justified, the soldiers ended their complete and open defiance of the officers and proceeded to secure what they felt was legitimately theirs in a fairly orderly fashion.

A deputation went to call on Bigot to arrange for the fulfilment of the officers' promises and presented the *commissaire-*

ordonnateur with accounts of sums due to all the men for injustices committed over the past few years. It is not clear how long the negotiations lasted but the deputies apparently returned on several occasions over a period of months. Bigot later bragged of how he stalled and prevaricated with the representatives, *"les amusant de belles promesses"* and avoiding payment for as long as possible until frightened into submission by veiled threats against his life.[40] His own accounts indicate that only 3,000 *livres* were given to the men. This would have amounted to an average of about six *livres*, the price of three or four bottles of wine, for each man in the garrison.[41]

Although there were no further dramatic confrontations like the one that took place on the morning of 27 December, Louisbourg remained in a state of alarm in the days that followed. The civilian population was terrified as groups of soldiers spoke openly of massacres and destruction and engaged in a form of *taxation populaire*, threatening merchants with swords and forcing them to sell them goods at what they considered a "just price."[42] Bigot and Duchambon described this situation when they first reported their predicament to the minister on 31 December. Their letter had a tone of urgency that verged on panic: *"Nous sommes ici leurs Esclaves, ils font tout le mal qu'ils veulent."*[43] Bigot outlined the elaborate precautions he took to keep this communication and its destination a secret. He was convinced that the troops would sack the town and turn it over to the English if they knew he was requesting that an armed force be sent from France to punish the rebels. And yet the fact that no one was killed or even injured, the absence in the records of complaints from merchants who actually sustained losses and, most of all, the soldiers' subsequent conduct during the siege, all lead to the conclusion that these men were remarkably restrained in the use of every weapon except their mouths. Certainly the soldiers were extremely angry. The situation was an explosive one that could easily have erupted into open violence but the mutineers seemed well aware that their bravado and threats frightened the authorities and had the effect of advancing their own interests. Moreover, it was no accident that the mutiny occurred at a time when the state of war and rumours of impending British attack strengthened the soldiers' position by making the officers and colonial officials feel all the more vulnerable.

Unfortunately, it is impossible to discover exactly what happened in the early months of 1745 since the best sources, the court-martials and Ensign Rasser's deposition, concentrate exclusively on the period up to and including the morning of the assembly. For the courts of military justice, it was this act of defying and threatening officers that constituted the crime of mutiny and they showed no interest in its aftermath. However, according to François Bigot, the only informant for the later period, the revolt lasted five months. *"Tout l'hiver se passa dans cette émotion,"* he wrote, stating elsewhere that the troops *"n'avoient pour ainsy dire reconnu aucune autorité"* from December to May 1745.[44] Bigot of course is not the most trustworthy of witnesses and he had an obvious interest in exaggerating the duration of the mutiny and his own role in handling it. It would be more accurate to describe this period as one of latent rather than open revolt. The men had recognized the officers' authority after their capitulation in the courtyard, but the latter must have exercised that authority with the greatest of caution. Unwilling to overturn the established hierarchy, the soldiers were nevertheless in a position of unaccustomed power at this time and they used the threat of violence to ensure that those in command treated them fairly according to their own standards. The officers and civilian officials did not dare oppose them and even avoided using *"le ton de leurs places."*[45] This was hardly a normal situation and, in Bigot's eyes, it constituted continued revolt.

Nor do we know how the soldiers organized themselves at this stage, how they chose their representatives or how they managed the business of compiling their demands for compensation and distributing the proceeds. Bigot mentions in passing that the men elected their own officers and he describes the deputies who negotiated with him simply as *"les plus séditieux."*[46] He felt that most of the rebel leaders were Swiss and that Abraham Dupâquier was most prominent among them. Bigot noted no dissension between the men of the *troupes de la marine* and those of the Karrer regiment, and, in fact, he gives the impression that they co-operated more fully in the period of negotiations than they had earlier. In any case, whatever the state of relations within the garrison may have been, the entire situation changed drastically with the intervention of an outside force six months after the outbreak of revolt.

When the New Englanders landed to lay siege to Louisbourg 11 May, 1745, Duchambon assembled the garrison and urged the troops to forget the past and unite with the officers and townspeople in facing the enemy. The men demurred at first and asked for a guarantee that no one would be punished for taking part in the mutiny. Naturally the governor consented and, together with Bigot, solemnly promised a complete pardon in the name of the king.[47] In the subsequent fifty-day siege the troops according to all reports acquitted themselves well.[48] At no time had they ever questioned or attempted to evade what they considered to be their duty as soldiers. Still, when they were called upon to repair the fortifications that were damaged by cannon fire, they would only work for double the normal labourer's wage and with immediate payment in cash.[49] Perhaps twenty or thirty soldiers were killed before the town surrendered at the end of June,[50] and among the first casualties was Laurent Soly, one of the principal Swiss instigators of the mutiny.

After the surrender of Louisbourg the garrison was evacuated and most of its members arrived at the French port of Rochefort in August, 1745. The French companies were later sent back to Isle Royale in 1749 when the colony returned to French rule, but a great many, perhaps the majority, of the men who had experienced the mutiny and siege died or deserted before the garrison was re-established.[51] No detachment from the Karrer regiment ever went back to Isle Royale as Duchambon and Bigot convinced Maurepas, the Minister of Marine, that it was the Swiss who had not only initiated the mutiny but also led the French soldiers in the days that followed the first outbreak.[52]

III

Although aware that the garrison had fought well, Maurepas felt that news of the soldiers discontent had determined the English to attack Louisbourg and he tended to blame the mutiny for the fall of the fortress.[53] Perhaps a certain desire to identify a scapegoat for the loss of Isle Royale accounts for the minister's insistence on the need for severe punishment to restore discipline among the colonial troops. In August, 1745, he instructed de Barrailh, the governor of Rochefort, to make discreet inquiries on the subject of the Louisbourg mutiny and to arrest those identified as ring-leaders by the colonial commander and *ordonnateur*. When court-martials were organized late in the fall, Maurepas ordered them to look into the soldiers' complaints against their officers.[54] There was no excuse for rebellion but Maurepas, who was well aware that irregularities had long been common in the Isle Royale garrison, intended to take some disciplinary action against those officers whose unfair treatment of the men had been particularly flagrant. The records give no indication that any officer was ever actually punished.

In view of the special status of the Karrer regiment, the Swiss mutineers could only be tried by court-martials composed of their own officers. These were held in the second half of November, 1745. A number of those accused were released but five men were convicted and sentenced to death.[55] Of these, one died in prison and another, Abraham Dupâquier, escaped. François Bigot was furious when he learned that the *premier chef* of the rebels had escaped the noose. "*Si celuy de qui dependoit sa sûreté eut été pendant six mois à la discrétion de ce misérable, comme je l'ay été,*" he wrote, "*il seroit encore en prison.*"[56] Maurepas was also displeased, all the more so as there were hints that Colonel Karrer and his officers may have intentionally provided the Lieutenant-Colonel's son with an opportunity to flee.[57] Some of Dupâquier's comrades were not so fortunate. Joseph Renard and Corporal du Croix were hanged on 7 December and their bodies were left on the gallows at Rochefort all day, "*afin de servir d'exemple a un chacun.*"[58] Two days later, Christophe Jout was decapitated hours after appearing before the court-martial where he expressed the hope that he too would be an example to others.

> ... il savoit bien qu'il alloit perdre la Vie ... mais son Exemple devoit apprendre aux off^s. command^t. pour le Roy de tenir la main a ce que le soldat ne fut point Vexé et que Luy fut distribué bons conformem^t. a l'intention de sa majesté les Vivres payés sur leur solde ....[59]

The court-martials of the French mutineers were delayed for a time when the accused brought up the pardon they had been promised by Duchambon and Bigot. Maurepas quickly intervened however, declaring that the king could not be bound by the promise since he had had no knowledge of it and insisting that examples be made of some of the men of the *troupes de la marine*. We have no accounts of the French court-martials but other records indicate that at least eight men were condemned. Five of these were hanged in January, 1746, one died in prison and two were sentenced to life terms as galley slaves.[60] In all, eight men were executed as a result of the Louisbourg mutiny, making it a more severely punished event than any of the revolts André Corvisier mentions in his study of the French army from 1700 to 1763.[61]

Because of the limitations of the historical sources, our knowledge of the mutiny is far from complete. Still, it seems sufficient to support a few conclusions about the basic nature of the event which should be reviewed as a preliminary to an analysis of the mutiny's origins. Occurring at a time when the state of war provided the soldiers with a favourable opportunity for successful action and touched off by an issue of spoiled vegetables, the revolt was essentially an armed assembly of protest intended to achieve some limited objectives. Almost all the men in the garrison were involved and they demanded material compensation for certain specific grievances. They did not attempt to depose their superiors but rather frightened them into complying with their wishes. If the mutineers' behaviour was restrained considering the circumstances, it must not be supposed that they acted with cool detachment in the pursuit of rationally defined goals. In fact, they were extremely angry. Simply by disobeying and threatening the officers, they committed an offence punishable by death. They would not likely have done so if their resentment was not deeply rooted and if they did not have more at stake than a few *livres*. Some of the rebels' spleen was vented against the merchants of the town and against François Bigot but the primary target of their ire was the officers. Whereas actions against Louisbourg's civilians were sporadic and relatively mild, only the officers had to face the assembled muskets and staunch hostility of their men.

IV

In attempting to explain the Louisbourg mutiny, historians have tended to emphasize two causal factors, the officers's exploitation of the men and the soldiers' miserable living conditions.[62] The mutineers certainly felt they had been cheated by their officers but nowhere in the documents concerned with the mutiny is there any hint (beyond the reference to a demand for more firewood) that they revolted because they were "disgusted with their living conditions."[63] It is true that the material conditions of life were very hard for the men of the Louisbourg garrison but generally they were no worse, and in many respects they were better, than those to which other eighteenth-century soldiers were subjected. A Louisbourg soldier did not always receive his rations in the prescribed amounts or qualities but he could easily supplement his diet by hunting and scrounging and never went hungry as his counterparts in France often did when they were in the field or in peacetime when sudden rises in food prices would occasionally make them unable to subsist on their fixed money allowance.[64] His annual issue of clothing was often defective and sometimes was not delivered for years in a row. Still, he was no worse off than soldiers in the French infantry and he could consider himself blessed in comparison to the men of the Albany garrison in 1700 who were, according to the governor of New York, in a "shameful and miserable condition for the want of cloaths that the like was never seen in so much that those parts of 'em which modesty forbids me to name, are expos'd to view."[65] He was not given an adequate supply of firewood and, although this did not make him unique among soldiers of the period, he may have suffered more from it than men who served in France because of the severe climate of Isle Royale. As for the "squalid and oppressive barrack conditions" that supposedly "led to the mutiny,"[66] the Louisbourg barracks were certainly not luxurious accommodation but they were probably more comfortable than the stuffy and disease-ridden barracks at Aix and less crowded than those in Marseilles where 30 or 40 men lived in a room with seven beds, "*comme du bétail dans une écurie.*"[67] In fact, the soldiers' rooms were repaired and the bedding improved in the early 1740s so that they would likely have been more comfortable in 1744 than they had been in earlier periods.[68] In general, the notion that the men of the Louisbourg garrison were particularly wretched by contemporary standards is difficult to accept in view of their exceptionally low mortality rates.

Misery and hardship were the common characteristics of all soldiers in the eighteenth century and of a great many civilians as well. Their presence alone accounts for neither the turbulence of the Louisbourg soldiers nor the loyalty of other, more wretched troops. Neither does it help to explain the timing of the mutiny which occurred when the men of the colonial garrison were, in some respects, better off than they had ever been in the past. The revolt should therefore not be dismissed simply as an *émeute de misère*; instead, it should be understood as the reaction of a group of men with a certain set of material interests and attitudes faced with a particular combination of circumstances. The main motive for the soldiers' uprising was the economic exploitation to which their officers subjected them. Variations in the intensity of this exploitation along with the mens' evaluation of the prospects for successful violent action help to explain the timing of the event.

V

More important however are the "structural causes" of the mutiny. These are the enduring characteristics of the soldier's position in the Louisbourg garrison which generally encouraged the formation of group habits of thought and action among the soldiers and kept them at odds with the officers. Obviously, the first pre-condition of concerted group action is the existence of a group with some common interest and awareness of itself. The structure of military life in Louisbourg from about 1720 to 1744 formed such a group of the soldiers and enabled them to react collectively to the situation that arose in 1744. Besides the positive factors promoting unity among the men, there were negative factors which intensified solidarity through common hostility to the officers. The colony's system of recruitment emphasized the division between soldiers and officers and was one of the most important of these negative factors.

Of course, officers and soldiers occupied very different positions in the social hierarchy of the eighteenth century. In the Isle Royale garrison, however, the gulf between the two groups was exaggerated, partly because of the very different backgrounds of their members. The officers of the *troupes de la marine* had very strong roots in the Louisbourg community. Most of those serving in 1744 had been born in the colony or had come from elsewhere in North America at an early age. They had extensive ties of kinship and marriage with their fellow-officers and with the Louisbourg merchants who were often their business partners as well. Their men, on the other hand, were almost all born in France and came to Isle Royale as isolated individuals. Parish and judicial records provide the places of birth in France of 67 men of the French companies between 1720 and 1745. Of these, 31 (46 percent) were born in towns and cities (12 in Paris alone), a disproportionate urban representation in a country where about 5/6 of the population was born in the country.[69] The backgrounds of members of the Karrer detachment were extremely diverse but they did not distinguish officers from soldiers in any clear way. However, the impersonal recruitment practices of both the French and Swiss elements of the Isle Royale garrison reinforced the alienation of soldiers and officers.

In the regular army, each captain was responsible for recruiting men to fill the vacancies in his company. Ideally he solicited recruits from the same region year after year and would have some knowledge of the populace and they of him.[70] In many cases, the family estate provided a captain with a steady supply of replacements and this "feudal recruitment" was, according to the most eminent historian of the French army, an important factor promoting cohesion in many companies where the officers and some of the men would be linked in a paternalistic relationship that often pre-dated their entry into the military.[71] In actual practice however, much of the manpower needs of the eighteenth-century army were supplied by professional recruiters whose only interest was in collecting the cash payment they earned for each body they delivered and whose unscrupulous methods for extracting signatures from young men earned them the pejorative title of *"racoleurs."* The impersonal choice of *"racolage"* divorced the act of recruitment from the responsibilities of command. While it is not uncommon in the regular army, it was all but universal in the colonial *troupes de la marine* and in the Karrer regiment.[72]

The men who eventually came to Louisbourg then, did not enlist in a particular company under a particular officer. In fact, few of them could have been certain when they signed their names that they would be sent to Isle Royale and not another colony. Until the 1720s, recruits for all the French colonies were gathered together at the Ile d'Oleron near Rochefort, and then embarked on ships bound for Canada, Isle Royale or the Caribbean with no regard for the wishes of the men involved.[73] In later years, a certain number of troops were raised each year specifically for the Isle Royale garrison but there was always a certain amount of shuffling and mixing of recruits at Rochefort so that a man destined for service in one colony could easily end up in another.[74]

In the *troupes de la marine*, recruitment was not only impersonal, it was also frequently involuntary. A few recruits sent to Louisbourg were victims of *"lettres de cachet"*;[75] others were taken straight from the prisons of La Rochelle,[76] and of these a substantial number were army deserters whose lives were spared on condition that they serve in the colonies.[77] A great many ostensibly voluntary enlistments were doubtless the result of the tricks and pressure tactics of *"racoleurs."* It would be a mistake, however, to conclude that such *"soldats malgre eux"* were ever a majority in the Isle Royale garrison. Some men joined the colonial troops to escape from legal or other difficulties in France.[78] Most probably enlisted out of a desire for adventure, a need for security and an assured subsistence or a sincere military vocation. They would likely have received a more substantial enlistment bounty from an infantry regiment, but they ended up in the *troupes de la marine* because, in many cases, their health, size or age would have made them unacceptable to any other branch of the French armed forces.[79] The number of soldiers appearing in the Isle Royale records who were under the official minimum height of 5 *pieds* 1 *pouce* or below the minimum age of 18 years, is proof of the laxity of recruitment standards in the colonial troops.[80]

Obviously, recruitment standards were not effectively enforced simply because sufficient numbers of volunteers could not be found otherwise. The colonial forces did not enjoy a good reputation in France and it was not so much because of their niggardly recruitment bounties or because service overseas was considered particularly hard. Men hesitated to join the *troupes de la marine* because they did not expect ever to return home once they had left Europe.[81] This popular "prejudice," although exaggerated, was not without foundation. While men joining the regular French army or the Karrer regiment were committed to serving a limited term (usually six years), most recruits for the colonial *troupes de la marine* signed "*engagements perpétuels*" which effectively bound them to remain soldiers until the king saw fit to release them.[82]

The sources do not allow any precise calculation of the duration of military service at Isle Royale. However, circumstantial evidence and the testimony of contemporaries make it clear that soldiers in the colony, *troupes de la marine* much more than Swiss, generally served for unusually long periods. Swiss and French had little hope of terminating their military careers except with an official discharge and the French *troupes de la marine* usually obtained one only after a great many years. In France and in the colonies, most men left the service through death, desertion or discharge and the following table shows the respective importance of each compared with similar statistics for a typical regiment of the French infantry.

These figures clearly demonstrate the preponderance of discharges as the end-point of soldiers' careers in the colonial garrison. This contrasts strongly with the situation which prevailed in the regular army where -- paradoxically, in view of the predominance of limited periods of enlistment there -- only one-third of the men left with discharges while roughly equal numbers died or deserted. The relative importance of discharges does not mean that the Isle Royale authorities were more generous in this regard than their counterparts in France; instead it is the result of comparatively low rates of death and desertion in the Isle Royale garrison.

Table 1
Soldiers Leaving the Isle Royale Garrison, 1721-1742.[83]

	Total	Death	Desertion	Discharge	Other
IR troupes de la marine, 1721-42	670 100%	130 19%	43 6%	470 70%	27 4%
IR detachment, Karrer regt., 1723-24; 1730-42	153 100%	37 24%	2 1%	112* 73%	2 1%
Vivarais-Infanterie regt., 1716-49	3,842 100%	1,374 36%	1,046 27%	1,290 34%	132 3%

*The officials at Louisbourg could not discharge men from the Karrer regiment but only record their return to France where presumably they were discharged.

Between 1730 and 1740 inclusive, the average annual rate of mortality among Isle Royale soldiers, French and Swiss, was slightly less than 20 per thousand.[84] The annual average in the Vivarais-Infanterie regiment was over 80 per thousand during the same period (34 per thousand if wartime years are excluded).[85] The men of the colonial garrison were of course spared the rigours and dangers of campaigning, but they also lived in a healthy climate and seem to have suffered much less than the infantry soldiers from epidemics and food shortages. The statistics are also affected by the artificial selection process that resulted from the government's policy of discharging the sickly and the lame.

Desertion from the French army was quite common in the eighteenth century. Soldiers who were dissatisfied with the service, and those who were momentarily annoyed with an officer or in danger of being punished for a crime could generally escape and disappear into the surrounding population with only a minimum of planning and luck.[86] Deserters from the Isle Royale garrison, on the other hand, found themselves in a wilderness that was an extremely hostile environment for Europeans with a few settlements that were far too small for a fugitive to avoid detection. In most of the 45 recorded cases therefore, men, usually in groups of two or more, attempted to reach the Acadian settlements at Beaubassin, some 250 miles from Louisbourg in the British colony of Nova Scotia. The journey was difficult and perilous and the destination unattractive. It must be assumed that these deserters had extremely pressing motives for leaving the garrison -- in fact, a few of them were fleeing justice after committing a theft -- or else an immoderate degree of determination of foolhardiness.[87] Of the 45, nineteen were apprehended and ten of these executed, a very high rate of capture by contemporary standards even if one assumes that only half the actual desertions were recorded. Moreover, the majority of the colony's desertions occurred at the outposts of Port Toulouse and Isle St. Jean which were much closer than Louisbourg to the mainland. Desertion, then, was hardly a practical option for Louisbourg soldiers who were unhappy with their lot.

The official policy on discharges was frequently repeated in the minister's despatches to Isle Royale governors:

> *l'Intention de sa majeste est que les congez ne soient donnés qu'aux Invalides et a ceux qui voudront se faire habitans, Je vous recommande de ne point en congedier d'autres sans des ordres exprès.*[88]

At least 24 men left the colony's *troupes de la marine* between 1721 and 1742 with "*congés de grace*" which their families had obtained by petitioning the minister and paying 150 *livres* to the Marine treasury.[89] A few other soldiers, Swiss and French, obtained discharges that were conditional on their remaining in the colony. The metropolitan authorities hoped to establish at Isle Royale a system which had contributed greatly to the development and population of Canada where soldiers had often been encouraged to marry and settle on the land with offers of discharges and material assistance.[90] Because of the inferior quality of Cape Breton soils however and because of the absence of established agricultural communities, the military settlement programme was a failure. As the colonial administrators were unwilling to lose good soldiers in what they considered a vain scheme, only a handful received discharges or permission to marry. The most important result of this for our purposes was that the Isle Royale soldiers were denied an exit route by which many men stationed in Canada were able to escape from a service that was not to their liking.

Most of the discharges at Isle Royale were given to men described as "disabled." When the documents occasionally give more details about individual cases, the most striking feature of the lists is the large number of soldiers who were sent home crippled from injuries received in accidents during the construction of the fortifications of Louisbourg.[91] Another form of discharge, the "*congé d'ancienneté*," though not mentioned in the minister's instructions cited above, was awarded to old soldiers who had served as long as forty years.[92] Depending upon the number of recruits available and the vacancies created by deaths, desertions and discharges of other sorts in a given year, as many as ten or twelve of these veterans might be released or none at all. Men on six-year enlistments had priority but even they were not always sent home as soon as their terms had expired.[93] There is no way of determining the length of time that the majority who had unlimited enlistments served but it seems that in most cases it was considerable. Unless he were particularly lucky, a man in the *troupes de la marine* of Isle Royale could expect to serve for decades or until he was the victim of a crippling injury. Still, the Louisbourg official who referred to service of this sort as "*un Espece d'esclavage*" was exaggerating.[94] There were a number of escape hatches such as the "*congés de grace*," the settler's discharges and perhaps a few fictitious invalid's discharges.[95] However, these opportunities for departure were rare and unreliable. For most of the colony's French soldiers, the prospect of leaving the service must have appeared remote and uncertain in the extreme. The situation was temporarily worsened after 1743 when, because of the threat of war, the awarding of discharges was entirely suspended in both the *troupes de la marine* and the Karrer regiment.[96]

It would certainly be a mistake however, to assume that every soldier wanted to escape the Isle Royale garrison. There is actually one case of a sickly young man who cried and begged his captain not to discharge him as an invalid.[97] The point is that, insofar as there was discontent and resentment in the garrison, it had few outlets. Contemporaries frequently remarked that the prevalence of unlimited terms of enlistment in the *troupes de la marine* was productive of low morale.[98] The prospects for promotion into the officer corps, which were nil, could not have improved matters.[99] Admittedly, six-year terms were the rule in the Karrer detachment which initiated the revolt. However, since all the Swiss in the colony were stationed at Louisbourg, desertion was even rarer among them than among the French. They were also less likely to benefit from settlers' discharges. If he were angry with his officers, homesick or dissatisfied with military life, the Isle Royale soldier, Swiss at least as much as French, was discouraged from responding in an individualistic fashion. More than a continental French soldier who could desert with little chance of being punished and more than a man attached to the Canadian troops who could exchange the military musket for the colonist's axe with relative ease, he had a permanent stake in his position as a soldier. Individual evasion of the military being more difficult at Isle Royale than elsewhere, collective action within the system was proportionately more likely.

Several characteristics of military life in Louisbourg operated in a more positive and direct way to encourage cooperative habits and a group spirit among the soldiers. To begin with, almost all of them were housed in one large barracks building. In the first half of the century, barracks were still a novelty and, in many French garrison towns and throughout Canada, troops were dispersed and billeted in the homes of civilians.[100] In Louisbourg, by contrast, every man was in close contact with his comrades and especially with the fifteen or twenty who shared his room and who together formed a group called a "chambrée." Besides sharing common living and sleeping quarters, the men of a *chambrée* ate together and cooked common meals in one large pot. They also tended to spend a great deal of leisure time together and the barracks room was a favourite spot for drinking, conversation and lounging. Not only was the *chambrée* an important unit in a soldier's life -- Renard, Soly and Dupâquier, the three principal instigators of the mutiny were apparently of the same room -- but the barracks environment, where officers seldom entertained, was well suited for the discussion of grievances and for conspiracies and plans for concerted action. The frequency of mutinies among naval forces has often been explained in terms of the solidarity bred by life in the fo'c'sle.[101] Similarly, the Louisbourg revolt can be seen partly as a result of the barracks situation which helped to foster a sense of community and also provided an environment favourable to secret organized action. The accounts of the mutiny show that the leaders took good advantage of its potential.

Outside the barracks, the men of the Louisbourg garrison, like soldiers everywhere, were in constant contact with their fellows while engaged in such activities as guard-duty and drills. What makes them unique however is the fact that so many of them devoted very little time to these military pursuits as they worked six months of every year building Louisbourg's fortifications. The construction of a European-style fortress in North America was an ambitious project and one which was never completed. Since civilian workers could not be persuaded to come to the colony, all the unskilled labour was performed by the troops of the garrison.[102] Not all the soldiers were employed in this way. Many were not strong enough for the heavy work involved and a number were always required for duty in the outposts and guardrooms. In the 1720s when many of the massive excavations were completed, more than half of the colony's soldiers worked on the fortifications.[103] By the years around 1740, the proportion of working soldiers may have been somewhat smaller but most of the men must have had some experience as construction workers. Canada also has a labour shortage and many men in the *troupes de la marine* stationed there were allowed to take jobs in the community. However, the soldiers from Canada were generally employed by private individuals, and so their work, like their system of lodging, had the effect of dispersing them.[104] Some Isle Royale soldiers also found employment with civilian parties but generally the voracious labour demands of state-financed construction at Louisbourg tended to concentrate them at one place under one employer.

If there were factors promoting a certain group feeling among Louisbourg's soldiers, there were nevertheless some divisions within the garrison that precluded the formation of a completely unified outlook. First of all, non-commissioned officers wielded considerable authority over the men in their daily affairs and received higher wages. The thirty members of the elite artillery company were also better paid than the other French soldiers. Because of their specialized duties, the cannoneers did not work on the fortifications and they were further set off from the others by their special barracks rooms and distinctive uniforms.[105] Most importantly, both the cannoneers and the French sergeants owed their special positions to the officers' appreciation of their superior merit (Corporals were chosen on the basis of seniority alone).[106] Not surprisingly, they stayed aloof from the mutiny.

The most significant complicating factor in the Louisbourg garrison however was the division between Swiss and French. The men of the Karrer regiment with its special privileges, traditions and procedures were separated from the others in many of the external formalities of military life, such as uniforms and drum signals, and also in some more essential matters, such as pay. Many of them were Protestants and most spoke German as a first language. The few glimpses of the soldiers' daily life afforded by judicial records give the impression that socializing between French and Swiss was not common. A Swiss or a French soldier would have had more extensive dealings with others of his own group, and especially those who were in his company and *chambrée*. In the 22 years the Karrer regiment was represented in the garrison however, its members would have had considerable contact with the men of the *troupes de la marine* as they worked together on the fortifications, served together in mixed guard details and were housed in the same building and treated in the same hospital. There is even evidence of a high degree of mutual trust between individual French and Swiss in the two recorded desertions from the Karrer detachment. In both cases, a Swiss soldier fled with a group of French deserters.[107] Generally, the two major components of the Louisbourg garrison lived separately but enjoyed harmonious relations. Certainly, there is no evidence of hostility of the sort that led to fist-fights and duels between the men of two infantry regiments that were stationed at Louisbourg in the 1750s. In the early stages of the mutiny, the French and the Swiss acted independently but their differing tactics were aimed at achieving essentially, though not exactly, identical objectives.

Although the men of the Louisbourg garrison did not form a completely cohesive group, they shared a common awareness of their distinct identity as soldiers that, along with the factors mentioned earlier, helps to explain the solidarity they manifested during the mutiny. The judicial records occasionally give indications of the importance they attached to the external signs of the warrior's profession. In one case, two men were convicted of breaking into a house and stealing a few items of little value. One of their prizes was a piece of ribbon which they had a tavern keeper's wife fashion into fifteen *cocardes* so that they and their comrades could wear these specifically military adornments in their hats.[108] Another incident resulted from a dispute between a butcher named Dupré and a Swiss soldier who wished to sell some partridges he had shot. At one point, the soldier threatened to hit his opponent with the butt of his musket but the butcher managed to wrestle the weapon away from him. Hurling insults behind him, the vanquished soldier retreated towards the barracks but returned later, accompanied by two Swiss armed with sticks, and demanded the return of his gun. When Dupré refused, the three attacked him, calling him *bougre* and shouting, "*Tu desarme un soldat.*" They beat him savagely, stabbed him in the chest and finally left him in the street, unconscious and gravely wounded.[109] The accounts of the victim and other witnesses give no hint that any national or religious animosity was involved in this incident. Instead, the brutal actions of the Swiss can best be interpreted as revenge against what they considered to be a serious offence on the part of a civilian who deprived a soldier of his weapon, the distinguishing mark of the military estate.[110] Similarly, anger over the treatment of the volunteers who participated in the Canso expedition -- anger which helped produce the outbreak in December 1744 -- should be seen as a product of the traditional notion that a victorious warrior ought to receive a share of the fruits of conquest.

Behind the actions of the mutineers seems to be the general belief that a soldier is an armed man who receives the king's money and his bread, as well as plunder on appropriate occasions, in order to fight his master's enemies and protect his possessions. When the men were given bad rations without what they considered legitimate reason, they felt not only deprived but insulted. Being made to work at unsoldierlike tasks without remumeration was also galling. The cannoneers received high wages for their special duties and skills, but the other soldiers felt they were entitled to their subsistence pay by virtue of performing strictly military service such as guard-duty.[111] Work in itself was not unacceptable as long as it was considered quite independent of a man's duties and status as a soldier and was paid for as such. What incensed the mutineers was having their officers treat them as mere labourers rather than as men-at-arms who occasionally worked for extra money. At his court-martial, Joseph Renard was asked if he had any complaints against his officers. He replied

> qu'il avoit grievemt. lieu de se plaindre des Torts a luy arrivés par la mauvaise qualité des Vivres qui faisoient partie de sa solde ainsy que de tous les ouvrages qu'on l'avoit forcé de faire a la descente de la garde et cela sans salaire quoique ces ouvrages Etoient Indépendans de son Service et de son devoir ....[112]

The authorities shared the soldiers' attitude to a large degree and they never questioned the proposition that men who worked on the fortifications should be given a supplement to their normal wages. The way in which this extra pay was remitted however was not always to the soldier-workers' satisfaction and the economic history of Louisbourg's military labour force sheds a great deal of light on the origins of the soldiers' hostility towards their officers which characterized the mutiny.

The construction of Louisbourg's fortifications was not administered directly by the crown but rather farmed out to a private contractor who was responsible, among other things, for paying the soldier-workers. The state nevertheless took an active role in the project, partly through the chief engineer, a military officer independent of the colony's military command, who superintended the works and was in charge of the discipline of the work force. The engineer and the contractor usually cooperated closely, but the governor also had some authority over the works and he and the other staff and company officers also exercised authority over the men.[113] Thus the administration was complicated and, in the 1720s when the soldier-workers still received their wages directly from the contractor, they were often able to take advantage of the fact that the engineer together with the contractor was often at odds with the governor and the officers, and neither party was able to claim their undivided obedience.

Although theoretically free agents in the labour market, physically fit soldiers who were not required for duty in the outposts and guardrooms were often obliged to work. One of their primary tasks was excavating and moving earth for the massive ramparts and ditches and they worked as day labourers or, more frequently, on a piece-work basis in gangs led by a "*chef d'attelier*" who was himself presumably a soldier.[114] The workers were allowed to negotiate pay scales collectively with the contractors and, in the early years, they occasionally staged demonstrations and refused to work in order to force their employer to raise the rates.[115] The governor could intervene in case of deadlock. He was not directly interested in keeping down construction costs but was more concerned about morale and about the difficulties of keeping the soldiers at the fortifications at a time when a boom in private construction provided them with an alternative source of employment. Therefore, he often settled disputes in favour of the men.[116] As the only substantial work force in the 1720s when public works in the colony were particularly extensive, the soldiers were in a relatively strong position and one that was in some ways strengthened by their military status, which meant that their subsistence was secure and their physical welfare the responsibility of the company captains. It is difficult to determine how much money the soldier-workers earned as a result, but the minister of Marine concluded from the reports of "strikes" and "*émeutes*" that they were becoming rich and consequently insubordinate.[117] It was one thing to establish pay rates however, and another to collect the actual wages. Owing to delays in forwarding funds, the contractor frequently found himself unable to pay the men in cash and resorted to the expedients of distributing notes which could only be redeemed at a discount, or paying in goods, especially wine. When funds were available, the workers were paid every two weeks, after which, according to the authorities, the majority went straight to the taverns and did not reappear for several days.[118]

As a wage earner the soldier-worker, was well-placed, but as a consumer he was extremely vulnerable. Since soldiers were not allowed to buy from merchants on credit, the custom was established from the earliest years of the colony's existence of giving each captain a monopoly on sales to the men of his company.[119] This commerce was considered a duty as well as a privilege as it consisted mainly of essential items such as shoes and stockings -- the standard military issues of these articles were never sufficient -- as well as tobacco, liquor and extra food.[120] The officers provided these "*fournitures*" at greatly inflated prices and, in order to collect their debts, simply had the 30 *sols* per month that remained of their men's military wages after deductions paid directly into their hands. This monopoly was not complete however, and in the 1720s the captains frequently complained of the contractor's practice of increasing his profits by advancing goods to the workers in lieu of wages.[121] Furthermore, these officers claimed the soldier-workers consumed much more merchandise than their military pay would afford and, although they had to be given clothing to protect them from the winter, they quickly squandered any cash they received from the contractor in the summer and neglected to repay their officers.[122] Thus, captains and contractors struggled for a greater share of the soldier-workers' earnings.

In the early years, the contractor had the advantage of being supported by the Marine ministry but the captains had the backing of the colonial governor. The officers scored their first victory in 1721 when they obtained permission for a sergeant to be present at paydays in order to compel workers in need of new clothing to purchase it on the spot.[123] The contractor successfully resisted these pretentions however, and in 1727 the French officers complained that their men were being paid mostly in merchandise and in advance. They asked that the wages soldiers earned working on the fortifications, like their military wages, be turned over from the contractor to the company captains who could deduct the value of each man's debts and pay him the balance in cash.[124] This was already the practice in the Swiss contingent but it was not until some time in the 1730-1735 period that the officers of the *troupes de la marine* gained such complete control over the fruits of their men's labour. How or why they defeated their opponent is not clear but it is certain that, from that time until 1744, the captains derived a substantial portion of their total incomes from the profits they made from their soldier-workers. They were not negligent in searching for ways to increase these.

The administration of the Isle Royale garrison was never very orderly before 1745 and there is no indication that the captains were obliged to keep close accounts or to report to anyone on how they disposed of the workers' wages with which they were entrusted. They soon began paying the men their cash balances only once a year at the end of the construction season, thereby all but eliminating the possibility that any of them could stay out of debt.[125] In view of the limited demand for shirts and shoes, they expanded their merchandising facilities, concentrating on an institution called the canteen. In the 1730s and forties, each captain operated a canteen where his men could drink wine and spirits on credit and at exorbitant prices. Complaints about the canteens and their effects on drunkenness and absenteeism multiplied around 1740 when there were even allegations that officers forced working soldiers to spend their earnings on drink.[126] When the newly-appointed governor Duquesnel arrived in the colony, he reported that the soldier-workers generally received no money whatsoever and he identified the situation as "*un viel mal.*"

> *Il faut attaquer les fournitures qu'on fait aux soldats et les Cantines, qui font que quelque travail que fasse un travailleur, il ne voit jamais un sol on luy fait tout Consommer, de la livrongnerie et le degout pour le travail, auquel ils ne vont que forcés.*[127]

In the late 1730s and early 1740s, the minister of Marine in France manifested a concern over abuses in the Louisbourg garrison that indicates he thought matters were more serious there than in Canada where the officers' routine appropriation of the military pay of working soldiers had been tolerated for years.[128] He had received reports about the confiscation of soldier-workers' pay and about other forms of exploitation, such as the captains' practice of taking the uniforms from the bodies of dead soldiers and "selling" them to new recruits.[129] Two new governors were appointed from outside the colony, de Forant in 1739 and Duquesnel in 1740, and instructed to remedy the situation. The officers were threatened with exemplary punishment unless they began treating their men more fairly and Maurepas actually went so far as to suspend the awarding of the *Croix de St. Louis* in the garrison in 1742.[130] Neither the minister nor the governors however could effectively oppose the firmly entrenched interests of the officers. The latter convinced them that their salaries were not sufficient to support a family in a difficult and expensive colony like Isle Royale. Consequently, no fundamental change was made in the system of exploitation which left a captain free to dispose of his men and their earnings as he saw fit.[131] Still, the governors exercised some restraining influence over the officers. However, when Duquesnel died in October 1744 and the command was assumed by Duchambon, a veteran of the Isle Royale officer corps, there is reason to suspect that the inhibitions that limited officers' profiteering at the soldiers' expense were abandoned.

The gap in outlook, background and material interests between the Louisbourg soldiers and their officers was considerable. The impersonal recruiting practices of the Karrer regiment and the *troupes de la marine* were not of a sort to reinforce the soldier's deferential attitude to his superiors nor his attachment to his company commander. Neither did the divided loyalties that accompanied the soldiers' employment under the fortifications contractor enhance the officers' authority. More important though was the unexampled economic tyranny which the officers, as paymasters, creditors and monopoly retailers, exercised over their men. As they gained exclusive control over the soldiers' earnings, they used their power for increasingly blatant exploitation which probably had a severe effect on their men's material prosperity. Whether it impoverished them or not however, it certainly appeared unjust to its victims and, more than anything else, it accounts for the discontent that eventually led to violence.

The company officers at Isle Royale showed more concern

for their own profits than for their men's morale but they had little incentive to do otherwise. In the regular French army, by contrast, captains who wished to minimize the considerable trouble and expense of recruitment had a selfish interest in preventing desertion and encouraging re-enlistment by keeping their men as contented as possible.[132] Colonial officers of the Karrer regiment as well as the *troupes de la marine*, on the other hand, had no regular recruitment responsibilities and those resident at Louisbourg were in relatively little danger of losing men through desertion and military settlement programmes, regardless of the level of morale.

As it was so difficult for soldiers, especially those who served in the *troupes de la marine*, to leave the colonial garrison, Louisbourg was very much a "pressure-cooker." As the officers' exploitation became more intense, there was no real "safety valve" of desertion which otherwise might have rid the community of its most disaffected elements. Instead, the likelihood of a major explosion increased. This is not to say that the relationship between stimulus and response was mechanical in any literal sense. Rather, the objective circumstances of the soldier's position in Louisbourg were such that aggressive group action was a relatively feasible reaction to severe discontent. Individual evasion was not a practical alternative as it was for many of the French troops stationed in France and in Canada. Moreover, factors such as the systems of work and lodging gave the men experience that enabled them to think and act collectively.

Already, in the 1720s, the soldier-workers had been involved in confrontations resembling modern strikes. Their opponent however was generally the fortifications contractor. When the company captains gained control of their wages in the following decade, the men were much less bold in dealing with such powerful and prestigious adversaries who had at their disposal the military system of discipline and punishment. As a result, there were no reported "*émeutes*" from the late 1720s until 1744. In the end, the soldiers only overcame their fear and deference when the exploitation they suffered became particularly severe and when the state of war temporarily strengthened their hand.

Nevertheless, although these structural and short-term factors that produced both unity and discontent among the soldiers made a confrontation likely in 1744, they do not entirely account for the outbreak of mutiny by themselves. Soldiers in the eighteenth century simply were not accustomed to defying their officers. Like other contemporary groups from among the popular classes, they only opposed their superiors openly when they were convinced that their cause was a righteous one. The "justifying ideology" that sanctioned the revolt and determined the form it took can, to some extent, be inferred from the mutineers' words and actions. Certainly the men felt their actions were legitimate. They showed no desire to command in the place of their officers, but only to force the latter to rule in a proper fashion. Therefore the mutiny as an open revolt ended quickly and the men returned to nominal subordination as soon as assurances were given that their grievances would be redressed. Throughout the period that followed, the leaders drew up accounts and negotiated payments in an orderly fashion without ever challenging the authority of the *commissaire-ordonnateur*. The soldiers had only resorted to force after milder forms of protest were ignored. This type of action was, of course, extremely destructive of military subordination, but it was intended only as a temporary emergency measure that would compel the authorities to correct the situation in which wages and other benefits were unlawfully withheld. The men seemed quite confident that their aims were not a threat to the hierarchical system since they merely demanded that actual practice in the garrison be consistent with official policy.

What the soldiers sought in 1744 was "justice" and the word itself occurs frequently in the court-martials and other records of the mutiny. On the surface, the justice they demanded was in the form of monetary compensation for material losses to cheating officers. On another level, they were asking to be treated with the respect due to a soldier. A soldier, these men apparently felt, earned plunder and subsistence wages by fighting and guarding. He might agree to perform other, unrelated duties in return for pay but he should not be used as a beast of burden or as a milk-cow by those who exercised military authority over him. From the mutineers' point of view, it was the officers who had subverted the military system over the years, and the soldiers who were obliged to restore a proper balance. Their procedures, as they assembled behind the barracks to the beat of drums and under the supervision of corporals, were eminently soldier-like and consistent with their limited objectives.

VI

Was the mutiny a success? In the short-term, the men's limited objectives were apparently achieved. They were given compensation for unfair wage deductions -- admittedly, the sources do not make it clear whether the soldiers were ever completely satisfied on this point -- and the officers and government officials treated them with respect. Trusting the authorities' promises of amnesty however, they were defeated in the end. It is possible that matters might have ended differently had the garrison not had the bad luck to be conquered six months after the first uprising and sent to France where the soldiers' power relation with the officers was reversed. A few men might have been saved from the hangman in this case and the officers might have been more restrained in their profiteering as long as their memory of the mutiny remained vivid, but the economic and power position of the soldiers would not have changed in any fundamental or enduring way. Since they had no intention of effecting any institutional or structural changes in the garrison, it is difficult to imagine their revolt resulting in anything more than a temporary modification of the existing order.

The mutiny was not without lasting results, however. The minister of Marine had attempted to reform the abuses in the Isle Royale garrison from as early as 1739 but, when the colony was re-established as a French possession in 1749, the recollection of the violence of 1744 must have added some urgency to his campaign to reform the military administration. As a result, the garrison was run in a much more regular fashion in the second period. There was still exploitation but it was controlled and systematized so that Captains were limited to profits of 25 percent on purchases made by their men.[133] Perhaps the soldiers found this parasitic system less annoying than the more blatant one that prevailed earlier. In any case, no further incidents of organized resistance at Louisbourg were recorded. However, most of the "structural causes" of the mutiny remained after 1749. The fundamental characteristics of military life in the colony were always of a sort that insurrection was possible, since they promoted solidarity among the soldiers and alienated them from the officers. Accordingly, in 1750 the engineer Franquet still observed among the soldier-workers *"un Esprit de Sedition et de revolte."*[134]

Notes

1. AN, AM, A¹, Art. 69, pièce 33, *Capitulation du Regiment Suisse de Karrer*, 25 September 1731.
2. See, for example, AN, Col., C¹¹B, Vol. 23, ff. 60-64, Duquesnel to Minister, 19 October 1741.
3. See, for example, *ibid.*, Vol. 20, ff. 104-05, de Bourville to Minister, 24 December 1738.
4. Three years earlier, they had gone without vegetables for an extended period although their bread ration was reduced at the same time. *Ibid.*, Vol. 24, ff. 87-89v, Bigot to Minister, 18 June 1742.
5. ASHA, XI *Deposition juridique reçu par ordre de Monsieur de Karrer ... de Mrs. les officiers des detachements de la compagnie colonelle ... en garnison cy devant à Louisbourg ... à l'occasion de l'émeute à l'Isle Royale au mois de decembre 1744*, 29 August 1745 (hereafter cited as "Rasser deposition"). The French may also have participated; the document is not precise on this point.
6. *Ibid.*
7. AN, Col., C⁷, 272, dossier Joseph Renard, transcript of the court-martial of Joseph Renard, 7 December 1745 (hereafter cited as "Renard court-martial"); *ibid.*, copy of the petition of a number of soldiers addressed to Duchambon, [22-23?] December 1744 (hereafter cited as "Soldiers' Petition").
8. Renard court-martial.
9. *Ibid.*
10. AN, Col., E, 157, dossier Abraham Dupâquier, transcript of the court-martial of Abraham Dupâquier, 9 December 1745 (hereafter cited as "Dupâquier court-martial").
11. Soldiers' Petition.
12. AN, Col., E, 233, dossier Christophe Jout, transcript of the court-martial of Christophe Jout, 9 December 1745 (hereafter cited as "Jout court-martial").
13. Renard court-martial.
14. ASHA, XI *Deposition juridique reçu par ordre de Monsieur de Karrer ... de Mrs. les officiers des detachements de la compagnie colonelle ... en garnison cy devant à Louisbourg ... à l'occasion de l'émeute à l'Isle Royale au mois de decembre 1744*, 29 August 1745 (hereafter cited as "Rasser deposition"). The French may also have participated; the document is not precise on this point.
15. AN, Col., E, 145, dossier Jean-Baptiste du Croix, transcript of the court-martial of Jean-Baptiste du Croix, 7 December 1745 (hereafter cited as "du Croix court-martial").
16. Rasser deposition.
17. Renard court-martial; Dupâquier court-martial. The testimony does not make it clear whether this was the same petition to Duchambon that was written several days earlier. Dupâquier testified that he wrote a note outlining grievances the morning of the demonstration. He may have been lying in order to be consistent with his story that there was no plot before 26 December. Since the specific complaints that Rasser recalled were not the same as those listed in the petition to Duchambon, it is quite possible that Dupâquier drew up a second petition shortly before the mutiny began.
18. Rasser deposition.
19. These are the same three complaints that Renard and Dupâquier later mentioned

at their court-martials.
20. AN, Col., C¹¹B, Vol. 9, ff. 72-78v, St. Ovide to Minister, 21 November 1727.
21. Renard court-martial.
22. Antony Steur seems to have been in this case when he passed the winter of 1739 at Spanish Bay hunting partridges for the benefit of Cailly, the Swiss commander. AN, Outre-Mer, G², Vol. 185, ff. 379-424, trial of Jean Larue dit le Gascon, accused of murder, 16 March-30 April 1738. For evidence of similar illicit practices in the French companies, see AN, Col., C¹¹B, Vol. 11, ff. 61-68, de Mézy to Minister, 4 December 1730.
23. George Juan De Ulloa And Antoine De Ulloa, *A Voyage to South America*, trans. J. Hopkins, 2 Vols. (London, 1806), Vol. 2, p. 380.
24. AN, Col., F³, Vol. 50, f. 415, an Account of the Canso Expedition, n.s., n.d., [1744].
25. G.A. Rawlyk, *Yankees at Louisbourg* (Orono, Maine: University of Maine, 1967), pp. 3-5.
26. AN, Outre-Mer, G², Vol. 188, ff. 304-05, Requette à M. Bigot de Marin Halest et 25 *autres volontaires*, 8 November 1744.
27. *Ibid.*
28. The King's Bastion and the barracks building formed an enclosed citadel usually referred to in French as "le fort." The "fortress," on the other hand, was the town together with the entire system of fortifications.
29. Rasser deposition.
30. Jout court-martial.
31. Rasser deposition.
32. AN, Col., C¹¹B, Vol. 26, ff. 231-34, "*Copie de la Lettre ecritte a Mr. le Comte de Maurepas par Mrs. Duchambon et Bigot a Louisbourg le 3ⁱᵉ X^{bre} 1744*," [31 December 1744] (hereafter cited as "Duchambon's and Bigot's letter").
33. Duchambon and Bigot reported that only the French sergeants and the thirty men of the elite artillery company refused to join in the mutiny. *Ibid.*
34. *Ibid.*
35. Anon., *Lettre d'un Habitant de Louisbourg*, trans., ed., G.M. Wrong (Toronto: Warwick Bro's and Rutter, 1897), p. 34.
36. AN, Col., C¹¹B, Vol. 23, ff. 13-14v, Duquesnel and Bigot to Minister, 10 October 1741.
37. De Ulloa, *op. cit.*, p. 375.
38. Soldiers' Petition.
39. Anon., *Mémoire pour Messire François Bigot, ci-devant Intendant de Justice, Police, Finance & Marine en Canada, Accusé: contre Monsieur le Procureur-General du Roi en la Commission, Accusateur* (Paris, 1763), Vol. 1, pp. 7-9.
40. *Ibid.*, p.8.
41. AN, Col., C¹¹C, Vol. 12, f. 167, "*Bordereaux de la recette et dépense faitte à l'Isle Royalle pendant l'année [1744]*," 2 April 1746.
42. Price-setting of this sort was a common feature of eighteenth-century insurrections, especially bread riots in England and France. See George Rudé, *The Crowd in History; A Study of Popular Disturbances in France and England* (New York: John Wiley & Sons, 1964), especially pp. 19-32; and E.P. Thompson, "The Moral Economy of the English Crowd in the Eighteenth Century," *Past and Present*, No. 50 (February 1971), pp. 76-136. Only one account of the mutiny (Duchambon's and Bigot's letter) reports any manifestation of this type of behaviour. The other documents mention vague threats to sack the town but they give no evidence of

hostility on the part of the soldiers directed specifically against the merchants.
43. Duchambon's and Bigot's letter.
44. Anon., "Memoire pour Messire François Bigot ...," I, p. 8; AN, Col., DFC, Am. Sept., no. d'ordre 218, Bigot, "*Relation du siege de Louisbourg*," 15 August 1745.
45. Anon, *Mémoire pour Messire François Bigot* ..., I, p. 8.
46. *Ibid.*
47. *Ibid.*, p. 9.
48. *Ibid.*; AN, Col., C¹¹C, Duchambon to Minister, 23 September 1745. Two Swiss deserted and one French soldier was executed for treason during the siege but this is not a sign of excessive disaffection by eighteenth-century standards.
49. AN, Col., F³, Vol. 50, f. 378v, Bigot, "*Sur la prise de Louisbourg*," August 1745.
50. One list of casualties reported a total of 50 deaths on the French side but this includes civilians as well as soldiers. AN, Col., F³, Vol. 50, f. 407, n.d., n.s.
51. AN, Col., D²C, Vol. 48, "*Liste des Soldats des Troupes servant. ci devant a l'Isle Royale désertés à Rochefort*," [n.d.], [n.s.]; AN, Col., B, Vol. 84-2, f. 289, Maurepas to de Serigny, 10 February 1746.
52. Duchambon's and Bigot's letter; AN, Col., B, Vol. 82-2, f. 377, Maurepas to Karrer, 14 September 1745.
53. AN, Col., B, Vol. 82-2, f. 369, Maurepas to de Barrailh, 20 August 1745; *ibid.*, f. 377, Maurepas to Karrer, 14 September 1745. In fact, news of the mutiny could not have reached New England in time to affect the plan to attack Louisbourg. Reports in the summer and fall of 1744 of low morale in the garrison however did encourage the New Englanders to attempt the invasion, Rawlyk, *op. cit.*, pp. 27-57.
54. AN, Col., B, Vol. 82-2, f. 403, Maurepas to de Barrailh, 23 November 1745.
55. AN, Col., C¹¹C, Vol. 9, ff. 118-21, Bigot to Maurepas, 11 December 1745.
56. *Collection de Manuscrits contenant lettres, mémoires, et autres documents historiques relatifs à la Nouvelle-France*, (Québec: Cote, 1884), Vol. 3, p. 271, Bigot to Minister, 2 December 1745.
57. AN, Col., B, Vol. 82-2, f. 412, Maurepas to Karrer, 10 December 1745; *ibid.*, f. 415, Minister to de Barrailh, 15 December 1745.
58. Du Croix court-martial.
59. Jout court-martial.
60. AN, Col., D²C, Vol. 53, "*Isle Royale. Rolle général des Troupes françoises commencé en 1739*," n.d., n.s.; Archives Maritimes, Port de Rochefort, IE, 141, Maurepas to Ricouart, 18 January 1746.
61. André Corvisier, *L'armée française de la fin du XVIIᵉ siècle au ministère de Choiseul. Le soldat* (Paris: Presses Universitaires de France, 1964), p. 883.
62. Guy Frégault, *François Bigot, Administrateur français* (Montréal: L'Institut, 1948), Vol. 1, p. 207; Rawlyk, *op. cit.*, pp. 71-72; and Robert J. Morgan and Terrence D. MacLean, "Social Structure and Life in Louisbourg," *Canada, an Historical Magazine*, Vol. 1 (June 1974), p. 66.
63. Rawlyk, *op. cit.*, p. 71.
64. Corvisier, *op. cit.*, pp. 834-36.
65. Quoted in W.J. Eccles, "The Social, Economic, and Political Significance of the Military Establishment in New France," *Canadian Historical Review*, Vol. 52 (March 1971), p. 6.
66. Morgan and MacLean, *loc. cit.*; cf. Trégault, *loc. cit.*
67. Quoted in Albert Bateau, *La Vie militaire sous l'Ancien Régime*, (Paris, 1889), Vol. 1, *Les Soldats*, pp. 85-88.
68. For example, new sheets and mattresses replaced the vermin-infested straw in

the barracks rooms in 1740. AN, Col., C¹¹B, Vol. 22, ff. 40-40v, de Bourville and Bigot to Minister, 20 October 1740.

69. This sample is too small to be statistically valid, but it does suggest that the proportion of urban recruits was much greater in the *troupes de la marine* than in the regular French army where about 30% of the men were born in towns. Corvisier, *op. cit.*, pp. 390, 394.

70. De Guignard, *L'École de Mars*, (Paris: Chez Simart, 1725), Tome 1, p. 682; Corvisier, *op. cit.*, pp. 163-78.

71. Corvisier, *op. cit.*, pp. 355-56.

72. On "*Racolage*," see *ibid.*, pp. 179-95; Georges Girard, *Racolage et Milice; Le service militaire en France à la fin du règne de Louis XIV* (Paris, 1922), pp. 75-161. Occasionally officers from the Isle Royale *troupes de la marine* on leave in France would raise some recruits for the colonies, but they did so to fill vacancies not in their companies but in their purses. There was an exception in 1730 when two companies were added to the garrison. The newly-appointed captains, de Gannes and Dailleboust, were sent to France to recruit some of the men they would later lead. These officers were born in Acadia and Canada respectively and it is unlikely that they engaged in the traditional sort of recruitment that required a certain degree of mutual confidence. Still, they at least had some long-term interest in the men they enlisted. AN, Col., B, Vol. 54-2, f. 520, "*Ordre du Roy au sr. de Gannes pour levée de Soldats*," 7 March 1730. The recruitment of Swiss soldiers for service at Isle Royale was also impersonal. Karrer officers enlisted men for the regiment as a whole and not for particular companies. The officers stationed at Louisbourg had no recruitment responsibilities as long as they stayed in the colony. AN, Col., F²C, Art. 3, ff. 323-26v, Décisions de la Marine, 29 June 1722.

73. See, for example, Port de Rochefort, IE, Vol. 86, ff. 241-46, Pontchartrain, 27 February 1715.

74. *Ibid.*, Vol. 116, f. 404, Maurepas, 10 June 1732.

75. These were special orders of the king that, in these specific cases, were granted at the request of parents who wished to have troublesome sons exiled. See, for example, AN, Col., C¹¹B, Vol. 8, ff. 55-64v, St. Ovide to Minister, 20 November 1726.

76. Port de Rochefort, IE, Vol. 101, ff. 617, 621-22, de Morville, 31 May 1723.

77. *Ibid.*, Vol. 87, ff. 645-51, Council, 28 May 1716; cf. Corvisier, *op. cit.*, p. 720.

78. Thomas Beranger *dit* La Rosée, for example, injured a peasant in a drunken brawl. When criminal proceedings were initiated, he fled to Rochefort and immediately joined the *troupes de la marine*. AN, Outre-Mer, G², Vol. 182, f. 215. "*Conseil Supérieur. Procedure criminelle ... a l'encontre du nommé Nicolas LeBegue d¹, Brulevillage et Thomas Beranger dt. La Rosée soldats acusés de vol*," 3 March-2 June 1733.

79. Isle Royale recruiters generally received only 30 *livres* per man. This sum was supposed to cover their expenses (including enlistment bounties) and provide them with a profit. See, for example, Port de Rochefort, IE, Vol. 116, ff. 360-61, Maurepas, 20 May 1732. Even if the entire amount were turned over to the recruits it would have compared unfavorably with the more substantial bounties offered by the recruiters who supplied the other branches of the French armed forces. Corvisier, *op. cit.*, pp. 328-39.

80. Of 21 men whose heights were recorded because they deserted or appeared in court between 1720 and 1745, four were under the minimum height. In the regular army, such short men were extremely rare. Corvisier, *op. cit.*, pp. 640-41. Underage

recruits were accepted even more readily, again in contrast with the more selective infantry. One governor remarked with satisfaction that the majority of the 40 soldiers arriving at Louisbourg in 1726 were 15 and 16 years old. AN, Col., C^{11}B, Vol. 8, ff. 55-64v, St. Ovide to Minister, 20 November 1726; cf. Corvisier, *op. cit.*, tables between p. 476 and p. 477.

81. AN, Col., C^{11}B, Vol. 33, ff. 89-91v, de Raymond to Minister, 12 October 1753.

82. See, AN, Col., B, Vol. 69, f. 68, Maurepas to Duval, 22 February 1739. The only systematic listing of terms of enlistment is a muster roll which dates from 1752. It indicates that, of 1,067 men in the Isle Royale garrison at that time, only 59 (5.5%) had six-year *"engagements limités."* ASQ, Papiers Surlaville, 55-8, *"Signallement general des trouppes de l'Isle Royale,"* [13 March 1752]. The proportion may have been slightly higher before 1744.

83. These figures were pieced together from a variety of sources. All of them, whether ration lists, reviews or isolated references in the governor's correspondence, were apparently based on the official headcounts prepared by a civilian bureaucrat and updated with information supplied by the major. The most consistent and useful source is the accounts of the keepers of the government storehouse. AN, Col., C^{11}B, Vol. 11-25, *passim, "Etat de la recette et consommation des vivres faittes dans les magasins du Roy à l'isle Royale ... subsistance des troupes ...."* They are complete for the 1730-41 period and they show the number of men supplied with rations in each company and in the Swiss contingent along with the date at which the number changed because of a death, desertion, discharge or the arrival of a recruit. These statistics are not completely reliable. Desertion in particular may have been somewhat underrecorded, but data on the regular army were subject to similar distortions. Figures on the Vivarais-Infanterie are from Corvisier, *op. cit.*, p. 585 (cf. pp. 583-88).

84. Calculated on the basis of information derived from the ration accounts (see note 83).

85. Corvisier, *op. cit.*, pp. 684-85.

86. *Ibid.*, pp. 700-03. Under similar conditions, groups of French and Swiss recruits destined for Isle Royale were decimated by desertion before they left France. Port de Rochefort, IE, Vol. 103, f. 319, Maurepas, 6 June 1724; AN, Col., B, Vol. 58, ff. 167v-68, Maurepas to de la Croix, 13 July 1733.

87. For an account of the difficulties encountered by one deserter who was eventually apprehended on the Nova Scotia mainland, see, AN, Col., C^{11}B, Vol. 7, ff. 78-93, *"Procedure criminelle extraordinaire instruite a l'Encontre du nommé michel Laugier d'alexandre accusé de desertion,"* 18 October 1724.

88. AN, Col., B, Vol. 53, ff. 584-84v, Maurepas to St. Ovide and de Mézy, 22 May 1729.

89. For example, *ibid.*, Vol. 65, f. 442v, Maurepas to St. Ovide and LeNormant, 26 February 1737. The governor and *commissaire-ordonnateur* were not allowed to accept money payments directly from soldiers anxious to purchase their freedom. The minister reserved to himself the right to order discharges *"par des considerations particuliers."* AN, Col., B, Vol. 74, f. 563v, Maurepas to Bigot, 6 June 1742.

90. AN, Col., F^3, Vol. 50, ff. 161-62v, Ordonnance, 26 June 1725; cf. Louise Dechêne, *Habitants et Marchands de Montreal au XVIIe siècle* (Paris and Montréal: Librairie Plon, 1974), pp. 80-88.

91. AN, Col., D^{2}C, Vol. 47, *passim.* Many of these *"invalids"* would have been unable to earn a living but only a small minority could ever hope to draw a pension.

92. AN, Col., C^{11}B, Vol. 7, f. 19, St. Ovide to Minister, 16 November 1724; *ibid.*, Vol. 20, ff. 317-17v, *"troupe"* (unsigned, undated mémoire), [1738].

93. AN, Col., B, Vol. 70, ff. 389-89v, Maurepas to de Forant, 7 May 1740.
94. AN, Col., C¹¹B, Vol. 7, ff. 267-71, de Mézy to Minister, 7 December 1725.
95. For one example of a healthy man discharged as an invalid, see AN, Col., B, Vol. 53, ff. 583v-87, Maurepas to St. Ovide and de Mézy, 22 May 1729.
96. *Ibid.*, Vol. 76, ff. 50-50v, "*Ordonnance du Roy qui suspend la delivrance des congés aux Soldats des Troupes des Colonies jusqu'au premier Janvier 1745,*" 20 March 1743.
97. "*... étant toujours attaqué de l'escorbut son capitaine voulu le congedier, mais le Repondant qui pour lors n'avait qu'environ seize a dix sept ans se mit a pleurer, disant que s'il était congédié il ne scaurait que faire pour gagner sa vie ....*" This soldier adds that his reluctance to leave the island produced a great deal of consternation among his comrades. AN, Col., C¹¹B, Vol. 17, ff. 296-315v, court-martial of Joseph Lagand *dit* Picard, charged with desertion, 24 October 1736.
98. *Ibid.*, Vol. 33, ff. 89-91v, de Raymond to Minister, 12 October 1753.
99. Only one man from the ranks, Jean Loppinot, received a commission in the colony's *troupes de la marine* before 1745. AN, Col., D²C, Vol. 47, "*Isle Royalle - Officiers de guerre,*" 8 May 1730. Loppinot was an exceptional case, having come with many of the original officers of the Isle Royale garrison from Acadia where his family was politically prominent. R.J. Morgan, "A History of Block 16, Louisbourg: 1713-1768" (manuscript on file, Fortress of Louisbourg, 1975), p. 59.
100. Corvisier, *op. cit.*, p. 94; W.J. Eccles, *Frontenac, the Courtier Governor* (Toronto, 1968), p. 220.
101. T.H. Wintringham, *Mutiny; Being a Survey of Mutinies from Spartacus to Invergordon* (London, 1936), p. 256.
102. F.J. Thorpe, "The Politics of French Public Construction in the Islands of the Gulf of St. Lawrence, 1695-1758" (Ph.D. thesis, University of Ottawa, 1973), pp. 232-62.
103. In September 1724, for example, when the strength of the colonial garrison was no more than 430, there were 236 soldiers (along with 17 civilians) employed in the construction of the fortifications. AN, Col., C¹¹B, Vol. 7, ff. 156-56v, de Verville, "*État des ouvriers ...,*" [September 1724].
104. Eccles, *Frontenac, the Courtier Governor*, pp. 215-18; C.J. Russ, "*Les Troupes de la Marine, 1683-1713*" (M.A. thesis, McGill, 1971), pp. 95-98.
105. AN, Col., C¹¹B, Vol. 26, ff. 236-38, Ordonnance, 20 June 1743.
106. *Ibid.*, Vol. 21, f. 55v, de Forant to Minister, 2 October 1739.
107. *Ibid.*, Vol. 18, ff. 85-87, LeNormant to Minister, 6 July 1736; *ibid.*, Vol. 23, ff. 60-64, Duquesnel to Minister, 19 October 1741.
108. AN, Outre-Mer, G², Vol. 182, ff. 148-357, "*Conseil Superieur Procedure criminelle ... a l'encontre du nommé Nicolas LeBegue dit Brulevillage, et Thomas Berranger dit La Rosée soldats acusés de vol,*" 3 March-2 June 1733.
109. *Ibid.*, Vol. 179, ff. 462-502, "*Conseil Superieur-Procedure Criminelle a l'Encontre de Reintender Sergent Suisse et deux autres Complices accuses de vol. [sic],*" 11 September-20 October 1727.
110. Babeau, *op. cit.*, Vol. 1, p. 240.
111. This attitude was also manifested, for example, among the French dragoons who, in the time of Louis XIV, refused to help collect taxes. "*Nous nous sommes engagés pour dragons, et non pour sergeants et porteurs de contraintes.*" *Ibid.*, p. 235.
112. Renard court-martial.
113. Thorpe, *op. cit.*, p. 251.
114. The sources shed little light on the organization and function of these gangs and only mention the "*chefs d'atteliers*" occasionally and incidentally. AN, Col., B,

MUTINY AT LOUISBOURG

Vol. 99, ff. 245-49, "*Instructions pour le S'. franquet D^{eur} des fortiffications de la N^{lle}, france sur les ouvrages que le Roy veut être executées à l'isle Royale,*" 12 May 1754.

115. The engineer and contractor reported these "*contestations tumultueuses*" and "*émeutes*" without providing details. AN, Col., C¹¹B, Vol. 5, ff. 235-37, de Verville to Council, 19 June 1720; *ibid.*, Vol. 6, ff. 127-30, Isabeau to Council, 30 November 1722.

116. *Ibid.*, Vol. 7, ff. 142-50, de Verville, Mémoire, [1724].

117. "... *les travaux que l'on fait dans cette isle donnant l'occasion au soldat de gagner de l'argent l'aysance qu'elle leur [sic] procure le rend delicat et difficile,*" AN, Col., B, Vol. 52-2, ff. 574v-77, Maurepas to St. Ovide, 18 June 1728. In 1719, the engineer estimated that a man could earn five *livres* per day and 465 *livres* in a season. AN, Col., C¹¹B, Vol. 4, ff. 66-68, de Verville to Council, 24 January 1719.

118. AN, Col., C¹¹B, Vol. 5, f. 136v, St. Ovide and de Mézy to Minister, 10 November 1720.

119. *Ibid.*, Vol. 1, ff. 73-76v, l'Hermitte to Council, 3 November 1714; AN, Col., B, Vol. 88-1, ff. 175-75v, Maurepas to Guillet, 15 October 1748.

120. AN, Col., C¹¹B, Vol. 12, f. 252, St. Ovide to Minister, 11 November 1732.

121. *Ibid.*, Vol. 5, ff. 386-88v, St. Ovide to Minister, 30 November 1721.

122. *Ibid.*, Vol. 4, ff. 285-85v, Petition of de Rouville to the Comte de Toulouse, 1719.

123. AN, Col., B, Vol. 44-2, f. 569v, Council to St. Ovide, 1 July 1721.

124. AN, Col., C¹¹B, Vol. 9, ff. 72-78v, St. Ovide to Minister, 21 November 1727.

125. *Ibid.*, Vol. 23, ff. 88-90v, Bigot to Minister, 15 October 1741; *ibid.*, Vol. 29, ff. 306-15, Franquet to Minister, 13 October 1750.

126. See, for example, AN, Col., B, Vol. 68, ff. 347-48v, Maurepas to de Forant and Bigot, 26 May 1739.

127. AN, Col., C¹¹B, Vol. 22, f. 93v, Duquesnel to Minister, 1 December 1740.

128. Russ, *op. cit.*, pp. 181-83. In Canada, even this relatively mild form of exploitation aroused the indignation and opposition of the bishop and clergy. If Canadian officers were more restrained in this regard than were their Isle Royale counterparts, the difference can be explained partly in terms of the more complex public elite of the St. Lawrence colony which was not so completely dominated by the military. However, the greater ease with which Canadian soldiers could leave the service, and the officers' consequent concern about morale, may have been more important.

129. AN, Col., B, Vol. 68, ff. 347-48v, Maurepas to de Forant and Bigot, 26 May 1739.

130. *Ibid.*, Vol. 74, ff. 592-92v, Maurepas to Duquesnel, 15 June 1742.

131. Although Duquesnel claimed that he abolished the canteens in 1741 (AN, Col., C¹¹B, Vol. 23, ff. 24-29, Duquesnel and Bigot to Minister, 20 October 1741), subsequent correspondence shows that he did no more than limit their operation. *Ibid.*, Vol. 24, ff. 52-52v, Duquesnel to Minister, 7 October 1742.

132. Babeau, *op. cit.*, Vol. 1, pp. 176-80.

133. AN, Col., C¹¹B, Vol. 28, ff. 44v-46, Desherbiers and Prévost to Minister, 21 October 1749.

134. *Ibid.*, Vol. 29, ff. 313v-14, Franquet to Minister, 13 October 1750.

Another Soldiers' Revolt in Ile Royale, June 1750

Allan Greer

Introduction

IS ANY FURTHER EVIDENCE needed that the history of the Atlantic region, the history of Canada generally, was not a matter of sweetness and light, peace and harmony? If so, then the following document may be of some interest. It recounts a violent and dramatic confrontation between soldiers and officers at the little outpost of Port Toulouse (present-day St. Peter's, Cape Breton Island) on 23 June 1750. The Ile Royale troops had a long history of turbulence; earlier, in 1744-45, the soldiers of Louisbourg revolted against their officers and assumed virtual control of the town for five months.[1] In 1750 the revolt was more short-lived.

Captain Duhaget, commander of the Port Toulouse garrison, some 100 kilometres southwest of Louisbourg, wrote this narrative, a letter to the colonial minister and our only source on the second mutiny, while recovering from a leg wound received during the exchange of fire.[2] There is little reason to question his basic outline of the events of the day. The soldiers here, like the men of Louisbourg six years earlier and like the sailors of the Battleship Potemkin 155 years later, were annoyed by the substandard quality of their rations. During an argument over food, a corporal struck a soldier and it was to protest this indignity that the men turned out in unauthorized battle formation. When Duhaget and the corporal ran for their weapons, they were fired upon and both were wounded. Bloodshed (probably unintended) immediately raised the stakes and, fearing a punitive expedition from Louisbourg, 23 rebels commandeered boats and set off for the English-held Acadian settlements. On the way however, there was an explosion on one of the boats and four or five of the fugitives were killed. Apparently the others either returned to give themselves up or were captured, since other documents indicate a mass court-martial. In September 1750, six men were convicted of mutiny and shot, while a large number of others were sentenced to servitude in the king's galleys.[3]

Why did the soldiers risk such brutal punishment? On this point, Duhaget is unhelpful and, quite likely, deliberately misleading. Anxious to avoid any blame, the commander insisted he had provided no grounds for complaint, implying that his men had revolted impulsively over a trivial incident. And yet the turn of events strongly suggests deep-seated tensions and suspicion. In general, the lot of an 18th-century soldier was a hard one: recruited in many cases by trickery or force, he served long terms with severe discipline, low pay and little opportunity to marry. A tremendous gulf separated soldiers and officers, but overt conflict was generally kept to a minimum in Europe by paternalism, by the socialization of new recruits to the military *esprit de corps* and by displays of the authorities' punitive power. These restraints did not operate as effectively in Ile Royale for a number of reasons. For example, there was a blatant system of exploitation here by which officers enjoyed a monopoly in supplying their men with liquor, clothing and other merchandise at grossly inflated prices. This certainly undermined any paternalistic relationship and was a major factor leading to the Louisbourg mutiny and, no doubt, to the Port Toulouse rising. Generally, the special circumstances of military life at Ile Royale tended to enhance a feeling of solidarity among the soldiers and to alienate them from the officers and other authorities.[4]

The result was two very serious revolts in the space of six years. The Port Toulouse rising in some ways seems the graver of the two. It was marked by open violence and it led to more merciless punishment. (Only three men were executed for the Louisbourg mutiny, compared with double that number for the later rising). On the other hand, the revolt at Louisbourg was more extensive, more prolonged, and more far-reaching in its challenge to authority. Taken together, these two incidents illustrate, in their results, the savageness with which the absolutist state dealt with rebels. More significantly, they also provide another example of the power of "traditional" attitudes, such as the notion of the dignity of the man-at-arms, to sustain collective resistance. Forced to live for years in lonely colonial exile, subjected to stern discipline and cheated out of their pay, the soldiers of Ile Royale defended their interests as best they could by petitions, by strikes and, when the circumstances called for more serious action, by open revolt.

Monseigneur

Vous aurés sans doutte apris par le compte que Mr. Desherbiers vous aura rendu, la revolte arrivée au Port toulouse, ou je commandois; cette Scenne s'est passée le 23 juin de la presente année.

Le seul pretexte de ces mutins fut, Monseigneur, sur ce que un caporal ayant commandé celuy d'entre eux qui etoit de cuisine pour avoir des herbes, et voyant au moment du souper, qui ne l'avoit pas fait, disant qu'il avoit des legumes; a quoy le caporal repartit il est d'usage dans nos troupes de les menager pour l'hyver; cette semonce déplut beaucoup audit soldat qui jurat le nom de Dieu, sur quoi le caporal luy detachat un seul coup de lianne dans la chambrée. Cinq ou six vinrent sur le champ se plaindre ainsy, me demandant si je voulois souffrir que les caporeaux et les sergents leurs donnassent des coups de cannes; je leurs repondis que je leurs rendrois bonne Justice, que mon intention n'estoit point que personnes les frapat plus que moy, mais aussy qu'ils ne manquassent point de respects aux officiers soldats. Ils parurent contants de ma reponse et s'en retournerent tout de suitte au quartier, ou le moment après je me rendis pour voir de quoy il etoit question. Je ne fus jamais plus surpris que d'entendre crier aux armes, et de voir qu'une partie les avoit desja pris; mon premier debut fut de crier bas les armes, et leurs demander s'ils ne me reconnoissoit [sic] pas pour leur commandant. Ils me repondit avec mutinerie que sitost qu'ils seroient rangé en bataille qu'ils me parleroient; J'employay tous les termes que je crus les plus propres pour les faire rentrer dans leurs devoirs, tant menaces que voix de douceurs; le caporal étoit pour lors a mes costés; huit de ses malheureux armerent pour lors leurs fuzils, et nous crierent de nous retirer sans quoy ils nous passeroient par les armes. Voyant la partie inegalle, et qu'il n'y avoit qu'un cris de nous retirer, sans quoy nous payerions notre entetement, je crus a propos de le faire, d'autant que je n'étois point armé. Je n'avois point concerté de precaution necessaire, et ne me serois jamais imaginé qu'on eûst pu pousser l'imprudence aussy loing; mon intention Monseigneur, n'estoit autre que de m'armer et de m'opposer a leurs mauvais desseins s'ils y persistoient. Le sergent et le susdit caporal me suivirent. Ses [sic] mutins previrent sans doutte ce que je premeditois, et au moment que je metois le pied dans la salle, qui n'étoit distante de la troupe que de huit a dix pas, un de la droitte se detachat et lachat un coup de fuzil, dont le caporal fut dangereusement blessé au bas ventre, les boyeaux luy sortant du corp. Le fuzil estoit chargé a deux balles. J'en receus une dans la cuisse qui me la perceat de part en part. Je me trouvay beigné dans mon sang et hors d'etat de m'opposer a leurs infamie. Ils me firent sitost qu'ils le surent, bien des excuses, et m'assurent qu'ils n'avoient point eu dessein de me blesser, qu'ils n'en avoient voulu qu'au caporal, que le malheur estant arivé, ils sentoient bien qu'ils n'avoient autre party a prendre que la fuitte, mais qu'ils ne pouvoient voyager sans argent et obligerent mon domestique a leurs donner les clefs de mes malles en le menaçant de luy bruler la cervelle.

Je ne vous retraceré point Monseigneur, les pertes que j'ay fait d'en ce jour. J'en ay rendu compte a Mrs Desherbiers et Prevost, et ces Mrs m'ont assuré qu'ils vous representeront combien il étoit juste que je fus remboursé de mes pertes; ils n'ont pas meme epargné le magazin du Roy.

Ils partirent enfin, le meme soir, après avoir enlevé deux petits batiments de dix a douze tonneaux, sur lesquelles ils s'embarquerent et tous leurs butin. Ils forcerent plusieurs habitants à les conduire sur les terres de l'acadie. A huit heures du matin estant dans le passage, l'esquif qui etoit chargé de poudre et de vivres sautat. Quatre de ces miserables perirent et ce qu'il y eut de plus malheureux, un des habitants nommé Briant sautat avec eux, et a laissé une pauvre veuve et huit enfants. Comme ces gens avoient laché au moment du depart, que toutte la garnizon de Louisbourg en devoit faire autant le meme jour, je depecha des le grand matin un expres a Mr Desherbiers, pour l'informer de ce qui c'estoit passé, et de ce qui c'estoit dit. Je serois inconsolable, Monseigneur, si j'avois donné la moindre occasion a cette revolte, et ay attendu que l'affaire eut eté jugé pour demander a Mr Desherbiers s'il avoit trouvé dans le procès quelque chose a mes charges; a quoy il m'a repondu n'y avoir rien trouvé, que il vous envoyeroit touttes les procedures et que vous seriés a meme d'en juger.

Il n'y en avoit que vingt trois qui ont trempé dans cette affaire, les autres ne l'ayant pas voulu, et n'osant se fier a leurs camarades, se refugierent dans les bois et revinrent des l'endemain matin. Sitost qu'ils seurent les autres partis, ils s'offrirent meme a courir après; mais ils avoient eu la precaution d'emporter touttes les armes et il n'i en avoit point pour les remplacer.

Mr Duboisberthelot, le seul officier que j'eus, m'avoit demander de s'absenter pour deux ou trois jours. Comme je luy avois permi il ne se trouva point dans cette affaire.

Le chirurgien major a jugé Monsigneur, que la nature de ma blessure exigeoit que je prisse les eaux de Barege et sur son certificat Mr desherbiers a bien voulu m'acorder un congé dont je profiterois; ce qui me mettra a meme en attendant la saison, d'avoir l'honneur de vous faire ma cour, et de vous rendre compte plus amplement de ce qui s'est passé.

J'ay l'honneur d'etre avec un profond respect, Monseigneur, votre très humble et tres obeissant serviteur,
Duhaget
a Louisbourg le 15e 8bre 1750.

Notes

1. Allan Greer, "Mutiny at Louisbourg, December 1744," *Histoire sociale-Social History,* Vol. 10 (November 1977), pp. 305-36.
2. AN, Col., C^{11}B, Vol. 29, ff. 319-25, Duhaget to Minister, 15 October 1750.
3. The general register of troops for Ile Royale lists a number of men sentenced to the galleys and many of these were probably involved in the Port Toulouse mutiny. About 11 others, all of them soldiers of Duhaget's company, there can be no doubt:
"*déserté le 24 juin 1750 et noyé le 29 dans son évasion*":
Jacques Gaultier dt. Bonnefoy, Etienne Pradeau dt. Francoeur, Pierre Coudreau dt. Nantois, Charles Quartier dt.Mayence, Robert Soubise dt. Laplace,passé par les armes," 9-12 September 1750:
Joseph Bonnet dt. Jolibois, Pierre Bonnaublanc dt. Acajou, Pierre Cousin dt. Fleury, Hilaire Pepin dt. Desmarest, Guillaume Jambert dt. Cahors, Jerome Sauvage dt. Malpec.
"Isle Royale. Rolle général des Troupes françoises commencé en 1739," AN, Col., D^{2}C, vol. 53.
4. Greer, "Mutiny," pp. 320-35. On military life in contemporary France, see Albert Babeau, *La vie militaire sous l'ancien régime* (Paris, 1889); André Corvisier, *L'armée française de la fin du XVIIe siècle au ministère de Choiseul. Le soldat,* 2 vols. (Paris: Presses Universitaires de France, 1964); and Georges Girand, *Le service militaire en France à la fin du règne de Louis XIV. Racolage et milice (1701-1715)* (Paris, 1922).

SOCIAL

Communities and Families: Family Life and Living Conditions in Eighteenth-Century Louisbourg

Kenneth Donovan

The Community Study

Although sociologists, psychologists, and anthropologists have long since conducted both empirical and theoretical research into the nature and function of contemporary families, it is only within the past two decades that French and English historians, and more recently their American counterparts, have come to recognize the central role of the family in moulding society. Seeing the paucity of community and family-oriented studies in general, a new generation of historians undertook to fill the void by producing so-called microstudies.[1] Taking a broader view of the family and the community as a whole, demographic historians have employed a new methodology which entails not only reconstructing but examining in detail the records of local communities.

Convinced that novel methods of demographic analysis could be used to investigate key problems in social history, these demographic historians sought the answers to such questions as how many children were in each family, at what ages did people marry, how much control did parents have over their children, and why did children remain in their parents' community. But merely uncovering particulars as to the size and composition of the domestic group would prove a fruitless exercise indeed were not such information applied to effects on behaviour. With such an end in view, New England scholarship in the late 1960s and early 1970s emphasized local or, more precisely, community studies. Of course, the authors of the New England community studies owe a tremendous debt to French and, to a lesser extent, British scholars, for they have pioneered sophisticated techniques of local analysis.[2] The demographic findings and the methodologies that have evolved in France and Europe as a whole, not to mention the United States, are relevant to an examination of Louisbourg.[3] Various French local works emphasize that the average colonial American's living standard was significantly above that of his western European counterpart. At the same time numerous studies of New England towns also underscore the often neglected similarities between American and French villages of the seventeenth and eighteenth centuries.[4] And to the extent that the history of Louisbourg is closely allied to France, the history of French families from the sixteenth through the eighteenth century provides a blueprint for an evaluation of the Louisbourg experience.

Utilizing such data as probates, land transactions, court records, and vital statistics, this relatively new scholarship tackled the social history of the local community from a radically new perspective by employing two basic statistical techniques: aggregate analysis and family reconstitution. Aggregate analysis is essentially the compilation of data on local communities and relies primarily on a chronological series of original records of birth, marriages, and deaths. After the information has been accumulated, historians can analyse it for various demographic trends including rates of population growth, decline, and mobility. Population trends in various communities thus can easily be compared. The principal limitation of this approach with regard to Louisbourg is the relatively short history of the fortress town. Louisbourg was occupied by the French a mere forty-two years, 1713-45 and 1748-58, hardly enough time for an on-going pattern of development to emerge, even if all the data were extant.

By far the most useful methodological tool for the study of Louisbourg is family reconstitution, for it is concerned with the lives of particular families within the communities as opposed to the more general patterns of population growth in various communities. But this is not to say that aggregate analysis should not be utilized in a demographic examination of Louisbourg, for the town should not be studied in isolation. In fact, this is one of the key areas where microstudies differ decisively from the traditional community study; unlike the latter which more often than not lapsed into ancestor worship, the new community studies, apart from using a new methodology involving quantitative analysis, are keenly appreciative of a broader historical context of which their respective works form only a minor part.

However, before any family reconstitution or community-oriented investigation may even be attempted, there must be a thorough set of records. Louisbourg, with some major exceptions, more than fits the bill, and a good case can be made for overkill, for in the archives of the Fortress of Louisbourg National Historic Park is the comprehensive parish record file with its records of baptisms, marriages, and deaths in Ile Royale. Moreover, there is an index of occupants of the reconstructed part of the town (approximately one-fifth of the fortress), with upwards of 45,000 references to roughly 1,000 names.[5] And there is the literary evidence. Frequently the latter is less important to the new methodology which stresses the value and importance of quantifiable data, nevertheless, the significance of subjective factors -- there are thousands of pages of official correspondence between Louisbourg and France -- must not be overlooked in any study of the Louisbourg community.

Based on the voluminous judicial records extant at Louisbourg, there is every reason to believe that the people of Louisbourg, not unlike those of New England, went to court more often than the average citizen today. Admittedly, the great majority of Louisbourg's citizens, perhaps as many as 70 per cent, were illiterate, but many appeared in court and some of their views have been preserved as testimony in legal proceedings. The clerks of the various courts, most notably the *plumitif* of the Superior Council and to a lesser extent the bailiff's court or royal court, recorded the statements of various defendants and witnesses. If Louisbourg citizens were prepared to drag their neighbours into court for the least offence, justice must have been relatively inexpensive. Civil cases of less than 200 *livres* that were judged summarily cost only 3 *livres*.[6] In protracted civil and criminal suits, however, justice was by no means moderately priced because fees were charged by officers of the court at virtually every level for the preparation of documents required by law. Of course, the court records necessarily convey a negative bias, if for no other reason than they tell us of what the community disapproved. Nevertheless, they are still one of the best sources for Louisbourg social history.

Another critical source for an examination of Louisbourg

family life is the inventory of estate. Although not unique to France and its possessions, French inventories were most exacting: under French civil law an inventory was required of the estate of each person who died with heirs. Naturally, when a spouse died, the co-ownership of the community of goods between a husband and a wife was dissolved. Since the inventory was primarily intended to protect the inheritance of the minors, an exact enumeration was made of all the goods and property and the appraisers subsequently set the value of the estate. After the inventory was complete, the estate was divided with the surviving spouse receiving half and the children equally sharing the remaining half.

By outlining the number of rooms and describing their contents, these inventories provide a wealth of information about the household of the deceased. Indeed, the difficulty in using them is knowing how to sort out the mass of data and make meaningful generalizations. At first glance, the inventories describe only those possessions owned by the colonists and hence give a formal view of family life. But the inventories actually provide clues to various questions about family interrelationships: Who owned what? How many rooms were in the house? Did the children sleep with their parents? Did the family eat at one or more tables? How much privacy did the family enjoy? In the end, the historian is faced with a formidable task, for to answer such questions he must come to terms, either by deduction, impression, or, where possible, quantification of the data, with certain personal and emotional patterns of behaviour which are critical for an overview of family life.

Even a cursory glance at the 187 Louisbourg inventories reveals a wide variance among households in terms of material possessions. Of course, this is understandable in view of the different social ranks of the people inventoried. Louisbourg inventories run the gamut of the town's society, including such notables as government officials, artisans, merchants, military officers, and ships' captains. By far the largest single occupation inventoried in Louisbourg are the lowly fishermen, with no less than 35 extant inventories. Of these 35, the majority are disappointingly small, usually comprising a couple of pages outlining the few worldly possessions of a drowned fisherman. Notwithstanding the fishermen's inventories, there are actually few inventories of the very poor in Louisbourg.

The comprehensive Louisbourg collection of artifacts also provides the opportunity of utilizing physical evidence. Historians have naturally felt more comfortable examining literary sources rather than physical remains. Although the answers may not be readily forthcoming and, at best, will be inferential, historians must ask questions about physical evidence to broaden our knowledge of social history. What Louisbourg historian could possibly ignore the thousands of pipe stems and wine bottles unearthed at the fortress site? This archaeological evidence reveals, to a much greater extent than the documents, that smoking and drinking spirits were cherished pastimes. Moreover, in terms of family life and household living conditions, archaeological evidence is particularly pertinent; occasionally it is the only available source for determining the size and appearance of a house and its contents.

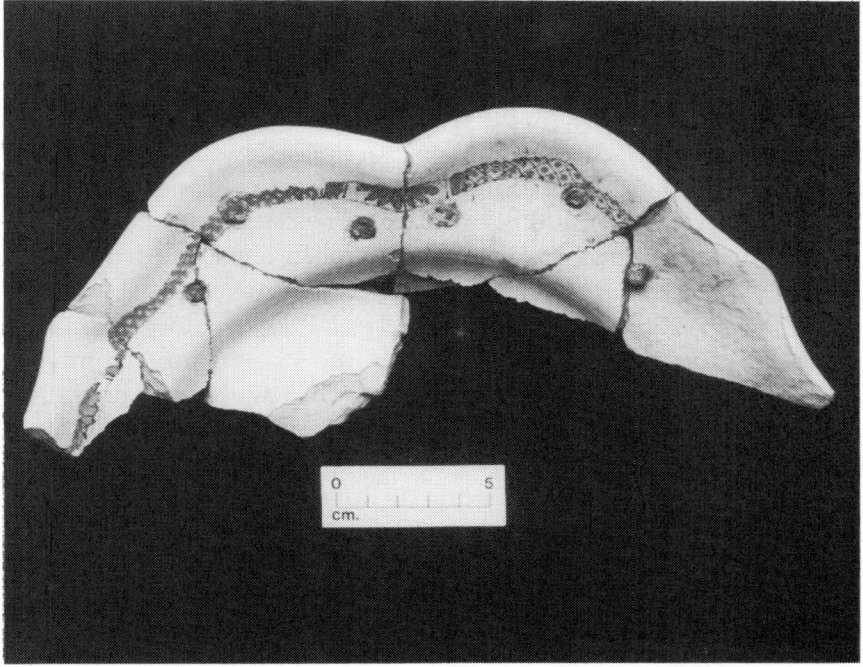

Figure 1. A faience platter with a scalloped rim section showing six lead staples embedded on either side of a break. Excavated from the fifth casemate on the right side of the King's Bastion, the platter has a white tin glaze with a dot, diaper, and hatch pattern separated by a foliate design. (Photo: Danny Crawford. Parks Canada, Fortress Louisbourg National Historic Park. Catalogue No. 1B.4N19.20).

The Louisbourg Community

Just how applicable is the community-oriented approach to eighteenth-century Louisbourg? A colonial aristocracy eventually emerged that was military, bureaucratic, and commercial, but Louisbourg's settlement had a communal character and small communities cannot sustain a vast range of social roles let alone a substantial differentiation of labour. Moreover, Louisbourg's founding settlement, comprising approximately 160 people (mostly soldiers), was small by today's standards. Within the context of eighteenth-century colonial North America, however, the settlement was anything but minute. By 1710 -- three years prior to the founding of Louisbourg -- there were only 60,000 people in all of Massachusetts and, more important, the average town had less than 100 adult males.[7] By 1737, Louisbourg, with approximately 1,500 people, was one of the most populous towns in North America.

In compliance with the terms of the Treaty of Utrecht, which officially ended the War of the Spanish Succession in 1713, Acadia and Newfoundland were ceded to Britain leaving France, Ile Royale (Cape Breton Island) and Ile Saint-Jean (Prince Edward Island). According to the terms of the treaty, the French were entitled to emigrate to French territory within a year, taking their moveable goods with them. Ile Royale was established as a French colony primarily because of the efforts of one man: Jérome Phélypeaux, Comte de Pontchartrain. A veteran administrator who succeeded his father as minister of marine in 1693, Pontchartrain sought to maintain France's preeminence in the North Atlantic fishery and hence, during the last two years of his tenure, Ile Royale became his first priority in colonial affairs. Thus, the settlement on Ile Royale, and particularly Louisbourg, was intended to replace Placentia as the headquarters for the fishery and serve as a haven for trading ships and privateers.[8]

Placentia was handed to the English and by early September 1713 its inhabitants had arrived in Ile Royale. The 116 men, 10 women, and 23 children all had a common background; they, and the people that followed them, formed the backbone of an eighteenth-century fishing community.[9] Established as a key French fishing settlement as early as 1662, Placentia had been provided with a garrison not only to protect the fishermen but to enable them to fish in nearby harbours. Although the great bulk of the vessels came out from France in the spring and returned in the autumn with their crews, Placentia had become an important depot for the fishery and consequently, as early as 1687 there were approximately 123 settlers or inhabitants who wintered in the colony.[10] By 1711, there were only 600 people in Placentia, of which fewer than half were full-time residents of the colony.[11] It was this small fishing community which would form the founding core of Louisbourg's population.[12]

These few hundred settlers seemed hardly enough, even if the majority of them transferred to Ile Royale, to fend off any concerted attack. What was essential to Pontchartrain was the assemblage of the largest possible force in one place and, although he was not unalterably opposed to the formation of other settlements, he pressed for concentration on the founding and subsequent fortification of Louisbourg.[13] Thus, after 1713 he called for the fishermen on the island of Saint-Pierre to move to Ile Royale and he waged a concerted effort to encourage the Acadians to emigrate to a land "of their nation."[14] To urge the Acadians to forsake their diked marshlands and emigrate to Ile Royale for purely patriotic reasons was for them a hollow argument; as Pontchartrain himself noted, Louisbourg had been chosen for one reason: "the abundance of the fish found there has determined that His Majesty should make it the first and principal establishment."[15]

It was all very well for the French Ministry of Marine to adopt a policy calling for the settling of Ile Royale, but obviously some incentive had to be offered to the Placentia fishermen and the Acadian farmers to encourage them to uproot their families and emigrate to an inhospitable new colony. That exceptional incentive was to be freehold tenure. To a settler of peasant stock, the thought of having legal title to his own land must have been nothing short of enthralling. Certainly there was no question that the people of Placentia were initially accorded a special status, at least in terms of land grants; they were the first settlers to be offered land concessions in Louisbourg, whereas the masters of vessels coming annually from France were to have access to the beaches in the nearby harbours of Mira and Scatary.[16] The Placentia refugees were to be granted land, not merely beach frontage, as compensation for leaving Newfoundland, the land of their birth.[17] Beach frontage was distributed to the people from Placentia in proportion to the amount of land that they owned in Newfoundland, and according to the number of *chaloupes* they possessed.[18] Furthermore, the granting of land in Louisbourg was all the more significant because throughout most of the eighteenth century in Newfoundland no private property had been granted except in association with the fishery.[19]

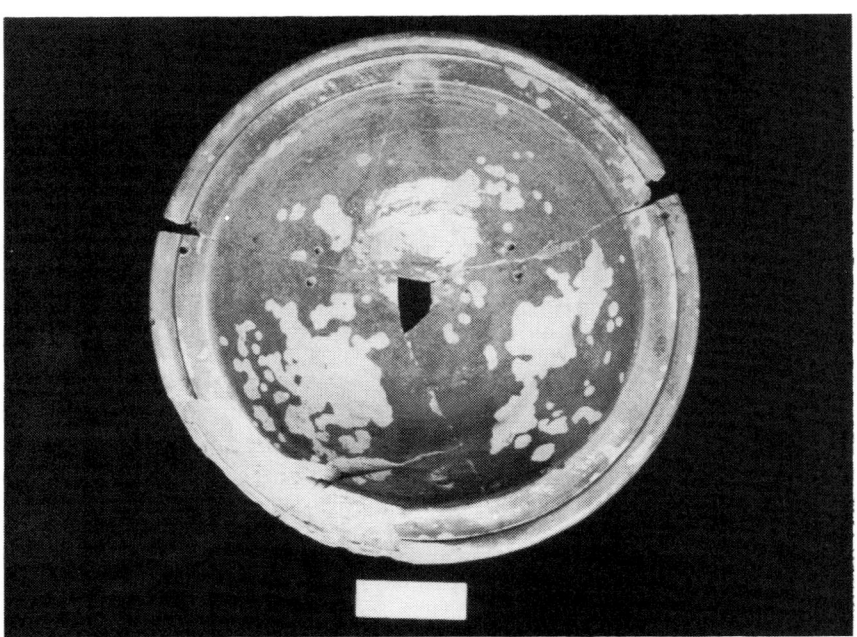

Figure 2. *A green glazed coarse earthenware bowl, radius 14.5 cm., from the Saintonge region, France. The bowl, excavated from the sixth casemate on the right side of the King's Bastion, has eight mend holes. (Photo: Danny Crawford. Parks Canada, Fortress Louisbourg National Historic Park. Catalogue No. 1B.4P11.14).*

Such was not to be the case in Louisbourg or Ile Royale because the Acadians had enjoyed the benefits of private property for over a century and if there was to be any hope of luring them to Cape Breton, they had to be offered their own land. Accordingly, Pontchartrain took steps to assure not only the Acadians but the settlers from Placentia that there would be no seigneurial concessions granted on Ile Royale in contrast to Canadian settlement along the St. Lawrence.[20]

The concessions of land on Ile Royale measured approximately two to four acres frontage by four to six in depth. However, Pontchartrain reminded Governor Costebelle that it served no purpose to give the settlers more land than they desired because other settlers would be prevented from establishing there. Furthermore, he did not want the land along the Mira River to be granted first because it was the most suitable land for cultivation.[21] And this was precisely the crux of the problem for the Acadians because there was so little arable land on the island. Above all, the Acadians were farmers and, over a century of relative isolation from France, they had created an indigenous culture. Why should they forsake their bountiful land to take up farming or fishing in Ile Royale?[22] The Acadians wished to settle, if any where on the island, at Port Dauphin which was better suited to farming. In the end, only 67 Acadian families, some 500 people, emigrated to Cape Breton between 1713 and 1734.

To the Acadians, Louisbourg's population must have appeared a tight corporate group, as indeed it was, since eighteenth-century man was much more group conscious than his present-day counterpart. People knew their role in society, and the pre-industrial man conformed to the norms of his group. Not surprisingly, the eighteenth-century French peasant identified himself with his most important group, the family, and then with his village.[23] There is no reason to suspect that the founding settlers of Louisbourg would think any differently. Had not their fishing village just been transferred wholesale to Louisbourg!

Even though the Acadians did not arrive as anticipated, by March 1714 there were more than 300 men at Louisbourg.[24] The transfer from Placentia appeared orderly enough (actually it caused tremendous hardship for the people involved), but Pontchartrain cautioned that the wives and children of the workers must not be sent to Ile Royale for the first year. These families would have to be looked after: "it would be better," he insisted, "if the families waited until next year to come because the workers will be established and in a state to receive them."[25]

Pontchartrain's suggestion that the families of the workers should delay their departure was not carried out completely, however; by early October 1714 Placentia had been fully evacuated.[26] The French departure from Placentia had been speeded up in order to avoid an imbroglio over the interpretation of the text of the treaty. Although the French had been granted a year to remove their valuables, some confusion arose over whether the year began, as the French presumed, the day they handed over their territory to the English or the day they signed the treaty? The latter was the English position and the French had little choice but to concede eventually. Pontchartrain therefore advised Governor Costebelle that it was necessary for the French to leave Placentia as quickly as possible.[27]

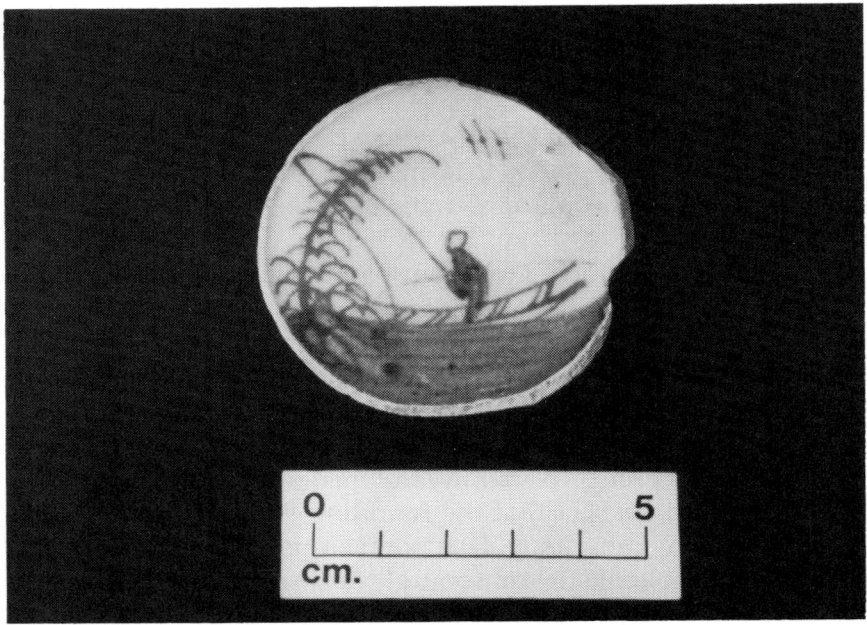

Figure 3. An English soft-paste porcelain bowl shaped for re-use. Special care has been taken to maintain the centre design of a boy fishing. Excavated from the Cassagnolles-Detcheverry storehouse in the Ile du Quay. (Photo: Danny Crawford. Parks Canada, Fortress Louisbourg National Historic Park. Catalogue No. 47L.90H2.1).

Since the people who came to Louisbourg clearly came to stay, the community-oriented concept appears all the more valid when applied to the fortress town. Of the eight officers who signed the original declaration claiming Ile Royale as a possession of Louis XIV, the descendants of no less than six participated in the defence of the fortress in 1745 and numerous descendants of former officers were present at the siege of 1758.[28] Prior to 1745 the original immigrants from Placentia virtually dominated the Superior Council, holding four of the five council positions.[29] Even the Ile Royale soldier, recruited as a member of the Compagnies Franches de la Marine, served to a much greater extent than his counterpart in France or Canada in terms of unlimited engagements which usually amounted to lifetime appointments.[30]

Yet, in the midst of this ostensibly staid society there was also a great deal of mobility, for the fishing proprietors, residents of the colony who owned the boats and shore facilities, hired hundreds of fishermen for each season. Although approximately one-third of these fishermen wintered in the colony, most of them came out each year from France. However, there was a critical distinction between the mobile sector of Ile Royale's population and Louisbourg society which was remote and restricted, at least for its full-time residents. Within such a relatively closed society, marriage alliances opened avenues to wealth and influence; the children of prominent families, of bourgeois merchants, administrators, or senior officers, easily intermarried. The resulting extended relationships and close bonds produced a feeling of local identity and a sense of exclusiveness towards outsiders.[31]

French economic policy accentuated the attitude of exclusiveness. Like his father, Pontchartrain retained the principal dogmas of mercantilism. In keeping with this policy the French endeavoured, mostly in vain, to establish a monopoly over Ile Royale's fishery. From the outset, Pontchartrain adopted measures intended to make the colony even more insular. Attempting to protect the settlement from exploitation, he stipulated as early as 1714 that tavern keepers, especially those from France who were retail merchants as well, would not be permitted to settle in Louisbourg because they lived off the work of others. But ultimately it was not so much French official policy as fortuitous circumstances and the business acumen of the Louisbourg merchants which contributed to their growing role in the colony's fishing industry and supply trade. Louisbourg's merchant-fishermen dominated Ile Royale's economy and they stimulated and helped to maintain a spirit of independence and nativism within the burgeoning town. As a result, colonial Louisbourg became a community, not merely in numbers, but in spirit and feeling.

Family Life and Living Conditions

Bountiful evidence, together with an expanded historical outlook and various quantitative techniques, render a community-oriented investigation of eighteenth-century Louisbourg most attractive. As important as the methodology, however, is the new conceptualization itself, for the family and generational development provides an excellent model for psycho-social analysis.

Louisbourg was constructed in a desolate spot. Notorious

for its dampness, the fortress was erected on a peninsula which takes the brunt of the southwest Atlantic winds; it is often shrouded in fog when the rest of the island, including the north shore of the harbour three miles away, enjoys sunshine. Relying only on a fully banked fireplace in a reconstructed period building at the Fortress of Louisbourg National Historic site can be a chilling experience in mid-winter. Insulation, as we know it, was unheard of in the eighteenth century, and given their relatively inefficient fireplaces it is only to be expected that the French spent much of their time trying to keep warm. Colonial officials continually bemoaned the hardships of Louisbourg winters to their superiors at Versailles. Writing in December 1727, Governor Saint-Ovide reported to the minister of marine that "wood is as necessary here as bread."[32] Louisbourg's inventories of estates confirm Saint-Ovide's contention; by October households had as many as fifteen cords of wood in preparation for the long winter months.[33] A 1735 account of the fuel used in the soldiers' guardroom of the King's Bastion barracks shows that they burned thirty cords of wood "in the 8 months of winter between the month of October and the end of May."[34]

In large measure, the townspeople relied on the troops of the garrison to supply fuel, for the soldiers were encouraged to earn extra income by cutting firewood. As might be expected the climate exacted its greatest toll during the winter, and it was continually being cited in correspondence as the cause of respiratory congestion and rheumatism. Charles Knowles, English governor of Louisbourg from 1746 to 1747, lamented in the spring of 1747: "I have struggled hard to weather the winter, which I've done thank God, tho was not above three times out of my room for 5 months ... I am convinced I shou'd not live out another winter at Louisbourg ...."[35] Like Knowles, James Johnstone grudgingly tolerated the Louisbourg weather. A former captain in Bonnie Prince Charlie's army during the Jacobite rebellion, as well as a translator and lieutenant in the Louisbourg garrison, Johnstone lived in the town from 1752 until the eve of the capitulation in 1758. In his memoir, Johnstone referred to "The bad climate of Louisbourg, where one does not see the sun sometimes for a month; the extreme misery which you experience from that ...." The climate, continued Johnstone, "contributed to cause me to acquire a taste for reading and studying philosophy, very seldom going out of my room except to attend to my duty...."[36]

COMMUNITIES AND FAMILIES

Patients in the Louisbourg hospital huddled around stoves in winter for warmth. In 1749 the hospital purchased "nine pine benches for the comfort of the sick around the stoves ...."[37] Nathaniel Knap, a carpenter from Newbury, Massachusetts, and member of the British force which had captured Louisbourg in 1758, described on 25 January 1759, how bitterly cold days brought work to a standstill: "This Day so cold that we Did but little work & had enough to do to keep ourselves warm by yee fire."[38]

Louisbourg's citizens coped with frigid temperatures by installing brick and iron stoves, surrounding their beds with heavy serge curtains, wearing mittens and gloves, and having their clothing lined. Despite such precautions, most adults and particularly children, could hardly be expected to remain out of doors for long periods of time during the winter months.[39] Such harsh climatic conditions, combining humid yet long, cold winters, forced the average family to live together even more intensely.

And what were the living conditions? On the whole, dwellings were smaller than those of today and parts were not used during winter. Moreover, most families were extended by in-laws, domestic servants, or slaves. This was certainly the case in Joseph Lartigue's family. Emigrating from Placentia in 1714, Lartigue soon made his mark in Louisbourg, employing sixteen fishermen and beach workers by 1715. Lartigue's household in January 1715 included his younger brother, who was a surgeon, his mother-in-law, two sister-in-laws, his brother-in-law, and a Madame Tossoire, as well as his wife, Jeanne Dhiarse, and a son and daughter.[40] Given the rigours of establishing a new settlement in a hostile environment, it was only natural that Lartigue would welcome his relatives into his home, at least until they could build their own houses.

What contributed to the extension of Louisbourg families was not only the lack of accommodation at the founding of the settlement, but also subsequent marriages among the townspeople. It became common practice in Louisbourg for prosperous fathers to offer as part of their daughter's dowry free room and board for one or more years. Of 566 marriages registered in the Louisbourg parish records between 1722 and 1758, there are marriage contracts for only 176. In 26 of the marriage contracts the parents offered to share their households with the newly married couple for periods ranging from one to ten years.[41] The case of Jeanne Beauché, widow of Jean Guyon Préville, is typical. When her daughter Jeanne-Angélique married

Joseph-Mathieu Guillet, a boat-builder from Cap Saint-Ignace, Canada, in 1741, Jeanne Beauché promised to provide free accommodation in her house "for two years which will begin the day of their marriage."[42]

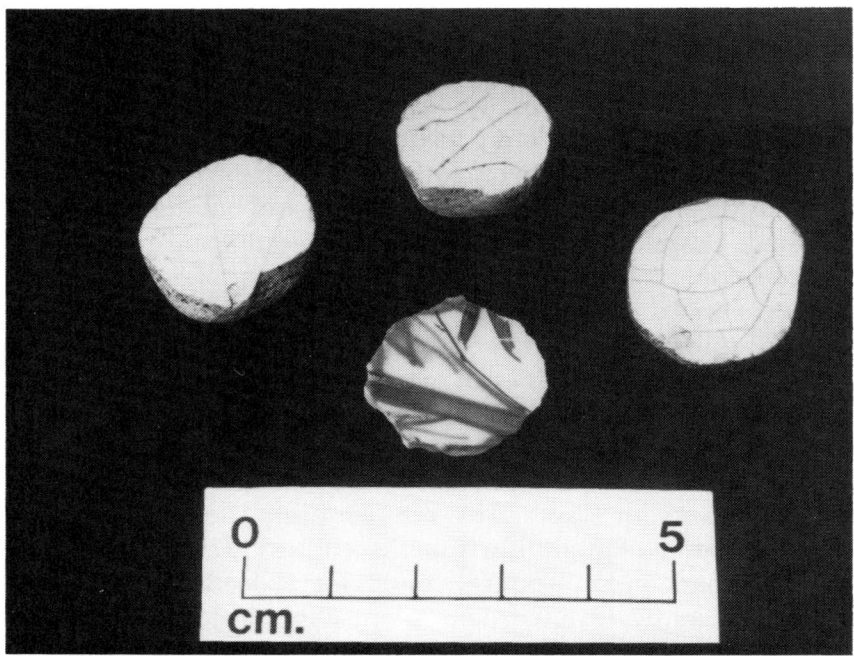

Figure 4. Three gaming pieces, excavated from the De la Perelle storehouse, carved from the base of a faience plate. At the bottom, there is a gaming piece chipped from the base of a Chinese export porcelain plate decorated in the Imari style. Excavated from the trash and collapse of the Guion-Claparede-Pugnant house. (Photo: Danny Crawford. Parks Canada, Fortress Louisbourg National Historic Park. Catalogue Nos. 17L.21C3.18 a, b, c, and 2L.17H3.2).

Some parents even offered free accommodation for their children as long as they desired it. Such was the case with Pierre Rousseau de Souvigny, a captain in the Louisbourg garrison, when his daughter Josephe married ensign François-Nicolas Chassin de Thierry in 1734. Son of Nicolas Chassin, controller general of the house of Madame la Dauphine, François-Nicolas obviously came from a well-to-do background and was a desirable suitor. Rousseau not only promised to provide accommodation for his daughter and son-in-law but, in case either family did not wish to continue sharing the same household, he offered his daughter and son-in-law a rent-free house on Rue Royale.⁴³ Numerous other parents, especially those of poorer families, welcomed their newlywed children into their homes on an informal basis, that is, without providing a written guarantee of occupation in a marriage contract.

Joseph Lartigue who opened his house to his brother and in-laws in 1715 seems to have welcomed the opportunity of extending his family. "I have a large family," asserted Lartigue in November 1737, "which is composed of my wife and nine children, four boys and five girls."⁴⁴ Lartigue's personal fortunes, however, had more than kept pace. Relinquishing his fishing operations in the early 1720s, he soon figured among Louisbourg's most prosperous traders. Equally important, he gained a seat on the prestigious Supreme Council in 1723, and eight years later was appointed keeper of the colony's seals. The crowning glory for this ambitious merchant came in 1734 when he was selected to be the first judge in Louisbourg's bailiff's court.

Obviously, a man of Lartigue's social and economic stature required a suitable dwelling, and his house, measuring approximately twenty-four by sixty-five feet, must have appeared appropriate. Located on the town waterfront just west of Block 1, Lartigue's 1-1/2 storey half-timber house and property was considered to be "the finest in the town."⁴⁵ The dwelling however was certainly crowded. Yet even though they had nine children and in all likelihood still employed a domestic, Lartigue and his wife promised, when their daughter Magdelaine married Léon Fautoux in early January 1738, "to lodge the married couple for five years free in their house in this town."⁴⁶ From our perspective, this offer seems remarkable. With thirteen people in one household, many of them adults, this house must have been a hive of activity. And yet this home, headquarters for the sessions of the bailiff's court, was considered comfortable. Colonial Louisbourg's standards of comfort were clearly inferior to our own. Crowded or not, the scrupulous Léon Fautoux, a prosperous Louisbourg merchant, took full advantage of his future parent's magnanimous offer. Within three years, he and Magdelaine had added another three children to the Lartigue household.⁴⁷

In July 1738, six months after Magdelaine had married Léon Fautoux, another of Lartigue's daughters, Marguerite, married Michel Rodrigue, who eventually became a prosperous Louisbourg trader and merchant. Michel and his new bride rented a house in the northeast corner of Block 17 of the town, not far from Judge Lartigue's house. Although a substantial house, measuring approximately twenty-six by fifty-four feet, space was at a premium in the 1-1/2 storey dwelling because Michel shared the house with his younger brother Pierre and probably with his brother Antoine as well. But both Pierre and Antoine were navigators and would have been at sea for considerable periods of time. In 1745, Michel Rodrigue was still renting the same house but his family had grown to include five young children, ranging in age from one to six years. After his mother had left for France in 1742, Michel, in his role as legal guardian, had probably invited his 12-year old brother, and his 14-year old sister to live with him. His two brothers were still residing with him. Moreover, he owned a black slave and employed a Micmac servant named Marguerite. There were a total of thirteen people living in the house.[48]

The Rodrigues, however, were by no means an untypical Louisbourg household, for many of the town's families were large and were extended by in-laws, domestics, or slaves. During its brief history there were upwards of 100 people enslaved in the town, and in 1737 alone Louisbourg households employed 229 domestics, 15 per cent of the total permanent population.[49] Certainly there was much less privacy than today, and the social consequences of such cramped living conditions upon the family and the community as a whole need to be examined further.

What was the relationship among family members and in-laws in an extended household? Because of limited accommodation and resources, some extended families shared such personal possessions as eating utensils, table napkins, furniture, and possibly even bedclothes. Witness the case of the merchant Blaise Bagoanere who married Catherine Daccarrette, daughter of prosperous Louisbourg merchant Michel Daccarrette, in 1733. Catherine died in 1742, two days after giving birth to their ninth child. Upon returning to Louisbourg in 1749, Blaise and his seven surviving children shared their half-timber house on Rue du Port with his brother Cyprien, also a merchant, and his wife Anne and their four young children. The Lagoanere families shared their household possessions: when Blaise died in September 1753, his estate could not be inventoried because Cyprien's family possessions were mixed with those of his brother. When he visited the house on the day of Blaise's death, François-Laurent de Domingué Mayracq, the king's councillor, noted:

> the said Mr. Siprien Lagoenere did tell us that since he shared the household with the said deceased part of his moveables, linen and other household items were mixed with those of the said deceased and that he could not produce them for us at present but that he would seek on their separation to produce them for us when required.[50]

Figure 5. An English bottle fragment, excavated from a latrine to the southwest of the DeGannes house, ground down so that the bottle could be kept as a container. The bottle fragment is similar to the English bottle on the left, which has a shape common prior to 1738. (Photo: Danny Crawford. Parks Canada, Fortress Louisbourg National Historic Park. Catalogue No. 17L.31B7.2).

In a number of marriage contracts the parents of the bride promised not only to share their house with the newlyweds but to feed them at their table. When fifteen-year-old Mathurine Santier, daughter of Louisbourg master butcher Maurice Santier, married Michel Valet, a 26-year-old beach master, in 1732, Santier and his wife "have promised and are obliged to lodge in their house and to nourish with their same bread, pot, and fire, the future husband

and wife with the children who will be issuing from their marriage during 4 entire and consecutive years, without taking any payment nor drawing on the dowry of their daughter, the said 4 years to begin the day of their wedding."[51] In 1752 Pierre Gauthier, second pilot on the king's frigate *Fidelle*, married Marie-Jeanne Lecluzeau, daughter of master surgeon, Guy Lecluzeau. As part of their daughter's dowry, the Lecluzeaus provided a bureau, a feather mattress, a bolster, a blanket, three pairs of sheets, two dozen serviettes, two tablecloths "and have further promised to furnish to the future newlyweds food at their table for 2 years ...."[52]

Pierre Gautier's presence at the Lecluzeau residence doubtless posed few difficulties for the Lecluzeau family since Gautier would have been at sea for much of the year. The same could be said for 23-year-old Louis Pellissier, a native of Languedoc and a lieutenant in the Artois regiment, who married 16-year-old Louise-Marguerite Vallée. Louise, daughter of Louis-Felix Vallée, an artillery officer, and Marie-Josephe Le Large, gave birth to a son fathered by Pellissier on 21 November 1757. Twenty-one days later Pellissier and Louise were married at her parent's home. The previous day Vallée and his wife had agreed, as part of their daughter's dowry, "to lodge and nourish at their home for ten years the future married couple as well as their children born or to be born, as well as to maintain all clothing and table cloths, firewood, laundry, medicines, and all types of treatment during the ten years."[53] At the time of this agreement Marie Vallée was four months pregnant and there were two boys and a girl living at home.

Why had the Vallées agreed to compromise their personal and family privacy over such an extended period, especially since they had granted their daughter a dowry of 10,000 *livres* during the first three years of her marriage? Moreover, Pellissier was heir to properties in France which he promised to bring into the marriage. Clearly, the overriding concern for Louis and Marie Vallée was the welfare and happiness of their 16-year-old daughter and her infant son. For the Vallées, inviting their daughter, husband, and child into their home was not so much a sacrifice of familial privacy as a workable compromise in living arrangements practiced in most Louisbourg homes.

Other extended families did not share personal and household possessions because the two families living in the same house may have separated their daily activities completely. Louis Emery, a king's pilot from Rochefort, married Marianne Chevalier in 1717. Marianne's father, Jean Chevalier, promised to provide the couple with a furnished bed, clothing, and linen plus "the half of a house."[54] In 1735 Marie-Angélique Henry, daughter of fishing proprietor Pierre Henry, married Pierre Delastre, a native of Martinique. For his daughter's dowry Pierre Henry agreed to give half of his house, fish sheds, beach, and staging on the condition that they maintained the stock, beach frontage, and equipment in good repair.[55]

In 1751 Jean Noel, a master cooper, married Marie-Anne Poirier, daughter of fishing proprietor Julien Poirier and Magdelaine Radou. As part of the dowry Elenne Turin, Marie's aunt, agreed

> to lodge the said future groom & bride in half of the house alloted to her by the division made with the said Mathieu Turin, her son, & to allow the bridal couple to enjoy the said 1/2 of the house for a period of six consecutive years beginning today unless the death of one partner or the other impedes the enjoyment of the said surviving member for the duration of the said 6 years ....[56]

Dual or multiple occupancy of a house in Louisbourg did not usually result in its division in two sections. Nevertheless, there is evidence of internal divisions of homes in which one or more families lived together. Many young married Louisbourg couples were given a separate room which was completely furnished. Thus, the newlyweds had the option of being self-sufficient within their room. In 1739 Anne Richard, the daughter of merchant Jean Richard and Anne Samson, married Jean-Baptiste Lascoret, a clerk to François Du Pont Duvivier. As part of their daughter's dowry, the Richards

> promised to feed & lodge with them free of charge the said future husband & wife for a period of three years & more over also promised to give to the said Anne Richard in advance settlement of the said future inheritance a fully furnished room consisting of a bed complete with bedding, Six chairs, an arm chair, six pairs of sheets, 4 dozen napkins, an armoire, 4 table cloths, a table, two silver table settings, a mirror, two dozen pewter plates, two pewter serving platters, a large pewter platter, a pair of andirons, a shovel, a pair of tongs, a pair of copper candlestick holders with their snuffers which are also made of copper. The said furnishings will then belong tothe community of the said future

bride & groom.[57]

To fulfil their contractual obligations, the Richards could have provided the Lascorets with food to eat in their own room since they had a fireplace, a table, serviettes, and dishes. Furniture and household possessions could easily be shared among one or more families because various provisions in the Custom of Paris, the French civil law, and particularly marriage contracts required heads of households to keep detailed lists of their personal possessions.

To people of the twentieth century with more living space per capita than at any previous time, Louisbourg's domestic living conditions were doubtless crowded. Yet household life was far from unbearable in colonial Louisbourg, because the people displayed a spirit of improvisation and flexibility. One solution to a crowded house is to expand it by constructing extra rooms, a costly undertaking. But an alternative was widely employed in Louisbourg: the erection of lightweight, inexpensive, and non-bearing partitions. Constructed of one-and two-inch boards which were aligned vertically and grooved together, the partitions were either nailed to the floor and ceiling or fastened with wooden mouldings, known as tringles. Since they were not framed into the surrounding walls and did not support overhead flooring joists, the partitions could easily be disassembled and placed where desired.[58] It was this flexibility that enabled Judge Lartigue to invite his newly married daughter and son-in-law into his home for five years. By using partitions, he could easily construct eight small bedrooms upstairs alone.

Louisbourg inventories and court records abound with references to partitions. They were even included in construction estimates for a number of the king's buildings.[59] Partitions were frequently cited in rental agreements. In April 1731, for instance, Antoine Paris rented a house situated at the corner of Rue d'Orléans to Jeanne Preville and stipulated in the lease that Madame Preville could construct partitioned rooms, but only at her own expense. Furthermore, the renovations would not cause her rent to be reduced and she could not remove the partitions when she vacated the house.[60]

These simple moveable walls had profound implications for personal interrelationships in Louisbourg households. Well-to-do Louisbourg parents could easily partition off more rooms and hence maintain an acceptable standard of privacy. But what is an acceptable standard of privacy? Clearly, privacy cannot be measured solely in terms of square feet per capita because privacy is both subjective and intangible. How much privacy any one family requires, be it extended or otherwise, depends on the individuals that comprise that family. Admittedly, the parents, children and in-laws of such Louisbourg families did not sleep together in one room; yet thin board partitions could only provide a minimal level of privacy, since it was easy to hear and see through them. Well aware of these deficiencies, some citizens attempted corrective measures. In 1756 the merchants Jean-Baptiste Silvain and Philippe Leneuf de Beaubassin had an English half-timber house constructed in Block 5 of the town. Silvain and Beaubassin instructed the building contractor that *"touttes les cloisons seront faitte de planche du pais, les plus epaisses qui Pourront se trouver."*[61] Heavy serge curtain hangings for beds also provided some privacy but not all parents could afford expensive serge curtains. By the early 1750s a used calico or red damask bed hanging sold for approximately 30 *livres*, almost the equivalent of a servant's wages for a year.[62] Thus, with bed hangings and partition walls providing little privacy, many Louisbourg children from an early age must have witnessed or heard their parents and others engaged in sexual intercourse.

How did Louisbourg households cope with such seemingly discomforting living conditions? Families in Louisbourg accommodated themselves admirably well, largely because the eighteenth-century family had many more functions to perform than its present-day counterpart. There were few institutions outside the family and hence, to a much greater extent than today, the family was the material, social, and psychological mainstay of society. Besides providing such basic necessities as food, shelter, and sexual release, the family functioned as a welfare institution, a school, a church, and a business. Is it any wonder, given the range of duties incumbent upon the family, that people adjusted themselves to apparently awkward living conditions?

Family life then was much less segmented than our own since individuals were more constantly together. Clearly, flexibility was an accepted facet of Louisbourg home life, and, in relation to domestic furnishings, it was further enhanced by a need for orderliness. With a limited number of square feet per capita, everything had to have its place. Thus, in the kitchen of widow Marie-Charlotte Berichon was a large table "under which is a bed for a boy to sleep."[63] At night Marie-Charlotte's youngest son or her servant presumably pulled the bed out from under the table to sleep and tend the fire.

The small bed under the table is representative of a number of specific pieces of furniture which were easily stored but readily accessible when needed. Feather mattresses were even more convenient than small bedsteads for they could be moved near a fireplace during the winter months. The furnishings of the Julien Auger *dit* Grandchamp inn in Block 2 of the town demonstrate the portability of lightweight feather mattresses. A native of Poitou and a former carpenter, Grandchamp died on 1 April 1741 at the age of seventy. Eighteen days after his death the inventory of the part of the inn reserved for guests revealed that eight feather mattresses and bolsters, together with seven wool blankets and a calico quilt, were stored downstairs in the main dining-room, measuring approximately nineteen by twenty-four feet. Besides a fireplace, the room contained a large and a small dining-room and eighteen straw chairs. The mattresses, bolsters, and blankets, valued at 375 *livres*, were the most valuable furnishings in the inn.[64] During the day, the mattresses were probably stacked against a wall, while at night they would have been spread on the dining room floor and the floor of the adjoining kitchen. In the attic, which was undoubtedly closed for the winter, there were seven "old bedsteads" which were valued at only 2 *livres* each. Various eighteenth-century European travel accounts reveal that it was common practice to spread straw as well as mattresses on the floors of inns, particularly those catering to a lower class clientele, to accommodate overnight guests.[65] The guests in the Grandchamp inn, a poorly furnished waterfront establishment, apparently were more than willing to bed down in the warmth of the dining-room.

Carrying one's mattress or *paillasse* and sleeping in a room near a fire was one means of keeping warm during the cold months but what about those rooms that did not have fireplaces? In Louisbourg brick and to a lesser extent iron stoves were popular in most households. Constructed each fall, the brick stove would be dismantled in the spring, and damaged bricks discarded and the iron door, top plate, and stove-pipe stored as a space-saving measure.[66] Moreover, the bricks, which usually survived for only one season, were the least expensive part of the stove. In 1738 surgeon Dominique Collongue had a stove installed in a patient's house. Of the 63 *livres* 10 *sols* expended on the stove, 23 *livres* were paid for the stove-pipe and door, 30 *livres* for the iron top plate, 4 *livres* 10 *sols* for 200 bricks, and 6 *livres* for assembling the stove.[67]

Iron stoves, while considerably more expensive, could also be assembled and dismantled quickly. The scientist and astronomer, the Marquis de Chabert, during his stay at Louisbourg in the winter of 1750, had stoves installed in his apartment in the governor's wing of the King's Bastion barracks.[68] Brick and iron stoves provided a degree of comfort unheard of in most of Europe. Throughout the eighteenth century, fireplaces were much more common in France than stoves, which were more prevalent in colder northern and eastern countries.[69] One priest serving in Canada was convinced that, in spite of the colder climate, interior living conditions were more comfortable in New France than the mother country because of the use of stoves. Writing from Sault-Saint-Louis, opposite the present-day town of Lachine on the St. Lawrence River, Luc-François Nau noted on 2 October 1735: "More precautions against the cold are taken here than in France. We are warmly clad, and our apartments are heated with stoves. All in all, I suffered every year more from cold in France than in Canada."[70]

Brick and iron stoves -- in Louisbourg practically every home had one -- were an obvious example of how individuals and families in the eighteenth-century town adapted their interior living conditions to suit the climate. Other pieces of furniture, while hardly distinctive to Louisbourg, were equally serviceable, especially in crowded homes. A common and extremely practical piece of furniture was the folding table. Antoine Paris had no fewer than five in his dining-room while Pierre Boisseau, a Louisbourg innkeeper, had "four tables with their folding feet or legs" in a cabinet next to the kitchen. The tables, valued at only 15 *livres*, were inexpensive and functional, for at mealtime they could easily be assembled either in the cabinet or the kitchen.[71]

Straw and cane chairs that could be stacked on top of each other were equally portable; there was no shortage of them in Louisbourg. Michel de Gannes, a captain in the Louisbourg garrison, had twenty-four chairs in his relatively small house.[72] A widower with possibly five children living at home by the time of his death in 1752, de Gannes doubtless brought out the chairs when guests arrived. When not used for entertaining, the seven straw and four cane chairs could easily be stored. Pierre Benoist, an ensign in the garrison, had no fewer than fourteen straw chairs tucked away in one bedroom, while Louis Delort, a member of Louisbourg's Superior Council, had eighteen straw chairs in his ante-chamber.[73] Equally popular was the *coffre* or flat-topped chest. At a time when few houses had closets, the chest served not only as a bureau for clothes but also as a seat or table, to say nothing of being a decorative piece of furniture.

Figure 6. A Chinese export porcelain bowl base, excavated from the Santier yard, shaped for re-use. (Photo: Danny Crawford. Parks Canada, Fortress Louisbourg National Historic Park. Catalogue No. 4L.56A3.5)

Many furnishings in Louisbourg homes served multiple purposes. Tapestries of various sizes were hung on walls, used as carpets or coverings for tables and, in colder weather, used as heavy blankets. Of course almost any fabric could serve as a blanket. On 9 September 1739 Étienne Clinchant, a seaman on the vessel *Providence*, died at the storehouse of Monsieur Lachoux where he was residing. The inventory of Clinchant's possessions included "an old cape, lined with linen, serving as a blanket."[74] Mattresses could also function as blankets. In February 1735, the widow Dastrait, proprietor of a tavern near Louisbourg's Dauphin Gate, had "a type of small mattress serving as a blanket" on one of her beds. The widow also demonstrated her resourcefulness when it came to starting a fire. Obviously, kindling was necessary but how did the French light their kindling? Paper was far too valuable and one alternative to wood chips was old dried leaves. In the main room of her inn the widow Dastrait had "twenty pounds of old leaves."[75]

In terms of the multiple use of furnishings in Louisbourg, necessity became the mother of invention. If families or individuals could not obtain or afford a particular furnishing or houseware they had little choice but to devise a workable alternative. For instance, in 1718 Pierre-Auguste de Soubras, Louisbourg's *commissaire-ordonnateur*, noted that 151 *aunes* (approximately 176 yards) of linen had been sent to Louisbourg to be used as burial shrouds. The linen was supposed to have been delivered to the Brothers of Charity at the hospital but it was eventually employed "for different uses such as lining the officers' rooms."[76]

Lining one's room with government-purchased linen was luxury hardly available to the poor of Louisbourg who had to rely on their own meagre resources. One such family was the Birons who lived on the north shore of Louisbourg harbour. A native of Poitou, Gabriel Biron *dit* Lagelée was a former soldier in the Louisbourg garrison who, after his discharge, was employed in the town as a labourer and gardener throughout the 1720s and 1730s. Biron and his wife lived in a one-room *piquet* house with a bark roof. The house, measuring thirteen by twenty-five feet, was a modest dwelling since in 1733 the house, courtyard, garden, and lot were valued at only 1,200 *livres*. The furnishings in the house, described as being "mostly worn out," were valued at only 500 *livres*. With few amenities, the Birons were accustomed to making do with what they had. Their tableware utensils, for instance, consisted of the following pewter: three platters, five plates, one porringer, and two small measures; they also had seven earthenware dishes, three faience goblets, one salt-cellar and a tin pepper-shaker. The stone fireplace in the cottage was as ill equipped as the dining-table. The fireplace equipment included "one frying pan, one grill, one spit, two trivets, four or five iron hooks serving as a pot hanger, the lot more than half worn out ...."[77] The Birons did not have an armoire but this posed little difficulty because they constructed a "cupboard serving as an armoire beside the fireplace."

Eighteenth-century Louisbourg, and the pre-industrial age in general, represented the antithesis of present-day planned obsolescence. Because practically all consumer goods were imported from France and New England, furniture and household ware were expensive and not to be discarded when worn or broken. Numerous Louisbourg inventories of estates contain furniture and housewares described as being "out of service" but obviously the items retained some value for they were kept and sold at the auctions of the estates.

One witness to the capitulation of Louisbourg in 1745 described how the French took even the most worthless furniture with them upon their expulsion from Ile Royale:

> all the furniture that was even of the most inconsiderable value was taken out of the Houses by the French such as a large Quantity of Empty old Chests, Trunks, Cupboards, Tables & Chairs which were fit for Nothing but Fuel, & they Stripped the Walls of Coarse Hangings & the Doors of their Locks & Hinges which were all Carryed away by them except such part as they met with a Price for agreeable to their Demand ....[78]

Even in homes of the well-do-do, old and broken furniture was not necessarily discarded. Jean Seigneur, a prosperous innkeeper residing in Block 2, had "an old armoire serving as a buffet."[79] Rather than dispose of the old armoire, valued at only 3 *livres*, Seigneur simply put shelves in it and presumably stored linen and other household wares in what had become a converted buffet. Similarly, Jean-Pierre Daccarrette, a well-to-do Louisbourg merchant, had a "large pine armoire which serves as a buffet" in his household.[80]

Archaeological excavations at Fortress Louisbourg confirm the reuse of various household wares. Numerous broken earthenware bowls from French contexts have been painstakingly repaired. One green, glazed, coarse earthenware bowl from the Saintonge region of France, with a radius of fourteen and one-half centimeters, had been repaired with four pairs of drilled holes on either side of a fracture which would have been wired together. In similar fashion, an excavated faience platter with a broken scalloped rim section had six lead staples embedded on either side of a crack.[81] The lead staples, joined on the back of the platter, were sanded smooth on the surface to preserve the appearance of the dish.

Other artifacts which have been adapted for reuse include

two English bottle fragments broken at the base of their necks. The jagged edges of the bottle were ground down so the bottles could be kept as containers. Even dishes that were broken beyond repair were not necessarily discarded, for parts of the dish could be remade for gaming pieces. Included in the Louisbourg artifact collection are three gaming pieces which were probably carved from the base of a faience plate, as well as one which was chipped from the base of a Chinese export porcelain plate decorated in the Imari style.[82] Some artifacts appear to have been reshaped for decorative purposes. One English soft-paste porcelain bowl base has been cut so as to maintain the centre design of a boy fishing, and a Chinese export porcelain bowl base had been chipped in the same style.[83]

Repaired earthenware bowls and faience plates, together with armoires converted to buffets, flat-topped chests, folding tables, stacking chairs, and moveable walls, to name but a few, were merely outward symbols of a people's willingness to improvise, especially in terms of their domestic relations. In view of this flexibility, it is perhaps more understandable how the citizens of Louisbourg, and indeed those of the eighteenth century in general, could cope with such seemingly squalid living conditions, ranging from the enclosed and fetid atmosphere of smoke-filled rooms to dirty floors and a generally inadequate standard of personal cleanliness.

Notes

1. Some of the important American local studies include: Kenneth A. Lockridge, *A New England Town: The First Hundred Years: Dedham, Massachusetts, 1636-1736* (New York: W.W. Norton & Company, 1970); Philip J. Greven, Jr., *Four Generations: Population, Land and Family in Colonial Andover, Massachusetts* (Ithaca: Cornell University Press, 1970); J.M. Bumstead, "Religion, Finance and Democracy in Massachusetts: The Town of Norton as a Case Study," *Journal of American History*, Vol. 57 (1970-71), pp. 817-31; J.M. Bumstead and J.T. Lemon, "New Approaches in Early American Studies: The Local Community in New England," *Social History*, (November 1968), Vol. 2, pp. 98-112; Richard L. Bushman, *From Puritan to Yankee: Character and the Social Order in Connecticut, 1690-1765* (New York: W.W. Norton & Company, 1970); and Michael Zukerman, *Peaceable Kingdom: New England Towns in the Eighteenth Century* (New York: Alfred A. Knopf, 1970). For a comprehensive overview of American local studies, see David J. Russo, *Families and Communities: A New View of American History* (Nashville: American Association for State and Local History, 1974).
2. Some of the most important works by French scholars who have developed such techniques include: Étienne Gautier and Louis Henry, *La population de Crulai paroisse, Normandie: Étude historique* (Paris: Presses Universitaires de France, 1958); Pierre

Goubert, *Beauvais et le Beauvaisis de 1600 à 1730* (Paris, 1960); and "Historical Demography and the Reinterpretation of Early Modern French History: A Research Review," in *The Family in History*, ed. T.K. Rable and R.I. Rotberg (New York: Harper & Row, 1971); Fernand Braudel and Ernest Labrousse, eds., *Histoire économique et sociale de la France* (Paris: Presses Universitaires de France, 1970); and Pierre Valmarry, *Familles paysannes au XVIIIe siècle en Bas-Quercy: Étude démographique* (Paris: Presses universitaires de France, 1965). See also Louis Henry, "Passé, présent et avenir en démographie," *Population*, Vol. 3 (mai-juin 1972), pp. 383-96. More recent works on the family in France include James F. Traer, *Marriage and the family in eighteenth-century France* (Ithaca: Cornell University Press, 1980), and Robert Wheaton and Tamara K. Hareven, eds., *Family and sexuality in French history* (Philadelphia: University of Pennsylvania Press, 1980).

In terms of historical demography and local analysis, the English have followed quickly on the heels of various French scholars. Among the most significant English works of recent years are: D.V. Glass and D.E.C. Eversley, eds., *Population in History: Essays in Historical Demography* (London: Edward Arnold, 1965); Peter Laslett et al., *An Introduction to English Historical Demography*, ed. E.A. Wrigley (London: Weindesfeld and Nicolson, 1966); and Peter Laslett, *The World We Have Lost*, 2nd ed. (London: Methuen & Co., 1971).

3. See J.M. Bumsted's thought-provoking article, "Puritan and Yankee Rediviva: Recent Writings on Early New England of Interest to Atlantic Scholars," *Acadiensis*, Vol. 2, No. 1 (Autumn 1972), pp. 3-21; and Stephen Patterson, "In Search of the Massachusetts-Nova Scotia Dynamic," *Acadiensis*, Vol. 5, No. 2 (Spring 1976), pp. 138-43. More than their English-speaking counterparts, French Canadian historians have led the way in terms of demographic studies. See Jacques Henripin's pioneering work, *La population canadienne au début du XVIIIe siècle* (Paris: Presses Universitaires de France, 1954); Louise Dechêne, *Habitants et marchands de Montréal au XVIIe siècle* (Paris and Montreal: Plon, 1974); and Hubert Charbonneau, *Vie et mort de nos ancêtres: étude démographique* (Montreal: Presses de l'Université de Montréal, 1975).

4. See especially Lockridge, *New England Towns*, viii, pp. 187-88; and Philip J. Greven Jr., *Child Rearing Concepts, 1628-1861* (Ithaca, Ill., 1973), p. 2.

5. *Canada: An Historical Magazine*, Vol. 1, No. 4 (June 1974), pp. 76-77.

6. T.A. Crowley, "Government and Interests: French Colonial Administration at Louisbourg, 1713-1758" (Ph.D. thesis, Duke University, 1975), p. 348.

7. Zukerman, *Peaceable Kingdom*, p. 47.

8. T.A. Crowley, "France, Canada and the Beginning of Louisbourg: In Search of the Great Fortress Myth" (Papers and Abstracts for a Symposium on Isle Royale during the French Regime, compiled for the Canadian Historical Association Annual Meeting, June 1972), p. 54.

9. J.S. McLennan, *Louisbourg from its foundation to its fall, 1713-1758* (Sydney, N.S.: Fortress Press, 1969), pp. 11-12.

10. H.A. Innis, *The Cod Fisheries: The History of an International Economy* (Toronto: University of Toronto Press, 1954), p. 123.

11. See J.D. Rogers, *Historical Geography of Newfoundland*, Vol. 5, pt. 4, of the *Historical Geography of the British Colonies*, ed. Sir Charles Lucas (Oxford, 1911), pp. 88-89.

12. AN, Col., E, 93, pièce 81, *Recensement des Habitants de Plaisance et des Isles St. Pierre rendus à Louisbourg avec leurs Femmes et Enfants*, 5 novembre 1714. There were a total of 32 people listed in the census. Twenty civilians were engaged in the fishery and they had transported 80 *chaloupes* to Louisbourg. There were also six

COMMUNITIES AND FAMILIES

officers who participated in the fishery and they had brought 25 *chaloupes* from Placentia to Louisbourg. See also AN, Outre-Mer, G¹, Vol. 466, pièce 52, *Recensement des Habitants avec leurs Familles qui rentent a Louisbourg et des Dependances cette Année 1716 avec le Nombre de Pêcheurs et Garçons qu'ils hivernent,* 1716. Three years after the initial settlement of Louisbourg there were 56 inhabitants in the harbour. Of these 56, 21 were listed as former residents of Placentia and they comprised the largest single group of the civilian population of Louisbourg. The 21 heads of families from Placentia employed 198 fishermen.

Louisbourg Settlers	Men	Women	Children	Hired Fishermen
Civilians from Placentia	21	19	74	198
Civilians not from Placentia	35	25	45	168
Total civilian population	56	44	119	366

13. AN, Col., B, Vol. 36, ff. 436-37, Pontchartrain à Costebelle, 22 mars 1714.
14. *Ibid.*, Vol. 35-1, f. 33, Pontchartrain à Gaulin, 29 mars 1713.
15. *Ibid.*, Vol. 36, f. 435, Pontchartrain à Costebelle, 22 mars 1714.
16. *Ibid.*, Vol. 36, f. 7, Pontchartrain à Boyles et Jurats de St. Jean de Luz & Siboure, 1 février 1714.
17. Ch. de La Morandière, *Histoire de la pêche française de la morue dans l'Amérique,* (Paris: G.P. Maisonneuve et Larosse, 1962), Vol. 2, p. 650.
18. AN, Col., B, Vol. 36-2, f. 422, Pontchartrain à L'Hermitte, 26 janvier 1714.
19. R. Cole Harris and John Warkentin, *Canada before Confederation: A Study in Historical Geography* (New York: Oxford University Press, 1974), p. 176.
20. AN, Col., B, Vol. 36, ff. 439-40, Pontchartrain à Gaulin, 22 mars 1714.
21. *Ibid.*, f. 439, Pontchartrain à Costebelle, 22 mars 1714.
22. J.B. Brebner, *New England's Outpost: Acadia Before the Conquest of Canada* (Hamden, Conn.: Archer Books, 1965), p. 67. See also W.S. MacNutt, *The Atlantic Provinces: The Emergence of Colonial Society 1712-1857* (Toronto: McClelland and Stewart, 1968), p. 13.
23. J.B. Cameron, "The French Village in the Eighteenth Century," *Forums in History,* ed. P.N. Stearns (St. Charles, Miss.: Forum Press, 1975), p. 4. "Early societies," noted the renowned French historian Marc Bloch, "were made up of groups rather than individuals. A man on his own counted for very little." See his *French Rural History, An Essay on its Basic Characteristics* (Berkeley and Los Angeles: University of California Press, 1970), p. 150.
24. AN, Col., B, Vol. 36, f. 93, Pontchartrain à Vauvré, 2 mars 1714.
25. *Ibid.*, ff. 103-04, Pontchartrain à Beauharnois, 7 mars 1714.
26. *Ibid.*, C¹¹B, Vol. 1, f. 108, Marly à Le Ch^{er} de Saujon, 19 novembre 1714.
27. *Ibid.*, B, Vol. 36, f. 435, Pontchartrain à Costebelle, 22 mars 1714.
28. McLennan, *Louisbourg,* p. 48. Not all sons of Louisbourg residents, however, could hope to obtain brides within the colony and thus they had to be prepared to emigrate if they wished to marry. See Barbara Schmeisser, "The Population of Louisbourg, 1713-1758" *Manuscript Report Series,* Vol. 303, (Ottawa: Parks Canada, 1976), p. 120.
29. Crowley, "Government and Interests," p. 327.
30. Allan Greer, "The Soldiers of Isle Royale, 1720-1745" (manuscript on file, Fortress of Louisbourg, 1976), p. 63.
31. See AN, Col., F³, Vol. 50, f. 150, "*Ordonnance du Roi,*" 30 juin 1723. The ordinance stipulated that men who had no wives or family in Ile Royale and were not born there were not permitted to buy beaches and land for fish stages or rent out those

they already owned. For further examples of this attitude towards outsiders, see MacNutt, *Atlantic Provinces*, p. 26; McLennan, *Louisbourg*, p. 49; and Robert J. Morgan and Terrence D. MacLean, "Social Structure and Life in Louisbourg," *Canada: An Historical Magazine*, Vol. 1, No. 4 (June 1974), p. 74.

32. AN, Col. C^{11}B, Vol. 9, f. 40, St. Ovide et Le Normant au Ministre, 15 décembre 1727.

33. AN, Outre-Mer, G^3, 2044, pièce 19, L'Inventaire et Description Generale de tous les Biens et Immeubles de Pierre Boisseau et la dite Veuve, sa Femme, 24 octobre 1755.

34. Charles S. Lindsay, "Louisbourg Guardhouses," *Canadian Historic Sites: Occasional Papers in Archaeology and History* (Ottawa: Parks Canada, 1975), p. 58.

35. Ann Arbor, Mich., William L. Clements Library, George Clinton Papers, 5, Charles Knowles to George Clinton, Louisbourg, 5 April 1747.

36. *Memoirs of the Chevalier de Johnstone*, trans. Charles Winchester (Aberdeen: D. Wyllie & Son, 1870), Vol. 1, p. 178.

37. AN, Col., C^{11}B, Vol. 29, f. 295, Etat des Ouvrages, 15 novembre 1750.

38. *The Diary of Nathaniel Knap of Newbury* (Boston: Society of Colonial Wars, 1895), p. 26.

39. For further information on children at Louisbourg, see Kenneth Donovan "Rearing Children in Louisbourg -- A Colonial Seaport and Garrison Town, 1713-1758" (Paper delivered at the Atlantic Society for 18th Century Studies, Mount Saint Vincent University, April 1979), pp. 26-28; and "Social Status and Contrasting Lifestyles: Children of the Poor and Well-to-do in 18th Century Louisbourg" (Paper delivered at the Atlantic Society for 18th Century Studies, College of Cape Breton, 1 May 1980).

40. AN, Outre-Mer, G^1, Vol. 466, pièce 51, *Recensements des Habitants établis dans le Havre de Louisbourg*, 14 janvier 1715.

41. The majority of Louisbourg marriage contracts were prepared within a week prior to the marriage. Prosperous Louisbourg parents may have been willing to invite their daughters and sons-in-law into their residences because, as in eighteenth-century France, they were accustomed to little privacy in their own homes. See Jean-Louis Flandrin, *Families in Former Times: Kinship, Household and Sexuality*, trans. Richard Southern (London: Cambridge University Press, 1976), p. 92. For the lack of privacy in New England, see David H. Flaherty, *Privacy in Colonial New England* (Charlottesville: University Press of Virginia, 1967), pp. 53, 55.

42. AN, Outre-Mer, G^3, 2046-2, no. 12, Contrat de Mariage entre Joseph Mathieu Guillet et Jeanne Angelique Guyon Préville, 14 juillet 1741.

43. *Ibid.*, 2039-1, no. 14, Contrat de Mariage entre François Nicolas Chassin de Thierry et Josephe Rousseau, 23 décembre 1734.

44. AN, Col., C^{11}B, Vol. 19, f. 267, Lartigue à Maurepas, 2 novembre 1737.

45. *Dictionary of Canadian Biography* (Toronto: University of Toronto Press, 1974), Vol. 3, p. 357.

46. AN, Outre-Mer, G^3, 2046-1, pièce 97, Contrat de Mariage entre Léon Fautoux et Magdelaine Lartigue, 13 janvier 1738.

47. The Fautoux children were born in October 1738, March 1740, and May 1741; see the Léon Fautoux family reconstitution file in the Louisbourg archives.

48. H. Paul Thibault, "L'îlot 17 de Louisbourg, 1713-1768," *Travail Inédit*, Tome 99 (Ottawa: Direction des Parcs nationaux et des Lieux historiques, 1972), pp. 80-81, 163-65.

49. AN, Outre-Mer, G^1, Vol. 466, pièce 73, Denombrement fait en 1737 des Personnes

COMMUNITIES AND FAMILIES

établies dans les Ports de L'Isle Royalle, 1737.
50. *Ibid.*, G², Vol. 202, dossier 294, pièce 2, Proces-Verbal d'Apposition des Scellés sur les Biens de feu Blaise Lageonere, 12 septembre 1753.
51. *Ibid.*, G³, 2038-1, pièce 88, Contrat de Mariage entre Michel Valet et Mathurine Santier, 24 décembre 1732.
52. *Ibid.*, 2047-2, pièce 10, Contrat de Mariage entre Pierre Gautier et Marie Jeanne Boudouin Lecluzeau, 15 janvier 1752.
53. *Ibid.*, 2045, pièce 108, Contrat de Mariage entre Louis Joseph Donna-Dieu Pellissier Dugrés et Louise Marguerite Vallée, 28 octobre 1757.
54. *Ibid.*, 2056, pièces 19 et 20, Contrat de Mariage entre Louis Emery et Marianne Chevalier, 24 juin 1717.
55. *Ibid.*, 2028-1, pièce 91, Contrat de Mariage entre Pierre Delastre et Marie Angelique Henry, 5 juin 1732.
56. *Ibid.*, 2041-1, pièce 87, Contrat de Mariage entre Jean Noel et Marie Anne Poirier, 19 décembre 1751.
57. *Ibid.*, 2046-1, pièce 170, Contrat de Mariage entre Jean Baptiste Lascoret et Anne Richard, 6 juillet 1739.
58. Eric Krause, "Domestic Building Construction Techniques of Ile Royale, 1713-1758" (manuscript on file, Fortress of Louisbourg, n.d.), section on partitions; see also "Preliminary Architectural Studies," 3 Vols. (manuscript on file, Fortress of Louisbourg, 1971-1972), Vol. 3, Linda Hoad, "Partitions, Lambris and Panelling" (1972), pp. 1-16.
59. AN, Col., C¹¹B, Vol. 16, ff. 206-17, Toisé des Ouvrages ... fait pour la Construction du Logement de l'Ingenieur En Chef, 30 septembre 1734.
60. AN, Outre-Mer, G³, 2038-1, no. 6, 10 avril 1731.
61. *Ibid.*, 2044, pièce 53, Marché entre Monsieur Beaubassin et Dubenca, Louisbourg, 30 mai 1756.
62. *Ibid.*, G², Vol. 202, dossier 283, Proces-Verbal de Vente d'un Coffre et Hardes fait a la Requête de Tanguy Mervin, Négoçiant, 6 septembre 1753.
63. *Ibid.*, Vol. 208, dossier 476, pièce 41, Apposition des Scellés dans la Maison du defunt Monsieur Berrichon après le Décès de son Épouse, 28 avril 1732.
64. *Ibid.*, Vol. 197-2, dossier 142, no. 5, Inventaire et Estimations des Meubles de la Succession de feu Julien Auger dit Grandchamp, 19 avril 1741.
65. See, for example, César de Saussure, *A Foreign View of England in the Reigns of George I and George II: The Letters of Monsieur César de Saussure to His Family*, trans., ed., Madame Van Muyden (London: John Murray, 1902), pp. 13-14, 25-26. For other references to overnight guests sharing the same room in French inns, see Laurence Sterne, *A Sentimental Journey Through France and Italy* (London, 1768; Penguin English Library edition, 1968), pp. 145-48; and Arthur Young, *Travels in France During the Years 1787, 1788 and 1789*, ed. Jeffry Kaplow, (1792; Gloucester, Mass.: Peter Smith, 1976), pp. 30-32.
66. For this paper I have examined 105 inventories of estates, 77 of Louisbourg householders. Thirty-three of the latter either had brick or iron stoves in their residences. See Kenneth Donovan, "Stoves in Louisbourg" (manuscript on file, Fortress of Louisbourg, September 1981). Besides inventories of estates, Louisbourg's official correspondence contains numerous references to stoves, see, for example, AN, Col., C¹¹B, Vol. 29, 15 novembre 1750. In a list of yearly official government expenditures there are references like the following: "*Le facon de dix poêles qui ont été construits dans les chambres des officiers estimés trois livres pièce*," ibid. f. 284. See ibid., f. 293, *ordonnateur's* residence, "*Reparation des poêles des appartements et bureaux,*

estimé pour fourniture et façon trente trois livres." For stoves imported into Louisbourg, see Chris Moore "Commodity Imports of Louisbourg, *"Manuscript Report Series,* Vol. 317 (Ottawa: Parks Canada, 1975), p. 83.

67. AN, Outre-Mer, G², Vol. 185, ff. 218-95, Succession de feu Joseph Dallemand, marchand, 12 novembre 1738.

68. AN, Col., C¹¹B, Vol. 29, f. 278v, Bordereaux des depenses, 15 novembre 1750. For further information on Chabert's stay at Louisbourg, see Kenneth Donovan, "Canada's First Astronomical Observatory, 1750," *Canadian Geographic,* Vol. 100, No. 6 (December 1980-January 1981): pp. 36-43.

69. Fernand Braudel, *Capitalism and Material Life, 1400-1800,* trans. Miriam Kochan (New York: Harper & Row, 1973), pp. 218-20.

70. Reuben Gold Thwaites, ed., *The Jesuit Relations and Allied Documents: Travels and Explorations of the Jesuit Missionaries in New France, 1610-1791* (New York: Pageant Book Co., 1959), Vol. 68, 1720-1736, p. 263.

71. AN, Outre-Mer, G³, 2044, pièce 19, Inventaire et Description Generale de tous les Biens et Immeubles de Pierre Boisseau et la dite Veuve, sa Femme, 24 octobre 1755. See also AN, Outre-Mer, G², Vol. 181, f. 62, Inventaire des Effets d'Antoine Paris, 20 février 1732. Pierre Benoist also had three folding tables in his house; see *ibid.,* Vol. 182, ff. 995, 1000, Inventaire après le Décès de dame Anne Levron à la Requête de Monsieur Pierre Benoist Enseigne des Compagnies de la Marine, son Mari, 19 décembre 1733.

72. AN, Outre-Mer, G², Vol. 201, dossier 254, pièce 2, Inventaire des Meubles de la Succession de Michel de Gannes de Falaise, 31 octobre 1752.

73. *Ibid.,* Vol. 202, dossier 296, Inventaire et Estimation des Biens, Meubles et Effets de la dite Communauté entre Barbe Le Neuf de la Vallière et feu Louis Delort, 22 décembre 1753; *Ibid.,* Vol. 182, f. 996, Inventaire.

74. La Rochelle, Archives départementales, Charente-Maritime, B, 6113, dossier 18, Louisbourg, Inventaire des Hardes d'Étienne Clinchant, Matelot du navire *la Providence* (Capitaine André Lachoue Dutestre de Saint-Malo) décédé dans le Magasin du Sieur Lachoue le 9 septembre 1739, 12 september 1739.

75. AN, Outre-Mer, G³, 2039-1, pièce 66, Inventaire, Estimation et Description de tous les Biens, Meubles et Immeubles de la dame Veuve Jean Dastrait, Jeanne Galbarette, 13 février 1735.

76. AN, Col., C¹¹B, Vol. 4, f. 31, 28 mars 1719, Soubras, *"Etat des Effets et Vivres qui manquent,"* 20 décembre 1718.

77. *Ibid.,* G², Vol. 182, ff. 556-69, Inventaire et Estimation des Biens de la Communauté d'entre Gabriel Biron dit Lagelee, Magdelaine Rimbeau, et ses Enfans de son premier Mariage avec Longue Epée, 16 juin 1733.

78. Massachusetts Historical Society, Louisbourg Papers, I, f. 25, Answer to the Memorial upon the Execution of the Capitulation of Louisbourg Presented by Commissary Seigneur at Bruxelles.

79. AN, Outre-Mer, G², Vol. 199, dossier 197, pièces 2, 4, 5, L'Inventaire des Effets mobiliers delaissés après le Décès de feu Jean Seigneur dit la Riviere, 3 février 1745, 12 mars 1745, 15 mars 1745.

80. *Ibid.,* Vol. 200, dossier 202, Papiers concernant la Succession de feu Sieur Jean Pierre Daccarrette, 18 février 1745.

81. I would like to thank Andrée Crépeau, Louisbourg archaeologist, and Jim Campbell, artifact collection supervisor, for their assistance in helping me to select and describe the artifacts cited in this paper. The Louisbourg artifacts catalogue number of the green, glazed, coarse earthenware bowl: 1B.4P11.14; the number of

the faience platter with the lead staples: 1B.4N19.20.

82. Louisbourg Artifact Collection, English bottle fragments: 17L.31B4.1 and 17L.31B7.2; three tin-glazed gaming pieces: 17L.21C3.18a, b, c; porcelain gaming piece: 2L.17H3.2.

83. The catalogue number of the English soft-paste porcelain bowl: 471.90H2.1; the Chinese export porcelain bowl base: 4L.56A3.5.

The People of Eighteenth-Century Louisbourg

A.J.B. Johnston

One of the truisms about history -- that is, history as the study of the past -- is that it always reflects the present. Whatever interests a given society at a fixed point in time -- be it a constitutional, religious, social or political question -- there are usually historians around who can find some precedent or background information to shed light on the particular question. Thus in recent decades, to cite just one example, we have witnessed the birth and growth of the field of women's history, as a direct response to the feminist movement.

Today, as we move into the 1990s, one of the questions facing Canadian society is the ethnic composition of the nation. With each passing year, the country moves farther and farther away from a vision of itself as simply an English-French duality. Accordingly, historians now find themselves going back to examine 200- and 300-year-old documents to determine just how diverse the country's population might have been in previous eras. Some of their findings will come as a surprise to more than a few readers.

For instance, how many Nova Scotians know that there was a Black man, possibly Mathieu da Costa, serving as a translator, travelling with the Sieur de Monts and Samuel de Champlain on their voyages along the Atlantic coast back in 1604-05? And how many ever learned that there were perhaps as many as 5,000 Blacks among the Loyalists who came to Nova Scotia after the American Revolution? Or that in 1788 there were approximately 200 "robust able black men" -- slaves from Bermuda -- working as fishermen on the Grand Banks?[1] What other ethnic "surprises" are there in our history from other parts of the region?

The time and place in Nova Scotian history that we focus on in this article is that of Louisbourg during the period 1713-58, when

THE PEOPLE

the fishing port and strategic stronghold was a major French colonial settlement in North America. The question we ask is simply the following: Who were the people of eighteenth-century Louisbourg?

The short answer -- they were French, Roman Catholic, and worked in the fishery or trade, or served in the military or laboured in someone's kitchen -- has long been sufficient. In light of the detailed questions people are now asking about ethnic origin and related matters, however, it is time for a more in-depth response. The intention of this article is to provide information on the following: (1) Louisbourg's population and gender ratio; (2) the origins of its inhabitants; (3) the religions they professed; and (4) the languages they spoke.

Throughout Louisbourg's forty-five-year history, there was always an imbalance between the sexes, with males greatly outnumbering females. This is as one would expect, for Louisbourg began as a pioneer settlement -- typically with few women -- and then developed into a garrison town and busy seaport, both of which functions called for large numbers of unmarried men: "In the 1720s, adult males outnumbered adult females eight or ten to one. The gap decreased somewhat as the years went by, but even leaving out the military population, the ratio of adult males to females was never lower than three to one."[2] One of the effects of this imbalance in the sexes was that Louisbourg brides married younger (average age at time of first marriage was 19.9 years) and men older (average age was 29.2 years) than was the case elsewhere in New France. In Canada, the eighteenth-century name for the French settlements along the St. Lawrence River, the average ages for first-time brides and grooms were 22.0 and 27.7 respectively.[3]

As for actual population totals, the following table summarizes some of the available data:

Table 1
Population of Louisbourg, Selected Years[4]

	1720	1724	1737	1752
Men (heads of household)	69	113	163	274
Fishermen	372	377	250	674
Servants (men & women)			229	
domestiques (males)				366
servantes (females)				71
Women (heads/wives)	50	84	157	299
Children	142	239	664	776
Habitants newly arrived				200

ASPECTS OF LOUISBOURG

	1720	1724	1737	1752
Households of governor and commissaire-ordonnateur				30
Civilian Total	633	813	1,463	2,690
Soldiers	317	430	543	1,250
Total Population	950	1,243	2,006	3,940

There is no single document that describes where the people of Louisbourg came from. There are many census returns, but only three of them list places of origin, and even then the birthplace is given only for those individuals who are identified as *habitants*, or heads of household. No such information is provided on the origins of the vast majority of the population: the hundreds of servants, fishermen and soldiers. Nor does the census data tell us about the birthplace of wives. Widows and single women who were heads of household are identified, but not ordinary married women.

The first Louisbourg census to include a "Place of Birth" column was that of 1724.[5] In that year, the census-takers recorded that the town had a permanent civilian population of 813 persons. Of that total, 113 were identified by name and place of origin. On the census of 1726, Louisbourg's civilian population was given as 963, of which 153 were listed as *habitants* with an identifiable place of origin.[6] Eleven years later, in 1737, the town's population had grown to 1,463, of whom 163 were listed by name.[7] What the town's population was during the 1740s is not known, but it was probably around 2,000 civilian men, women and children. That estimate is roughly halfway between the recorded population of 1,463 for the year 1737 and the total of 2,690 for the year 1752.[8] Keep in mind, however, that none of these figures includes totals for the garrison, or for fishermen and others who might have been in town only on a seasonal basis.

In spite of their limitations, these three Louisbourg census returns -- 1724, 1726 and 1734 -- are of interest, in that they provide data on the origins of the town's principal inhabitants during one ten-year period. In particular, the data underline that as Louisbourg grew steadily over that decade, it attracted fishing proprietors, merchants, artisans, cabaret owners and so on from a wide variety of regions in France, New France, and even foreign countries.

Though the graphs of Figure 1 are largely self-explanatory, there are a few points worth making about the data they summarize. First, nearly everyone within the "Southwest France" category

THE PEOPLE

came from the largely Basque, coastal region near the Spanish border. These individuals tended to be from Saint-Jean-de-Luz, Hendaye, Bayonne and Bidart. Second, about half of the people from "Midwest France" were from major urban centres such as Bordeaux, Nantes, La Rochelle and Rochefort. The rest were from smaller towns and villages in Poitou and in the Saintonge, Armagnac and Perigord regions. Third -- not surprisingly -- nearly everyone in the "Ile de France" category came from Paris. Fourth, almost everyone from "Brittany/Normandy" was from a coastal settlement; Saint-Malo was the predominant place of origin.

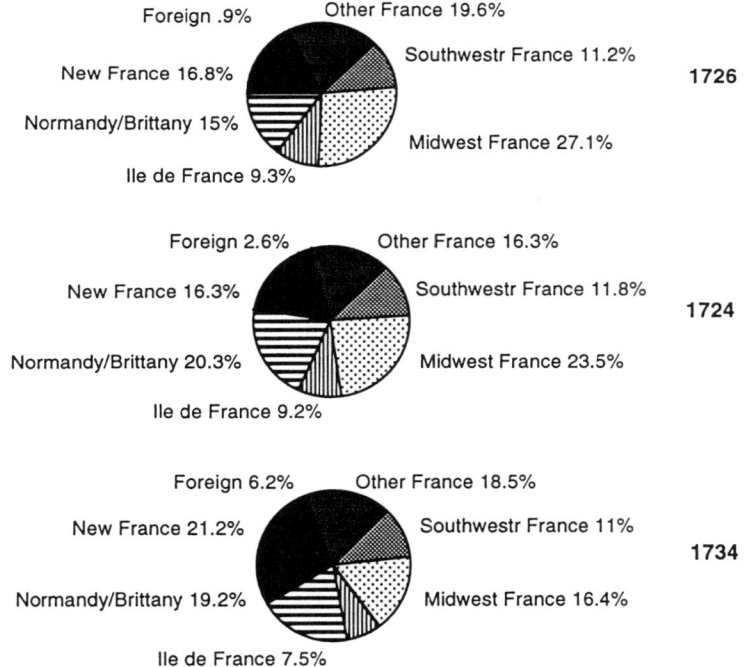

Figure 1. *Places of Origin of Louisbourg's* Habitants, *1724, 1726 and 1734*

Fifth, within the "New France" category, in 1734 there were ten heads of household in Louisbourg who had been born in Acadia: eight from Placentia, and two born on Ile Royale itself. Sixth, the "Other France" category included individuals from all over the rest of France, from Picardy to Lyon and from Toulon to Champagne. One town that stood out, on each of the three census returns, was Limoges; there were never any fewer than six *habitants* in Louisbourg who hailed originally from that city. Last, the "Foreign" category in

1734 included three people from Switzerland and two each from Belgium, Flanders and German states. It is important to remember, however, that this list of "foreigners" was only for individuals who were heads of household; there were many other outsiders serving as soldiers, working as servants, or employed in some other capacity.

Keeping in mind that the three census documents analysed above reveal only the birthplace of the *habitants* category, it is important to use other sources to obtain an image of the rest of the Louisbourg population. On a 1752 listing of 199 ordinary fishermen in Ile Royale, 48.7 per cent of the *pêcheurs* came from the southwest (largely Basque) corner of France, while 37.6 per cent were from Norman and Breton ports along the Gulf of Saint-Malo.[9] If one can assume that these two relatively small areas produced most of Ile Royale and Louisbourg's ordinary fishermen throughout the colony's history, then we get a quite different picture than that provided by the *habitants* on the census.

Marriage records are another source that must be considered. As part of the priest's notations accompanying each wedding entry, he was required to include the birthplace of the bride and groom. One virtue of such records is that a woman's place of origin is not subsumed under her husband's, as is usually the case in an eighteenth-century census. A weakness, on the other hand, is that wedding data reveals nothing about people who are unmarried, or already married when they came to live in Louisbourg. Another flaw is that a roll-up of marriage data over several decades does not offer a "snapshot" of the town at any particular point in time. Nonetheless, it is useful to compare the origins of Louisbourg brides and grooms with the census data already presented. Using Barbara Schmeisser's tabulations,[10] the following graphs can be drawn up:

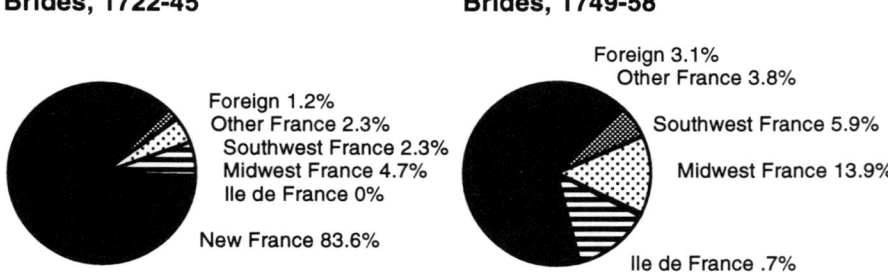

Brides, 1722-45

Foreign 1.2%
Other France 2.3%
Southwest France 2.3%
Midwest France 4.7%
Ile de France 0%
New France 83.6%

Brides, 1749-58

Foreign 3.1%
Other France 3.8%
Southwest France 5.9%
Midwest France 13.9%
Ile de France .7%
New France 59.2%

THE PEOPLE

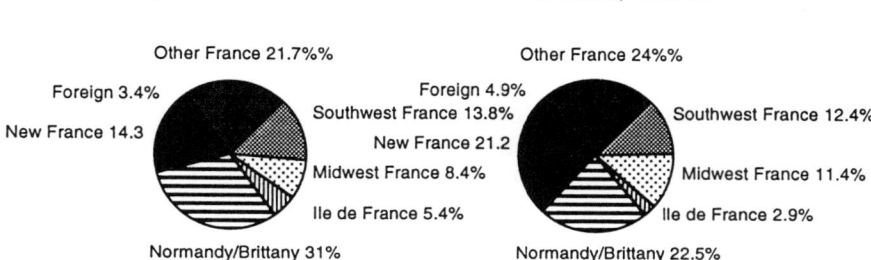

Figure 2. Places of Origin of Louisbourg's Brides and Grooms 1722-45 and 1749-58

The two brides' graphs present a dramatically different picture from that obtained from the census data concerning Louisbourg's heads of households (compare with Figure 1). Unlike the men of the town, the women of Louisbourg were predominantly from the New World. Demographic pressures led most girls born in the colony to wed while still in their teens. By way of contrast, the grooms' graphs are similar to those for the *habitants* of the census returns, one exception being that there is a lower percentage of grooms from "Midwest France" and a higher percentage from "Other France."

The evidence examined thus far gives us the following picture of eighteenth-century Louisbourg: the ordinary fishermen were overwhelmingly from the Norman/Breton coastline along the Gulf of Saint-Malo and the Basque region of southwest France; about eighty per cent of the household heads were from France (see graphs for details); and a clear majority of the brides were colonial-born (Placentia, Canada, Acadia, or Ile Royale).

A close look at all available parish records (marriages, baptisms and burials) for the periods 1722-45 and 1749-58 yields further insight into the origins and ethnic background of Louisbourg's civilian population. The limitation with parish records as a source is their "hit-or-miss" quality. Practising Roman Catholics who married, had a child baptized, or died while at Louisbourg are mentioned in this source, but there is no way of knowing how many other inhabitants or transients went unrecorded. Nonetheless, the parish records do provide us with an indication of the minimum number of individuals in Louisbourg from non-French backgrounds.

There are, for instance, references to a handful of Protestants from English, Irish or Scottish backgrounds who converted to Catholicism while in the capital of Ile Royale. Similarly, there is also mention, over a period of decades and usually in the form of an adolescent's baptism, of nearly two dozen Blacks. These were generally slaves sent to the colony from the Antilles. Adult Blacks who were already practising Catholics had less likelihood to turn up in the parish records, unless they gave birth or married. It is noteworthy, however, that there were a few free Blacks in Louisbourg, at least during the 1750s. In 1753, Jean-Baptiste Cupidon purchased his beloved's freedom in order to marry her.[11] The number of Blacks, freed or enslaved, who might have been in Louisbourg at any fixed point in time, however, is difficult to say.

While Blacks predominated, a few North American Indians also ended up in Louisbourg as slaves. Some of these may have actually been Pawnee Indians, for they are identified as *"Panis"* in the documents, but then again that term came to be applied to most enslaved Indians, whether or not they were really Pawnees.[12] As for the native people of the Atlantic region, the Micmacs, they were rarely seen in town. They generally lived and hunted in the southern part of the island, in the vicinity of modern-day Chapel Island and St. Peters, as well as inland around the Bras d'Or Lakes. Nonetheless, "the occasional baptism of a native child, the entry into domestic service of a young Micmac girl, and the infrequent visits of their scouts or chiefs," testifies that Micmacs did sometimes come to Louisbourg.[13]

Of the various non-French minorities at Louisbourg, the group that may have proved the most compatible was probably the Irish Catholics. They had both religion and a distrust of the English in common. Some forty to fifty Irish surnames turn up in the Louisbourg parish records. Most were servants, but there were a few with craftsmen's skills. There was even an occasional Irish priest who came to serve on Ile Royale. In 1750, no fewer than eight Irish families sailing from Newfoundland to Halifax jumped ship and sought refuge in Louisbourg. The freedom to practice their faith, Roman Catholicism, seems to have been the attraction.[14]

Louisbourg, of course, was not just a community of fishermen and merchants, tradespeople and servants. As a fortified stronghold and important garrison town, it also had a sizeable military population. Soldiers formed anywhere from one-quarter to one-half

THE PEOPLE

of the total population, depending on the time period examined. Unfortunately, when it comes to origins, it is usually difficult to ascertain where the ordinary enlisted men came from, other than that they were recruited in France. For the period 1720-45, years in which there may have been well over a thousand soldiers in Louisbourg, historian Allan Greer has been able to determine the birthplaces for only seventy-five.[15] Of those, only three were born outside France: one in Acadia, one in Switzerland and one in Ireland.

The presence of two "foreigners" -- the Irishman and the Swiss -- fighting on the side of the French should come as no surprise. It was common in the eighteenth century for armies to recruit and accept troops from wherever they could get them, provided they met certain height and health standards. There were many Irishmen and Scots in French regiments, and even more Germans in British ones. The word "mercenary" was then a descriptive term, not a pejorative.

One foreign mercenary regiment even found itself at Louisbourg. This was the Swiss-based Karrer Regiment, which served in the fortress between 1722 and 1745. With up to as many as 150 men, or about twenty per cent of the entire garrison at that time,[16] the Karrer troops were known collectively as *les Suisses*, though many, perhaps even a majority, were actually from German-speaking areas outside Switzerland. Many, if not most, were also Protestant. This made for an interesting irony: here was Louisbourg -- a French Catholic stronghold -- defended in part by a good many German and Swiss Protestants.[17]

The Karrer Regiment did not return to Louisbourg in 1749, when Ile Royale reverted to French jurisdiction according to the terms of the Treaty of Aix-la-Chapelle (1748). Yet that did not mean there were no more non-French soldiers in the town. According to a detailed troop roll drawn up in 1752, that listed the approximately one thousand Compagnies Franches soldiers in the garrison at that time,[18] there were fifty-three foreigners serving in the garrison, or about five per cent of the total military population. The origin of those men was as follows:

Spanish	-	21	Savoyard	-	3
Catalan	-	1	Saxon	-	12
Portuguese	-	1	Italian	-	1
German	-	7	Piedmontese	-	2

Prussian	-	2	Neapolitan	-	1
Austrian	-	2	Genoese	-	1
Brabant	-	3	Hungarian	-	1
Flemish	-	1	Luxemburger	-	1
Dutch	-	1	Berber	-	1
Swiss	-	1	Irish	-	1

The Spaniards would seem to have been numerous enough to form something of a sub-culture within the garrison. Similarly, the different Germanic-speaking individuals may also have used their language among themselves and similarly kept alive other aspects of their original culture.

The impression of Louisbourg's military population would therefore be the following: it was always predominantly French-born, but in the period up to 1745 there was a large Swiss and German minority, as high as about twenty per cent. During the early 1750s, there was still a five-per-cent scattering of non-French soldiers.

There is no doubt that Louisbourg was officially and overwhelmingly Roman Catholic. Overwhelmingly, because the vast majority of the town's inhabitants were of that persuasion. Officially, because the context of the time was one in which the French state lent its full support to its national church (known as the Gallican Church), just as the church gave the same support back to the monarchy. The king named all French bishops, including the one for New France, paid their salaries, and had them take an oath of loyalty. The only religious ceremonies and celebrations that were permitted to be held in public were those associated with Roman Catholicism. Furthermore, only practising Catholics could hold public posts. The partnership between church and state has been succinctly expressed by historian Guy Frégault: "The men of the State were Catholics; the men of the Church served the State."[19]

While most of Louisbourg was thus Roman Catholic -- nominally if not devoutly -- there were exceptions. Most noticeably, there were the German and Swiss soldiers of the Karrer Regiment. We have no way of knowing exactly how many of these were Protestants, but there were enough to cause occasional difficulties within a town that was supposed to be exclusively Catholic: "In 1724, Governor Saint-Ovide warned the minister of marine that France's Micmac allies regarded the Protestant troops "as suspects." Three years later, the governor complained that the Karrer officers refused to lead their soldiers in the *Fête-Dieu* (Corpus Christi) procession in the town."[20]

There were a few other Protestants in Louisbourg as well, beside the soldiers in the Karrer Regiment. The names of several individuals originally from England, Scotland or New England turn up in baptismal records when they converted to Catholicism. There is even a reference to a Jewish conversion.[21]

Aside from French, which was obviously the dominant language, Basque, Breton, German, Swiss German, Spanish, English, and perhaps Irish, Provençal and occasionally Micmac were sometimes spoken in Louisbourg.[22] There were also a few people, notably the foreign-born soldiers listed above, who on occasion might have spoken Dutch, Italian and Portuguese.

The largest single, non-French-language community consisted of the several hundred fishermen and few merchants who spoke Basque. The Récollet priests who served the parish were repeatedly asked to bring over a Basque-speaking priest from southwest France, but this they never did.[23] When unilingual Basques had to give evidence in court cases, interpreters were used to translate their testimony.

How many of the people from Brittany spoke Breton, a Celtic language said to be more akin to Welsh than to any other, is unknown, because there is no record of Bretons demanding to have their language spoken. This is likely because most of them spoke French in addition to Breton, and also because the parish priests were all initially from Brittany, and some of them at least would have been able to speak their ancient Celtic tongue.

The German- and Swiss German-language communities were comprised of soldiers and, in some cases, their wives. German-speakers were most numerous during the 1740s when the Karrer Regiment was present. While much smaller, there continued to be a German presence on the island in the 1750s, even after the departure of the Karrer Regiment. This presence was localized in the Village des Allemands established on the Mira River in the 1750s. Its inhabitants were mostly German Catholics who had abandoned the new settlement at Lunenburg on mainland Nova Scotia.[24]

In conclusion, the people of Louisbourg, aside from being predominantly French and Roman Catholic, were a mix of men, women and children, with males largely outnumbering females. There were a few hundred Basques and Germans, a few dozen Blacks and Irish, and a scattering of Spanish, English and Scottish. There were more than a few Protestants, especially during the 1730s and 1740s, and perhaps even a few Jews. There were many in the fishery who spoke Basque -- and perhaps others who used Breton -- while in the military there were a lot of German- and Swiss German-speakers in the 1740s. Spanish was probably the most common "second" language in the garrison during the 1750s.

All in all, the French stronghold that Louisbourg was, the seaport community was also home to a wide range of minority populations. Some differed from the majority in terms of ethnicity, others in terms of religion, and still others in terms of the language they spoke.

Notes

1. Hilary Russell, "Opportunities to Introduce the History of People of African Descent at Existing National Historic Sites" (manuscript on file, Ottawa, National Historic Sites Directorate, 1990). For details, see Robin Winks, *The Blacks in Canada: A History* (Montreal, 1971); and James W. St. G. Walker, *The Black Loyalists: The Search for a Promised Land in Nova Scotia and Sierra Leone, 1783-1870* (New York, 1976).
2. A.J.B. Johnston, *Religion in Life at Louisbourg, 1713-1758* (Montréal and Kingston: McGill-Queen's University Press, 1984), p. 5.
3. *Ibid.*, pp. 122-44; for figures on other regions in New France, see Hubert Charbonneau, *Vie et mort de nos ancêtres: Etude démographique* (Montreal: Les Presses de l'Université de Montreal, 1975), pp. 158-64; Gisa Hynes, "Some Aspects of the Demography of Port Royal, 1650-1755,"*Acadiensis*, Vol. 3, No. 1 (Autumn 1973), pp. 3-17.
4. AN, Outre-Mer, G^1, Vol. 467 (1720), part 3A; *ibid.*, 466, pièce 67 (1724); *ibid.*, no. 71-suite (1737); ASQ, Poly 55-49 (1752); J.S. McLennan, *Louisbourg from its foundation to its fall, 1713-1758* (London: MacMillan, 1918), p. 371, also provides population totals.
5. AN, Outre-Mer, G^1, Vol. 466, pièce 67, Recensement ... 1724.
6. *Ibid.*, pièce 68, Recensement ... 1726.
7. *Ibid.*, pièce 71-suite, "*Dénombrement de L'Isle Royalle*," 1737.
8. Barbara Schmeisser, "The Population of Louisbourg, 1713-1758," *Manuscript Report Series*, Vol. 303 (Ottawa: Parks Canada, 1976), p. 10.
9. B.A. Balcom, *The Cod Fishery of Isle Royale, 1713-1758* (Ottawa: Parks Canada, 1984), pp. 55-56; and A.J.B. Johnston, "The Fishermen of Eighteenth-Century Cape Breton: Numbers and Origins," *Nova Scotia Historical Review*, Vol. 9, No. 1 (1989), pp. 62-72.
10. Schmeisser, "The Population of Louisbourg," passim.
11. AN, Outre-Mer, G^3, 2041-2, pièce 78, 1 mars 1753.
12. Cornelius J. Jaenen, *Friend and Foe. Aspects of French-Amerindian Cultural Contact in the Sixteenth and Seventeenth Centuries* (Toronto: McClelland and Stewart Limited,

THE PEOPLE

1976), p. 139.
13. Johnston, *Religion in Life*, pp. 8-9.
14. *Ibid.*, p. 8; A.A. MacKenzie, *The Irish in Cape Breton* (Antigonish: Formac Publishing Co. Ltd., 1979).
15. Allan Greer, "The Soldiers of Isle Royale, 1720-1745," *History and Archaeology*, Vol. 28 (Ottawa: Parks Canada, 1979), pp. 30-31.
16. *Ibid.*, pp. 13-23; see also Margaret Fortier, "The Ile Royale Garrison, 1713-45," *Microfiche Report Series*, Vol. 67 (Ottawa: Parks Canada, 1981).
17. Johnston, *Religion in Life*, pp. 7-8.
18. The troop roll in question is the "*Signalement général des troupes...,*" drawn up by Michel Le Courtois de Surlaville. NAC, MG 18, F^{30}, Dossier 1.
19. Guy Frégault, *Le XVIIIe siècle canadien: Études* (Montreal: Editions HMH Ltée, 1968), p. 148.
20. Johnston, *Religion in Life*, p. 8.
21. Gaston Du Boscq de Beaumont, ed., *Les derniers jours de l'Acadie (1748-1758). Correspondances et mémoires* (Geneva, 1975), p. 63.
22. Christopher Moore, "Harbour Life and Quay Activities," in "Street Life and Public Activites in Louisbourg: Four Studies for Animators," *Manuscript Report Series*, Vol. 317 (Ottawa: Parks Canada, 1977).
23. Johnston, *Religion in Life*, pp. 47-48.
24. W.P. Bell, *The "Foreign Protestants" and the Settlement of Nova Scotia. The History of a Piece of Arrested British Colonial Policy in the Eighteenth Century* (Toronto: University of Toronto Press, 1961), pp. 375-77.

The Gardens of 18th-Century Louisbourg

Anne O'Neill

The Fortress of Louisbourg National Historic Park is a project of the Government of Canada, begun in 1961 and just now nearing completion. It is a massive undertaking, a reconstruction of a portion of the 18th-century French town as it was during the 1740s when, because of its strategic and economic importance, it was a flashpoint of Anglo-French rivalry in North America. Louisbourg's span of history was short, founded in 1713 and captured first in 1745 and then for the second and final time in 1758; but at its peak it was a centre for French trade, commerce, fishing and military power in the New World. Situated on a barren peninsula dividing a deep, well-protected harbour from the rugged North Atlantic, the town's population by the 1740s is thought to have been around 3000, including a military garrison of about 700. The Louisbourg project consists of much more than a collection of reconstructed buildings. It also includes interpretive exhibits, publications, films, furnished period houses and, most popular of all, costumed animation of the events and routines of 18th-century daily life.

One aspect of the re-creation and interpretation of life in Louisbourg is the project to reconstruct some of the original gardens. The project began without the benefit of any professional horticulturist or botanist. Instead, a group of interested staff members with diverse gardening backgrounds and considerable enthusiasm began researching and planning the gardens, with advice from historians, draughtsmen, architects and various other specialists in the Park.

During researches in the extensive Louisbourg documentation it was discovered that during the period 1713-1758 there were over 100 gardens in the town.[1] Cartographic evidence from over 60

THE GARDENS

maps and plans of the town indicated that the gardens were divided into squares or rectangles, often with borders around the circumference. In some cases, maps of the same year present a different layout for the same garden,[2] which indicates that some garden plans may be merely an artist's rendering rather than an actual diagram of an existing plot. For instance, one plan shows the King's Garden divided symmetrically into rectangles at a period when according to official correspondence, it was not under cultivation.[3] Unfortunately, no detailed design for any individual garden has yet been discovered.

The average dimensions of the gardens were found to be 61.4 *pieds* long by 45.6 *pieds* wide (1 *pied* = 1.066 ft or 32.47 cm). The smallest one mentioned was 22 *pieds* by 16 *pieds*.[4] Obviously, these gardens were far from the immense and elegantly formal estate gardens found in France during this period. No mention of *"jardins fruitiers"* or *"jardins d'agrément"* were found in the documents, although in several instances, *"jardins potagers"*[5] or *"jardins en légumage et à herbes"*[6] are cited. It is not surprising that the Louisbourg gardens would be of a practical nature considering the limited space within the fortress walls and the continuing lack of self-sufficiency that plagued Louisbourg throughout its history.

As for the actual cultivation standards of these gardens, their soil quality, care and maintenance undoubtedly varied. It was 1741 before the occupation of professional gardener was listed in the census returns,[7] and most gardens were cultivated by individual fishermen, tradesmen, merchants, military officers or servants who may or may not have had sufficient gardening expertise to maintain attractive and productive gardens. Some documents record the ordering of topsoil for improvement of specific gardens,[8] but this seems to have been the exception rather than the rule.

The majority of gardens in Louisbourg were backyard *potager* gardens, surrounded by *piquet* fences,[9] with varying standards of cultivation. A journal kept during the New England occupation of the town (1745-1749) states: "There were also many very fine gardens ... The King's Garden just by the Citadel ... the garden in the Magazin General ... the Hospital, etc., and many others but not Eaquel to these."[10]

Once the basic type of gardening done in Louisbourg was determined it was necessary, without any extant individual plans, to decide on specific layouts for our sample gardens. Keeping in mind the background, social status and personalities of the various property owners, gardens were designed according to the rules, regulations and philosophy of 18th-century French gardening as outlined in *La nouvelle maison rustique* by Louis Leger, published in France in 1755.[11] The first volume of this two-volume work concentrates specifically on all aspects of French country gardening during our period and offers a wealth of detailed advice, as well as a sampling of designs for typical *potager* gardens.

In the actual selection of plant materials several sources were used: *La nouvelle maison rustique,* for a list of the most popular *potager* garden plants; plant lists from New England[12] (deemed acceptable because of the connection through trade between Louisbourg and the American colonies); documents, letters, and census returns mentioning the names of specific plants;[13] 18th-century cookbooks for the insight they offer on the most commonly used herbs for cookery; and archaeological seed analysis.[14] This last source has revealed certain types of foodstuffs available here, although whether these were grown locally or imported cannot be ascertained. During the 18th century experimentation with local indigenous species was encouraged by the king, so it is reasonable to surmise that some plant materials would have been transplanted into gardens and tested for useful qualities. Both native species and French introductions of the period are incorporated into our gardens after they have been historically authenticated.[15]

To date, four gardens have been reconstructed at Louisbourg with a fifth partly designed. These are representative gardens only, and serve as a visual enhancement to our interpretation of 18th-century life. Research is continuing and our gardens will adapt as new or additional information is uncovered, in keeping with the mandate of authenticity displayed in all aspects of the Fortress of Louisbourg project.

Notes

1. AFL, Louisbourg Map Collection, Nos. 1730-2, ND-24. AN, Outre-Mer, DFC, IV-164, 1730; BN, Cabinet des Estampes, Vd 20a-54, n.d.
2. *Ibid.,* 1751-8, 1751-17. AG, 14-1-30, 1751; AN, Outre-Mer, DFC, IV-225, 1751.
3. AN, Col, C^{11} B, Vol. 14, ff. 114-116v, St. Ovide au Ministre de la Marine, 21 octobre 1733.
4. AN, Outre-Mer, G^3, 2058, pièce 40, Bail à loyer de Dominique Detcheverry à Thimothé Latapy, 31 octobre 1726.

THE GARDENS

5. AN, Outre-Mer, G³, 2044, pièce 54, Bail d'une Maison de J.F. Chesnay à Jean Minaud, 11 juin 1755.

6. AN, Outre-Mer, G², Vol. 209, dossier 512, pièce 4, Inventaire de Philibert Pineau, 22 novembre 1757.

7. AN, Col., C¹¹B, Vol. 26, f. 20v, François Bigot au Ministre de la Marine, 1 octobre 1740.

8. AN, Col., C¹¹B, Vol. 22, ff. 157-157v, François Bigot au Ministre de la Marine, 1 octobre 1740; *ibid.*, Vol. 10, f. 154v, de Mézy, Verrier, et St. Ovide au Ministre de la Marine, 20 avril 1728.

9. AN, Outre-Mer, G³, 2044, pièce 54, Bail à loyer de Pierre Sentier à Arnaud Barrouillet, 11 juin 1755.

10. Louis Effingham De Forest, ed., *Louisbourg Journals 1745* (New York: The Society of Colonial Wars, 1932).

11. Louis Leger, *La nouvelle maison rustique ou economie général de tous les biens de campagne*, 7th edition (Paris: Saugrain Fils, 1755), Vol. 1.

12. Rudy Favretti, *Early New England Gardens* (Sturbridge, Mass.: Old Sturbridge Village, 1974).

13. AN, Outre-Mer, G², Vol. 182, pp. 1052-57, Procès entre F. Vallée et J. Brisson, juin-août 1733; Harvard University, Baker Library, Thomas Hancock Papers, Bastide to Hancock, 30 April 1748; ASQ, *Papiers Michel LeCourtois de Surlaville*, Poly 55-49.

14. J.H. McAndrews, "Seed and pollen analysis, Fortress of Louisbourg" (manuscript on file, Fortress of Louisbourg, 31 October 1978); John E. Duncan, "Seed identification of archaeological seed from Fortress of Louisbourg" (manuscript on file, 1977).

15. J.S. Erskine, *The French Period in Nova Scotia, A.D. 1500-1758 and Present Remains* (Wolfville, N.S.: John Erskine, 1975).

1

ECONOMICS

The Cod Fishery of Isle Royale, 1713-58

B.A. Balcom

Fishing and the Economy of Isle Royale

Perhaps more than most places, the history of the colony of Isle Royale has been shaped by military and political factors rather than by economic ones. As the former factors have figured so prominently in the colony's historiography, they require only a brief mention here. The colony was founded in 1713 to offset French territorial losses in Acadia and Newfoundland by the Treaty of Utrecht and comprised the islands in the Gulf of St. Lawrence -- principally Isle Royale (Cape Breton), Isle St. Jean (Prince Edward Island), and Isles de la Magdaline (Magdalen Islands). As both the colony and its principal island share the name of Isle Royale, Isle Royale will be used in this report to describe the colony unless the island is specified. Barely 30 years after its founding the colony was occupied by the English -- its capital besieged and captured, its fishing outports burned, and its population deported. After an English occupation of 4 years, the French retook possession of the colony in 1749. The second French period was considerably shorter than the first. In 1758 the English captured Louisbourg for the second and final time. The French lost final possession in 1763, by which time Louisbourg's fortifications had already been demolished.

French appreciation of Isle Royale's economic and strategic potential received written expression during the early years of the 18th century. Although the 1706 colonization proposal by Antoine-Denis Raudot, intendant of New France, is the one most frequently cited by historians,[1] it was only one of a number of such memoirs written at that time by Frenchmen interested in the island's development.[2] In general, these memoirs stressed the economic potential of the island's fisheries and its interior resources such as timber and coal. Isle Royale was also foreseen as an entrepôt within the French imperial system. Raudot wisely foresaw that for the future colony to succeed in this role, its trade would have to be international and not just imperial in scope. Finally, these memorialists viewed a French establishment on Isle Royale as a protection for French fishing efforts, a containment to English expansion, and an operational base in time of war for French naval ships and privateers acting against English shipping and coastal colonies. These strategic considerations have had an unfortunate historiographical legacy in which Isle Royale, and in particular Louisbourg, features as an expensive but ineffective "Guardian of the Gulf of St. Lawrence."[3]

Modifications occurred as the projections contained in these early memoirs materialized. Three main areas of economic endeavour developed but the colony's land resources, both extractive industries and agriculture, failed to achieve more than marginal significance in the colonial economy. In their place, government expenditure on Louisbourg's fortifications and other public spending on the colonial administration and on a relatively large garrison assumed major proportions. Within the private sector, trade and fishery formed the two major areas of economic activity. However, free enterprise was so enticing that both garrison officers and civil administrators actively engaged in both trade and the fisheries, and, with the private contractors, may be considered the principal recipients of any government largesse.

Given Isle Royale's short and turbulent history, it is not surprising that the colony's population remained relatively small during both French periods. As seen in Table 1,[4] the colony's resident population never exceeded 9,000 and towards the end of the first period it barely exceeded 5,000. The population was also surprisingly urban in character with approximately 35% of the population concentrated in Louisbourg. It is important to note that this urban concentration was exaggerated by the inclusion of the colony's military garrison, of which over three-quarters were stationed in Louisbourg. Indeed, the tripling of this garrison in the second French period further exaggerated the colony's urban character. Although the garrison had considerable interaction with the private sector, with its soldiers as a labour force and its officers as entrepreneurs, it still remained largely separated from the private sector. Another important segment of the population was the large labour force employed in the fishery. The transience of this labour force led to large seasonal fluctuations in the population and meant that the resident *habitant-pêcheurs* or fishing proprietors had a production capacity considerably greater than their numbers indicated at some points in the year.

Table 1
Colonial population, various years

Year	Population (including military garrison)			
	(1) Louisbourg	(2) Isle Royale	(3) Isle Royale plus Isle St. Jean	(1) as % of (3)
1719	853	ca.2,012	2,262	37.7
1726	1,296	3,528	3,950	32.8
1734	1,616	3,955	4,527	35.6
1737	1,963	4,618	5,181	37.8
1752	4,174	5,845	8,814	46.9

The best documented, but also the most exaggerated, aspect of the colony's economy was public expenditure. In addition to the well-known expenditure on the colony's fortifications and military garrison, the French government also maintained the civil administration, including the courts. The crown also contributed funds for the construction and maintenance of other public works, such as the hospital, the lighthouse, and a careening wharf. The extent of this expenditure has been considerably magnified by some historians. The total cost of the fortifications has been placed as high as 30 million *livres* instead of the approximate actual cost of 4 million *livres*.[5] This latter amount was less than the sum of 3 years' production in the colony's fishery at local production values. In fact, during most years the amount spent on fortifications was less than the outfitting costs of a 6-month voyage for a large warship of the period.[6]

The colony's government usually operated on a balanced budget based on a system of controls to prevent abuse.[7] In the fall local officials prepared a statement of anticipated expenses for the coming year, which was sent to the Minister of Marine for approval. This statement was scrutinized during the winter and payment, in the form of either cash or goods, was sent in the spring to Isle Royale for the approved items. These payments then appeared under one of three headings on the colony's balance sheet. First there were charges for the labour and material used on the fortifications. Second there was the colonial budget to cover the annual expenditures of the colony, such as the salaries and supplies for the garrison and

ASPECTS OF LOUISBOURG

bureaucracy. Finally there were extraordinary expenses which covered special or unforeseen costs. Table 2[8] shows the colony's annual receipts and expenditures for the years 1721-57. It should be noted that the colony's receipts were supplemented on occasion by the sale of government supplies to private individuals and to French military units operating in Acadia on a separate budget.

When compared with Canada, Isle Royale received a far larger budget than its population warranted. With a considerably smaller population, Isle Royale's budget was over half as large as that of Canada, some six to eight times as much in terms of per capita funding.[9] As Isle Royale was more dependent on trade than Canada, the island colony had a higher per capita balance of payments. Government expenditure helped equalize this balance of payments, particularly during the second period, when increases in government expenditure greatly outstripped increases in the private sector. It is important to remember, however, that a considerable sum in the colony's budget did little to employ local services or encourage domestic production. In addition to the cash sent for salaries and local purchases, a large portion of the budget was spent on goods in France. Although the shipment of these goods enabled the colony to support a larger government sector than would otherwise be the case, they added little direct wealth to the local private sector.

Table 2
The budget of Isle Royale: receipts and expenses, 1721-57

Year	Receipts				Expenditure	Surplus (+) or deficit (-)
	Colony	Extra-ordinary	Fortifications	Total		
1721	151,871	11,084	80,000	242,955	242,954	
1722	124,740	4,020	80,000	209,661	192,353	+17,308
1723	144,289	6,817	130,000	281,105	267,761	+13,344
1724	151,485	9,601	150,000	311,087	298,831	+12,256
1725	116,941	3,960	150,000	270,901	270,899	
1726	136,911	8,879	150,000	295,701	295,790	-89
1727	144,889	14,939	150,000	309,829	309,790	
1728	--139,056--		150,000	289,056	286,746	+2,310
1729	--155,112--		150,000	305,112	292,324	+12,798
1730	154,283	4,007	152,700	311,162	311,162	
1731	149,965	5,067	128,900	300,427	300,427	
1732	167,362	420	128,900	296,682	296,682	
1733	179,784	583	130,335	310,704	310,703	
1734	179,441	575	128,900	313,587	313,586	
1735	209,091	492	128,900	338,484	338,481	

THE COD FISHERY

Year	Receipts				Expenditure	Surplus (+) or deficit (-)
	Colony	Extraordinary	Fortifications	Total		
1736	205,389	2,437	128,900	337,370	337,370	
1737	216,012	1,133	128,900	346,045	346,044	
1738	215,123	218	128,900	349,455	349,455	
1739	--176,005--		128,900	304,905	309,904	
1740	224,586	2,892	128,900	355,830	355,845	
1741	247,314	5,284	128,900	380,701	380,702	
1742	232,269	4,974	128,100	365,346	365,345	
1743	352,650	14,709	128,100	495,461	495,468	
1744	335,825	83,553	128,100	547,480	547,436	+44
1749	1,082,569	6,241	48,420	1,137,231	1,194,724	-57,492
1750	851,478	532,634	143,200	1,527,312	1,463,086	+64,266
1751	846,791	89,761	28,400	964,952	1,369,560	-404,608
1752	1,184,095	350,259	80,000	1,614,354	1,305,355	+308,998
1753	422,035	349,938	51,720	823,693	892,834	-69,141
1754	456,300	208,693	82,000	806,993	960,907	-150,914
1756					1,069,574	
1757					1,113,691	

Like government expenditure, commerce developed into one of the economic mainstays of Isle Royale. Although the available primary documentation prohibits evaluating in absolute terms the contribution of commerce to the colony's economy, it is possible to show its relative importance to Isle Royale by comparison with other colonies. In Canada and Isle Royale, a single staple product (furs and fish, respectively) dominated each colony's exports. The per capita value of total exports for Isle Royale in 1737 was approximately eight times greater than that of Canada for the years 1735-39. Indeed, a comparison between Isle Royale and the neighbouring British colonies for approximately the same period reveals a similar pattern.[10] Only Newfoundland, which had a similar dependency on the fishery, came close to Isle Royale's level of per capita exports. This does not mean that Isle Royale was more prosperous but it does reflect the greater importance of trade to the Atlantic colony. Isle Royale was also more dependent on imports for the necessities as well as the luxuries of life. The resulting high level of exchanges provided Isle Royale, and Louisbourg in particular, with international markets and supply sources and fostered a strong shipping and merchandising sector.

The fishery formed a strong nucleus around which the rest of the colony's commerce revolved. This industry produced a large quantity of dried cod for export to markets in Europe and the West Indies. The fishery demanded a large material input, principally salt, and, as it was labour intensive, its workers placed heavy demands on the local economy for provisions and clothing. The French adopted a simple development strategy of minimizing these production costs through cheap imports. There were inherent risks in this economic system, however. Poor fishing seasons caused fluctuations in the general level of commerce and induced hardship. Similarly, interruptions of supply, such as crop failure or war, created shortages which adversely affected the whole economy.[11] It is important to note that these fluctuations and shortages were temporary in nature and until combined with an enemy attack, they never seriously threatened the colony's economic core. Indeed, the steady demand for Isle Royale's staple product, fish, gave the colony a stability often lacking in other developing areas.

The fishery also aided Louisbourg's development as the colony's entrepôt. The dispersed pattern of fishing settlements along the island's Atlantic coast necessitated a distribution and collection centre. Such a centre maximized shipping efficiency by ensuring the sale and purchase of complete cargoes in one port equipped for a large turn-over of goods. The outports, lacking the necessary volume of trade, were linked to the entrepôt through the *cabotage*, or coastal trade, which employed smaller vessels. Because of its early emergence as the largest population centre, its good harbour facilities, and its relatively central position in the colony, Louisbourg became the colony's commercial centre. Distance and market size slightly weakened its trading monopoly over the outports; Niganiche (Ingonish) and Petit Degrat, both relatively large and distant centres, were the only outports that regularly received trading vessels from abroad. The scale of this commercial activity was small, however, and posed no threat to Louisbourg's supremacy.

Geography also enhanced Louisbourg's position as an entrepôt within the French imperial system. In an age when navigational instruments determined latitude but not longitude, it was common practice to sail along a selected latitude until a landfall was reached. Cape Breton's easternmost point was on the same latitude as the major French ports of Rochefort and La Rochelle, making Louisbourg a convenient destination for French ships sailing to North America.[12] Louisbourg was also used as a trans-shipment point in France's Quebec trade. By trans-shipping cargo at Louisbourg, vessels from France avoided the time-consuming and potentially hazardous navigation of the St. Lawrence. Cargoes were efficiently carried from Louisbourg to Quebec in smaller vessels locally owned in the two ports. Louisbourg also benefitted as a pivotal spot in France's intercolonial trade. Although this trade incorporated triangular patterns for movement of goods between France, the West Indies, and Isle Royale, individual ships, like their British counterparts, probably engaged in a "shuttle" service between two of these points.[13] Louisbourg merchants extended this trade pattern to include trans-shipments to Acadia and New England as well as to Quebec.

France's Atlantic ports, especially St. Malo and St. Jean de Luz, were Isle Royale's most important trading partners.[14] These ports drew not only on a large and varied domestic production but supplemened these supplies with re-exports from France's extensive foreign trade. In this way Isle Royale not only obtained French foodstuffs, clothing, wine, and fishing supplies but foreign goods ranging from Irish salt beef to Chinese porcelain. Dried fish and fish oil, some of which went to Spain and the Mediterranean, accounted for as much as 90% of the value of Isle Royale's export shipments. Lumber and coal made up much of the remainder. Distance had a limiting effect on some aspects of Isle Royale's trade with France; in particular, alternative sources for perishable commodities, such as fresh foods and livestock, had to be found.

Isle Royale's commerce also merged with the trading patterns of Canada and the French West Indies. Canada sent Isle Royale foodstuffs and lumber, some of which were re-exported to the West Indies. The French West Indies shipped return cargoes of sugar, sugar by-products, coffee, and other tropical goods, some of which could be passed on to Canada. Trade with Canada was never large and after the late 1730s, crop failures, growing domestic consumption, and other events limited Canada's exports to Isle Royale even further.[15] In contrast, Isle Royale's West Indian trade, based on a reciprocal demand for goods, flourished. Cod accounted for 70-80% of Isle Royale's exports to the Caribbean. Timber, coal, and re-exports of New England products, notably horses during the second French occupation, added variety to the trade. Rum and molasses formed the bulk of Isle Royale's West Indian imports. Such products filled a strong local demand such as quenching that common predilection of North American seafarers for rum, as well as forming the basis of Isle Royale's New England exports.

Acadia and New England were Isle Royale's two remaining

trading partners. These areas, both under British control during this period, bridged Isle Royale's trade gaps within the French colonial system. Both regions provided perishable foodstuffs and livestock which, because of distance and other factors, were largely unavailable from French sources. Isle Royale's Acadian trade was principally with the French Acadian farmers whose self-sufficient farming economy restricted the nature and extent of commerce. This trade remained small in scale and consisted of foodstuffs, livestock, furs, and some fish being exchanged for manufactured items. New England's exports were similar, with the important addition of construction materials, whereas re-exports of Caribbean products dominated the return cargoes. New England also remained an important source of schooners for Isle Royale's fishery and coastal trade.[16] The ease with which New England merchants obtained trading permits during both French occupations did much to minimize smuggling between the two regions.

As shown in Table 3,[17] the nature and extent of Isle Royale's trade with these five different regions varied considerably. These variations changed over time and were affected by a growing disparity in the colony's balance of payments. France remained Isle Royale's largest market and supplier but by 1754 this trade greatly favoured the mother country. After France, the French West Indies was Isle Royale's largest trading partner. It is particularly important to note the great increase in this branch of trade during the second French occupation. A similar growth pattern occurred in the colony's commerce with New England. Although data for 1754 are missing, Isle Royale's imports from and exports to New England stood at 488,037 and 654,680 *livres*, respectivly, in 1752. This was a considerable increase over the 102,198 *livres* worth of goods the colony imported from this region in 1737. Trade with Canada and Acadia was relatively small and remained of only marginal importance to Isle Royale's commerce as a whole.

Table 3
Values of Isle Royale's imports and exports in *livres*, by region, 1737 and 1754

Region	Imports (*livres*)		Exports (*livres*)	
	1737	1754	1737	1754
France	1,022,597	1,437,256	1,082,394	788,757
West Indies	247,049	1,188,917	147,828	656,353
New England	102,198	n.d.	n.d.	n.d.
Canada	23,851	39,607	72,855	75,575
Acadia	22,994	n.d.	n.d.	n.d.
All regions	1,418,860	2,665,780	1,499,448	1,510,685

THE COD FISHERY

In the prosecution of these various trades, Isle Royale received visits from a substantial volume of ships. J.S. McLennan concluded that after eliminating local traffic an annual average of 154 vessels visited the colony's ports, particularly Louisbourg, during the decade 1733-43. Only three ports in the more populous British colonies to the south surpassed this total.[18] Variations in average vessel size for the different trades make tonnage figures a more accurate reflection of the volume of trade with each area than a straight vessel count. During the first French occupation the annual volume of shipping amounted to some 8,000 *tonneaux*.[19] The larger vessels from France usually accounted for less than half the number of ships but well over half the tonnage. During the early part of the second French occupation, the volume of shipping jumped to 13,000 *tonneaux*. The increase was due to a quadrupling of the West Indian and New England tonnage to parity with that of France.

On the basis of Isle Royale's export dependence on the fishery, Christopher Moore has determined that the colony's balance of payments remained favourable until the late 1730s.[20] After that date a decline in fishery production resulted in a weakening of Isle Royale's trade position. During the second French occupation higher prices partially affected lower fishery production, but the increase in population and consequent increase in import demands further worsened the colony's balance of payments. Indicative of this decline in Isle Royale's trade position was an apparent tightening in the colony's money supply. Although bills of exchange were a major form of financial transaction, there were still considerable amounts of specie in circulation. Although it is impossible to quantify changes in this system, literary sources indicate the availability of specie to all classes during the first French occupation. By the 1740s the colonial administration was expressing concern over the increasing scarcity of cash.[21] Although Isle Royale was not reduced to issuing card money like its sister colony of Canada had to on occasion, the decrease in the money supply indicated a cash outflow to pay for goods and services.

The outflow of cash from the colony was aggravated by the French reluctance to diversify its economy and thus substitute domestic production for imports. Although French mercantilist policy prohibited local involvement in some areas of production, other areas, particularly in primary industry, were open for expansion. Certainly the colony had potential for greater development in agriculture, lumbering, and coal mining. A hundred years later, the Scots, utilizing a farming technology similar to that of the French, established an extensive subsistence agriculture.[22] The English were quick to set up a colliery at L'Indienne (Lingan) during their brief occupation from 1745 to 1749.[23] The local construction industry provided a ready market for lumber while the colony's fishing, coastal, and even international trades provided a steady demand for vessels.

Numerous reasons have been advanced to explain in part the reluctance of the French to exploit more fully these economic opportunities. The French preference for grain over the more regionally suited potato hindered the development of farming beyond mere garden plots.[24] Competition with foodstuffs imported from France, New England, Quebec, and Acadia further restricted agricultural development. Similar competition existed with regard to construction materials and shipbuilding. During the first French occupation coal mining was relatively small scale, with local consumption seemingly limited to the artillery forge and presumably some private forges, plus small amounts for export. After 1749, however, coal started to become a major fuel and the English coal yard, on the eastern end of the quay, was retained by the French.

Indeed, too often historians have expected to see major development in what was essentially a new colony. Like all French colonies, Isle Royale suffered from the general lack of emigration from the mother country.[25] Although this was offset to some extent by large seasonal influxes of transient fishermen, there is nothing to indicate that these fishermen formed an effective pool of potential settlers. Given a slow immigration rate, the colony's short and turbulent history militated against any substantial development or diversification of the economy. After all, Isle Royale enjoyed barely three decades of peace before it was captured and its population deported in 1745.

There are indications, however, that had the French enjoyed a longer second occupation after 1749 there would have been a greater diversification of the colony's economy. The influx of Acadian settlers into Isle St. Jean and even into the interior of Isle Royale would have inevitably led to a greater agricultural self-sufficiency. Similarly, the government-encouraged settlements of Rouillé and Village des Allemands on the Mira River, while hardly successful, indicated increased government interest in other sectors of the economy. As in agriculture, the French also increased their exploitation of the colony's coal resources during the second occupation. However Isle Royale's truncated history precludes any analysis of its economy except on a short-term basis.

Within the short term the concentration of production factors within the fishery resulted in an economy dominated by the staple production of a single commodity -- dried cod. Although this concentration left Isle Royale exposed to the fluctuations of international supply and demand, it nevertheless provided the colony with an export item generally in demand in the world market. With the fishery providing a cash income, Isle Royale was able to pay for its necessary imports and thus avoided the "starving time" that initially plagued so many developing colonies. This did not mean that there were not fluctuations in the fishery that caused occasional hardships. With so much dependence on the success of the fishery, fluctuations in the local level of production or in its market value or in the prices of imports had damaging effects on the colony's economy.

The French Fishery and the Establishment of Isle Royale

The beginnings of the French cod fishery in the northwestern Atlantic considerably pre-dated the founding of Isle Royale in 1713. Indeed, a French Basque memoir dated 1710 claimed that the Basques had been the first to exploit the North American cod stocks and that it was the acquisition of a Basque "rutter" or pilot's log book that had enabled Columbus to undertake his discoveries.[26] Initially drawn to North America in pursuit of whales, the Basques quickly took advantage of the abundant cod stocks -- first for shipboard and domestic consumption and later for export. Although the archives attesting to these facts have been burned, the Basques maintain that North American coastal nomenclature supports their claims. Although the early date mentioned in these Basque claims may have been exaggerated, recent historical research has verified the existence of a viable Basque whale fishery in the Gulf of St. Lawrence and along the Labrador coast from the 1540s to the end of the century.[27]

Basque participation became one of the continuing trends in France's North American cod fishery. Both Nicholas Denys and Duhamel Du Monceau described the Basques as being the most skillful of the French fishermen. This Basque participation resulted in their presence at Plaisance and later at the founding of Isle Royale. Michel Daccarrette was one such Basque who had initially settled at Plaisance (Placentia) and had joined the wholesale transfer of that population to Isle Royale where he became a prominent fishing proprietor and merchant.[28] St. Jean de Luz annually outfitted numbers of trading and fishing vessels for Isle Royale, and Basque merchants, like Bernard Detcheverry, operated from this port and were a common feature of the Louisbourg business community.[29] Similarly, skilled Basque fishermen found a ready market for their services among the colony's fishing proprietors. The numerous entries of Basque names in the account books of the widow Dastarit, an innkeeper in Louisbourg's Fauxbourg district, confirms the frequency of this practice.[30]

Like the Basque monopoly on the whale fishery, which disappeared with the development of the Spitzbergen whale fishery in the 1620s, the initial Basque hegemony in the northwestern Atlantic cod fishery vanished with European exploration of the region. By the middle of the 16th century all the major western European powers -- France, Spain, Portugal, and England -- were engaged in this fishery. Thereafter the international competition for superiority would continue to the present day. As the intricacies of this struggle have been chronicled numerous times,[31] it suffices at this point to add that by the beginning of the 17th century the two main competitors were England and France.

The reasons for this struggle were both economic and political in nature. Economically, dried or salted cod became a major foodstuff in Europe and later in the colonies, so that its production was profitable. Moreover, the fishing industry became a source of consumption for domestic products while fish surpluses could be exported abroad to pay for the country's necessary imports. In this manner, the cod fishery became almost a textbook example of the emerging mercantilist model. Strategically the cod fishery trained large numbers of fishermen/sailors and so became the famed "nursery of seamen" for use in national navies during wartime. At a time when European expansion overseas emphasized the need for naval strength, the strategic implications of the cod fishery could not be overlooked.

All of these economic and strategic considerations were based on the cod's suitability as a preservable food item. The deterioration of fresh cod came from autolysis or self-digestion of the

THE COD FISHERY

tissue by the enzymes and from putrefaction or bacterial decomposition.[32] Fortunately, both these conditions were easily overcome by reducing the moisture content of the flesh either through salting or drying, or a combination of the two.[33] In any case, the whole or "round" cod was first "dressed," i.e. the head and entrails were removed; the backbone was split about a third of the way up from the tail and removed so that the fish lay flat; and usually the black membrane lining the abdominal cavity was rubbed away to produce an attractive finished product. In Iceland and Norway the fish was simply exposed to cold weather drying which produced the famed hard-dried, stock fish. In more southerly regions, where warm weather speeded decomposition, salting was required in addition to air drying. Cod could be preserved solely by a heavy salt pickle or could be salted and then dried. The longer the fish was kept salted before drying the more salt was required. As salt is hygroscopic, heavily salted fish could only be dried to a certain extent before they absorbed moisture from the air. Consequently, lightly salted fish could be dried "harder" than the heavier salted ones. Generally speaking, lightly salted hard-dried cod was the preferred cure on the international market.

The difficulties that attended the curing of good quality dried fish were legion.[34] Failure to bleed the fish and rough or excessive handling encouraged bacterial decomposition. Improper splitting and failure to remove the abdominal lining resulted in a less attractive product. Insufficient salting failed to retard decomposition and excessive salting burned the fish. Mineral impurities in the salt imparted a bitter taste to the fish, delayed the penetration of the salt into the fish, and drew moisture from the air to the finished product.[35] The presence of red haliophilic bacteria in solar salt caused "reddening" of the finished cure, and the presence of brown mold caused eventual putrefaction.[36] Although it is uncertain if the above were present in 18th-century supplies of French solar salt, they certainly plagued 19th-century fishermen. If the fish dried too quickly a salt crust formed on the surface and if they dried too slowly the fish became "slimy."[37]

Slow drying also caused putrefaction, which allowed soft spots to develop in the thicker parts of the fish.[38] On hot days the drying fish could become "sunburnt," with the protein of the fish coagulating like the boiled white of an egg. In general it must be remembered that curing salt fish was a highly skilled art and that any error in the dressing, salting, or drying processes lessened the value of the finished product.

Naturally, given the long history of the fishery and differences in fishing practices, a specialized nomenclature has developed to identify distinct types of fisheries. The most familiar related pairings in this terminology included green and dry, shore and bank, boat and vessel, and migrant and resident. These terms referred respectively to differences in the processing of the catch, the fishing grounds used, the fishing equipment employed, and the labour force engaged. In addition, the term sedentary referred to the prosecution of the fishery from a permanent shore establishment by either resident or migrant fishermen. As the type of fishing gear or the kind of processing of the catch was frequently related to the fishing grounds being used, single terms of the specific pairs were occasionally used interchangeably. For example, the terms green, bank, vessel, and migrant might be used individually to describe a fishery that was actually a composite of all the terms. Without advocating the use of cumbersome multi-adjectives, careful attention has to be paid to the specific meaning of terms describing particular fisheries.

The green fishery referred to the preservation of fish solely through heavy salting whereas the dry fishery, at least in its North American context, referred to a technique by which the fish were first salted and then dried. With abundant and cheap supplies of domestically produced solar salt the French had a relative advantage over the English in the green fishery.[39] French fishermen also had the advantage of a large Catholic market for salt cod which had to be principally satisfied through the green fishery because of the earliness of the Lenten season.[40] As green salted fish gained consumer acceptance, a large and continuous domestic demand for the product, particularly in Paris, proved a mainstay for the French green fishery.

The English, with a smaller domestic salt supply and a greater reliance on exports, concentrated their efforts on the dry fishery, which required lesser quantities of salt. The dry fishery necessitated shore establishments, however, so the English forcibly advanced their claim to the exclusive use of the Avalon peninsula in Newfoundland.[41] Their success in advancing these claims has suggested that the English concentrated on the dry fishery and the French on the green. However, the French were also concerned with

THE COD FISHERY

the dry fishery, as shown by their establishments at Plaisance and later at Isle Royale and by the tenacity with which they lobbied for shore drying rights in the repeated peace negotiations with Britain during the 18th century. The reason for the French interest in the dry fishery was the better preservative qualities in warm climates of dried over green cod. This made dried cod the more desirable commodity for export to the Iberian, the Mediterranean, and later the West Indian markets.

The particular fishing ground used was often directly related to the method of processing the catch. Within the northwestern Atlantic cod fishery there were two types of fishing grounds -- the inshore and the bank. The inshore fishing grounds hugged the coastline and were generally within a dozen miles (1 mile = 1.609 km) of the shore. The bank fishing grounds were actually the submerged plateaus of the continental shelf and were usually 50 miles or more from shore. They included Grand, Green, and St. Pierre banks off Newfoundland, the western banks off Nova Scotia, and Orphan and Bradelle banks in the Gulf of St. Lawrence, as well as the bank surrounding the Magdalen Islands. As no contact with land was needed, the green fishery supported fishing trips of several months' duration to the offshore banks until the requisite amount of fish was caught. The dry fishery lent itself to the exploitation of the inshore fishing grounds with fishermen making daily trips to and from inshore grounds. A combination of these two fisheries also existed in which a relatively long trip of perhaps a month would be made to the banks, after which the heavily salted catch was brought to land for drying.

Understandably, the type of fish processing and the fishing grounds utilized determined the selection of the boat or vessel employed. The green fishery on the offshore banks favoured the use of larger, more seasonal vessels. The inshore dry fishery encouraged the use of small boats or shallops as the fish were taken ashore daily and carrying capacity was less of a consideration. In addition, a number of small shallops had a better chance than a single vessel in finding the dispersed schools of cod. The prosecution of a dry bank fishery necessitated the use of an intermediate-sized vessel. The fore-and-aft rigged schooner or *goélette*, averaging some 35-50 tons (1 ton = 0.907 tonne), proved large enough for the successful exploitation of the bank fishery yet small enough to make the relatively frequent trips to shore without underutilization of cargo space.

Theoretically, both resident colonists and migrant seasonal fishermen from the mother country could participate in all branches of the cod fishery. However, because the catch of the green bank fishery was transported directly to the home market on board the fishing ship, the migrant vessel fishermen probably had the advantage. Participants in the dry fishery often produced a small quantity of green fish towards the end of the season while waiting for final processing of the last batch of drying fish. Both resident and migrant fishermen conducted the dry fishery using either shallops or schooners. As the cod fishery did not usually begin until the end of April or the beginning of May, migrant fishermen easily arrived in the colony in time to make the necessary shore preparations for processing the catch. Permanent residents had an obvious advantage in selecting the best shore properties, an advantage that led to bitter rivalries between migrant and resident fishermen.

The sedentary fishery was closely associated with the development of a resident fishery but was actually dependent on possession of legal title to the land. This fishery usually included dry processing and was conducted from a permanent shore establishment. This procedure was ideally suited to colonial residents and contrasted sharply with the usual land division on a "first come first serve" basis as practised in the migrant fishery. However, there was the danger in the sedentary fishery that legal title to the land would pass into the hands of migrant fishermen who would occupy the land only seasonally. Without some control on non-resident land tenure, colonial development could be greatly hindered.

As might be anticipated from these concerns over the sedentary fishery, the various branches of the cod fishery had differing effects on the development of the North American seaboard. The French green vessel fishery conducted on the offshore banks had no land contact at all, aside from the infrequent trips inshore for fresh water or to repair storm damage. The migrant dry fishery resulted in only marginal colonial development as occupation was only seasonal and French-based fishermen tried to discourage competition from resident fishermen. The resident dry fishery provided permanent settlement but it did not encourage economic diversification. As the dried cod represented the finished product, no additional economic activity was undertaken except in the marketing sector. Although the fishery provided a market for goods and services, some items, like salt, and in some areas, food, were not produced locally. Even in those instances where colonial production was feasible, cheap imports from established areas and the limited size of the market often mitigated against the local firm. Often colonial production was limited to vessel and boat building and the strongest economic stimulus was to the service sector, supplying the labour force and maritime-oriented trades such as coopers and cordwainers.

Although a typically high level of imports, as in 18th-century Isle Royale and 19th-century Newfoundland, discouraged diversification of domestic production, the large volume of dried cod exports encouraged a strong merchandising sector. As the fishing outports were quite independent of each other in terms of actual dried fish production, the merchandising sector provided economic bonds within the colony. The scale of operations of individuals and companies affected the strength of these bonds. Large-scale operations such as those conducted by the Jersey firms in 18th and 19th-century Gaspé and Cape Breton meant that trade links with the mother country were stronger than those with other outports in the colony. Small-scale operations prevented such business harmony and encouraged the development of a local business community. However, the typically small size of outport markets and production worked against the establishment of direct trade links in every outport. Instead, colonial entrepôts developed where the scale of operations warranted direct trade, with the movement of goods to and from the outports being conducted through the coastal trade. This system, which was practised in Isle Royale, ensured that an outport's direct economic bonds were to the colonial entrepôt rather than to its neighbouring outports.

Bearing these considerations in mind, it is necessary at this point to review briefly the development of the French fishery up to the founding of Isle Royale in 1713. After the beginning of the 16th century there was a gradual expansion in the northwestern Atlantic cod fishery and in the development of the international fish trade. France, with the advantage of a large domestic market, was able to concentrate on the bank, green fishery. Indeed, this extensive fishery remained a continued feature of France's cod fishery throughout Isle Royale's existence.[42]

At the same time, the growth of the international dried fish trade encouraged France's participation in the inshore dry fishery. By the middle of the 17th century the French dry fishery was divided between two regions in Newfoundland. The "Petit Nord" stretched along the west coast of the Great Northern Peninsula, and the coast of Chapeau Rouge eventually stretched from Plaisance to Cape Ray but the fishery was concentrated along the Burin Peninsula.[43] In Acadia, development of an extensive migrant fishery was somewhat hindered by a less abundant inshore fishery, a further distance from France, and the occasional vexations caused by the claims of the land proprietors.[44] The French also conducted the dry fishery on the Gaspé peninsula and on the Labrador coast.

More important to the establishment of Isle Royale was the founding of Plaisance in 1662. At Plaisance the establishment of a resident fishery subsequently protected by a small garrison formed a blueprint for the later development of Isle Royale. A small French resident fishery on the south coast of Newfoundland between Trepassey and Cape Despoir had actually preceded the official founding. In 1660, Nicholas Gargot was chosen as the first governor of Plaisance. The development of the nascent colony was slow as residents had to fight stiff competition from migrant fishermen and the efforts of the colonial officials and garrison officers to monopolize the beach areas of Plaisance. Probably as the result of superior fishery facilities, the French resident fishery concentrated at Plaisance. In 1687, 256 of the 640 French inhabitants on the south coast were at Plaisance, which was protected by a garrison of only nine soldiers.[45] War with England during 1688-97 and again during 1702-13 prevented the development of this resident fishery and led to the colony's demise. By the treaty of Utrecht in 1713, the French ceded Plaisance to the English but were confirmed in their possession of the Petit Nord in Newfoundland and of Cape Breton Island.

The French swiftly moved to transfer their settlement from Plaisance to the new colony of Isle Royale, and by early September of 1713 the initial group of 149 men, women, and children had made the transfer. Efforts to broaden this population base by tempting large numbers of French Acadians to forsake the new British regime in Nova Scotia met with only marginal success. The agrarian background of the Acadians did not lend itself to easy absorption into a maritime economy, and the agricultural prospects of Isle Royale, even when coupled with promised freehold land tenure, failed to induce many to emigrate. This early unsuccessful attempt at diversification proved an accurate forerunner of the fishery's supremacy in the new colony.

Having had experience with sedentary fisheries in Gaspé, Acadia, and the Petit Nord as well as at Plaisance, the French Ministry of Marine quickly set up a legal framework for a resident fishery at Isle Royale. Initially the former residents of Plaisance were to be offered properties in Louisbourg, while the migrant fishermen had access to the beaches at Mira and Scatary.[46] The concessions made to the new inhabitants were to be based on their former properties in Plaisance and in proportion to the number of shallops they owned. Married fishing proprietors, whose families would ensure the colony's development, became the object of French official protection. As abuses on the ownership of fishing properties became apparent, the regulations respecting land tenure became increasingly restrictive. For example, single fishing proprietors were forbidden to rent their properties and migrant fishermen were forbidden to conduct the sedentary fishery at all.[47]

Similarly, the areas of commercial activity open to migrant fishermen and merchant captains were restricted to protect the fishing proprietors. An ordinance passed in 1720 required captains of all vessels arriving in Louisbourg to make an exact declaration of the cargo on pain of confiscation.[48] They could sell fishing gear and provisions to anyone, provided they informed the authorities, but were allowed to sell liquor only to merchants or fishing proprietors and not to tavern keepers. Merchants engaged in the fishery were able to retail liquor directly to their own employees only. A later regulation prohibited foreign merchant captains from engaging the fishermen of fishing proprietors and from purchasing supplies from other vessels.[49] This latter measure was designed to limit competition between residents and non-residents and thereby keep prices down. Later, general regulations allowed foreign merchants to sell only aboard vessels, prohibited captains from leaving fishermen in the colony to undertake the autumn fishery, and also attempted to prevent captains from buying the cargoes of vessels from France, Canada, or the West Indies.

Regulations were also passed that directly protected the financial position of the fishing proprietors. In 1743 an ordinance was passed that provided for the comprehensive regulation of the Isle Royale fishery.[50] The wages paid to hired fishermen were specified to eliminate expensive competition for labour, not to provide a minimum wage for the fishermen. Similarly, the hired fishermen were made liable for unnecessary damages to fishing equipment and for any good fishing days lost through negligence on their part.

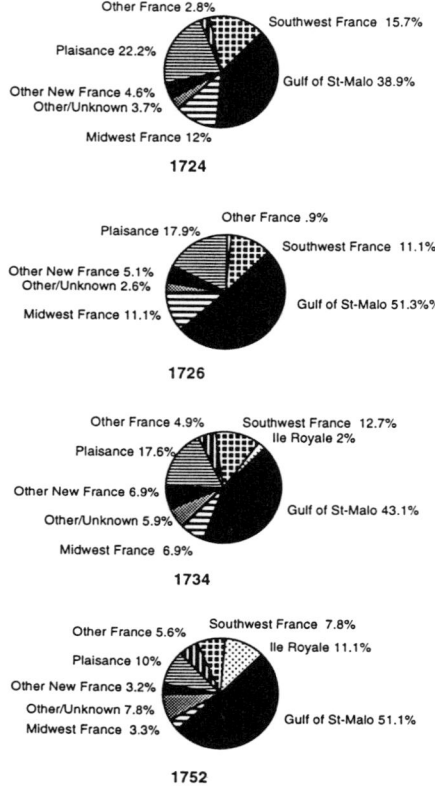

Figure 1. *Export volumes of the Isle Royale cod fishery, 1718-55 (in* quintaux) *(Source: See, B.A. Balcom,* The Cod Fishery of Isle Royale, 1713-58 *[Parks Canada, 1984], pp. 16, 50).*

In addition to this legally fostered resident fishery, migrant vessel fishermen operated from rented shore properties or from temporary establishments on land that was not formally conceded. It was the transfer of France's migrant as well as resident fishery on Newfoundland's south coast to Isle Royale that gave the nascent colony such a great impetus in dried fish production. As shown in Figure 1, the colony's dried fish production had already reached its highest level by 1718-19. Unfortunately, the shortness of the time period and gaps in the statistical material prohibit the use of more sophisticated quantitative techniques in determining trends. However, even a simple bar graph as in Figure 1 is useful in determining levels of production in some periods. Indeed, three periods emerge: one of relatively high production from 1718 to the late 1730s, marked by annual fluctuations and perhaps depression in production in the 1720s; a second of markedly declining production in the 1740s; and a final period of low production during the second French occupation.

The first of the two obvious periods of lower production took place during the 1740s. A decrease in the per unit landings of both shallops and schooners amplified a reduction in the actual numbers of these vessels employed. This decrease in per unit production was particularly severe in the winter shallop fishery which dropped from a high of 180 *quintaux* (a measure of weight equal to 100 *livres* or 48.95 kg or 100 lb., the English quintal or hundredweight weighs 112 lb. or 50.97 kg) per shallop in 1739 to a low of 30 *quintaux* per shallop in 1743. The reduction in the number of shallops and schooners operating in the Isle Royale fishery became more acute prior to the outbreak of war in 1744, as pre-war tensions caused French outfitters to cancel voyages. Any such cancellations had a twofold effect on the colonial fishery as fishing proprietors encountered shortages of transient labour and supplies from France. A similar pattern of pre-war reductions in dried fish production has also been noted in Newfoundland during the 18th century.[51]

The second period of low production in the Isle Royale fishery occurred during the 1750s. Per unit production in both the shallop and schooner fisheries reached the high levels of the 1730s, but total volumes remained low. Initially, the resident fishery remained low as the fishing proprietors had to overcome the difficulties of re-establishing their operations. Within a few years there was a marked expansion in the resident fishery, which was quickly reversed as the threat of war again loomed in the mid-1750s. The failure of the migrant fishery in Isle Royale to reach its former level of participation was the decisive factor in determining the low levels of production in the 1750s. This lower level of migrant participation also had a restrictive effect on the resident fishery. In 1750 the *commissaire-ordonnateur*, Prevost, reported that a labour shortage was limiting the fishing proprietors' catch. The decline in the number of migrant fishing vessels also reduced the amount of transportation available to transient fishermen who worked seasonally in the colony. The outbreak of hostilities in 1755 ended any chance for further development of the French fishery in Isle Royale.

With the exception of these two periods of low production,

the Isle Royale fishery had an annual output of between 120,000 and 170,000 *quintaux* of dried cod. Although production was lower during the 1720s than in the years before and after, the statistical gaps for this decade make conclusions of a depression in output somewhat tentative. A more important trend, which is investigated more fully later in this paper, is the expansion of resident over migrant dried fish production. The total domination of the Isle Royale fishery by residents during the second French occupation contrasts with the strong migrant input prior to the first siege. Leaving this trend aside, the major factors influencing the annual fluctuations in the colonial industry were shortages of labour and supplies, price variations, and weather conditions.

The dominant position of the fishery within Isle Royale's economy cannot be questioned. In an export-oriented economy the fishery accounted for almost 90% of the colony's total exports in 1737 and for almost two-thirds of the total in 1754.[52] This was particularly important in light of the fact that much of Isle Royale's remaining exports actually consisted of re-exports of goods from other areas. If exports only of domestically produced goods were included, the dominance of the fishery would have been nearly absolute.

Within the fishery, production was almost entirely concentrated on one item -- dried cod. Other food fish, such as herring or mackerel, were used only as bait and were not prepared for export, although they were the object of extensive domestic French fisheries. As seen in Table 4, dried cod accounted for over 92% of the estimated value of Isle Royale's fishery during both French occupations.[53] When the value of cod oil, a by-product of the cod fishery, was added to that of dried cod, the concentration of this single fish commodity became even more apparent. Indeed, the only competition to the cod fishery came from "Magdalen oil" derived from the killing of *vache marins* or walruses on the Magdalen Islands. The production of this oil never amounted to 1% of the total value of the fisheries in any year.

Care must be taken in using these figures, however. They were generally compiled by the *commissaire-ordonnateur* and were based on an estimate of the number of shallops and schooners fishing in the colony, multiplied by an average catch for each type, respectively. The amount of cod oil was then proportionately derived from the estimated total catch and a figure was also added for the Magdalen oil. The amounts of dried cod and oil were then multi

THE COD FISHERY

Table 4
The "in France" value of the Isle Royale fishery in *livres*

Year	(1) Cod (livres)	(2) Cod oil (livres)	(3) Magdalen oil (livres)	(4) Total fishery (livres)	(1) as a % of (4)
1716					
1717					
1718	3,130,000	313,000		3,443,000	90.9
1719					
1720					
1721	2,512,000	168,000		2,680,000	93.7
1722					
1723	3,029,000	183,920		3,212,920	94.3
1724					
1725					
1726	2,818,000	140,900		2,958,900	95.2
1727	2,293,000	91,680		2,385,280	96.1
1728					
1729					
1730	3,312,600	165,600	12,000	3,490,200	94.9
1731	3,350,800	167,550	35,000	3,553,350	94.3
1732					
1733	3,307,300	181,830	11,000	3,500,185	94.5
1734	2,796,200	153,780	12,100	2,962,080	94.4
1735	2,849,900	156,750	13,200	3,019,850	94.4
1736	3,022,200	166,210	14,300	3,202,710	94.4
1737	2,986,000	164,230	22,000	3,172,230	94.1
1738	3,049,400	189,640	22,000	3,239,040	94.1
1739	2,873,200	157,960	30,250	3,061,465	93.8
1740	2,463,000	147,780	19,200	2,629,980	93.6
1741				2,585,440	
1742				1,782,680	
1743	1,774,400	106,440	42,000	1,922,840	92.3
1744	1,388,600	83,280	9,600	1,481,480	93.7
1750	1,811,200	108,660		1,919,860	
1751	1,911,600	114,600		2,026,200	94.3
1752				1,771,970	
1753	1,969,000	98,450	17,000	2,083,500	94.5
1754				2,054,075	
1755					

plied by an official value for each commodity. It was at this point that the accuracy and utility of these statistics weakens, because the use of official values failed to reflect price changes. With one exception, dried cod was consistently valued at 20 *livres* per *quintaux* and oil typically varied from 110 to 120 *livres* per *barrique*. Although their prices purported to reflect the value of these commodities in France, their value in Isle Royale was, of course, considerably less.

The Isle Royale value followed the current price along the coast according to the practice established at Plaisance. Although Peter Warren noted in a 1739 review of Isle Royale's fishery that the government annually set the price at about 9 shillings or 8 *livres* per *quintal*, this type of price control appears to have happened only once.[54] In 1724 St. Ovide and de Mésy set the price at 12 *livres* for fishermen selling to their fishing proprietors, but this probably represented a temporary measure.[55] Certainly, sales of dried cod at lower prices were recorded, particularly when the fish in question were not completely dried. It would appear that 10 *livres* per *quintal* represented an average price for the first French occupation. Consequently, by halving the values appearing in Table 4 an approximate colonial value for the fishery can be obtained. However, the use of constant official values has prohibited any meaningful comparison between price and the volume of fishery production.

The values of Isle Royale and Canadian staple exports can be compared, however, utilizing the adjusted evaluation of Isle Royale's fishery. In Table 5[56] the values of total exports from Canada and of fishery exports from Isle Royale are compared. (In the case of Isle Royale's export values these have been reduced by half to approximate the colonial value of the catch.) Isle Royale's fishery exports compared favourably with the total exports of the more populous colony of Canada. It is important to note, however, that A.J.E. Lunn, who originally compiled the Canada figures, felt the amounts were under-estimated. While higher per capita import costs offset commercial gains in Isle Royale, this small colony, on the basis of its fishery, had a combined import and export trade equal in value to the trade of the larger colony of Canada.

Just as the scale of its fishery assured Isle Royale of an important position within the French imperial trade system, it also gave the colony prominence within France's North American fishery. It has been estimated that the annual average of France's total northwestern Atlantic fishery effort may have reached 8 million *livres* between 1720 and 1760 and that Isle Royale accounted for 1.5 to 3.5 million *livres* of this total.[57] Although Isle Royale did not dominate French fishery production it did constitute a major source of supply.

The volume of Isle Royale's fishery production also made Isle Royale a significant competitor within the international cod fishery. In their estimates of the volume rather than the value of Isle

Table 5
Value of total exports from Canada and of fishery products from Isle Royale for various years (in *livres*)

Year	Total exports - Canada (*livres*)	Fishery products - Isle Royale (*livres*)
1726		1,479,450
1727		1,192,640
1729	1,483,198	
1730	1,398,327	1,745,100
1731	1,776,675	
1732	1,483,192	
1733	1,389,047	1,750,092
1736	1,677,696	1,601,355
1739	2,103,868	1,530,732
1740	2,111,107	1,314,990
1753		1,041,750
1754		1,027,037

Royale's fish production, the colonial administrator's reports were probably more accurate. Reports prepared in 1734 and 1735 by the Admiralty in Louisbourg provided greater detail with regard to the winter fishery but were otherwise in close agreement with those prepared by the *commissaire-ordonnateur*.[58] Similarly, there was a reasonably close concurrence between the stated exports of fish in 1737 and the amount of fish produce reported by the *commissaire-ordonnateur*.[59]

Using these figures on Isle Royale's fishery production, comparisons can be made with the fish production of the neighbouring British colonies. Between 1736 and 1739, when Isle Royale's fishery reached its height in volume of production, the colony produced an annual average of 149,120 *quintaux* of dried cod. For the same period the British fishery at Newfoundland, both shore and bank, produced an estimated annual average of 380,400 quintals. In 1745, when war had led to a decrease in production, New England still produced 230,000 quintals.[60] Although Isle Royale did not match the larger British colonies in terms of production it was nevertheless regarded as a serious competitor and a keystone of the French fishery in North America.

The fishery was Isle Royale's strength and its weakness. It stimulated the colony's export-oriented economy and enabled Isle Royale to become an entrepôt within the French imperial system. Even at colonial prices its value in the late 1730s was the equivalent of a subsistance wage for every man, woman, and child in the colony.

In spite of fluctuations in production the fishery provided a fair degree of economic stability to the young colony. However, this concentration on the fishery detracted from the development of other sectors that would have broadened the economic base and increased self-sufficiency. The fishery concentrated the population in areas less suited for diversification into agriculture and lumbering. The labour pool attracted by the fishery was schooled in a maritime economy rather than a land economy. Perhaps most importantly, the fishery encouraged the importation of cheap supplies that kept the costs low but also provided stiff competition for fledgling domestic production.

Notes

1. AN, Col., C¹¹C, Vol. 8, ff. 40-52, "*Memoire sur les affaires presente du Canada et l'établissement du Cap Breton, 1706*" by Raudot, Intendant of Canada.
2. See Christopher Moore, "A Catalogue of Memoires" (manuscript on file, Fortress of Louisbourg, 1973) for references to additional such memoires.
3. Christopher Moore, "Isle Royale in Canadian History" (paper presented for Professor J. Levitt, University of Ottawa, 1976), pp. 13, 21, and 28.
4. Christopher Moore, "Merchant Trade in Louisbourg, Isle Royale" (M.A. thesis, University of Ottawa, 1977), p. 14.
5. Frederick J. Thorpe, "The Politics of French Public Construction in the Islands of the Gulf of St. Lawrence, 1695-1758" (M.A. thesis, University of Ottawa, 1973), p. 149.
6. *Ibid.*, p. 14.
7. Moore, "Merchant Trade in Louisbourg, Isle Royale," pp. 30-34.
8. *Ibid.*, p. 32.
9. *Ibid.*, p. 33.
10. *Ibid.*, p. 15.
11. Harold Innis, "Cape Breton and the French Regime," Royal Society of Canada *Transactions*, Section 11 (1935), p. 64.
12. Christopher Moore, "The Maritime Economy of Isle Royale," *Canada: An Historical Magazine*, Vol. 1, No. 4 (June, 1974), p. 40.
13. James F. Shepherd and Gary M. Walton, *Shipping, Maritime Trade and the Economical Development of Colonial North America* (Cambridge: University Press, 1972), p. 51.
14. Christopher Moore, "Commodity Imports of Louisbourg" (manuscript on file, Fortress of Louisbourg, 1975), p. 28.
15. Innis, "Cape Breton and the French Regime," pp. 65-66.
16. J.S. McLennan, *Louisbourg from its foundation to its Fall 1713 - 1758* (Sydney, N.S.: Fortress Press, 1969), p. 223.
17. Moore, "Merchant Trade in Louisbourg, Isle Royale," p. 25.
18. McLennan, *Louisbourg from its foundation ...*, pp. 221-22.
19. Moore, "Commodity Imports of Louisbourg," pp. 16-19, 26.

20. Moore, "Merchant Trade in Louisbourg, Isle Royale," pp. 34-38.
21. *Ibid.*, p. 37.
22. Andrew Hill Clark, "New England's Role in the Underdevelopment of Cape Breton Island during the French Régime, 1713-1758," *The Canadian Geographer*, Vol. 9 (1965), p. 5.
23. Peter Bower, "Louisbourg: A Focus of Conflict 1745-1748" (manuscript on file, Fortress of Louisbourg, 1970), pp. 439-44.
24. Clark, "New England's Role in the Underdevelopment ...," pp. 5-6.
25. *Ibid.*, pp. 3-4.
26. AN, Col., $C^{11}C$, Vol. 7, ff. 3-9, *Memoire concernant la Decouverte, les Establissement et la Possession de l'Ile de Terre Neuve et l'Origine des Pescheries*, 1710.
27. Selma Barkham, "The Basques: Filling a Gap in our History between Jacques Cartier and Champlain," *Canadian Geographical Journal*, Vol. 96, No. 1 (February/ March 1978), pp. 8-19.
28. T.J.A. LeGoff, "Michel Daccarrette," *Dictionary of Canadian Biography* (Toronto: University of Toronto Press, 1974), Vol. 3, pp. 156-57.
29. Moore, "Merchant Trade in Louisbourg, Isle Royale," p. 43.
30. AN, Outre-Mer, G^3, 2039-1, *pièce 66, Inventaire de la dame Veuve Dastarit, 13 février 1735*.
31. See Harold Innis, *The Cod Fisheries, The History of an International Economy* (Toronto: University of Toronto Press, 1954), for the most detailed account of this rivalry.
32. N.L. MacPherson, *The Dried Codfish Industry* (St. John's: Department of Natural Resources, 1935), pp. 16-17.
33. For more detailed accounts of fish drying see Atlantic Experimental Station for Fisheries, Halifax, "The Preparation of Dried Fish," *Canadian Fisherman* (December 1925); D.L. Cooper, "Fish Drying," *Progress Reports of the Atlantic Coast Stations*, No. 20 (August 1937); Ruth F. Grant, *The Canadian Atlantic Fishery* (Toronto: Ryerson Press, 1934), pp. 72-74; and MacPherson, *The Dried Codfish Industry*, pp. 16-43.
34. MacPherson, *The Dried Codfish Industry*, pp. 43-44.
35. Ernest Hess, "Studies on Salted Fish: 8. Effects of Various Salts on Preservation," *Journal of the Fisheries Research Board of Canada*, Vol. 6, No. 1 (1942), pp. 1-9; and MacPherson, *The Dried Codfish Industry*, pp. 24-25.
36. Ernest Hess and N.E. Gibbons, "Studies on Salted Fish: 10. Effect of Disinfectives and Preservatives on Red Haliophilic Bacteria," *Journal of the Fisheries Research Board of Canada*, Vol. 6, No. 1 (1942), pp. 17-23.
37. H.P. Dussault, "Bacteriology of Light Salted Fish: Sliming," *Progress Report of the Atlantic Coast Station*, No. 55 (March 1953).
38. S.A. Beatty, "Putty Fish," *Progress Reports of the Atlantic Coast Stations*, No. 31 (February 1942).
39. Innis, *The Cod Fisheries ...*, p. 50.
40. *Ibid.*, pp. 48-49.
41. Gillian T. Cell, *English Enterprise in Newfoundland 1577-1660* (Toronto: University of Toronto Press, 1969), p. 5.
42. Charles De La Morandière, *Histoire de la pêche française de la morue dans l'Amerique Septrionale* (Paris: G.P. Maisonneuve et Larosse, 1962), Vol. 2, pp. 613-37.
43. C. Grant Head, *Eighteenth Century Newfoundland: A Geographer's Perspective*, Carleton Library Series (Toronto: McClelland and Stewart, 1976), pp. 11-13 and 15-16.
44. Robert Guitard, "Le déclin de la Compagnie de la Pêche sédentaire en Acadie de 1697

à 1702," *La Société Acadienne: Les Cahiers*, Vol. 9, No. 1 (March 1978), pp. 5-21.
45. Head, *Eighteenth Century Newfoundland* ..., pp. 11-13.
46. AN, Col., B, Vol. 36, f. 47, Pontchartrain à Boyles et Jurats de St. Jean de Luz & Siboure, 1 février 1714.
47. Ibid., F^3, Vol. 50, ff. 150-50v, Ordonnance du Roi qui defend aux Habitants non mariés à L'Isle Royale de louer les Graves et Vignaux à n'y appartinans à Mendou le 20 juin 1723.
48. Ibid., $C^{11}B$, Vol. 5, ff. 157-58, Ordonnance de Police sur divers cas du 27 avril 1720, St. Ovide et de Mezy.
49. Ibid., B, Vol. 45, ff. 929-31, Ordonnance qui confirme celle rendue par les Srs. de St. Ovide et de Mézy le 15 7bre 1721. Le Roy, Paris, 12 Mai 1722.
50. Ibid., F^3, Vol. 50, ff. 254-59, Reglement concernant l'Exploitation de la Pêche de la Morue à l'Isle Royale. Le Roy, Versailles, 20 juin 1743.
51. Head, *Eighteenth Century Newfoundland* ..., p. 65.
52. Moore, "Merchant Trade in Louisbourg, Isle Royale," p. 25.
53. References for Isle Royale Fishery Returns: (1716) AN, Outre-Mer, G^1, Vol. 446, Pièce 54. Récensement Général de l'Isle Royale, 1716; (1718) France. AN, Col., $C^{11}B$, Vol. 3, ff. 206-8. St. Ovide au Ministre, 17 décembre 1718; (1719) AN, Col., $C^{11}B$, Vol. 5, ff. 43v-44. St. Ovide au Conseil, 29 novembre 1719; (1721) AN, Col., $C^{11}C$, Vol. 15, pièce 210. Conseil au St. Ovide et de Mézy, 7 décembre 1721; (1723) AN, Col., $C^{11}B$, Vol. 6, f. 245. Etat des Navires qui sont venus, 12 décembre 1723; (1726) AN, Col., $C^{11}B$, Vol. 8, f. 230, Isle Royalle, 1726; (1727) AN, Col., $C^{11}B$, Vol. 9, f. 259, Isle Royalle, 1727; (1729) AN, Col., $C^{11}B$, Vol. 10, f. 211. Liste Generale des Batteaux, Gouelettes et Chaloupes, 16 décembre 1729; (1730) AN, Col., $C^{11}B$, Vol. 11, f. 69, Isle Royalle, 4 décembre 1730; (1731) AN, Col., $C^{11}B$, Vol. 12, f. 64. Isle Royalle, 1731; (1732) AN, Col., $C^{11}B$, Vol. 13, f. 242. Liste Generale des Batteaux, Gouelettes et Chaloupes, 22 décembre 1732; (1733) AN, Col., $C^{11}B$, Vol. 14, f. 232. Isle Royale 1733 and AN, Col., $C^{11}B$, Vol. 14, f. 234. Estat des Batteaux, Gouelettes et Chaloupes, 1733; (1734) AN, Col., $C^{11}B$, Vol. 16, f. 257. Isle Royalle, 1734 and AN, Col., $C^{11}B$, Vol. 16, f. 119. Estat des Batteaux, Gouelettes et Chaloupes, 1734; (1735) AN, Col., $C^{11}B$, Vol. 17, f. 90. Isle Royalle, 1735; and AN, Col., $C^{11}B$, Vol. 17, f. 127. Etat des Batteaux et Chaloupes, 1735; (1736) AN, Col., $C^{11}B$, Vol. 18, ff. 170-71v. Isle Royale, Pesche et Commerce de l'année 1736; (1737) AN, Col., $C^{11}B$, Vol. 20, ff. 21v-22v. Isle Royale, Pesche et Commerce, 1738 (for 1737) and AN, Col., $C^{11}B$, Vol. 20, f. 326. Etat général des Batteaux et Chaloupes, 1737; (1738) AN, Col., $C^{11}B$, Vol. 10, f. 220. Isle Royalle, 1738 and AN, Col., $C^{11}B$, Vol. 26, ff. 225-26. Isle Royale, Pesche et Commerce, avril 1740 and AN, Col., $C^{11}B$, Vol. 20, f. 334. Estat des Batteaux et Chaloupes, 24 décembre 1738; (1739) AN, Col., $C^{11}B$, Vol. 21, f. 152. Isle Royalle, 1739 and AN, Col., $C^{11}B$, Vol. 26, ff. 225-26. Isle Royale, Pesche et Commerce, avril 1740; (1740) AN, Col., $C^{11}B$, Vol. 23, ff. 160-60v. Isle Royale, Pesche et Commerce, 1740; (1741) AN, Marine, G, Vol. 53, p. 244. Le Produit de la Pêche de l'Isle Royale en 1741; (1742) AN, Col., $C^{11}B$, Vol. 26, ff. 217-18v. Isle Royale, Pesche et Commerce, 1743 and AN, Marine, G, Vol. 53, p. 248. Le Produit de la Pêche; (1743) AN, Col., $C^{11}B$, Vol. 26, ff. 209-10v. Isle Royalle, Commerce et Pêche, janvier 1744 and AN, Col., $C^{11}B$, Vol. 26, ff. 217-18v. Isle Royalle, Pêche et Commerce, 1743; (1744) AN, Col., $C^{11}B$, Vol. 26, ff. 227-28v. Isle Royalle, Pêche et Commerce, 1744; (1750) AN, Col., $C^{11}B$, Vol. 29, f. 206. Prevost au Ministre, 10 décembre 1750; (1751) AN, Marine, G, Vol. 55, ff. 274-75. D'après l'Etat envoie par le Sr. Prevost; (1752) AN, Col., $C^{11}B$, Vol. 33, f. 437v and AN, Col., Série $C^{11}B$, Vol. 33, f. 496. Etat Général des Batiments et Chaloupes en 1752 and AN, Marine, G, Vol. 55, p. 279; (1753) AN, Col., $C^{11}B$, Vol. 33, f. 436, Isle Royalle, 1753; (1754) AN, Col., $C^{11}B$, Vol. 34, ff. 180v-81. Prevost au

THE COD FISHERY

Ministre, 19 décembre 1754.

54. PRO, Admiralty 1, Vol. 2652, Peter Warren, Boston, 9 July 1739, n.p. Conversion to *livres* based on average rate of exchange for 1739 given in John J. McCusker, *Money and Exchange in Europe and America, 1600-1775: A Handbook* (Williamsburg: University of North Carolina Press, 1978), p. 96.

55. AN, Col., F³, Vol. 50, f. 160, *Sur les Representations que nous été faite par les Maitres, Habitant, Pecheurs, et les Marchands ...,* St. Ovide et de Mézy, 21er 7bre 1724.

56. A.J.E. Lunn "Economic Development in New France 1713-1760" (Ph.D. thesis, McGill University, 1942), p. 477. Isle Royale values are taken from Table 4 in this work but have been halved to approximate colonial values.

57. Frederick J. Thorpe, "The Politics of French Public Construction in the Islands of the Gulf of St. Lawrence 1695-1758" (M.A. thesis, University of Ottawa, 1974), p. 2.

58. The Admiralty reports are found in AN, Col., C¹¹B, Vol. 16, f. 119; and *ibid.*, Vol. 17, f. 127; the civil authorities' reports are in *ibid.*, Vol. 16, f. 257; and *ibid.*, Vol. 17, f. 90.

59. See *ibid.*, C¹¹C, Vol. 9, ff. 50-95; and *ibid.*, C¹¹B, Vol. 20, ff. 21v-22v.

60. Innis, *The Cod Fisheries ...,* p. 161.

The Fishermen of Eighteenth-Century Cape Breton: Numbers and Origins[1]

A.J.B. Johnston

The importance of the fishery to the overall economy of Nova Scotia is well-known. From groundfish to shellfish, inshore or offshore, there is barely a settlement along the province's craggy coastline that does not have a stake in one of the various fisheries. Techniques have changed over the years and many more species are now harvested than in the past, but the fishery has always been the foundation of the Nova Scotia economy. Throughout the seventeenth and eighteenth centuries there was one fish species, cod, that was more important than all the others in the harvest from the seas. For generations, whether the area was known as Acadie or Nova Scotia, no other industry came close to the cod fishery in terms of its impact on employment and the economy.

During the colonial era there were actually several fisheries in the waters off Nova Scotia. On national lines, there were the fisheries based in different European countries, which employed tens of thousands of mariners. The vast majority, whatever the nation, stayed only as long as was necessary. They were seasonal employees, sometimes never setting foot on land. Within the French and English fisheries one could also make distinctions based on location (Newfoundland versus Cape Breton, or inshore versus offshore) and on technique ("dry" versus "wet" or "green").

There is now a large literature on the various fisheries of Atlantic Canada.[2] The focus in this article, however, is on only one particular fishery: that undertaken by the residents of Cape Breton during the French Regime. At that time the island was known as Ile

Royale, and its administrative centre was the fortified stronghold of Louisbourg.

Though for decades historians regarded Louisbourg and Ile Royale only in terms of its military context, the colony is now recognized as having had an economic as well as a strategic *raison d'être*. No longer is the eighteenth-century French possession considered simply as an advanced defence post for the rest of New France. Recent studies of the island's economy during the period of French occupation, 1713 to 1758, have demonstrated just how important fishery and trade were to the so-called "Guardian of the Gulf."[3] The strongest sector of the Ile Royale economy was undoubtedly the cod fishery. In B.A. Balcom's recent study, the author concluded that the "cod fishery was the economic base of Ile Royale" and that it "dominated the colony's import and export trades."[4] Given that pre-eminence in the island's economy, together with the traditionally labour-intensive fishery, it comes as no surprise to learn that a major proportion of the colonists on Ile Royale gained their livelihood as either fishermen or shore-workers. This article sets out to determine just how many men were employed in the Ile Royale fishery, where on the island they lived, and where they were from originally.

The best available information on the population of Ile Royale comes from the colonial censuses. Figure 1 summarizes the main census data. It also reveals the degree to which the people employed in the fishery--owners (*"habitant-pêcheurs"*), fishermen, and shore-workers--dominated the resident population on the island, at least during the first period of French occupation, from 1713 to 1745.

During the first period of French occupation, over one-half of all adults[5] on Ile Royale worked in the fishery, on either a seasonal or a full-time basis.[6] It is worth underlining that the total adult figure used to compile the data for Figure 1 *includes* the garrisons at Louisbourg and elsewhere on the island.[7] Also worth mentioning is that, counted under the "civilian" heading, are many people (particularly the wives of the fishing proprietors and their sons over fifteen) who were likely part of the colony's fishing population as well. If their numbers could be determined and then subtracted from "civilians" and added to "fishermen," the dominance of the cod fishery would loom even larger. (Surely, it goes without saying that many of the non-fishing civil population also depended on the fishery, whether as merchants selling supplies, tradesmen doing work, or *cabaretiers* providing food and drink).

The census data on the second period of French occupation, from 1749 to 1759, is not as complete as it was during the 1720s and 1730s, at least in so far as it provides information on the fishing population. There is only one year, 1752, for which we can assemble figures to compare with those from the first period.[8] What the data from that year indicates (see Figure 1) is a sharp decline in the fishing population on the island, both relatively and absolutely. There were several factors at work here, the most important of which was the renewal of Anglo-French hostilities in the region. Having watched Louisbourg fall in 1745, and then the British found Halifax in 1749, the French authorities anticipated future conflicts. Accordingly, they doubled the size of the Ile Royale garrison based at Louisbourg.

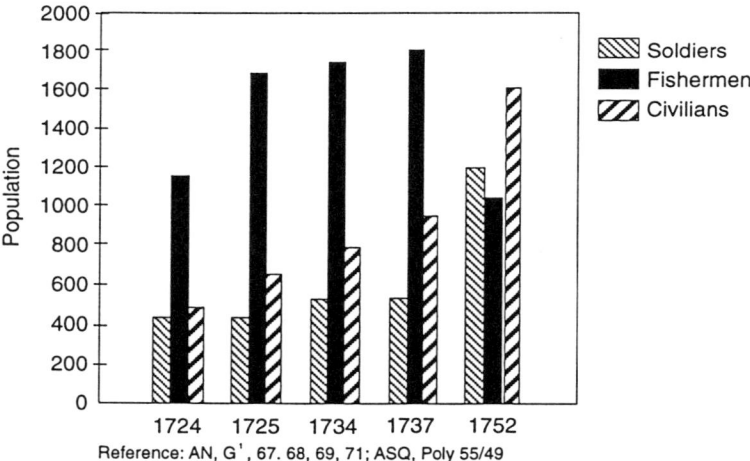

Figure 1. *Adult Population of Ile Royale 1724 - 1752*

Fishermen were influenced by much the same politico-military climate. Many who had been deported to France in the aftermath of Louisbourg's capitulation in 1745 chose not to return to the colony in the 1750s. At Niganiche (Ingonish), a community that had boasted over six hundred inhabitants before 1745 siege, there were only a couple of dozen French settlers during the second period.[9] Other prominent fishing settlements, like Baleine, Lorembec (Lorraine), Scatary, and St.-Esprit, did welcome back more fishermen, but in greatly reduced numbers. In 1734 those four outports had a total population of 973. In 1752 the figure for the same places was only 439.[10] B.A. Balcom has shown that Ile Royale fish catches were down significantly during the 1750s and attributed this to a sharp drop in the offshore migrant fishery.[11] Judging by the census data, that slump in the island's fishery was also due to a steep decline in its resident fishing population. Where one can identify over 1,800 resident fishing adults in 1737, the total for 1752 is under 1,100.

The very same Anglo-French belligerence that kept some fishermen away from Ile Royale in the 1750s led other groups to settle in the colony. Hundreds of Acadians from Nova Scotia came to the island between 1749 and 1755, boosting the populations of some settlements and giving birth to others, like Pointe de la Jeunesse (Grand Narrows) and Baie des Espagnols (Sydney).[12] In addition, there were new communities established along the Mira River, by discharged French soldiers and by German Catholics who fled Halifax and Lunenburg in search of a place to practice their faith openly. All of these groups added to Ile Royale's civilian population, though in truth they did very little for its economy. Most lived at government expense, surviving on rations.

Let us return to the first period of French occupation, when the fishing population was so utterly dominant. A glance at Figure 2 reveals that during that period the preponderance of fishermen on Ile Royale did vary from settlement to settlement. Those ports that had the natural advantages for fishing (proximity to cod stocks and a protected harbour) became fishery centres soon after 1713, when the French colony was established. Once settled, those harbours tended to remain active in the fishery, at least until the first conquest in 1745.

There were only a few communities, such as Port Dauphin (Englishtown) and Port Toulouse (St. Peters) that had small fishing populations. In both cases, there were good reasons why there were relatively few fishermen. Port Dauphin was simply too far from the fishing banks to be a base for the fishery. Port Toulouse, on the other hand, developed a fairly diversified economy, specializing in the coastal carrying trade. In 1726, for instance, Port Toulouse had fifty-nine heads of household, but only six were directly connected with the fishery, and there were only another twenty-two active fishermen.[13] By way of contrast, Port Toulouse had thirty-three household heads that were listed as navigators. Aside from Port Dauphin and Port Toulouse, however, the dominance of the fishery was nearly complete on Ile Royale. Indeed, in many small outports virtually every adult derived his or her living from the fishery. In Baleine and Lorembec, for example, communities just up the coast from Louisbourg, there were respectively 118 of 142 adults and 109 of 125 adults who were directly dependent on the fishery. Similarly, the economy of Niganiche, the colony's second most populous settlement, was almost completely rooted in the cod fishery. Twenty of thirty-nine heads of household were fishermen or fishing proprietors, and 444 of its total adult population of 541 worked in the fishery.[14] Louisbourg, of course, as befitting a military, commercial and administrative centre, had the most diversified economy on Ile Royale. Yet here again, there were far more fishermen than any other civilian occupational group. Using the same 1726 census as an example, there were then 677 adult civilians. Of that number, over half (thirty-five heads of household and 314 "*matelots, pêcheurs* and *graviers*") worked directly in the fishery.

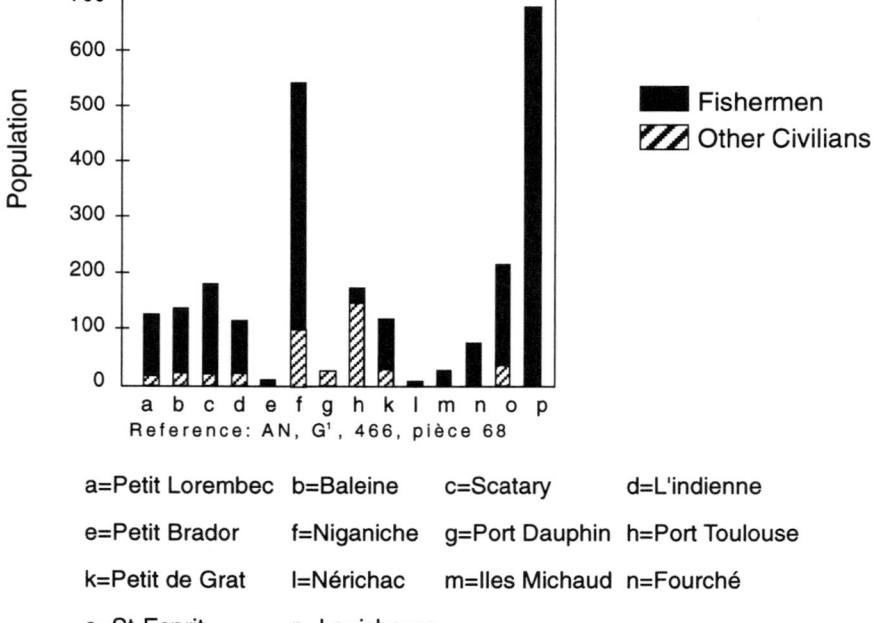

Figure 2. Fishermen of Ile Royale in relation to other adult civilians, 1726

In his study of the cod fishery, B.A. Balcom used the 1752 census by Sieur de la Roque to ascertain the places of origin for 199 of the colony's fishermen. He found that the majority of them were from Normandy, Brittany and Gascony. In fact, most came from relatively small areas: seven dioceses on the Gulf of St.-Malo produced 37.6 per cent of the fishermen, while two largely Basque dioceses along the southwest coast (around Bayonne and St.-Jean-de-Luz) were the places of origin for another 48.7 per cent of the fishing population.[15] In light of the differences outlined above between the fisheries of the first and second periods of French occupation, one wonders how accurately those 1752 figures reflect the situation during the 1720s and 1730s. The enumerations before 1752 were not as detailed as that of Sieur de la Roque, so one cannot so precisely pin-point the origins of the ordinary fishermen of the 1720s and 1730s. Instead, the *recensements* of those early years simply had a

Table 1
Origins of Heads of Household involved in the Ile Royale Fishery, Selected Years.[18]

	1724	1726	1734	1752
Gulf of St.-Malo	42	60	42	46
Midwest France	13	13	7	3
Southwest France	17	13	13	7
Other France	3	1	7	5
Plaisance	24	21	18	9
Ile Royale	--	--	2	10
Other New France	5	6	7	3
Other/Unknown	4	3	6	7
	108	117	102	90*

* *There are no heads of household from Louisbourg included on the original source, the de la Roque census of 1752.*

column set aside for the total number who worked under a particular employer, without giving any indication of names or places of origin. Nonetheless, the data from three returns, those of 1724, 1726 and 1734, is sufficiently extensive to enable a researcher to identify the birthplace of every head of household in the colony who was identified as a *"pêcheur," "maître de grave," "habitant-pêcheur"* (or in the case of a woman, a *"habitant faisant pêche."*[16] These were the people who employed the ordinary fishermen and shore-workers; sometimes only a few, at other times several dozen. The census information reveals that in 1724 there were 108 heads of households involved in the Ile Royale fishery, 117 in 1726, and 102 in 1734. The figure for 1752 stood at ninety, but that was without any entries for Louisbourg, so the actual total was probably twenty or thirty higher.[17]

ASPECTS OF LOUISBOURG

Therefore, despite a drop-off in the second period in both the productivity of the fishery and in the total number of fishermen involved, there seems to have been about the same number of fishing heads of household on the island (see Table 1).

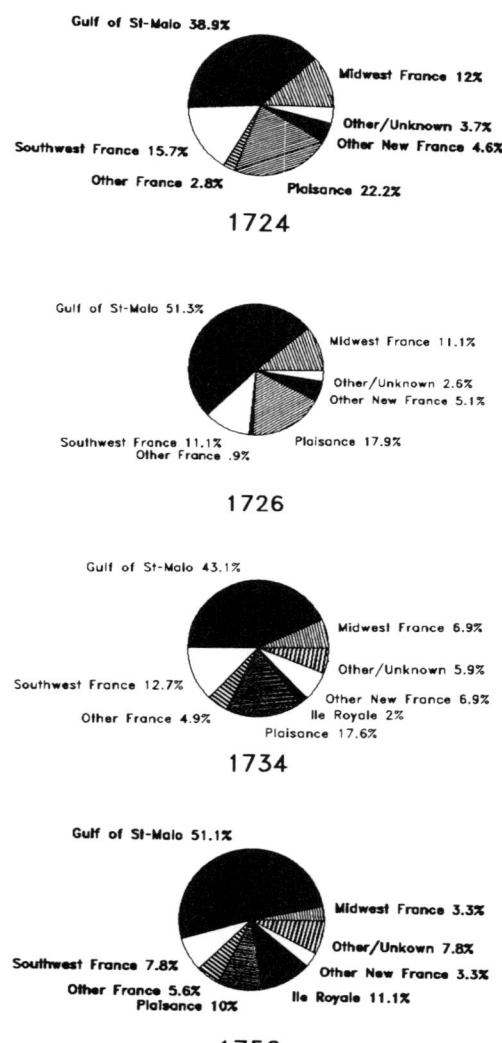

Figure 3. Origins of Heads of Household involved in Ile Royale Fishery

THE FISHERMEN

Looking exclusively at places of origin (Table 1 and Figure 3), one quickly sees that during the period before 1745 the fishing heads of household came from four main areas: the Gulf of St.-Malo, Plaisance (Placentia, Newfoundland), southwest France, and midwest France (basically from Nantes to Bordeaux). Of these four areas, the Gulf of St.-Malo easily outdistanced the others. The picture changes somewhat during the second period, with a noticeable increase in Ile Royale-born fishermen and a decline in those from everywhere else except the Gulf of St.-Malo, which maintained its thoroughly dominant position.

It is not surprising that large numbers of fishermen and fishing proprietors had moved to Ile Royale from gulf ports such as St.-Malo and Granville (and also from inland towns such as Avranches, Coutances, Dol-de-Bretagne, St.-Brieux and Dinan). There was a strong connection between gulf fishermen and "Atlantic Canada" throughout the colonial period.[19] Yet the proportion of fishing heads of household from that small region, roughly half of Ile Royale's total, is extremely high. The evidence from the seventeenth-century French fishery in Newfoundland shows no such similar dominance.[20] And if there was any correlation at all between the heads of household and the ordinary fishermen out in the boats, then the figures suggest that there were many more Gulf of St.-Malo *pêcheurs* on Ile Royale during the 1720s and 1730s than the 37.6 per cent recorded in 1752. In fact, the 1752 figures only weigh as heavily as they do in favour of southwest France because of a single settlement. Sieur de la Roque entered on the listing for Petit Degrat two large groupings of non-resident fishermen, totalling eighty-two men, all of whom were from the southwest corner of France (indeed nearly all of them were from St.-Jean-de-Luz). At virtually every other fishing community on the island fishermen from the Gulf of St.-Malo predominated.

The next largest fishing group after the individuals from the Gulf of St.-Malo were those who had been born in Plaisance, the Newfoundland fishing establishment from which the colony's founders had come in 1713. This was a group whose numbers could only decline as the years went by. But as the Plaisance fishermen became less numerous, the totals of others born in New France (particularly Ile Royale) were increasing. The third and fourth most common place of origin for the resident Ile Royale fishing population was in southwest and midwest France. The numbers from both regions were significantly below those from the Gulf of St.-Malo, even if they were combined into a grouping that would be entitled "Atlantic France."

One final question that intrigued me in going through the census data was the thought that there might be some link between place of origin and place of residence on Ile Royale. Keeping in mind the settlement pattern on St.-Pierre et Miquelon,[21] where settlers from a particular region clustered together (and apart from others from different regions), I hypothesized that something similar might have happened on Ile Royale. People from the same region (be it the Gulf of St.-Malo or Plaisance) might have chosen -- because of language, custom, economic advantage, family ties or some other reason -- to live near one another in their new setting. Alas, the evidence proved otherwise. In only one instance, at Petit Lorembec, was there a consistent indication of the fishing population being from a single area. In 1724, all five heads of household were from the Gulf of St.-Malo; in 1726 it was nine of ten. In 1734 there were nineteen fishing heads of household there, thirteen of whom were from the Gulf of St.-Malo, while in 1752 eleven of sixteen were from that region and a twelfth from nearby Bayeux. In the other Ile Royale settlements, however, the population was more of a mix of people from different places, though generally fishing proprietors from the Norman/Breton gulf predominated.

There are two main points that emerge from this brief article. First, during the 1713-45 period of French occupation on Ile Royale, the fishing population (fishing proprietors, fishermen, and shore-workers) was far and away the largest component group on the island. There were more adults involved in the fishery than all the other civilians and soldiers combined. This situation changed drastically during the second period of occupation (1749-58). Because of increased Anglo-French hostility, as an aftermath to the War of the Austrian Succession and in anticipation of the Seven Years War, there were dramatic increases in both the garrison and the ordinary civilian population of Ile Royale, the latter growing largely as a result of Acadians relocating there. But the threat of capture at sea, or simply disruption of their work, was enough to convince many fishermen not to re-establish on Ile Royale when the island was reoccupied by the French after 1748. As a result, the resident fishing population of Ile Royale dropped significantly during the 1750s.

The second point concerns the places of origin of the heads of household on the island who were involved in the fishery. Regardless of the year selected, a clear majority of those individuals came from ports and inland towns along the Gulf of St.-Malo. Others came from midwest or southwest France, and from communities elsewhere in New France, but in nothing like the numbers from that part of the Normandy/Brittany coastline. This preponderance of Bretons and Normans among the fishing heads of households was greater on Ile Royale than it had been in the old French colony at Plaisance, back in the late seventeenth and early eighteenth centuries.

Notes

1. The author would like to thank his colleagues, B.A. Balcom and Kenneth Donovan, for their comments and assistance.
2. See Harold Innis, *The Cod Fisheries: The History of an International Economy* (Toronto: University of Toronto Press, 1954); Charles de la Morandière, *Histoire de la pêche française de la marine dans l'Amérique septemtrionale* (Paris: G.P. Maisonneuve et Larose, 1962); A.H. Clark, *Acadia, The Geography of Early Nova Scotia to 1760* (Milwaukee: The University of Wisconsin Press, 1968); B.A. Balcom, *The Cod Fishery of Isle Royale, 1713-1758* (Ottawa: Parks Canada, 1984); and most recently, Michel Mollat, ed., *Histoire des pêches maritimes en France* (Paris: Editions Privat, 1987).
3. The most recent in-depth study of the Louisbourg economy is John Robert McNeill's *Atlantic Empires of France and Spain: Louisbourg and Havana, 1700-1763* (Chapel Hill: The University of North Carolina Press, 1985). See also Balcom, *Cod Fishery* and Christopher Moore, "The Other Louisbourg: Trade and Merchant Enterprise in Ile Royale, 1713-58," *Histoire sociale/Social History*, Vol. 12, (1978), pp. 79-96. It must be said that J.S. McLennan pointed out the importance of fishing and trade in *Louisbourg from its foundation to its fall*, first published in 1918. McLennan did not, however, provide an in-depth study of the colonial economy. On Louisbourg's place in the overall context of the French defence of the eastern coast of Canada, see Fred J. Thorpe, *Remparts lointains: la politique française des travaux publics à Terre-Neuve et à l'Ile Royale 1690-1758* (Ottawa: Université d'Ottawa, 1980). For a detailed study of Louisbourg's fortifications, see Bruce W. Fry, *"An appearance of strength" The Fortifications of Louisbourg*, 2 vols. (Ottawa: Parks Canada, 1984).
4. Balcom, *Cod Fishery*, p. 65.
5. To obtain the total "adult" population, I have not included two categories listed on the original census. These were the entries for "*garçons au dessous 15 ans*" and "*filles.*" I did, however, include any entries under the "*servantes et domestiques*" heading, as well as any "*garçons au dessus de 15 ans.*" Were I to exclude teenaged boys fifteen and up, the predominance of the fishermen would loom even larger among the adult population. In fact I suspect that many of these young males, particularly in households where a parent or guardian was a "*habitant-pêcheur,*" were directly involved in the fishery. Nonetheless, I have not added any to my details.
6. This statement is based on the census returns for 1724, 1726, 1734, and 1737. AN, Outre-Mer, G^1, Vol. 466, pièces 67, 68, 69 and 71-suite.

7. Allan Greer gives the totals, ideal and real, for the colony's garrison in "*The Soldiers of Isle Royale, 1720-45,*" *History and Archaeology*, Vol. 28 (Ottawa: Parks Canada, 1979). The military figure for 1752 comes from: ASQ, Surlaville Papers, Poly 55, No. 49.

8. One must use ASQ, Poly 55, No. 49 which gives information on Louisbourg and AN, Outre-Mer, G¹, Vol. 466, nos. 81-82 for details on the other settlements on Ile Royale.

9. Sieur de la Roque does not record anyone as being at Niganiche. But there were still fishermen there. See "État general des havres ..."(1751), in BG, Carton 1, no. 25; J.S. Bourinot, "Cape Breton and its Memorials of the French Regime," Royal Society of Canada *Transactions*, Section 2 (1892), pp. 173-175.

10. Barbara Schmeisser, "The Population of Louisbourg, 1713-1758," *Manuscript Report Series*, Vol. 303 (Ottawa: Parks Canada, 1976), p. 8.

11. Balcom, *Cod Fishery*, pp. 16-17.

12. A.J.B. Johnston, "Before the Loyalists: Acadians in the Sydney Area, 1749-54," *Cape Breton's Magazine*, Vol. 12 (June 1988).

13. "*Recensement général des habitants Établis à l'Isle Royalle fait en l'année 1726,*" AN, Outre-Mer, G¹, Vol. 466, pièce 68.

14. *Ibid.*

15. Balcom, *Cod Fishery*, pp. 55-56.

16. On the question of women in the fishery, I was able to identify four women who were fishing proprietors in 1724, one in 1726, and seven in 1734.

17. The 1752 de la Roque census, published in the *Report on Canadian Archives for the Year 1905* (Ottawa: S.E. Dawson, 1906), does not include data on Louisbourg. I was able to ascertain how many fishermen there were in the capital of Ile Royale by using another census, the "*Recensement numérique de Louisbourg par rues et totaux Généraux ...,*" in ASQ, Poly 55, no. 49. That census, unfortunately, does not list heads of household and their occupations.

18. AN, Outre-Mer, G¹, Vol. 466, pièces 67, 68, 69, 81-2.

19. For an introduction to the magnitude and importance of the fishery conducted by *pêcheurs* from the Gulf of St.-Malo, see J.F. Brière, "Le trafic terre-neuvier malouin dans la première moitié du XVIIIe siècle (1713-1755)," *Histoire social/Social History*, Vol. 11 (1978), pp. 356-374.

20. For a comparison with the seventeenth century, see John Mannion and Gordon Handcock, "The 17th Century Fishery," in Cole Harris, ed., *Historical Atlas of Canada* (Toronto: University of Toronto Press, 1987), Vol. 1, Plate 23.

21. Michel Poirier, *Les Acadiens aux Isles Saint-Pierre et Miquelon, 1758-1828* (Moncton: Editions d'Acadie, 1984), p. 47.

The Price and Profits of Accommodation: Massachusetts - Louisbourg Trade, 1713-1744

Donald F. Chard

War ravaged much of New England in the last decade of the seventeenth and the first decade of the eighteenth centuries. Northern areas were particularly hard hit: Maine was so badly ravaged that its population in 1717 was still less than it had been in 1660. In the 1690s, residents of some frontier towns were forbidden to flee their homes because of the need for a buffer against French and Indian attackers and because Bostonians resented the presence of penniless refugees on their doorsteps. When a second conflict broke out with the French in 1702, many of the same problems recurred. By 1706, some Bostonians felt very threatened. Samuel Sewall, prominent Boston merchant, experienced nightmares about the situation:

> Last night I dreamed I saw a vast number of French coming towards us, for multitude and Huddle like a great Flock of Sheep. It put me into a great consternation, and made me think of hiding in some Thicket. The impression remain'd upon me after my Waking. GOD Defend.[1]

Sewall had good reasons to fear the French. In 1707 Boston's trade declined drastically because of the activities of French privateers. One observer reported that "Boston hath been a place of great trade, but the warr have extremely impoverished them, so that the trade is not now one-third of what it was."[2] Port Royal, then capital of Acadia and refuge for a number of the privateers harassing New England, fell to the English in October 1710, but not before a fierce assault on New England shipping by French marauders. In the last year in which the French controlled Port Royal, privateers from there seized some thirty-five English vessels, including nine within five days no more than fifteen leagues from Boston.

It is little wonder, then, that when the War of the Spanish Succession ended in 1713 there was fear in North America that New England would enjoy little relief from French rivalry. Samuel Vetch, first English governor of Nova Scotia, and a leading advocate of English expansion in North America, warned the Board of Trade that France might apply to Cape Breton Island all the money formerly devoted to Acadia and Newfoundland, and that Louisbourg would become a major privateering center. Vetch's fears appeared to have been realized when Nova Scotia Indians, allied to the French authorities on Cape Breton Island, prevented Massachusetts fishermen from establishing themselves anywhere in Nova Scotia except at Canso, across the strait from Cape Breton Island. The situation worsened until 1715, when Indians forced Cyprian Southack of Boston to abandon his fishing establishment on Nova Scotia's south shore. Indians seized some twenty-seven New England fishing vessels in the course of the year, and Massachusetts had to send two commissioners to Nova Scotia to negotiate a release of the vessels.

French occupation of Cape Breton Island and influence in Nova Scotia worried some New Englanders, but to others it spelled opportunity. Massachusetts' merchants quickly grasped the potential of trade with Ile Royale, as the French named their colony, and they pursued that trade avidly until the beginning of the War of the Austrian Succession in 1744.

In accommodating themselves to the French, Massachusetts merchants had to cope with a series of obstacles. This was the main price of accommodation. There were three main threats to accommodation between 1713 and 1744, the first of which came in 1718 when fishing interests precipitated a confrontation with the French over control of Canso. French mercantilist policy posed the second major threat to accommodation and trade and was most serious in the late 1720s when metropolitan French officials attempted to reduce drastically, if not eliminate, trade between English colonies and Ile Royale. The third challenge came from British mercantilist policies and was of greatest concern to New Englanders in the early 1730s.

Although the price of accommodation, in terms of wrangling with opponents of trade, was considerable, it was clearly outweighed by the profits. For over thirty years, New England merchants traded with their counterparts at Louisbourg. Some of the Massachusetts merchant kings of the period were involved in the trade: men such as the Pepperrells (father and son), and Peter Faneuil. By the last decade before war disrupted trade, forty to fifty New England vessels visited Ile Royale each year. The English sold a wide assortment of goods to the French, but foodstuffs, building materials, and ships dominated the list. At Louisbourg, New Englanders obtained large quantities of molasses to fuel Boston's rum distilleries. They also secured rum itself, indigo, coal, and French manufactured goods.

Trade with Ile Royale began within a year of the founding of Louisbourg in 1713 and was based on the inability of the French empire to supply the colony of Ile Royale as capably as could New England merchants. French settlers began to arrive at Louisbourg in the summer of 1713. That winter they suffered greatly from inadequate provisioning. They began slaughtering their cattle in December, and by spring only two of the original twenty-one cattle were still alive. Some settlers developed scurvy that winter. Relief from France was slow in reaching the island in 1714. Drift ice remained off the coast until the end of May, making it impossible for French supply vessels to get to Louisbourg until then. The first French vessel to arrive in 1744 was in the ice fields for twenty days. Another vessel, carrying provisions to the outlying settlements of Miré (Mira), was wrecked in passage. Unexplained delays in the departure of vessels from France further exacerbated the situation.

Whether or not they recognized that a French colony dependent on them for supplies was less of a long-term threat than a colony which could be sustained by the French empire, Massachusetts' merchants moved quickly to secure a portion of the Louisbourg market. Acadians who visited Ile Royale in 1714 reported seeing New England vessels at Louisbourg and elsewhere. One of the vessels was from Boston; another was from Casco Bay. Both ships carried boards, salt, cattle and other goods. Among the customers for the cargoes was Joseph Monbeton de Brouillon (called Saint-Ovide), then king's lieutenant and from 1717 to 1739 Governor of the colony. Saint-Ovide purchased for himself the entire contents of four Boston merchantmen in 1714.[3]

As soon as the trade began, some British officials in North America sought to halt it. Samuel Vetch's successor as Governor of Nova Scotia, Francis Nicholson, mentioned the trade to Governor

Joseph Dudley of Massachusetts several times in 1714 and expressed apprehension that New Englanders would send more vessels in the spring of 1715. Nicholson also expressed a belief that the French would have to draw on New England for supplies if they were to develop a sizeable establishment on Cape Breton Island. To forestall this eventuality, Nicholson advised New England governors and customs agents to use "all lawfull ways and means" to prevent French development of Cape Breton. Anticipating the methods by which some of the trade would be conducted, Nicholson said that he supposed that vessels bound for the island would enter for "Newfoundland or some place here abouts ...."[4]

Nicholson's complaints met with a prompt response in Massachusetts. The Council read his letter two days after it was written and then launched an investigation into the matter. It ordered the examination of three French officers then in Boston to determine the nature of their business in the city. The French apparently satisfied the Council that their presence did not constitute a threat to the interests of Massachusetts or the British empire generally. Nevertheless, on 3 January 1715 the Massachusetts Council drew up a proclamation forbidding any correspondence, trade, commerce, or any other dealings with the French of Canada, Cape Breton or any other French colony. The proclamation specifically prohibited the shipping of provisions, lumber or any other supplies to the French. This action would at first seem to indicate a determination of the Massachusetts government to give Nicholson its wholehearted support. But, on closer scrutiny, it appears that the Council had reservations about placing overly strict or lengthy restrictions on trade with the French. The proclamation was to be in effect only "until His Majesty's Pleasure be known therein." In March 1715, the Council advised customs collectors in Massachusetts to use all possible methods to discover any vessels whatsoever trading to Cape Breton, Canada, or any other place inhabited by subjects of the French king, but to judge from the rarity of seizures, the customs officials could not have had the means to carry out their instructions.

At Louisbourg, trade was accepted and encouraged. Major Jacques L'Hermitte, engineer at Louisbourg in 1714 and 1715, reported at the end of 1714 that trade with Boston had been open all summer and that Governor Costebelle had accepted it. French records for this period, although fragmentary in dealing with Louisbourg shipping, suggest that Massachusetts regulations had no effect on trade between the two colonies. L'Hermitte suggested that New Englanders sold goods at Louisbourg at lower prices than could French merchants, which gave Louisbourg merchants a considerable incentive to trade with the New Englanders.

Although they wanted trade with Massachusetts and the other New England colonies, the French authorities at Louisbourg wanted the trade confined within certain limits. By 1716, Louisbourg authorities had imposed controls on New England vessels calling at that port. When four or five New England vessels put in to Louisbourg because of bad weather and a need for food and water, a sergeant and two soldiers boarded each ship, and obliged each vessel to leave within twenty-four hours.

Contacts and trade elsewhere were more difficult to police. One French official complained of a *"liaison trop grande"* between fishermen of the two nations. The situation was particularly troublesome at Port Toulouse, because of the lack of conscientious enforcement of trade regulations there and because of the settlement's proximity to Canso.

Louisbourg officials could not find an easy solution to the problems of the Port Toulouse-Canso area. A report of early 1717 indicated that both French and English lived at Canso, and there were suggestions that Governor Costebelle tolerated the situation. To these allegations Costebelle replied that toleration of the situation was necessary to keep the strait between Cape Breton Island and Nova Scotia open to the French. As for trade in the area, he suggested that it was necessary because of problems in receiving supplies from merchants in French ports such as Bayonne, Nantes, and St. Jean de Luz. The Council of Marine in France was apparently unsatisfied with such explanations. The Council, noting in a memoir of September 1717 that trade was easily and commonly conducted at Port Toulouse, proceeded to forbid all commerce with the English by inhabitants of the village. Issuing decrees was easier than enforcing them. The Louisbourg authorities probably could not rely on the garrison at Port Toulouse to regulate trade. The soldiers there were reportedly so undisciplined that they passed much of their time in taverns and worked only when it pleased them to do so. It was said to be impossible to get them to perform even the most pressing tasks. Only the suppression of the taverns, one report advised, would bring about a restoration of order.[5]

While Louisbourg officials brooded about English-French

contacts, Massachusetts officials and entrepreneurs took steps to protect their interests. Their actions threatened the Anglo-French entente which had developed after the Treaty of Utrecht, but New Englanders were prepared to take the risk despite the implications for trade. In 1718 some Massachusetts residents with fishing interests at Canso began to agitate for the eviction of the French from the area and for a forceful assertion of Britain's claim to jurisdiction over Canso as a territory dependent on Nova Scotia.

Cyprian Southack, former commander of *Province Galley* of Massachusetts, operator of a fishing station at Canso, and the sponsor of the abortive enterprise at Port Roseway, played a key role in the affair. In registering the first known complaint about French activity in the Canso area, Southack declared that "a great many French commanders of ships with their men," had come from Cape Breton to fish at Canso and to the west. Southack also charged that one particular Frenchman from Cape Breton had built a house and stages at Canso and "makes all the mischief he can ... against the English interest."[6] Other complaints followed. In June 1718, Governor Shute of Massachusetts received a memorial declaring that about 300 Frenchmen had taken possession of the area and erected houses in it. "There is a ship from France in the harbour and more dayly expected, they have seized the best places for making fish, and threaten the English with a removal, pretending that they act by the advice and direction of the Governor of Cape Breton."[7] A memorandum by Cyprian Southack supported the complaint.

Prompted by the spate of complaints about French encroachments and French-encouraged Indian hostility, Governor Shute dispatched H.M.S. *Squirrel* to Canso and Louisbourg in August 1718 to investigate the matter. Captain Thomas Smart commanded the vessel, accompanied by Cyprian Southack. The investigation resulted in the seizure of French property at Canso and the eviction of French residents, after a protest was lodged with Louisbourg authorities.

Protests by individual French merchants and the French government, discussion of the affair by an Anglo-French boundary commission, and reprisals by Indians and French inhabitants of Ile Royale all ensued from Massachusetts' action in 1718. But the Massachusetts government had made its point. In light of the Anglo-French entente it dared not attempt the destruction of Ile Royale, but it was determined to establish firm control over Canso. The price Massachusetts paid, in terms of raids on the establishment at Canso, did not shake English control of the area, and by 1720 the Louisbourg trade was once more of sufficient volume to worry Massachusetts' Governor Shute.

In early 1720, Shute asked his legislature to ban trade with Ile Royale. In a message to the Council, Shute claimed that Massachusetts and New Hampshire "constantly supplied the French of Cape Breton with provisions and other stores," and suggested that a French and Indian raid on Canso in August might not have been possible if goods had not reached Ile Royale from New England. Some three weeks after Shute's statement, three members of the Council formed a committee with members of the House of Representatives to consider the Governor's request. They subsequently drew up a bill to effect a ban, but the House of Representatives refused its assent. In March 1721 Shute renewed his appeal for a ban: "I must again recommend it, hoping it will have a better fare this session, lest otherwise it should be thought by the Government at Home that we have more regard for some private man's interest than to his Majesties Treaties or the Public Good."[8] Once more Shute's arguments fell on deaf ears. The Council passed legislation "to prevent Carrying on an illegal Trade to Cape Breton alias Louisbourg," and when the bill was sent to the House a message was attached to impress that body with the need for passage of the bill. The message noted that Governor Phillips of Nova Scotia had complained to Governor Shute about supplies going to Cape Breton from New England. Phillips warned that he would be obliged to represent the state of affairs to the authorities in Britain. Moreover, the message to the House alleged that an unidentified French officer from Cape Breton had admitted that except for supplies received from New England, the French would have had to abandon the colony. Such information failed to sway the House, which rejected the bill, declaring "We then did not, neither do we now know, or are informed of any within this Government, that do Trade there ...."[9]

Although the volume and the value of New England's trade with Louisbourg in the early 1720s is difficult to determine with precision, it was of sufficient importance to attract several prominent Massachusetts merchants. This fact may explain, at least in part, the reluctance of the Massachusetts House of Representatives to ban the trade. For instance, one of the Bowdoins, possibly James Bowdoin, was involved in trade with Ile Royale in 1720. That year,

Bowdoin consigned a cargo of pork to William Pickering of Salem. Pickering, one of the first New Englanders to do business at Canso after the end of the War of the Spanish Succession, conveyed the pork to Cape Breton.[10] Pickering later disappeared with his vessel, and it is not known if anyone else maintained the trade for Bowdoin. The fact of Bowdoin's involvement in the Cape Breton trade is significant. Not only does it prove an interest in the Cape Breton trade by prominent Massachusetts merchants, but it also anticipated the entrance of Peter Faneuil in the trade in the 1720s, in which trade Faneuil became extensively involved.

Massachusetts' trade with Ile Royale was also extensive enough that it involved merchants of the other New England colonies, as the case of Joshua Peirce illustrates. Peirce, a native of Portsmouth, New Hampshire, had five or six schooners fishing at Canso by 1723. By 1726, he was selling livestock and lumber at Louisbourg, and by 1728 he was engaged in cooperative ventures to the West Indies with a Louisbourg merchant named Dolebra. In the autumn of 1728, Peirce arranged to send his partner a brigantine loaded with items such as boards, bricks, sheep, and cattle. Peirce instructed Dolebra to sell the cargo at Louisbourg and then to send the vessel to Martinique under a French master. From there, the vessel was to return to Boston, where the English captain would assume command again.[11] The arrangements were sophisticated and somewhat clandestine, prompted no doubt by French edicts of 1717 and 1728 which excluded all foreign commerce from French islands in the West Indies in order to make both imports of the islands the monopoly of the French empire. It is clear from Peirce's activities that Boston merchants sometimes used merchants of other colonies to facilitate their trade with Ile Royale, and through Ile Royale with the French West Indies.

On occasion, Peirce used Canso to mask the nature of his activities. In 1733 one of Peirce's vessels, carrying goods from Louisbourg to Boston, entered Canso to disguise the origin of its cargo of molasses and other French goods. Peirce explained to his Boston buyer that there would now be no danger of the goods being seized at either Portsmouth or Boston.[12] Such precautions may not really have been necessary, as Boston merchants enjoyed a special relationship with the customs collector there. On the death of John Jekyll the elder, who held the customs collector's post from 1717 to 1733, the *Boston Weekly Newsletter* reported that by his "courteous Behaviour to the Merchant, he became the Darling of all fair Traders ... with much humanity (he) took pleasure in directing Masters of Vessels how they ought to avoid the Breach of the Acts of Trade."[13]

On the whole, French imperial trade regulations posed a greater nuisance to Massachusetts merchants than did British regulations. In 1722 the King of France decreed that trade with the English for "Livestock and lumber" was permissible when there was need for these items at Louisbourg, but at the same time he declared that trade in other items was forbidden except under "the most pressing and indispensable need."[14] Regulations such as those of 1722 (and the earlier edicts of 1717) appear to have been more honored in the breach than in the observance, to judge from the complaints of inhabitants and officials alike at Ile Royale, and from the occasional reiteration of trade regulations by authorities in France. In 1724, for instance, a number of inhabitants of Ile Royale complained to the Minister of the Marine that a great number of English (New England) ships came to Ile Royale and, under the pretext of bringing permitted goods, brought prohibited materials such as tar, pitch, salt, lard, tobacco, and even cloth. In 1726, authorities in France repeated their orders to Louisbourg officials on trade with foreign vessels. The entry of any merchandise from foreign colonies was forbidden except for livestock, provisions, building materials, and in case of need, flour. Guards were to be placed on all foreign ships to ensure that they complied with these regulations.

Despite these oft-repeated instructions, St. Malo merchants complained in 1727 that Governor Saint-Ovide allowed foreigners to trade in prohibited goods. They also claimed that New Englanders received gold and silver when there was any at Louisbourg, and fish when there was not. One St. Malo merchant charged that Saint-Ovide maltreated and imprisoned him and the crew of his ship *Prudent* for having brought about the arrest of a New England ship trading at Louisbourg. In his defense, Saint-Ovide claimed that the merchant had boarded the ship in question with fifteen to twenty armed men and had maltreated the captain.[15]

According to Louisbourg Admiralty officials, Saint-Ovide also interfered with their activities. In April 1727, Admiralty officials seized the brigantine *Travellor*, whose captain admitted making a false declaration of goods landed, having neglected to declare £243 worth of tobacco and other unspecified items. Saint-Ovide had intervened and returned the confiscated goods. Not long after this, the Minister of the Marine warned Saint-Ovide that "It is to your interest that there should be no more complaints on this score."[16] Saint-Ovide defended his actions by asserting that everything he had done had been for the good of the community and had not benefited any individual.

In 1727 new regulations, precipitated in part perhaps by the difficulties early in the year, heralded a stiff challenge by authorities in France to Massachusetts-Ile Royale trade. Maurepas, Minister of the Marine from 1724 to 1749, and a mercantilist of considerable conviction, decided to ban all trade between the French and English colonies in North America. His edict of November 1727 was, however, not registered at Louisbourg until October 1730, until which time trade continued. Within a few months of imposition of the ban some merchants were complaining about it. St. Jean de Luz merchants declared in December 1730 that they needed English ships to carry on the fishery and that the ban deprived them of the vessels.[17]

Louisbourg officials soon began using loopholes in French trade regulations in order to guarantee access to the colony's New England suppliers. In 1731, Governor Saint-Ovide allowed four New England ships to trade at Ile Royale on the grounds that the contractor working on the fortifications was in great need of bricks and planks. The Governor also acknowledged having permitted New Englanders to sell cattle, sheep, poultry, Indian wheat, apples, and onions, because the colony allegedly suffered shortages of food. Louisbourg authorities also permitted New Englanders to sell five ships there in 1731, and thirteen in 1732.[18]

In 1733, Louisbourg officials continued to sanction trade with New England on the grounds that there were shortages in the colony. In the first eight months of 1733 some thirty-two English ships, mostly from Massachusetts, arrived at Louisbourg. Trade continued at this level for the next ten years. From 1733 to 1743, an average of fifty ships a year reached Louisbourg from Acadia and New England. The average tonnage of the New England vessels at Louisbourg in 1742, one of the few years for which figures are available, was 40.5 tons.

Throughout the period, Massachusetts merchants traded at Louisbourg confidently. The merchant community did not reflect the concern Boston newspapers expressed at the continued erection of fortifications on Cape Breton Island. In September 1733, the *Boston Gazette* published a report that the French were still adding to Louisbourg's defenses although they allegedly already had nearly 200 guns mounted on the batteries there. The French were also said to have started fortifications at Port Toulouse. The newspaper expressed concern about the works in case of war between France and Britain. It noted that "poor Canso ... lies neglected, without so much as one gun for its defense, and in the neighbourhood of so powerful a rival in the fishery."[19]

Boston merchants doing business at Canso took a rather different view of the military establishment at Canso, as is apparent from a 1732 memorial of Massachusetts and New Hampshire merchants to the Governor of Nova Scotia. The merchants complained that the Canso garrison committed depredations on the fishing establishment and on warehouses there. Among the signers of the petition were such prominent merchants as Peter and Andrew Faneuil, Stephen Botineau, Charles Apthorp, Jacob Wendall, and Joshua and Nathaniel Peirce. Governor Phillips responded to their complaints by establishing a court of sessions at Canso, composed of justices of the peace authorized to meet weekly. Several of those who had complained of the disorderly garrison, such as Joshua Peirce and Thomas Kilby, received appointments as justices.

Just as New England merchants were sensitive to anything at Canso or Cape Breton which might have interrupted or otherwise impeded trade with the French, their representatives in the Massachusetts government demonstrated a like determination to silence or counteract publicity about illegal trade. Thus, they showed great concern at statements Jeremiah Dunbar made before a committee of the House of Commons in 1730, to the effect that New England timber reserved for the Crown was being cut by private individuals who then exported it from Boston to the French colonies. Dunbar reportedly charged that "most of the principal people in that country were involved," and that "some of the richest men in Boston got their estates by exporting timber and importing French sugar, rum, and silks." Cape Breton was not mentioned in the report, but Dunbar had reportedly said that there were merchants in Boston who were factors for the French and, in that capacity, had ships built and registered in their own names. Afterwards they transferred the ships to masters sent to Boston by the French to bring the vessels to the French colonies.[20] This was basically the same technique Joshua Peirce used in his dealings with his partner at Louisbourg.

An anxious Massachusetts House of Representatives set up a committee to investigate the report, because they felt that it contained "sundry injurious restrictions and false insinuations of the people of this Province their trade and Business ...." Dunbar, then residing in Boston, was summoned before the committee, where he declared that parts of the statements attributed to him were false, that he had said nothing about illegal imports of French silks. The committee then called on Samuel Waldo and Joshua Winslow, who had been present at the Commons hearings at which Dunbar had testified. They stated that the report in the possession of the Representatives contained the substance of what Dunbar had said, including the comment about silks. Dunbar again denied the charge, but the committee concluded that he had misrepresented "His Majesty's good subjects of New-England to the Honourable the Commons of Great Britain."

No doubt Dunbar's charges had embarrassed the Massachusetts government, despite their denials of his charges. Governor Belcher subsequently took a strong stand against illegal trade. In 1731, Belcher reiterated the provisions of the Treaty of Neutrality of 1686, which authorized the confiscation of any French or English vessel caught fishing or trading in the territorial waters of the other sovereign's colonies. His actions suggests that some Massachusetts authorities wanted to give appearance of opposition to illicit trade, but the proclamations were at the same time an admission that such trade took place. Belcher noted that "divers French Vessels have entered the Ports of this Province under Pretence of being disabled and hindered from proceeding on their voyages."[21] The real purpose of the calls, Belcher suggested, was to carry on illegal trade. Belcher also reminded the colony of an act passed in 1701 entitled "an act for the preventing of Danger by the French residing within this Province." According to the terms of this act, French residents of Massachusetts were not permitted to live in seaports or on the frontier without a license from the governor and council.[22] Belcher's move can only have been directed against the Huguenot community in Massachusetts, members of which had traded with the French in Acadia during the War of the League of Augsburg in the 1690s, and traded with the French at Louisbourg in Belcher's own day.

Curbs on Huguenot contacts with the French would not,

however, have stopped trade with Ile Royale, because there were also prominent non-Huguenot merchants such as the Messrs. William Pepperrell trading there along with a host of less well known individuals. The Pepperrells traded with Ile Royale for more than a decade, despite some losses, such as the wrecking at Port Toulouse of a vessel in which they had an interest in 1721. The master of the vessel, a sloop called *Prosperous,* saved only the clothes on his back.[23]

This voyage to Cape Breton by Pepperrell interests was not an isolated venture. The same year in which *Prosperous* was lost, Pepperrell sent *John and Mary* to the same area. He instructed the captain, John More, to dispose of his cargo to either the French or the English. The cargo was typical of those destined for the Canso-Port Toulouse area. It consisted of 2,500 feet of boards and planks, 5,500 staves, four calves, some cows, twenty-four sheep, one hogshead of rum, and two hogsheads of tobacco. Pepperrell specifically directed More to call at Port Toulouse and "See and bring home what our Vessels have got to send home." Moreover, Pepperrell instructed More to sell the vessel if he could get £200 sterling or goods of that value for it.[24]

In 1723, the Pepperrell operations in the Canso-Port Toulouse area suffered another loss with the death of Captain John Watkins, son-in-law to the senior Pepperrell. Watkins was killed at Canso by either French or Indians. When he learned of the event, Pepperrell wrote to Major William Cosby, commander of the Canso garrison, to ask his assistance in settling Watkins' affairs and securing his effects, described as very considerable. In 1726, the Pepperrells still conducted business at Port Toulouse, as is made clear by their correspondence dealing with the disposal of a vessel left at Port Toulouse upon the death of Captain John Dearing, with whom the Pepperrells were joint owners.[25]

In the 1730s, undaunted by their earlier reverses in dealings in the area, the Pepperrells made use of Louisbourg to facilitate trade with the French West Indies, particularly with Martinique. Details of this trade are sketchy, but the Pepperrells had sent ships to the West Indies via Louisbourg by at least 1729, when Hughes Grangent, a Martinique merchant, wrote Pepperrell that a small boat belonging to the latter had arrived at Martinique from Louisbourg. Grangent, who owed Pepperrell and a third party, Benjamin Clark, over £5,000 Massachusetts currency, indicated that he would remit rum and molasses to Boston in payment. In Grangent's account of the transaction there are references to four different New England ships taking part in his trade with Pepperrell.[26]

Doing business with Grangent was sometimes difficult. In January 1731, Grangent complained to Pepperrell of the latter having held up two brigantines, thus making their entry at Louisbourg difficult for some unspecified reason. As an alternative to sending the vessels to Louisbourg, Grangent suggested sending them to St. Lucia. In reply, Pepperrell stated that there had been a delay in fitting out the vessels because of an outbreak of smallpox at Boston. There were other obstacles in the way of the transaction as well. Grangent still owed Pepperrell over £500 "New England money," and Pepperrell insisted on payment of the debt before he would send the ships: "I shall write to Mr. Daccaratt Junior at Lewisbourg on Cape Brittain and if he will send us effects [I] will dispatch the two brigs. But I shall not advance any more money." To make sure that the point was clearly understood, Pepperrell remarked that he did not "care to Venture to Send them to St. Lucia or Louisbourg untill the money is Secured in some English place, it is too Great a risque ...."[27]

Other New England merchants, such as Peter Faneuil of Boston, managed to conduct trade with the French with less apparent difficulty. For Faneuil, the Cape Breton trade may have been only a small part of his overall operations, but he nevertheless pursued it avidly. Faneuil's first known venture to Louisbourg occurred in 1728 when he received sixty-one barrels of sugar, and over thirty-two tierces of molasses from Louisbourg. In 1729 Faneuil received shipments of rum, sugar, molasses, sweetmeats, cotton, wool, cocoa, wine, brandy, and silks from Louisbourg. The goods were sent there by merchants in Guadeloupe and La Rochelle.[28]

From at least 1729 to 1733, Peter Faneuil did business at Louisbourg with Abraham Tabois. Tabois, otherwise unidentified, was a middleman for Faneuil, forwarding goods to Faneuil on the account of merchants in La Rochelle and possibly for West Indian merchants also. By 1733, Faneuil had developed an arrangement with Joshua Peirce whereby he acted as an intermediary and a shipper of goods from Louisbourg to Boston. Joshua's brother Nathaniel carried molasses and other goods from Louisbourg to Boston for the Faneuil interests in November 1733.[29]

Whether or not the Peirces still handled business at Louisbourg for Faneuil in the late 1730s is unclear. The Peirces made voyages to Canso as late as 1737, but by that time Peter Faneuil had appointed Thomas Kilby as his agent at Canso and conducted much of his Louisbourg trade through him. In selecting Kilby as his agent, Faneuil obtained the services of an individual with an intimate knowledge of the Canso area, an individual who, if not then well acquainted with Louisbourg would soon become very familiar with it. After completing his studies at Harvard in 1726, Kilby became a merchant, with interests at Canso, where he was granted land some time prior to 1729, and named a justice of the peace in 1730.[30]

Kilby looked after both trade at Louisbourg and fishing matters at Canso. In a letter of June 1737, Peter Faneuil instructed Kilby to supervise the loading with fish of a ship bound for Bilboa, and to secure cargoes for three other ships. In the same letter, Faneuil also instructed Kilby to go to Louisbourg and dispose of a sloop and its cargo there or to send the sloop back to Boston. Faneuil advised Kilby that he would give him credit for a sum of money at Louisbourg, implying that he had maintained contacts there since the earlier ventures under the auspices of Joshua Peirce. In addition to selling the sloop and her cargo, Kilby was instructed to see if any indigo, rum or molasses was available, "or anything ye will turn to account here ...." At the same time, Faneuil requested Kilby to find out what was in demand at Louisbourg, and advise him, so that the appropriate goods might be sent there. Shortly afterwards, Faneuil sent Kilby a cargo of lumber, salt, and other goods, and instructed him to dispose of them and to buy indigo.[31]

Prices at Louisbourg were not always favorable, but must generally have been good. In July 1737, Faneuil wrote Kilby that "the French were starving for want of provisions they may thank themselves for it for when we used to carry it to 'em they would give nothing for it ...." Although Faneuil grumbled about the prices he received for his goods at Louisbourg previously, that did not stop him from doing business there, nor did it keep other New Englanders away in any great numbers. In 1736, there were thirty-five vessels from New England and Acadia at Louisbourg (most of them New England vessels), and the year before that there were fifty-two English colonial vessels there.[32]

In the summer of 1737, demand at Louisbourg was good, and prompted the involvement in a trading venture of Peter Warren, who would in 1745 lead the naval squadron which assisted William Pepperrell in seizing the town. A shortage of provisions at

Louisbourg in 1737 prompted Governor Saint-Ovide to write to Faneuil and promise that any Englishmen who came with provisions would have his protection.³³ Upon receipt of this news, Faneuil and Captain Peter Warren decided to send Kilby a sloop with a cargo of biscuit to sell to the French. In exchange for the food Faneuil wanted rum, molasses, and cash. Faneuil gave Kilby explicit directions to purchase Cape François rum, which was available from "Mr. Morpain ... and no one else." Faneuil estimated that he and Warren would clear between £400 and £500 on the voyage, and clearly outweighed any qualms they may have had at dealing with a noted former privateersman.

Faneuil's correspondence with Kilby reveals several facets of his involvement with Louisbourg. Faneuil's interests were extensive enough to require his agent's presence at Louisbourg frequently and facilitated Faneuil's trade with France. Not content merely with purchasing whatever French goods were available at Louisbourg, Faneuil went beyond that and corresponded with two Bordeaux merchants, Etienne Sigal and P. Griffon. This suggests that although Louisbourg merchants handled some aspects of transactions between New England merchants and their counterparts in France and the French West Indies, there were occasions on which the principals would discuss their transactions directly and eliminate the middle-man at Louisbourg or relegate him to a minor role.

Although there is little correspondence by New England merchants trading with Louisbourg in the 1740s, there is evidence that the trade continued to grow then, for a variety of reasons. For one thing, Ile St. Jean (present-day Prince Edward Island), failed to become a reliable source of foodstuffs for Ile Royale. In 1741 the continued failure of the French empire to meet all the needs of Ile Royale is apparent in the fact that fifty New England vessels called at Louisbourg and in 1742 approximately the same number arrived. Severe shortages kept demand for English colonial produce high. In June 1742, François Bigot, then a highly placed official at Louisbourg, wrote that misery had grown in the colony and that there was little or no bread and no vegetables whatsoever available. Officials in France made it clear to Bigot that he should send to France for supplies when Canada could not provide them. Bigot agreed to follow the order, but observed that it would be expensive for the colony because goods which came from France were always more expensive than those from New England.³⁴

Again in 1743, shortages at Louisbourg led officials there to seek large amounts of foodstuffs from the English colonies. Not only could the colony of Canada not export food to Louisbourg, but its officials requested Louisbourg officials to obtain supplies from New England for Canada. Gilles Hocquart, intendant of Canada, requested 4,000 or more quarts of flour, because caterpillars threatened the wheat crop in Canada. In August, word reached Louisbourg that the threat was not as severe as at first anticipated. By that time Louisbourg officials had sent to Canso for the flour, 800 to 900 quintals of biscuit, a cargo of corn, vegetables, and 4,000 quintals of cod.[35]

That the French would turn so quickly to Canso for supplies reveals much about the evolution of trade between Ile Royale and New England between 1713 and the 1740s. At first, contacts had been somewhat haphazard. There is no evidence of the involvement of Massachusetts merchants of any consequence prior to Bowdoin's involvement in 1720. By the late 1720s merchants such as the Peirces, Pepperrells, and Peter Faneuil had developed contacts at Louisbourg which enabled them to obtain goods there from France and the French West Indies. Faneuil maintained an agent at Canso to look after his affairs there and at Louisbourg. Both Faneuil and the Pepperrells also corresponded with merchants in the West Indies, and Peter Faneuil corresponded with merchants in France, indicating that while Louisbourg was a useful place through which to obtain the products of other parts of the French empire, by the late 1730s Louisbourg merchants may have played a secondary part in the trade.

French officials at Louisbourg accepted the trade from the very beginning as a necessary means of providing the inhabitants of the colony with provisions and building materials, and in order to guarantee a market for goods coming to Louisbourg from other parts of the French empire. Authorities in France came to accept this state of affairs even though it contradicted the mercantilist precepts on which French imperial trade policy was based.

As for the New Englanders, led by Massachusetts merchants and mariners, they pursued the Louisbourg trade relentlessly until the eve of the War of the Austrian Succession in 1744. They also managed to obtain a near monopoly on the shipping of English colonial goods to Louisbourg. Only two of the English colonial vessels whose visits to Louisbourg were recorded by the French for 1742 and 1743 came from outside New England, and the bulk of the

New England vessels came from Massachusetts. At first, New Englanders conducted trade with Ile Royale openly. Early attempts by governors of Massachusetts and New Hampshire to stop the trade failed, as did efforts to control the trade in the 1730s by such means as the Molasses Act of 1733.

Mercantilist-inspired Navigation Acts, and similarly inspired French trade regulations bowed to colonial realities which dictated that colonists would trade wherever they could do so with profit. Merchants of both Massachusetts and Ile Royale would undoubtedly have subscribed to the words of Joseph Robineau de Villebon, the French governor of Acadia, who immediately on his arrival in the colony in 1691 had to make considerable adjustment to colonial realities. He explained to his superiors that "Without these compromises it would be impossible to exist in this country ...."

Notes

1. "Diary of Samuel Sewall," 4 April 1706, Massachusetts Historical Society *Collections*, 5th Series (New York: Farrar, Straus and Giroux, 1973), Vol. 6, 157.
2. Colonel Robert Quary to the Council of Trade and Plantations, 10 January 1708, *Calendar of State Papers, Colonial Series, America and the West Indies*, Vol. 23, No. 1273.
3. Public Archives of Nova Scotia, MG7, 52, 53, Declaration of Denis & Bernard Godet of Annapolis Royal, 1 September 1714; B. Pothier, "Joseph de Monbeton de Brouillon, dit Saint-Ovide," *Dictionary of Canadian Biography* (Toronto: University of Toronto Press, 1974), Vol. 3, p. 454.
4. Public Archives of Nova Scotia, MG7, 49, Governor Francis Nicholson of Nova Scotia to Governor Joseph Dudley of Massachusetts, Boston, 25 December 1714.
5. AN, Col., $C^{11}B$, Vol. 11, f. 274, De la Forest (? to the Minister of Marine), 12 September 1717.
6. PRO, CO 217/2, ff. 188, 189, Cyprian Southack to Lieutenant Governor John Doucett of Nova Scotia, Boston, 9 January 1718.
7. *Ibid.*, f. 283, Memorial to Governor Shute, the Council and General Court of Massachusetts by Oliver Noyes et. al., Boston, June 1718.
8. PRO, CO 5/794, p. 123, Massachusetts Council Minutes, 15 March 1721.
9. PRO, 6/794, f. 85, Massachusetts House of Representatives to Governor Shute, November 1720.
10. Salem, Mass., Essex Institute, Pickering & Derby Papers, 10, Giles Hall to Mrs. Hannah Pickering, Boston, 11 September 1723.
11. Harvard University, Baker Library, Peirce Letter Book, Peirce to Dolebra, Portsmouth, 10 September 1728.
12. *Ibid.*, Peirce Letter Book, Peirce to Peter Faneuil, Portsmouth, 9, 30 November 1733.
13. T. Barrow, *Trade & Empire, The British Customs Service in Colonial America 1660-1775* (Cambridge, Mass.: Harvard University Press, 1967), p. 169.
14. AN, Col., $C^{11}B$, Vol. 14, f. 235, Memorial of the King to Saint-Ovide and de

MASSACHUSETTS - LOUISBOURG TRADE, 1713-1744

Mézy, 12 May 1722.
15. *Ibid.*, Vol. 10, ff. 24, 25, 29, Complaint enclosed in a letter from the ministry of the Marine to Saint-Ovide, 17 May 1728.
16. AN, Col., B, Vol. 52, f. 582v, Maurepas to Saint-Ovide and de Mézy, 18 June 1728.
17. AN, Col., C¹¹B, Vol. 11, ff. 111-13, Officers of the Admiralty, Louisbourg, 5 December 1730.
18. *Ibid.*, Vol. 13, ff. 7, 110, de Mézy to the Minister of the Marine, Louisbourg, 3 February 1732, list of New England ships sold at Louisbourg in 1732.
19. *Boston Gazette*, 17 September 1733.
20. *New England Weekly Journal*, 8 January 1733.
21. *Boston Gazette*, 16 August 1731.
22. *Ibid.*
23. Boston, New England Historical and Genealogical Society, Pepperrell MS., Book 2, E. Pearse to William Pepperrell, London, 6 December 1721.
24. Portland, Maine Historical Society, Pepperrell Papers, Box 212, 1718-1721, Orders and Bills of Lading, July 1721; *Ibid.*, Pepperrell Papers, Collection 35, No. 12, p. 5, William Pepperrell to Captain John More, Piscataqua, 25 July 1721.
25. *Ibid.*, William Pepperrell, Sr. to Captain Thomas Richards, 8 August 1726.
26. *Ibid.*, Acct. of Mes. H. Grangent with Wm. Pepperrell & B. Clark, 13 November 1729.
27. *Ibid*, H. Grangent to William Pepperrell, Martinique, 11 January 1731.
28. Baker Library, P. Faneuil Ledger, 1730-1732, 3, Invoices nos. 119, 120, 121, 1, 10 September and 17 November 1729.
29. *Ibid.*, Peirce Letter Book, J. Peirce to P. Faneuil, Portsmouth, 9, 30 November 1733.
30. PRO, CO 217/6, f. 150, Governor Richard Philipps to John Henshaw *et al.*
31. Baker Library, Faneuil Letter Book, Faneuil to Thomas Kilby, Boston, 20 June 1737.
32. AN, Col., C¹¹B, Vol. 18, f. 170, Account of Trade for 1736.
33. Baker Library, Faneuil Letter Book, Faneuil to Kilby, Boston, 19 April 1737.
34. AN, Col., C¹¹B, Vol. 24, ff. 87-89, Bigot to the Minister, Louisbourg, 18 June 1742.
35. La Rochelle, Archives Départementales, Charente-Maritime, B, Amirauté de Louisbourg, registre B272, ff. 510-515, 555-560.

The Other Louisbourg: Trade and Merchant Enterprise in Ile Royale 1713-58[1]

Christopher Moore

Studies highlighting the economic rather than the military history of eighteenth-century New France have never given much attention to Louisbourg and Ile Royale. Ile Royale has typically been characterized as "little more than a buffer zone protecting the approaches to Canada." Even when its purchases of Canadian foodstuffs have been noted, the colony has been judged too small a market to be significant in New France's trade. Louisbourg remains the costly ineffectual fortress where economic activity was the preserve of corrupt officials and New England smugglers.[2]

    In fact, Ile Royale was a major participant in the surge of French maritime trade that followed the Treaty of Utrecht. Within a few years of its foundation in 1713, the new colony was producing and exporting stocks of cod worth about three times as much as Canada's annual beaver fur exports (Tables 1 and 2), though Ile Royale was only one of several areas where the French fishing fleets exploited the cod resource. Cod production on this scale allowed Ile Royale to build a maritime trade that rivalled Canada's in absolute value and far exceeded it on a per capita basis. Furthermore this trade saw a significant degree of colonial participation, and a merchant community quickly developed in Ile Royale. The growth of that community and its response to the harder times which began about 1740 provide material for a useful comparison of the commercial experiences of the two branches of New France, the one in the Saint Lawrence river valley and the newer, smaller one on Cape Breton Island.

Table 1[3]
Fish Catches at Ile Royale (in quintals)

Year	(1) Residents' Catch	(2) Total Catch	(3) 1 as % of 2
1718	76,000	156,000	48.5
1719	85,120	156,520	54.3
1721	78,000	125,600	62.1
1723	72,000	121,160	59.4
1726	104,000	140,000	74.2
1727	80,305	114,680	70.0
1730	121,454	165,630	73.3
1731	128,645	167,540	76.7
1733	108,904	165,345	65.8
1734	107,272	139,810	76.7
1735	109,017	142,495	76.5
1736	112,957	151,110	74.7
1737	119,857	149,300	80.2
1738	116,859	152,470	76.6
1739	100,161	143,660	69.7
1740	82,228	123,150	66.7
1742		83,410	
1743	61,249	88,720	69.0
1744	44,612	69,430	64.2
1751		95,580	
1752		83,130	
1753	78,940	98,450	80.1
1754	86,240	97,729	88.2

Table 2[4]
European Value of Cod and Fur Exports (in *livres*)

Four Year Averages	Estimated European Ile Value of Ile Royal Cod	Canadian Furs at La Roche
1718-21	3,183,000	465,783
1722-25	3,212,920	635,951
1726-29	2,672,090	1,221,272
1730-33	3,502,912	1,181,830
1734-37	3,089,218	967,903
1738-41	2,976,828	1,098,208
1742-45	1,729,000	1,946,980
1746-49		1,160,707
1750-53	1,950,615	1,413,625
1754-57		1,985,348
1758-61		506,125

Ile Royale's only product was dried cod. The patterns of settlement and labour recruitment dictated by the fishing industry limited the development of other industries and of subsistence agriculture. As the colony grew larger, its demand for imported supplies of all kinds increased. As a result Ile Royale used its large volumes of cod to pay for imports not only of its food supplies but also of virtually all the other components of its material culture. Within five years of its foundation, Ile Royale was selling its cod and buying supplies through trade with five regions: France, the French West Indies, Canada, the British American colonies, and Acadia. France sent preserved food, wine, fishing equipment, cloth, and a wide range of European manufactures in exchange for cod, much of which it sold in Spain and the Mediterranean. The West Indies sent rum and other sugar products, buying cod, livestock, and building materials. Canada sent wheat, dried vegetables, and a little tobacco and bought French and West Indian goods. The British colonies, principally Massachusetts,[5] sent fresh food, large quantities of lumber and brick, and several vessels annually, to be exchanged for rum and molasses. Acadia marketed its furs, fish, livestock, and wheat at Louisbourg and bought European hardwares. This network, a diversified trade which added re-export business to the exchange of locally produced cod for imported supplies, was firmly established in Ile Royale by 1720.[6]

Ile Royale's success within this framework can best be examined by reference to the colony's economic position around 1737. Not only was the period 1735-40 one in which trade was relatively well documented, it was also the culmination of a quarter century of stable conditions and growing volumes of trade, soon to be superceded by a period of challenge and change.

By 1737 immigration and demographic growth had given Ile Royale and its dependency, Ile Saint-Jean, a population of 5181 residents. Nearly 2,000 of these colonists lived in Louisbourg.[7] As the colonial capital, designed and fortified by military engineers, Louisbourg was home to most of the colonial administration[8] and to a garrison of nearly 600 soldiers, mostly of the colonial regular troops. It was also the colony's commercial centre, far outstripping the other settlements as a destination for trading vessels. Louisbourg had the port facilities, administrative agencies, and commercial support industries which trade required and it had become the home of most of the colony's merchants. Coastal shipping linked Louisbourg and the outports, most of which appear to have been economic satellites of the capital.

In 1737 trade with France, the Antilles, New England,

TRADE AND MERCHANT ENTERPRISE

Canada, and Acadia brought 130 trading vessels to Ile Royale, mostly to the port of Louisbourg.[9] With a combined tonnage in excess of 7,500 *tonneaux*, the ships brought cargo worth a recorded value of 1,418,680 *livres*. Fifty-one vessels from France carried the greatest proportion of these goods: 1,022,600 *livres*, or 72 percent of all imports. The French West Indian islands were the second most important source of imports. In nineteen ships from Grenada, Martinique, Guadeloupe, and Saint-Domingue came cargo worth 247,050 *livres*, 17 percent of all imports. The other three regions trailed far behind. The British colonies sent 103,000 *livres*, about 7 percent of imports. Canada and Acadia together sent about 4 percent of Ile Royale's imports, with sales of 23,850 *livres* and 22,990 *livres* respectively. The small Canadian sales of 1737 cannot be taken as typical, for a severe crop failure had almost eliminated Canada's ability to export grain that year. During the 1720s and 1730s, Ile Royale had come to depend on large imports of wheat and flour from Canada, the colony's major supplier of these products. Forewarned that Canada would not fulfil this supply role in 1737, Ile Royale turned to France and New England for its wheat requirements. Wheat products worth at least 100,000 *livres* were brought from France and about 25,000 *livres* worth of the same goods came from New England to replace the missing supplies from Canada, which had sent wheat products worth 150,000 *livres* or more in each of several previous years. Hence France and New England were unusually well represented in the imports of 1737, while Canada's sales were much smaller than usual. Comparing the 1737 figures with partial data for other years suggests that had Ile Royale drawn its normal amounts of grain from Canada in 1737, Canada would have provided about ten percent of Ile Royale's total imports.[10]

The cargoes exported from Ile Royale were less completely recorded. Vessels from Europe hauled away cargo worth 1,082,400 *livres*, 147,000 *livres* worth was purchased by vessels from the West Indies, and Canadian vessels bought 72,000 *livres* worth, but the destinations of these cargoes were not specified. Cod was overwhelmingly the most important item in these recorded exports: 1,448,000 *livres* out of 1,459,500 *livres*. Unfortunately, exports to New England and Acadia went unrecorded in the 1737 trade records. Sugar, rum, and other Caribbean goods, omitted from the export record, were the most valuable exports to New England. Judging by the amount of these products imported, the volume of shipping between Ile Royale and New England, and New England's purchases in other years, the missing exports to New England and Acadia should have approached 200,000 *livres* in 1737.[12]

Table 3[11]
Recorded Value of Imports & Exports of Ile Royale

Year	France	Antilles	Imports American Colonies	Canada	Acadia	Total
1732				202,500		
1733				67,300		
1735				241,300		
1736				167,000		
1737	1,022,579	247,049	102,198	23,851	22,994	1,418,680
1739	770,209	288,870	50,478	142,452	25,865	1,277,881
1740	641,302	269,315	49,147	196,403	27,130	1,183,298

Year	France	Antilles	Imports American Colonies	Canada	Acadia	Total
1741	582,269	282,911	40,343	282,514	56,946	1,244,986
1742	726,742	414,722	(.......... 284,717 ....)			1,429,181
1743	817,555	566,078	(.......... 417,818 ....)			1,802,443
1752	1,124,137	1,180,246	488,037	13,276		2,805,696+
1754	1,437,256	1,188,917		39,607		2,665,780+

Year	France	Antilles	Exports American Colonies	Canada	Acadia	Total
1737						1,499,448+
1739						1,258,987
1740	1,175,756	242,804	70,678	53,439	19,208	1,571,885
1741	859,715	477,849	42,355	43,114	35,998	1,459,031
1742	943,365	256,326	(.......... 189,547 ....)			1,389,238
1743	878,565	482,917	(.......... 458,032 ....)			1,819,514
1752			654,680			
1754	778,757	656,353			75,575	1,510,685+

Though the statistics are certainly imprecise, the 1737 trade figures summarized above give valuable evidence of the size and structure of the trade network Ile Royale had built in its first quarter century. Table 3 records a total trade of 2,918,000 *livres*, with imports and exports almost even. If the corrections suggested by *ordonnateur* LeNormant de Mézy are made, the total rises to nearly three and one half million *livres*. Moreover, there are enough figures from earlier years to confirm that 1737 was atypical only in the low level of imports from Canada.

Ile Royale's volume of trade in 1737 was large enough to

make it one of the most trade-oriented colonies on the continent. With a population about one-ninth that of Canada, Ile Royale was shipping nearly the same value of merchandise as its older counterpart. As a result, Ile Royale's earnings from its export sales were approximately 370 *livres* per colonist in 1737, when the comparable Canadian figure was about 40 *livres*. Among eighteenth-century North American colonies, only Newfoundland could show per capita exports as large or larger than Ile Royale's (Table 4). Such a large volume of trade does not mean Ile Royale was richer than other colonies, for it produced almost nothing but cod and had to pay for imports of almost all it consumed. Rather, the per capita figures demonstrate the importance of trade to Ile Royale. Reliance on external trade was basic to the economy and society of Ile Royale.

Table 4[13]
Per Capita Exports, Various Colonies, 1735-72

Colony & Year	Exports (*livres*)	Population	Per Capita Exports (*livres*)
Ile Royale, 1737	1,700,000	4,618	368
Ile Royale, 1754	2,000,000	5,900	338
Canada, 1735-39	1,776,000	39,000	45
Canada, 1739	1,461,000	39,627	37
Newfoundland, 1740s	6,000,000	7,000	857
Newfoundland, 1770	7,200,000	12,000	600
New England, 1768-72	9,780,000		17
Middle colonies, 1768-72	11,440,000		22
Upper south, 1768-72	23,620,000		59
Lower south, 1768-72	12,280,000		65

Ile Royale's trade was roughly in balance in 1737. Data for the years before 1737, moreover, suggest that favorable trade balances were common. Growing volumes of shipping between 1719 and 1737 suggest that the colony's imports were growing steadily along with the population.[15] The amount recorded in 1737 was probably one of the largest annual imports. Records of the fish catch (Table 1), on the other hand, show that the amount of fish available for export had often been as large or larger than in 1737, so export surpluses likely were common in previous years. In addition to the generally favorable trade balances, substantial government spending contributed to Ile Royale's balance of payments. In 1737, government spending in Ile Royale totalled 346,045 *livres*, just slightly more than the average figure for the decade 1731-40, which in turn had grown from the average of the previous decade (Table 5). For the decade 1731-40, annual government investment in Ile Royale averaged about 77 *livres* per colonist, at a time when the larger Canadian colony received about nine *livres* per head.[16] This generous funding, which saved Ile Royale from the budget deficits which were chronic in Canada, also provided an important source of specie. The

Table 5[14]
The Budget of Ile Royale (in *livres*)

Year	Receipts				Expenditure	Surplus (+) or deficit (-)
	Colony	Extra-ordinary	Fortifications	Total		
1721	151,871	11,084	80,000	242,955	242,954	
1722	124,740	4,020	80,000	209,661	192,353	+17,308
1723	144,289	6,817	130,000	281,105	267,761	+13,344
1724	151,485	9,601	150,000	311,087	298,831	+12,256
1725	116,941	3,960	150,000	270,901	270,899	
1726	136,911	8,879	150,000	295,701	295,790	-89
1727	144,889	14,939	150,000	309,829	309,790	
1728	--139,056--		150,000	289,056	286,746	+2,310
1729	--155,112--		150,000	305,112	292,324	+12,798
1730	154,283	4,007	152,700	311,162	311,162	
1731	149,965	5,067	128,900	300,427	300,427	
1732	167,362	420	128,900	296,682	296,682	
1733	179,784	583	130,335	310,704	310,703	
1734	179,441	575	128,900	313,587	313,586	
1735	209,091	492	128,900	338,484	338,481	
1736	205,389	2,437	128,900	337,370	337,370	
1737	216,012	1,133	128,900	346,045	346,044	
1738	215,123	218	128,900	349,455	349,455	
1739	--176,005--		128,900	304,905	309,904	
1740	224,586	2,892	128,900	355,830	355,845	
1741	247,314	5,284	128,900	380,701	380,702	
1742	232,269	4,974	128,100	365,346	365,345	
1743	352,650	14,709	128,100	495,461	495,468	
1744	335,825	83,553	128,100	547,480	547,436	+44
1749	1,082,569	6,241	48,420	1,137,231	1,194,724	-57,492
1750	851,478	532,634	143,200	1,527,312	1,463,086	+64,266
1751	846,791	89,761	28,400	964,952	1,369,560	-404,608
1752	1,184,095	350,259	80,000	1,614,354	1,305,355	+308,998
1753	422,035	349,938	51,720	823,693	892,834	-69,141
1754	456,300	208,693	82,000	806,993	960,907	-150,914
1756					1,069,574	
1757					1,113,691	

relative abundance of coinage in Ile Royale, which never needed the card money substitutes on which Canada relied in this period, is further evidence of a favorable balance of payments.

Though France was Ile Royale's major trading partner in the years up to 1737, the trade figures of that year show how actively the colony traded with several other widely dispersed regions. The flexibility which this variety of trade routes gave to Ile Royale was demonstrated in 1737 by the colony's success in avoiding harm when imports failed to arrive from one of its suppliers, in this case Canada. Even in Canada's best wheat exporting years, Ile Royale was in no sense an appendage of the larger Canadian colony. Ideally located for trade with European and colonial destinations and abundantly endowed with a product for which demand was unfailing, Ile Royale had developed a diversified trading system in which Canada was a small but useful part.

Ile Royale's vigorous trade was based on the production of dried cod, in which Ile Royale replaced and soon surpassed the ceded colony of Plaisance in Newfoundland. Since the methods of the cod fishery had been established long before the foundation of Ile Royale, the new colony was able to produce large volumes of cod without a long period of experimentation. In 1713 and 1719, cod catches amounted to about 156,000 quintals, totals not surpassed until 1730, when the catch rose to 165,000 quintals. The 1737 catch was 147,000 quintals.[17]

As significant as the volume of cod produced was the proportion of the total catch taken by the local residents. Fishing fleets based in France came annually to Ile Royale as well as to other regions in Newfoundland and on the continental coast, but in 1719 the residents took just over half of all the fish caught at Ile Royale and established a lasting ascendency over the visitors. In 1721 residents took 62 percent of Ile Royale's total catch, and their share continued to grow. By the 1730s, resident fishermen usually took about three-quarters of the catch. Local control of the cod resource had been established.

The residents' share, worth well over one million *livres* in most years, was shared by between 80 and 100 competing firms run by individual colonists. Most of these entrepreneurs had few more than the minimum practical number of boats and employees, and they relied on credit when purchasing the food, salt, fishing equipment, and other supplies that their businesses required. Since the cost of these supplies amounted to perhaps one-third of the gross earnings of the fishing industry,[18] the supply trade created by the local fishing proprietors was substantial, providing opportunities for merchant commerce in the colony. From the start, Louisbourg had a thriving merchant community.

In merchant trade as in the fishing industry, residents had to compete with visitors, but again the residents' share was large. In Ile Royale's early years, few French firms were so involved with Ile Royale as to justify their placing an employee or partner there. Their interests were limited to shipping ventures to Louisbourg, where wholesale business could be handled by the ship's captain or cargo director. "*Pas un seul marchand de france un peu aisé n'a voulu s'y établir*," wrote the colonial officials in 1726. Instead the colony developed its own community of resident merchants, mostly former residents of Plaisance with experience in the fishing business or immigrants hoping to begin commercial careers in the new colony.[19]

Rather than limit themselves to supplying goods and disposing of catches for the proprietors of fisheries, several of the early merchants became participants in the fishing industry. As the distinction between merchants and fishing proprietors broke down, the merchant-fishermen came to dominate the fishing industry. In 1724, merchants who owned fishing properties were only 12 percent of all owners, but they employed enough men and vessels to take nearly 20 percent of the residents' catch. By 1734, 25 merchants, 24 percent of all fishery owners, had the capacity to take 37 percent of the residents' catch (Table 6). By owning larger than average fish-

Table 6[21]
Merchant Participation in the Local Fishing Industry

	1724	1726	1734	1753
Resident Owners	82	86	106	119
Merchant Owners	10	18	25	18
% of total	12.2%	20.9%	23.6%	15.1%
Residents' employees	1,056	1,551	1,625	
Merchants' employees	209	362	711	
% of total	19.7%	23.3%	43.7%	
Residents' shallops	68	278	263	225
Merchants' shallops	28	63	96	85
% of total	17%	23%	36%	37.9%
Residents' schooners	36	21	28	62
Merchants' schooners	4	1	13	37
% of total	11.1%	4.8%	46.4%	59.6%
Merchants' potential share of catch	15.4%	20.9%	37.9%	48.8%

ing operations, the merchants assured themselves of a secure supply of cod. At the same time, they could extend their activities by supplying goods to and purchasing catches from smaller, less diversified operators. Though by 1734 more than half the Louisbourg merchants owned fisheries, it was not essential to do so. Merchants also found other commercial opportunities in supply to the government,[20] in ship chandlery, in retail trade, and in the sale of goods on commission.

After fishing and wholesale trade, the third sector of Ile Royale's commerce was transportation. This was the field in which the residents had the smallest share during Ile Royale's first quarter century. Though local residents, particularly merchants, were the most active participants in Louisbourg's vigorous market in commercial vessels, they sold almost as many as they bought, buying vessels from New England for resale to French and West Indian buyers.[22] Though a few Louisbourg-owned vessels traded with Québec, the Antilles, and even Europe, locally owned ships were more often used for fishing and coastal trade than for long distance trade.

Since the local merchant fleet was small, the colony depended on visiting vessels to bring its supplies and carry away its cod. This control of the transportation system was the non-resident traders' most important source of influence in the trade of Ile Royale. Since most of the ships and cargoes arriving at Louisbourg were externally owned, the visitors competed with the local merchants for the business of the local fishing industry and the other colonial markets, earning from shipping charges as well as from sale revenue. Louisbourg merchants found a share of this business, however, by holding interests in the cargoes, buying cargo outright, or acting as commission agents, earning five to eight percent on cargoes sold or purchased for non-resident shipowners. Commission earnings were rarely a merchant's only income, for accepting consignments on commission and paying commissions on one's own consignments were normal aspects of the cooperation between merchants. At Louisbourg the largest and most stable of such arrangements involved established local merchants with interests in fishing, wholesale trade, and even in shipping ventures. An employer-employee relationship was rarely implied between a local merchant and his trans-Atlantic correspondents.[23]

By 1737 the business of Ile Royale -- the fishery, wholesale and retail trade, and shipping -- supported nearly 50 resident merchants in Louisbourg. The business training, scope of operations, and wealth of these merchants varied widely. Retail shopkeepers with only a small volume of business sometimes had only a rudimentary commercial education. Most merchants, however, were trained in book-keeping and other business skills. Louisbourg's close contacts with France gave them access to the latest business methods and financial instruments, which were essential to the management of complex international exchanges typified by long delays, voluminous correspondence, and delicate credit arrangements. The volume of such businesses was frequently large. The largest merchant fishing businesses could produce up to 100,000 *livres* worth of cod annually from their own properties, in addition to their revenues from other merchant operations. One merchant regularly handled commission consignments worth nearly 100,000 *livres*, and several firms were estimated to have a net worth of at least that size. Even small profit margins would have provided these merchants with substantial incomes, though comprehensive data on the business volume and wealth of the merchant community are lacking.[24]

The importance of the merchants and their trade was recognized in the colony. The large and influential government presence in Ile Royale rarely hindered merchant operations by legal or administrative restrictions. Once the practicality of trade with the British colonies had been demonstrated, for instance, Ile Royale secured loyal exemption from the general prohibition on foreign trade by French colonies. Some restrictions were maintained, but the essence of the colony's foreign trade was open and licit and could freely be reported in the official trade reports.[25] The colonial administrators responded to the Minister of Marine's advice that they make the colony's commerce "*le principal objet de vos soins et de votre attention,*" but they did so by assisting commerce, often in response to merchants' lobbying efforts, rather than by controlling it.[26]

Mercantile values appear to have been influential and respected in Louisbourg. Merchants jealously protected their reputations as "*négociants d'honneur*" and promoted the dignity of their symbol, the pen.[27] More significantly, the social structure of the colony promoted the dissemination of commercial values. No self-sufficient landed population or seigneurial elite existed to counter the merchants' influence and, though the officer corps of the colonial regular troops enjoyed prestige, the fishery did not invite military control the way the Canadian fur trade did. As the government accepted responsibility for defence, justice, and a widening range of social services in Ile Royale, the need for fixed reciprocal duties within a traditional social hierarchy faded, making room for a society based on commercial exchange. In that context, successful merchants became some of the colony's most prominent and influential people. They monopolized civilian appointments to the Superior Council,[28] held many administrative posts, and participated in all the social and economic activities of Ile Royale.

The first quarter century of Ile Royale's growth, while not free of all difficulties, shows a generally stable and vigorous trade structure supporting a thriving merchant community in Ile Royale. Shortly after 1737, however, serious strains were placed on the maritime trade (and hence the entire economy) of Ile Royale.

The Canadian crop failure of 1736-37 was a harbinger of one of the problems. That crop failure was temporary -- large agricultural exports from Canada to Ile Royale were renewed in 1739, 1740 and 1741 -- but new crop failures beginning in 1742 soon put an end to Canadian grain exports.[29] Since Ile Royale had come to rely on Canadian grain in the 1730s, Canada's declining exports posed a dilemma for administrators and merchants in Louisbourg: would Canadian grain production revive, or should trade be reoriented in search of a new supplier of grain? Flour was bulky and expensive when brought from Europe, but it was dangerous to turn to New England, which could cut off exports of the vital food in time of war.

At about the same time, a more serious crisis struck. Discussing potential new markets for Ile Royale's cod in 1739, the new *ordonnateur* François Bigot had noted that war between Britain and Spain would make fortunes for the fishermen of Ile Royale, who could take over the British place in the Spanish markets.[30] Yet when the hoped-for war began that year, the colony was unable to profit by it, for a severe decline in fish catches which had begun in 1739 grew more and more serious during the 1740s. The 152,000 quintals produced in 1738 fell to 123,000 quintals in 1740, 83,000 quintals in 1742, and 69,000 quintals in 1744. The inshore fishery dominated by the residents was affected most, driving their share of the total catch from a characteristic 76 percent in 1738 to 69 percent in 1743 and 64 percent in 1744 (Table 1).

There are grounds for suspecting that overfishing contributed to this sudden setback, for the major feature of the falling catches was a slump in catch per vessel ratios. Summer catches of 260 quintals per shallop in 1739 fell to 150 quintals per shallop in 1742, while winter catches fell from an unprecedented 180 quintals per shallop in 1739 (110 to 120 was more normal) to 90, 40, and 30 quintals in 1740, 1743, and 1744.[31] It seems clear that falling yields rather than war or external economic factors caused the total catch to fall. Climatological or biological influences on the cod cannot be ruled out in this declining yield, but it is equally possible that the intensified fishing activity of the long peace since 1713 had reduced local fish populations in areas convenient to the drying shores and accessible to the technology of the time.[32] Since similar setbacks hit several heavily exploited regions along the Atlantic coast within a decade of Ile Royale's crisis, overfishing and a subsequent fall in total yields may have been a general phenomenon of the Atlantic cod fishery in the mid-eighteenth century.[33]

Whatever the cause, the effect on Ile Royale was severe. For years, the proprietors of fisheries had claimed their efforts brought marginal returns, and government investigators had tended to agree.[34] Falling yields on the same investment in the 1740s meant increasing hardship for the proprietors, their employees, and the merchants who served the fishing industry: that is, virtually all the civilians of Ile Royale. For the economy as a whole, the rising problem of replacing Canada with a new source of food imports was compounded by the threat to export earnings posed by the fall in fish production.

The 1740s also saw a decline in the importance of France among Ile Royale's trading partners. This may have been related to the colony's trading difficulties. Trade with the British colonies had to increase once food shortages forced Ile Royale to rely on New England grain. To pay for these grain purchases, Ile Royale exported more sugar products to New England, and so imports from the Caribbean rose. In return, more cod had to be shipped southward, despite Ile Royale's declining production. To supply the necessary cod, cod exports were diverted from the European market to the West Indies, and France began to lose its position of dominance among Ile Royale's trading partners (Table 3).

At this time, Ile Royale probably attempted to sustain the supply of cod available for export by increasing its clandestine purchases of New England cod. This trade had always been rigorously prohibited and severely punished as a threat to the colonists' main livelihood and as an impediment to the training of French seamen. Nevertheless, with local cod production in crisis, New Englanders temporarily excluded from their traditional Spanish markets, and increasing amounts of West Indian sugar and rum available to pay for New England goods, the amount of contraband probably increased. It was not directly reported in trade figures but, after comparing Ile Royale's fish catch records with its trade figures for 1742, the Ministry of Marine noted that though the fish catch had fallen to 83,000 quintals, nearly 90,000 quintals had been exported.[35] Clandestine imports were not an effective replacement for the colony's missing catch, for total cod exports remained much smaller than usual. In any case, New England fish was only available in bulk while Britain remained at war with Spain and at peace with France, a situation that only lasted until 1744.

The 1740s were an unstable period for Ile Royale. The colony's trade fluctuated greatly as the potential for increased trade with the Caribbean and New England was explored, but the problems of declining fish production and insecure food supplies were not overcome. It seems likely that as fish catches fell, the favorable trade balances achieved in the years up to 1737 became unattainable.[36] Food shortages were severe in several years.[37] By 1743 currency shortages were reported. A visiting merchant who lamented *"la triste scituation du commerce à l'ile royale"* may have been speaking for many.[38]

The war between Britain and France which began in the spring of 1744 compounded the colony's economic difficulties, cutting off trade with New England, threatening all the trade routes, and adding the risk of capture to the other troubles of the fishing industry. Though privateering briefly offered a substitute for peacetime trade, the invasion and conquest of Ile Royale in the spring of 1745 and the deportation of the colonists completed the ruin which the depressed conditions of the 1740s had threatened.

When French occupation of Ile Royale was renewed in 1749, a large proportion of the surviving colonists returned, and by 1752 the populations of Louisbourg and of the colony as a whole were larger than ever.[39] With cod fishing resumed and trade re-established, record volumes of trade passed through Louisbourg, pushing annual tonnages from prewar figures of 7,000 - 8,000 *tonneaux* to 13,000 *tonneaux* in 1752.⁴⁰ Per capita export values had fallen slightly, from about 370 *livres* in 1737 to about 340 *livres* per colonist in 1754, but the import-export trade built on the cod fishery remained basic to the colonial economy. Nevertheless some significant structural changes had taken place, both in the directions of Ile Royale's trade and in the activities of the local merchants.

After 1749 France no longer dominated Ile Royale's exchanges. Imports from France had grown slightly from their 1737 levels, but less cod was being shipped from Ile Royale to Europe, leaving Ile Royale with a substantial deficit in its exchange with France. At the same time, imports and exports to and from the French West Indies and New England had soared. The West Indian economy, fundamental to the eighteenth-century expansion of French overseas commerce, had begun its fastest growth in the 1730s.⁴¹ As the sugar and coffee production of Martinique, Saint-Domingue, and the other islands increased, so did their demand for food supplies. By increasing exports of cod to these islands, tentatively in the 1740s, more surely in the 1750s, Ile Royale linked its trade to the most rapidly expanding sector of French overseas commerce. By 1754, the Caribbean islands were nearly as important a market for Ile Royale's cod as Europe was, buying half a million *livres* worth of cod annually. Ile Royale's trade with New England had grown nearly as quickly. Confirmed as Ile Royale's principal supplier of grain in the 1750s, New England was also the main market for the West Indian sugar products which came in to pay for the islands' purchases of Ile Royale cod.⁴² A sort of triangular trade developed between the three regions: via Louisbourg, the West Indies sent sugar products to the British colonies; New England shipped foodstuffs and construction materials to Ile Royale; Ile Royale shipped cod to the West Indies. This tripartite exchange had existed since the foundation of Ile Royale (and before at Plaisance⁴³) but its size and importance were transformed in the 1750s. Ile Royale's trade with the West Indies and with New England underwent a fivefold increase between 1737 and 1754, and the two regions together far outweighed France in Ile Royale's total trade. This new volume of trade with the West Indies and the British colonies provided the increase in Ile Royale's total trade, for trade with France was nearly static and trade with Canada and Acadia was in decline. The New England-Caribbean exchange did not give Ile Royale a trade surplus sufficient to match its deficit with France. With cod exports remaining below the levels of the 1730s, the colony's trade balance was in deficit in the 1750s. Shortages of currency were still noted, but large government expenditures may have produced an overall balance of payments.

Significant changes had occurred in the cod fishery as well. Until 1745, visiting fishing vessels from Basque, Breton, and Norman ports had always taken a sizeable share of Ile Royale's total catch. In the 1750s this link between resident and migrant fishermen was virtually broken. Evidently defeated by the poor catches of the early 1740s and the war years of the rest of the decade, many of the French fishing vessels abandoned the Ile Royale fishery to the resident fishermen, who took nearly ninety percent of Ile Royale's total catch in 1754. An important factor in the residents' increasing control was the appearance of a resident-owned schooner fleet. Up to 1740, residents had rarely owned more than one-third of the fishing schooners used at Ile Royale and their share had fallen in the 1740s. In the 1750s, however, residents owned a majority of the schooners as well as most of the shallops.[44] As a result they dominated both the inshore and the offshore fisheries. Total catches remained below the levels reached in the 1720s and 1730s because of the shrinking participation of non-resident vessels, but catch per vessel ratios recovered to acceptable levels and the residents' catch began to approach the levels it had reached before the crisis of the early 1740s. (Table1).

The merchant community of Louisbourg participated in both these changes. By 1755, 66 merchants, including many of the pre-war merchants or their heirs, were active in Louisbourg. Many still operated on a small scale and a few were employees of French firms with new, trans-Atlantic operations, but the major resident merchants were more important than ever in the local economy. In particular, their share of the fishing industry was larger than ever. In 1753, 18 merchant fishermen were only 15 percent of all fishery proprietors but they employed 38 percent of the resident industry's shallops and no less than 60 percent of the schooners. These vessels had the potential to take 48 percent of the total resident catch (Table 6). In addition, local merchants remained active in serving the rest of the fishing industry, in supplying the growing needs of the local garrison and administration, and in the usual wholesale and retail trades. Since their control of the cod supply assured them a place in the growing triangular exchange between Ile Royale, New England, and the Caribbean, they were well situated to benefit from the colony's growth in total trade. There was also one new characteristic of the Louisbourg merchants in the 1750s. They became shipowners.

This new development probably stemmed from the residents' nearly complete control of the fishing industry. Before the war, French fishing fleets played an essential transportation role in the fishing industry. Residents depended on them to bring salt, fishing equipment, and migrant workers, and to haul away a substantial part of the catch when they returned to Europe. As non-resident participation in the Ile Royale fishery faded in the 1750s, the local merchants began to provide the transportation themselves, probably using the same schooners which they had begun to employ in the offshore fishery. The Caribbean, now a major cod market, was an important destination, but the impact was also noted in France. Unfortunately Louisbourg sources, while they provide a variety of references to local firms establishing trading fleets,[45] yield no statistical series by which to measure the growth rate of this new business. It is sources from French ports that suggest the vigour with which the colonists entered the shipping industry in the 1740s and particularly in the 1750s. The best data come from Bayonne and the Basque fishing ports, which since the foundation of Ile Royale had sent large fleets of vessels there. From 1713 to 1742, only 12 Louisbourg-owned vessels had entered Bayonne, Saint-Jean de Luz, Ciboure, and the other Basque ports. They were an insignificant proportion of the total traffic between the two regions. From 1743 to 1745, 13 more Louisbourg vessels arrived. Between 1749 and 1757 the number of Louisbourg visitors increased to 92, making Louisbourg the major outfitter of shipping between the two regions.[46]

Since the Basque region was a market for cod and also a source of workers for the fishery, the residents of Ile Royale had strong incentive to maintain this link when the Basques themselves ceased to provide sufficient shipping. Figures from Bordeaux show that Louisbourg-owned vessels also began to appear there. Only nine Louisbourg vessels were recorded at Bordeaux from 1725 to 1745, but there were 11 more in four years during the 1750s.[47] Louisbourg did not begin to dominate in trade between Ile Royale and Bordeaux as it did in shipping to the Basque ports, but the Bordeaux data imply that colonial shipping to large commercial centres as well as to fishing ports was increasing.

The restructuring of Ile Royale's economy in the 1750s, reflected in increasing local control of the cod fishery, the growth of a local merchant fleet, and the swing toward the Caribbean market, was not long lasting. In 1755 naval conflict was renewed between Britain and France. In 1758 conquest and deportation again brought the colony to a halt, this time permanently. But the importance of Ile Royale's trade and its restructuring after 1749 is not measured simply by its duration. Ile Royale's performance can be a useful benchmark against which to compare Canada's economic experience in the same period. It is also instructive about economic behaviour in New France generally.

In Canada, export industries were proportionately much less important than in Ile Royale, and residents held a smaller share in the major export industry. Since beaver furs were shipped and marketed by a French-based monopoly, the Compagnie des Indes Occidentales, Canadians interested in maritime trade were limited to exporting the colony's surplus grain supplies, a trade which grew from 1713 to the mid-1730s but did not compare in value to either furs or fish. In a recent article, James Pritchard has argued that the collapse of the small but significant group of Canadians active in import and export shipping before mid-century stemmed from the decline in grain production that began in 1737. As falling agricultural production, population growth, and war transformed Canada from "a growing self sufficient agricultural and trading community" into "a large military fortress and garrison that required external aid," the Canadian traders, still a small group and dependent on agricultural exports, were unable to respond to the changed circumstances. Pritchard argues that their collapse "destroyed any signs of the appearance of an indigenous merchant group in Canadian society" before the conquest.[48]

Another indigenous merchant group, that of Louisbourg, faced a somewhat similar crisis between 1737 and 1745. Insecure food supplies and a serious decline in fish production reduced Ile Royale's ability to export, bringing hardship to the whole colony and threatening the position of the local merchants. In Ile Royale, however, production control of the major resource, cod, remained in local hands and the local merchants had greater flexibility in responding to change. By increasing their control of the fishing industry, by developing a locally-owned trading fleet, and by responding to new market opportunities in the Caribbean, the Ile Royale merchants appear to have overcome the commercial threat to their position.

The economic significance of Ile Royale has not often been noted, partly because records other than those kept at Louisbourg tended to group Ile Royale and Canada together, blurring the distinction between the two economies. Historians have done the same, considering Ile Royale a military outpost on the periphery of New France rather than a separate and distinct society. Close inspection reveals in Ile Royale a vigorous economy based on large scale external trade and supporting an influential indigenous merchant community. The success of Louisbourg's merchants during Ile Royale's short existence suggests that capital accumulation and entrepreneurial enterprise could thrive within the legal and political structures of New France, given the right economic conditions. The case of Ile Royale suggests that economic factors, notably the success or failure of the colonists in securing control of an export industry sufficient to pay for their imports, were the decisive causes of the contrasting experiences of Canada and Ile Royale in the development of an indigenous merchant community and mercantile values.

Notes

1. Several sections of this article are based on material in my thesis, "Merchant Trade in Louisbourg, Ile Royale" (M.A. thesis, University of Ottawa, 1977). I am grateful to my thesis director Fernand Ouellet and to my former colleagues in the research staff of Fortress of Louisbourg National Historic Park for advice and criticism.

2. This interpretation, developed in the histories of Garneau, Parkman, and Wrong, has been challenged only by J.S. McLennan, *Louisbourg from its foundation to its fall* (London: Macmillan, 1918). Canadian wheat shipments to Ile Royale are studied in J.S. Pritchard, "Ships, Men and Commerce: a Study of Maritime Activity in New France" (Ph.D. thesis, University of Toronto, 1971). The quotation is from W.J. Eccles, *The Canadian Frontier 1534-1760* (New York: Holt Rinehart Winston, 1969), p. 3.

3. Statistics delivered yearly to the Ministry of Marine by the office of the *ordonnateur* at Louisbourg. Specifically: AN, Col., $C^{11}B$, Vol. 3, f. 206 (1718); Vol. 4, f. 223 (1719); $C^{11}C$, Vol. 9, f. 9 (1721); $C^{11}B$, Vol. 6, f. 245 (1723); Vol. 8, f. 230 (1726); Vol. 9, f. 259 (1727); Vol. 11, f. 69 (1730); Vol. 12, f. 64 (1731); Vol. 13, f. 243 (1732); Vol. 14, f. 232 (1733); Vol. 16, f. 120 (1734); Vol. 17, f. 90 (1735); Vol. 18, f. 170 (1736); Vol. 20, f. 21v (1737); Vol. 20, f. 220 (1738); Vol. 21, f. 152 and Vol. 26, f. 225 (1739); *ibid.*, and Vol. 23, f. 160 (1740); Vol. 26, f. 216 (1742); Vol. 26, f. 209 (1743); Vol. 26, f. 227 (1744); AN, Marine, G, Vol. 54 (1751-52); AN, Col., $C^{11}B$, Vol. 33, ff. 436, 437, 495 (1752-54). Note: The residents' catch for some years was determined by multiplying the number of resident-owned vessels by the recorded average catches of schooners and shallops that year. The European value of Ile Royale cod was estimated at 20 to 25 *livres* per quintal. This was roughly twice the wholesale price in Ile Royale. In

TRADE AND MERCHANT ENTERPRISE

addition, each 100 quintals of cod produced one *barique* of cod oil worth 100 to 110 *livres* in Europe.

4. Cod: Same as Table 1; Beaver: A.J.E. Lunn, *Economic Development in New France 1713-60* (Ph.D. thesis, McGill University, 1947), p. 464.

Note: The estimated values of cod exports for 1720, 1722, 1724, 1725, 1728, 1729, 1732, 1741, and 1745 are unknown and do not figure in the table. Canadian sales are the values recorded in La Rochelle by the Chambre de Commerce. The Ile Royale figures are projected revenues rather than actual earnings. Local officials based the projection on annual estimations of current European prices.

5. Except for a few ships from New York, New England vessels monopolized this trade. AN, Col., F²B, Vol. 11, Tableaux de Commerce, *passim*.

6. The earliest yearly record of shipping, for 1719, shows arrivals from all five regions. AN, Outre-Mer, G¹, Vol. 466, pièce 59, Recensement des vaisseaux ... 1719.

7. AN, Outre-Mer, G¹, Vol. 466, pièces 67-76, Recensements de l'Ile Royale.

8. As a part of New France, Ile Royale was theoretically under the authority of the Governor-General in Québec, but the local government reported directly to the Ministry of Marine in France. Ile Royale and Canada were virtually separate colonies within New France.

9. The following statistics of Ile Royale's trade in 1737 are based on AN, Col., C¹¹C, Vol. 9, ff. 50-95, "*État des cargaisons* ...." See below, Table 3.

10. On the crisis in wheat supply, see AN, Col., C¹¹B, Vol. 19, f. 1, St. Ovide et LeNormant, 2 juin 1737 and *ibid.*, f. 129, LeNormant, 28 décembre 1737. For Canadian imports in other years see Table 3.

11. AN, Col., F²B, Vol. 11, Tableaux de Commerce (1732-36, 1752-54; C¹¹C, Vol. 9, ff. 50-95 (1737); B, Vol. 70, f. 400 (1739); *ibid.*, Vol. 72, f. 442 (1740); *ibid.*, Vol. 74, f. 581 (1741); *ibid.*, Vol. 76, f. 510 (1742); *ibid.*, Vol. 78, f. 405 (1743).

Note: A plus sign in the totals column indicates that the total given is incomplete due to missing data. The combined figures given for trade with Canada, Acadia, and the American colonies in 1742 and 1743 are largely composed of exports to and imports from the American Colonies, since trade with Canada and Acadia was limited.

12. *Ordonnateur* Le Normant de Mézy, under whose supervision the 1737 table figures were compiled, discussed the omissions in the table in AN, Col., C¹¹B, Vol. 19, f. 143, 31 décembre 1737.

13. Canadian exports 1735-39: Lunn, op. cit.; Canadian exports 1739: Jean Hamelin, *Economie et société en Nouvelle-France* (Québec: Presses de l'Université Laval, 1960), p. 33; Canadian population estimate: Guy Frégault, "Essai sur les finances," in *Le XVIIIᵉ Siècle: Études* (Montréal: HMH, 1963); Newfoundland: based on data in C. Grant Head, *Eighteenth Century Newfoundland* (Toronto: McLelland and Stewart, 1976), pp. 65, 82, 141; and Thirteen Colonies: James F. Shepherd and Gary Walton, *Shipping, Maritime Trade and the Economic Development of Colonial North America* (Cambridge: at the University Press, 1972), p. 47.

Note: Sterling values for the British colonies have been converted to *livres* at 20 *livres* per pound. The accuracy of the figures for the Thirteen Colonies is questionable, since the same source seriously underestimates the exports of Canada and Newfoundland in the 1768-72 period. However, even a substantial increase in these regions' exports would not bring them close to the per capita figures for the fishing colonies.

14. AN, Col., C¹¹C, Vols. 11-14, Bordereaux des Recettes et Dépenses, except for 1756, which is from *ibid.*, F³, Vol. 51, p. 473.

15. Moore, *op. cit.*, Table 1.4.
16. *Ibid.*, Table 1.8. Figures for Canada taken from Frégault, *op. cit.*.
17. One quintal is 100 *livres* (50.9 kg) of dried cod. See Table 1.
18. The cost of supplies relative to total catch is discussed in Moore, *op. cit.*, pp. 56-58.
19. AN, Col., C^{11}B, Vol. 8, f. 21, St. Ovide et De Mézy, 1 décembre 1726. There is no evidence that any of the major merchants of Louisbourg's first quarter century arrived with wealth.
20. Most government spending in Ile Royale was for wages and services, not for merchandise. As a market for the local merchants, the administration did not compare with the fishing industry until the 1750s, since the colonial depot at Rochefort supplied most of the administration's needs.
21. Census data, AN, Outre-Mer, G^1, Vol. 466, except for 1753 figures, which are taken from material in the Fonds Surlaville, PAC, MG 18, F^{30}, "*Troupes de l'Ile Royale.*"
22. Moore, *op. cit.*, Table 2.11.
23. Several examples of commission sales are discussed in Moore, *op. cit.*, pp. 68-71.
24. The fishing business of the Daccarrette family, with 34 shallops producing 300 quintals each at 10 *livres* per quintal, was within the range of 100,000 *livres* by 1726. T.J.A. LeGoff, "Michel Daccarrette," *Dictionary of Canadian Biography* (Toronto: University of Toronto Press, 1974), Vol. 3, pp. 156-57. Merchant Léon Fautoux's large consignments from his correspondents are detailed in Dale Miquelon, "Léon Fautoux," p. 216 in the same volume.
25. AN, Col., B, Vol. 57-2, f. 760, Maurepas à Saint-Ovide, 19 juin 1732. The principal restrictions maintained were on imports of cod and of commodities which could be imported from Canada.
26. AN, Col., B, Vol. 61, f. 592v, Maurepas à Saint-Ovide et De Mézy, 4 mai 1734. A major lobbying effort preceded the imposition of limits on wages paid to fishermen. *Ibid.*, F^3, Vol. 50, f. 254, Règlements concernant l'Exploitation de la Pêche ..., 20 juin 1743.
27. AN, Outre-Mer, G^2, Vol. 200, dossier 210, f. 76, Labrouche vs Duboé, 16 juillet 1751; *ibid.*, Vol. 188, f. 377v, Claparede vs Duchambon, 23 décembre 1751.
28. Of the 13 councillors not appointed *ex officio*, 6 were merchants. All the others were officers or administrators.
29. Pritchard, *op. cit.*, pp. 323-27.
30. AN, Col., C^{11}B, Vol. 21, f. 112, Bigot à Maurepas, 6 novembre 1739.
31. Moore, *op. cit.*, Table 2.08.
32. Similar declines in the Newfoundland fishery which are best explained by overfishing are analysed in C. Grant Head, *Eighteenth Century Newfoundland* (Toronto: McClelland and Stewart, 1976), pp. 20-21 and 66-68.
33. Head, *op. cit.*, makes the case for Newfoundland. The large New England fishery at Canso virtually disappeared in the 1730s. Stagnation in New England catches is suggested by data in Harold Innis, *The Cod Fisheries* (Toronto: University of Toronto Press, 1954), p. 161.
34. AN, Col., C^{11}B, Vol. 14, f. 62, Représentation des Habitants qui font la Pêche, septembre 1733; *ibid.*, Vol. 21, f. 297, LeNormant, 1739.
35. AN, Col., B, Vol. 76, f. 510, Maurepas à Bigot, 30 juin 1743.
36. Trade statistics for these years show surpluses, but clandestine cod imports were not included and other omissions may have been tolerated. Since trade figures for the 1740s exist only in summary form, their omissions cannot be checked as

those of 1737 can.

37. AN, Col., C¹¹B, Vol. 25, f. 179, Bigot à Maurepas, 27 novembre 1743.

38. AN, Col., C¹¹B, Vol. 25, f. 199, Bigot à Maurepas, 13 octobre 1743; La Rochelle, Archives Départementales, Charente-Maritime, B, Amirauté de Louisbourg, registre 275, lettre de 28 novembre 1740.

39. AN, Outre-Mer, G¹, Vol. 466, pièce 77, Recensement de 1752.

40. Moore, *op. cit.*, Table 1.4.

41. Paul Butel, *La croissance commerciale bordelaise dans la seconde moitié du XVIIIe siècle* (Thèse de doctorat, Université de Paris, 1973), p. 90.

42. AN, Col., F²B, Vol. 11, Tableaux de Commerce. See Table 3.

43. Examples of Plaisance's trade can be seen in Outre-Mer, G³, Vol. 2055, Notariat de Plaisance.

44. Moore, *op. cit.*, Table 2.07.

45. For instance, references to shipping owned by two Louisbourg firms in AN, Col., E 227, Dossier sur Imbert et Lannelongue; *ibid.*, E 159, Dossier J-B Dupleix-Sylvain, pièce 12.

46. Laurier Turgeon, *Les échanges franco-canadiens de 1713 à 1758: Bayonne, les ports basques et Louisbourg, Ile Royale* (M.A. thesis, Université de Pau, France, 1977), p. 37.

47. James Pritchard, "The Pattern of French Colonial Shipping to Canada before 1760," *Revue Française d'Histoire de l'Outre-Mer*, Tome 63, #231, 2e trimestre, (1976), pp. 186-210.

48. James Pritchard, "The Pattern of French Colonial Shipping to Canada before 1760," *Revue Française d'Histoire de l'Outre-Mer*, Tome 63, #231, 2^e trimestre, (1976) pp.186-210.

PRESERVATION CONSERVATION RESEARCH

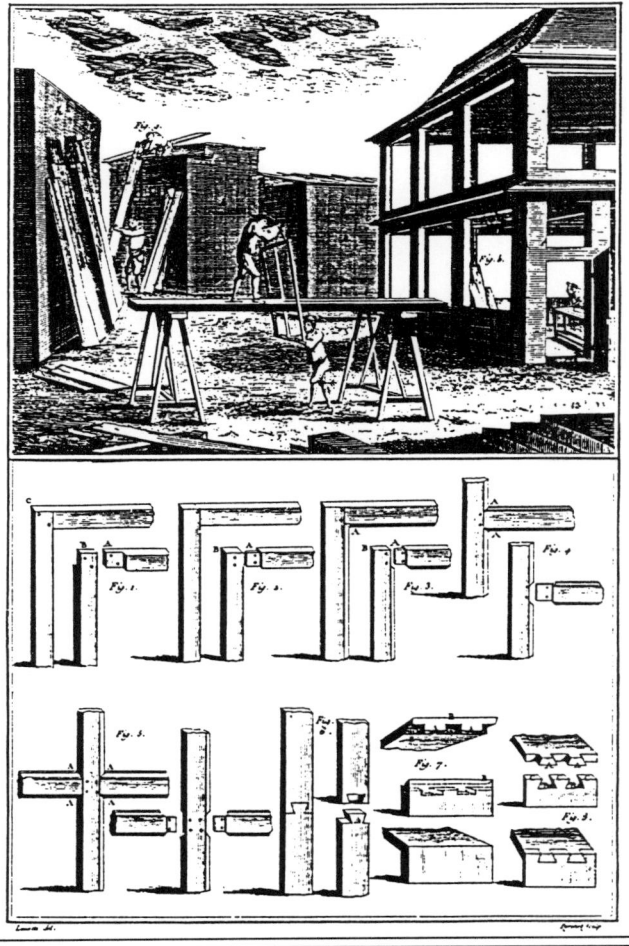

Preserving History: The Commemoration of 18th-Century Louisbourg, 1895-1940

A.J.B. Johnston

During the first half of the 18th-century Louisbourg was one of the best known settlements in North America, celebrated for its fortifications, fishery and trade. In the second half of the 20th century the site of the original French town has again become renowned, this time as the Fortress of Louisbourg, Canada's most ambitious historic park. For most of the long intervening period, however, Louisbourg was a largely forgotten spot, its population small and its significance on the world stage clearly behind it. The few people who gave the place much thought were historians or antiquarians interested in the Anglo-French struggle for North America. Fewer still were inclined to visit there in person, although those who did believed the trip worthwhile for the romantic exhilaration offered by walking among the ruins.

Late in the 19th century there emerged a new sensibility about Louisbourg and its ruins. Individuals in the Maritimes and elsewhere began to feel that the area deserved both commemoration and preservation. The first monument was erected in 1895; soon afterwards an organization was formed to preserve the most prominent ruins and to erect additional memorials. Other efforts followed, involving more cairns and plaques, land acquisition, and the establishment of a museum. In 1928 Louisbourg was designated a National Historic Site, and in 1940 it became the Fortress of Louisbourg National Historic Park.

The study of the transformation of Louisbourg from an abandoned ruin to a historic park offers a case study in the history of heritage preservation in Canada. In the 19th century France and Great Britain had both taken steps to provide for the protection of historic properties. In the United States wealthy philanthropists, coalitions of concerned citizens, and local historical societies often came to the fore with money to support preservation efforts. But Canadians appeared to lack the same concern with heritage preservation or, more importantly, they lacked the willingness to donate money for historical matters. Private efforts to preserve and commemorate Louisbourg advanced slowly and with great difficulty. However, a small group of early enthusiasts persevered in the face of apparent indifference and inaction on the part of governments, and ultimately succeeded in establishing Louisbourg as an official historic site. In their efforts they encountered some typically Canadian difficulties in the construction of a national identity and they contributed to the evolution of a Canadian approach to heritage preservation.

When the British captured Louisbourg in July 1758, preparation began immediately to remove the French inhabitants. By the end of the summer most of the Louisbourgeois had been sent to France. For the next decade Louisbourg was a British garrison town,[1] though in 1760, in accordance with the wishes of Prime Minister William Pitt, who feared that Louisbourg might again be handed back to France as part of a peace settlement, the town's fortifications were systematically destroyed. Eight years later, the garrison was withdrawn. More than half of the 500 inhabitants who lived there in 1767 departed when the soldiers left the following year. Louisbourg became, in the words of the Governor of Nova Scotia, Lord William Campbell, a "decayed city ... going to ruin."[2] Most of the people who chose to stay in the area decided to move to properties across and around the harbour. The area inside the walls of what had been French Louisbourg came to be known as "Old Town," a place of scattered houses, grazing animals, and ruins. The usable brick, stone, and lumber of the French period were incorporated into new structures, at Louisbourg or elsewhere, even as far away as Halifax. By 1805, when the Rev. John Inglis, later Anglican Bishop of Nova Scotia, visited Louisbourg, the historic townsite presented a desolate picture: "A more complete destruction of buildings can scarcely be imagined. All are reduced to confused heaps of stone after all the wood, all that was combustible was either burnt or carried away .... The great size of the heaps of stone indicated the magnitude of the edifices. [I saw] the ruins of several barracks and hospitals, of the Intendant's and the admiral's house and various other publick buildings .... [The current residents] are exceedingly poor. In the town and vacinity [sic] there are fourteen families ...."[3]

Although the situation changed little in the course of the 19th century, visitors' perspectives on the site did seem to alter. No longer were people content simply to describe what the place looked like.[4] In full romantic style visitors from the 1830s onward found historic Louisbourg to be a place of "melancholy contrast,"[5] "melancholy desolation,"[6] "perfect desolation,"[7] and "grassy solitude."[8] It was the perfect location for philosophical rumination on the passage of time and the meaning of life. Few could resist making the obvious observation: *sic transit gloria mundi*. Given the romanticism of the era, the absence of appeals to protect or clean up the site is not surprising. It was precisely the juxtaposition of old ruins with fences, fish flakes, houses and sheep, the contrast of a glorious past with a humble present, that so captivated tourists. Moreover, to Anglophiles and other imperialist-minded visitors of the period, a French fortress turned to ruins may have struck them as being particularly appropriate. Had the ruins been threatened with destruction by some new development scheme,[9] or had there been large numbers of curio-seekers taking home souvenirs, some of the 19th-century visitors might have advocated preservation or renovation measures. But since isolated Louisbourg was not under any pressure to change and grow there was no apparent need to safeguard its ruins.

Commemoration was a different issue. Monuments, memorials, and statues were erected to historic events or figures throughout the 19th century in Europe and North America. A column to Nelson, put up in Montreal in 1809, and Brock's Monument, erected on Queenston Heights in 1824, were among the earliest to be raised in British North America.[10] By the 1880s, monument-raising was enjoying a definite vogue.[11] The most popular subjects to which people erected monuments or statues during the late 19th and early 20th centuries, were the War of 1812 (14), the Boer War (11), Queen Victoria (9) and the Northwest Rebellion (6). Other suitable subjects were the early explorers and religious figures, heroes and battles of the Seven Years' War, the Loyalists, local disasters, and individual acts of heroism. The funds for the memorials usually came either from private societies (like the Women's Christian Temperance Union who established a Loyalist fountain in Saint John in 1883), general subscriptions (such as the teachers and "friends of education" who put up a monument at Truro in 1872 to educator Alexander Forrester) or wealthy individuals (like Governor-General Matthew Whitworth-Aylmer, who had a truncated column erected in 1832 to mark the spot where Wolfe died). The federal government rarely became involved in such matters, though it did so on occasion, putting up statues in Ottawa and commemorating certain events and individuals in other locations as well. In 1895, for instance, it marked the Battle of Chateauguay and in 1904, Sieur de Monts.

While there was considerable enthusiasm in Canada during the last quarter of the 19th century for raising monuments to the past, Louisbourg was not one of the sites selected. The two sieges fought there, particularly the one in 1758, were widely acknowledged to have been historically important. Nonetheless, the area had not yet attracted anyone with either the money or, with one exception, the interest to push for some type of commemoration. Clerics, historians, and journalists offered their descriptions and comments on its ruins, but no fund raisers or organizers came forward to start campaigns to protect or mark the former French town. The only published call for a monument at Louisbourg appeared in *Picturesque Canada* (1882) in the entry on Cape Breton written by Rev. Robert Murray, editor of the *Presbyterian Witness* and J.S. McLennan, a Montreal-born industrialist involved in the development of Cape Breton coal mines. In the section on Louisbourg, almost certainly written by McLennan, the author asked "Should not some memorial be raised which would show that Canadians ... are still mindful of the great deeds done on Canadian soil? There could be no fitter site than ... Louisbourg, where French and English dust co-mingles in peace ...."[12] More of an observation than a request, the call for a "memorial" remained unanswered. But particularly noteworthy was the author's appreciation of the bicultural significance and appeal of the Louisbourg site. It was an idea that would be developed more fully in the future.

When Louisbourg did finally receive its first memorial it came not from Canada, or even from France or Great Britain, but from the United States. One of the many organizations established in the United States during the 19th century[13] to promote history and patriotism was the Society of Colonial Wars. The first society bearing that name was formed by a "group of gentlemen" in New York in 1892. By the following year there were other Colonial Wars societies in Pennyslvania, Maryland, Massachusetts, Connecticut and the District of Columbia, as well as a General Society, based in New York City, which was formed by delegates from each of the state organizations. The purpose of these groups was to perpetuate the memory of events from the pre-revolutionary period in American history.[14] One of their first projects was to erect a suitable monument at Louisbourg to mark the 150th anniversary of the New Englanders' conquest of the French town in 1745. A monument was designed (a 26-foot column), a location selected (just outside the King's Bastion ruins) and a date set for the unveiling (17 June 1895).

As the details of the unveiling ceremony were being completed, word of the proposed commemoration reached unsympathetic ears in Atlantic Canada. Three French-language newspapers (*Evangéline, Courrier des Provinces Maritimes* and *Moniteur Acadien*), and one English Catholic weekly (Antigonish *Casket*) protested the idea of a group from a foreign country raising a monument on Canadian soil to what had been a Canadian defeat. They considered the project an "aggressive demonstration" by a "few Americans of the old school" that would be felt as an "insult" by all French-Canadians.[15] One distinguished French-Canadian who certainly did feel that way was New Brunswick author and Senator, Pascal Poirier. Speaking in the Senate, Poirier informed his listeners that the memorial proposal had "aroused an unpleasant feeling" in the Maritimes and that it violated the norms of "international decency." He added his personal voice to the others protesting the commemoration and asked what the federal government would do to prevent it. Prime Minister Sir Mackenzie Bowell, a member of the Senate, replied simply that the government knew very little about it since the monument was being erected by a private society on private land.[16]

Two weeks before the scheduled unveiling new protests were made, from a group not normally regarded as being overly sympathetic to the sentiments of French-Canadians: the United Empire Loyalists Association of Canada. Meeting in Montreal, the association resolved that the monument "will necessarily prove offensive to a great section of the Canadian people, and especially to the Acadians" and therefore should be reconsidered. Their protest, likely motivated as much by anti-American sentiment as anything else, was forwarded to the solicitor-general, J.J. Curran, who referred the matter to Prime Minister Bowell, "who took no action."[17]

Notwithstanding the various complaints, the monument was unveiled as planned, and with considerable government participation. Not only was it arranged to have two vessels anchored in the harbour for the occasion, identified as the HMS *Canada* and the "Dominion cruiser" *Curlew*, but the memorial itself was unveiled by Lieutenant-Governor Sir Malachy Daly of Nova Scotia on behalf of the Governor-General of Canada, the Earl of Aberdeen. Aberdeen sent his regrets that he could not be there in person, as did United States President Grover Cleveland. Twenty-five hundred people attended the festivities, which included two hours of speeches by various Canadian and American dignitaries. Most of the speakers were clearly aware of the protests that had surfaced in the months leading up to the unveiling and did their best to answer charges that the monument celebrated the defeat of the French. Nearly every person who addressed the crowd referred at least once to the achievements and valour of France and French-Canadians. Such remarks seem to have been inserted largely to mollify possible critics, for speaker after speaker emphasized what was in reality the main theme of the occasion: the unity and greatness of the Anglo-Saxon race.[18] Just as England and New England had cooperated to conquer Louisbourg in 1745, so it was hoped that there would always be, in Lieutenant-Governor Daly's words, "fraternal good will ... between New England and Old England; and that every Canadian who may gaze upon it [the monument] may learn the lesson plainly taught by it, that what Colonists have done before, Colonists can do again." The address of Sydney native Sir John G. Bourinot, chief clerk of the House of Commons, who could not attend in person but whose speech was nonetheless read to the assembled multitude, was perhaps the most explicit expression of Anglophile and Whig sentiments. He wrote that though it was not "the humiliation of France we celebrate ... it was a happy day for Canada ... for English as well as French Canadians -- that the fleur-de-lys fell from the fortress of Louisbourg and Québec."[19]

Two days after the gala event Pascal Poirier rose in the Senate to repeat his objections, and to express his disappointment that the monument was unveiled by a representative of the crown. He also asked questions about the ownership of land at Louisbourg. Poirier found it difficult to believe that the area did not belong to either the Nova Scotia or Canadian government, as other former British ordnance lands had been transferred to the governments at

Figure 1. Top: View of the Louisbourg Ruins as depicted by J.E. Woolford in 1818 (Dalhousie University Library). Bottom: Unveiling of Society of Colonial Wars Monument, 1895 (Cape Breton Regional Library - Louisbourg).

the time of Confederation. He urged the federal authorities to clarify the status of the site. Prime Minister Bowell explained that for reasons unknown the Louisbourg fortifications had not been included in the ordnance lands transferred to the Canadian Department of Militia and Defence in 1882. (By 1895 the site of historic Louisbourg was divided into more than 20 different lots, all owned privately).

As for the Society of Colonial War ceremony, Bowell understood that "due praise" had been given to the French by the various speakers. On the general question of historic site preservation and monument-raising the Prime Minister commented that initiatives in that area were praiseworthy as they tended to "nationalize our people."[20]

Senator Poirier continued to press for action at Louisbourg. In 1902 he travelled to Cape Breton on behalf of the Royal Society of Canada to view the ruins and surrounding area. The society took this action partially in response to a letter from Professor Benjamin Rand of Harvard University that had been read at their May 1900 meeting. Rand described Louisbourg as "the most interesting historical ruin in the eastern part of North America," and urged the Government of Canada to acquire it "as a public park for all time to come." Poirier presented his report at the annual meeting of the Society, and published an article in *Acadiensis* that made the same basic points.[21] Poirier described historic Louisbourg as "a field of desolation and ruin ... occupied by squatters" and vandalised by souvenir-seeking tourists. Worse still, the site might soon undergo massive redevelopment by American concerns. The harbour was Canada's closest to Europe (already it served as the winter port for Cape Breton coal) and there was talk that "United States capitalists" were building a road from Canso to the area, where they had "taken an option of all the ground where the old Louisbourg fort stood." Poirier could envisage the entire historic area being sacrificed to the interests of foreign capitalists and he deplored the prospect. He asked when Canada would enact legislation such as France had done in 1887 to protect its properties of historic and artistic value. Surely if the government of Canada could spend $80,000 to purchase the Plains of Abraham, it could spend what was needed to stop the "wanton devastation" and preserve "at least the remaining ruins of old glorious Louisbourg."[22]

One who shared Pascal Poirier's concern for the preservation of the Louisbourg ruins was Captain D.J. Kennelly, ironically one of the industrialists who was reshaping the face of Cape Breton at the turn of the 20th century. Born in Ireland, employed in India by the East India Company and the Royal Indian Navy, Kennelly also trained as a lawyer in England before coming to Cape Breton during the 1870s. Initially, he represented a group of London capitalists who were interested in constructing a railway from New Glasgow to Louisbourg (thereby linking Cape Breton to the other train networks of the eastern seaboard), and then in establishing an express steamship service between Louisbourg and Milford Haven, England. The hope was that Louisbourg, not New York, would thereby become the North American terminus of trans-Atlantic passenger travel.[23] Funds were never secured to implement the idea, but Kennelly stayed in the area and became the general manager of the Sydney and Louisburg Coal and Railway Company, as well as a large shareholder in the Cape Breton Coal, Iron and Railway Company.[24] He is credited with introducing the first coal-cutting machines into eastern Canadian collieries and with being the first Cape Breton businessman to employ a stenographer and typewriter.[25] Modern though his business ideas were, Captain Kennelly was also fascinated with ruins and relics.

Kennelly came to acquire more than a dozen pieces of property in the Louisbourg area.[26] Two of the lots, purchased between 1901 and 1903, were within the confines of the old French town; upon them stood the most prominent of the 18th-century ruins, the arches of the casemates of the King's Bastion. Starting with the need to protect those structures Kennelly began in 1903 an international campaign entitled the Louisburg Memorial Fund. The premise of the fund in Kennelly's mind was that it was a "sacred duty" of the 20th century to preserve "remnants" of the past and as far as Louisbourg was concerned, to "keep in memory" the "heroic dead." Specifically, he called for the stabilization of the casemate ruins, the fencing and improvement of nearby burial grounds, and the erection of a large masonry tower within which there would be a museum as well as marble panels listing the names of the ships, regiments and officers who fought in each siege.[27] In front of the tower he planned to erect a bronze equestrian statue of Edward VII, "The Peacemaker." Beneath the tower Kennelly envisioned "underground Mortuary Chambers to contain the relics of the dead found on the site and ... for the remains of Canadian heroes of the future."[28]

Kennelly convinced a remarkable number of prominent people to lend support to his scheme. The patron of the Louisburg Memorial Fund was Edward VII; vice patrons, of whom there were more than 40, included Sir Charles Tupper, Robert Borden, the governors of five American states, six Canadian lieutenant-governors, 14 British peers, and the president of Harvard University. Premier G.H. Murray of Nova Scotia was the president of the fund, and committee members included five other premiers, three Canadian senators (including Pascal Poirier) and various wealthy Americans. President Theodore Roosevelt did not join the organization, but did send his "cordial good wishes" for success. Kennelly contented himself with the title Honorary Secretary.[29]

Captain Kennelly estimated that it would cost $25,000 to accomplish his programme of preservation and commemoration. He hoped that the governments of Canada and Nova Scotia would contribute $5,000 each[30] and that the rest could be obtained through a fund-raising drive. To that end, he promised that everyone who gave ten dollars or more would have his portrait preserved in the museum; lesser contributors would have their names listed. By late 1905 he had raised more than $1,200, about half of which came from Great Britain, mostly from the regiments that had served at Louisbourg.[31]

In April 1906 Kennelly took his campaign to the Nova Scotia legislature, where he secured the passage of "An Act to incorporate the Trustees of the French Fortress and Old Burying Ground at Louisburg as an Historical Monument of the Dominion of Canada and as a Public Work."[32] Kennelly boasted that it was the first time in Canadian history that a historical monument in the country had been "legalized." The act named 11 individuals (one British, one American and the rest Canadian) as the formal trustees of the Louisbourg ruins and burial ground and gave them the power to acquire whatever land they needed "for the purpose of said memorial, historical monument and public work." It also empowered them to make whatever regulations they deemed necessary, as long as they were not contrary to provincial law, to manage the site. Finally, it spelled out the fines (from four to 40 dollars) or jail terms (up to 60 days) to be assessed for vandals and public nuisances.

Kennelly also devoted attention to the ruins he wished to protect. In 1903 he began to "preserve" the casemates of the King's Bastion by removing layers of earth and stone and replacing them with cement. This project continued during each of the next three summers, with Kennelly personally supervising all aspects of the work. He even had a small building containing sleeping quarters erected beside the ruins so that he could stay as close as possible to the site.[33] Although Kennelly had created, on paper, a large organization to oversee the project, and he was only one of 11 legal trustees, the captain seems to have carried out his preservation efforts according to his own desires. A fellow trustee, lawyer and former

Mayor of Sydney, Walter Crowe, stated that Kennelly spent the funds that came in "according to his own notion, without consulting or reporting to anyone."[34] Crowe told Kennelly that he was "going at the thing in the wrong way," but the former naval captain chose to disregard him.[35]

Captain Kennelly died in August 1907, aged 76, and the first attempt to preserve what was left of 18th-century Louisbourg died with him. The fund-raising stopped and the work on the ruins came to an end. Although there were ten other trustees to carry on the project, no initiatives were forthcoming from them for the next five years. When at last a meeting was called by Walter Crowe in January 1913, no one but Crowe was able to attend.[36] Undoubtedly Kennelly had realized that none of the trustees possessed the same commitment to Louisbourg that he did. Yet he obviously hoped that somehow his project might be brought to completion. In his will of 23 August 1907 he bequeathed his fortress properties and $88,000 worth of bonds in the Cape Breton Coal, Iron and Railway Company to the premier, chief justice and another justice of the Supreme Court of Nova Scotia, as trustees, to finish the work he had started.[37] Unfortunately, that bequest was impressive only on paper. The bonds were without any market value[38] and the land gift served only to delay and complicate subsequent development. Later court action was required to have the sections in Kennelly's will pertaining to Louisbourg declared null and void. According to the decision of the Supreme Court of Nova Scotia in 1919, Kennelly's Louisbourg lots were to be sold "for the best available price."[39] They were not sold, however, and remained tied up in Kennelly's estate until 1924.

Despite Kennelly's obvious achievements, a decade after his death historic Louisbourg was still a jumble of ruins and shanties. Indeed it is questionable whether Kennelly's efforts had improved the site or made it worse. His preservation work was judged in 1920 to have been "somewhat amateurish," with insufficient waterproofing and drainage,[40] and his proposals for a memorial tower and equestrian statue left the area with two foundations that had "nothing to do with Old Louisbourg and are an eyesore and an anachronism."[41] In 1930 they would be "razed to ground level and the waste material removed."[42]

Not long after the death of D.J. Kennelly and the ensuing collapse of the Louisburg Memorial Fund, new appeals were made for the federal government to take action at Louisbourg. Speaking to the Nova Scotia Historical Society in 1908, J.S. McLennan, by this time a retired industrialist and the publisher of the Sydney Post, declared that "the preservation of historic sites is too large a task for private or co-operate undertaking. Indeed, part of its significance would be lost were it not for the action of the people through their governments."[43] McLennan's thoughts were echoed by others: L.B. Runk addressing the Pennsylvania Society of Colonial Wars in 1911, and Beckles Willson in the *Canadian Magazine* in 1914.[44] Both called for government acquisition of the historic area and a general cleanup of the grounds. McLennan possessed a far grander vision of what could be accomplished. Well into his research on the French occupation of Louisbourg,[45] McLennan knew the rich documentary and cartographic record the town had left behind. He argued that it was possible "to reconstruct the city as it was ... [it] is only a question of intelligence and outlay." Though later he would ask for more, in 1908 McLennan urged the reconstruction of only a single building, the intendant's house, which would serve as a museum.[46] Beyond that he hoped to see the streets, major structures, siege positions, and courage of individuals marked or commemorated in some way.

It was one thing to recommend that a historic site be acquired by the federal government; it was quite another to find a department or agency with the inclination or capability to oversee such sites. Since 1885, when the government acquired the Banff Hot Springs, the Department of the Interior had administered selected natural areas as National Parks.[47] Historic sites, however, were not initially part of Interior's mandate, or of that of any other ministry. The Department of Militia and Defence controlled a number of fortifications which had long since outlived their military usefulness, and which would eventually become historic sites and parks, but there was no set procedure for that transformation. Fort Howe (Saint John) and Fort Anne (Annapolis Royal), both believed to have been sites of "stirring events in the early history" of the country,[48] had been added *ad hoc* to Interior's National Park system in 1914 and 1917, but those steps were taken without specific legislation or policy guidelines concerning the acquisition and administration of historic sites. The only body actively examining the question of historic site development at the time was a non-governmental body, the Historic Landmarks Association (which became the Canadian Historical Association in 1922). The Landmarks Association had been created by the Royal Society of Canada in 1907 to prepare for the Quebec Tercentenary celebrations the following year. Beyond that it was to work for the preservation and commemoration of historic landmarks across the country. Yet while the Historic Landmarks people had the knowledge of Canadian history to make appropriate recommendations, they lacked the money and power to take significant action on their suggestions.

A partial solution to the problem was found in 1919, when the Historic Sites and Monuments Board of Canada [HSMBC] was created. Instrumental in the establishment of the Board was J.B. Harkin, an Ontario-born journalist who in 1911 had become Commissioner of the Dominion Parks Branch of the Department of the Interior. As both the public servant in charge of Canada's parks and a member of the Historic Landmarks Association, Harkin was aware of the need to bridge the gap between the worlds of administration and historical knowledge. His solution, suggested in 1919, was for the federal government to appoint "an honorary board or committee ... of men from all parts of the country who are authorities on Canadian history, to advise the Department in the matter of preserving those sites which preeminently possess Dominion wide interest." Arthur Meighen, Minister of the Interior at the time, approved the principle and the first members of the board were selected: two from Ontario, one each from Quebec, Nova Scotia and New Brunswick, as well as two civil servants, including Harkin. The first meeting of the new advisory body took place in Ottawa in October 1919.[49]

One of the first sites to be considered by the HSMBC was Louisbourg, which was considered historically important because the siege there in 1758 had played a pivotal role in determining the outcome of the Anglo-French struggle for North America. Anxious though the board was to have the historic area of Louisbourg preserved, it was uncertain what course of action to recommend because of the complicated land situation there. Ownership was divided among more than two dozen local families, D.J. Kennelly's estate, and the Cape Breton Railway Company.[50] The Department of the Interior had title searches and general investigations carried out during 1920 and 1921, and in May 1921 the board made its recommendations: first, that the Kennelly properties be acquired by the government and second, that a caretaker be hired for the summer months "to stop people from taking away relics."[51] One month later the Parks Branch acquired its first land at Louisbourg: two lots (comprising 69 acres) that had formerly belonged to the Cape Breton Railway Company were transferred to the Department of the Interior by the federal Department of Railways and Canals.[52] While Louisbourg was not yet an official historic site, a beginning had been made.

To those who cared most deeply about Louisbourg, the initial land acquisition was far from sufficient. McLennan, who had been made a Senator in 1916, complained privately and publicly of the "negligence" the Department of the Interior was showing toward both Louisbourg and Fort Cumberland.[53] Harkin of the Parks Branch responded with assurances that Louisbourg was a top priority and definite progress was being made, but McLennan was not satisfied. He urged, as he had more than a decade earlier, that a special commission be formed to look after the historic sites of the Maritimes.[54] Otherwise, argued McLennan and New Brunswick physician, historian and museologist Dr. J.C. Webster, the neglect of the region's sites would continue. To a certain extent, their complaint that Maritime history was being ignored or forgotten by the rest of the country was but one more variation on the widespread sense of alienation present in the region during the 1920s, and which produced the Maritime Rights movement.[55] A more practical idea than a Maritime commission on historic sites perhaps was the proposal to give the National Battlefields Commission at Quebec control over sites such as Louisbourg.[56] The Minister of Militia and Defence, Sam Hughes, had stated that was to be the government's approach to Louisbourg,[57] but government officials were reluctant to create a new commission or to expand the mandate of the Battlefields Commission. The fear, as expressed by Harkin, was that such commissions might propose elaborate schemes and large-scale expenditures, which would prove "embarrassing" to the government. The option preferred by Harkin and other officials within the Parks Branch was to create a simple advisory committee, without executive or financial power, to offer advice to the HSMBC. The board in turn would pass on recommendations to the government for its consideration.[58] Accordingly, in 1923 the two Maritime members of the HSMBC, Major J. Plimsoll Edwards of Halifax and J.C. Webster of Shediac, were designated a special sub-committee to report on the situation at Louisbourg. Both men were already on record as favouring greater commemoration and development at Louisbourg.

Edwards had told the other board members that Louisbourg "was one of the most important [historic sites] in Canada, and its present condition was a disgrace." Webster had expressed similar views in public, and privately he told McLennan that the only reason he had joined the HSMBC was because Charles Stewart, the Minister of the Interior, had personally assured him "that a new forward policy will be adopted in the Lower Provinces."[59]

Webster and Edwards arrived in Cape Breton in the summer of 1923 to tour the Louisbourg site and meet with two of the local people most interested in its development: Senator McLennan and Archdeacon T.F. Draper, Anglican minister at Louisbourg. Their persuasiveness, combined with the "disgraceful"[60] condition of the historic area, convinced the two visitors of the need for prompt and extensive action. The programme they recommended went far beyond anything that had been suggested to date. Webster and Edwards, seconded by McLennan and Draper, proposed the acquisition of the entire site of historic Louisbourg (town, fortifications, detached batteries, lighthouse), the removal of all buildings and fences, the appointment of a permanent caretaker and the construction of a residence for him, and the employment of a military engineer to mark, with two-foot-high stone markers, the streets and principal buildings of the 18th-century town. In addition, the fortifications were to be put "in some sort of order."[61]

The proposals were impressive, far more impressive than either the HSMBC or the Parks Branch could support. Board chairman Brigadier-General E.A. Cruikshank, a noted historian of central-Canadian topics, wrote Harkin that as far as he was concerned, for the time being four cairns should be erected at Louisbourg and nothing more. The more elaborate ideas did not merit discussion until Parliament voted a special appropriation for "commemoration on a grandiose scale."[62] Harkin was undoubtedly relieved to receive Cruikshank's views, for the Parks Branch was in no position to pay for the development Webster and Edwards were urging. The bulk of the branch's funds were committed to the natural parks in the west. Only five per cent or less was being spent on historic sites,[63] and this imbalance was a source for some bitterness among historical enthusiasts. As Webster commented in 1924, "It is all very well to preserve the buffalo, but when our historic centres suffer on their account the people are justified in raising a storm."[64] Webster may have been comforted somewhat when former Prime

Minister Arthur Meighen told him that he would "help pass a special appropriation for Louisbourg" in the next session of Parliament.[65]

Preservation efforts at Louisbourg proceeded very slowly. The failure to acquire and protect the historic ruins meant that they continued to deteriorate. Nothing illustrated that more clearly than what happened in 1923 to the ruins of the 18th-century French lighthouse. In 1922 fire destroyed the Louisbourg light erected during the 19th century near the site of the old French lighthouse. Construction of the replacement light began in 1923, but the federal Department of Marine and Fisheries, which held responsibility for coastal navigational aids, decided to rebuild on the site of the original 18th-century lighthouse. At the time, the ruins of the old French lighthouse consisted of seven to eight feet of exterior wall, an intact entrance doorway, and several steps of the circular staircase. According to Archdeacon Draper, "the greatest part of this was ruthlessly torn down" in preparation for the new structure. The 200-year old ruins were dismantled stone by stone until the workers came across the original foundation tablet. At that point the engineer in charge was called in and he decided to select another location for the new lighthouse. As Draper put it, "it was a case of shutting the door after the horse was stolen."[66] Dr. Webster added his lament, informing the Parks Branch that he was inclined to "lay the matter before the Premier" and that he would not be sorry if the press raised a "howl" about it. The fact that a government department had been responsible for the destruction made it a particularly "sickening story."[67] In Ottawa, Harkin shared the dismay and through the Deputy Minister of the Interior a request was made to the Department of Marine and Fisheries to have the remaining lighthouse ruins and any artifacts found there transferred to the jurisdiction of the Parks Branch.[68]

The Parks Branch began to address the ownership problem in the mid-1920s. The first of the private lots to which it sought to acquire clear title were those tied up in D.J. Kennelly's estate, and upon which stood the ruins of the casemates of the King's Bastion. Walter Crowe was employed to oversee the passage of a bill through the Nova Scotia legislature that would transfer the property left to the Trustees of the French Fortress to the control of the Department of the Interior. Crowe contacted all the trustees to obtain their approval for the scheme, drafted the legislation, found an MLA to introduce and support it, and then answered questions about it at the committee stage. In May 1924 the Parks Branch had finally acquired the much-photographed symbol of Louisbourg's vanished glory.[69] With the transfer of the Kennelly lots to the federal government the Parks Branch possessed more than 70 acres of historic Louisbourg, or roughly one-fifth of the total area recommended for acquisition. Crowe, and to a lesser extent J.C. Webster, urged Harkin to work to have the site declared a National Park, and to add on to it as the years went by. Harkin demurred, stating that it was not "an opportune time" because of the demand "for economy in public expenditure."[70]

While unwilling to see Louisbourg declared a National Park, the federal government did grant the site its first official recognition as a historic place in 1926. On 10 August 1926, before about 400 onlookers, four commemorative plaques, on cairns, were unveiled at selected locations around the harbour.[71] Each of the plaques was bilingual, although there had initially been some doubt whether French versions of the text were called for.[72] But when an official within the Parks Branch pointed out that Louisbourg was "as much ... or even more" a French site than an English one, and that the full support of francophone MPs would be needed to obtain a special appropriation for the development of Louisbourg, it was decided to erect bilingual plaques.[73] In a similar vein, in choosing the date for the 1926 unveiling the dates of the two capitulations of Louisbourg were considered but deliberately rejected so as not to "wound the feelings of our French-Canadian friends."[74]

Foremost among the French-Canadians of the 1920s who were interested in the fate of historic Louisbourg was Henri Bourassa, the Quebec nationalist, journalist and politician. In August 1927 Bourassa stopped at Louisbourg in the company of a large group of French-Canadians from Quebec and Ontario who were touring the Maritimes. It was his second visit to the site -- he had been there 30 years earlier -- and he was "amazed" by the deterioration of the ruins during the intervening period. Standing on the remains of one of the bastions, Bourassa addressed a crowd of 200 Acadians, the English population of modern Louisbourg, and his companions from central Canada. Bourassa vowed to "bring before Parliament ... the necessity of preserving what is left of the historic Fort Louisburg." He kept his promise the following year, rising in the House of Commons to complain of the "terrible state of abandonment" at Louisbourg, and of the need to clean up and protect the site. The Minister of the Interior, Charles Stewart, commented only that "This is being done."[75]

Indeed, at long last, some major steps were being taken at Louisbourg. In 1928 the federal government appropriated $19,000 for the purchase of most of the private properties at historic Louisbourg and an additional $3,000 for the initial development of the acquired land. By the end of August, 13 properties had either been obtained or had options taken on them. With the terrain now in its hands, the government was finally prepared to make the long awaited announcement; Stewart officially designated Louisbourg a National Historic Site. Appropriately, discussion began within the Parks Branch on how best to develop its latest site.[76] Two quite different approaches were recommended. The first was chiefly a landscaping approach, designed to maximize the aesthetic and emotional experience of visiting the ruins. The second approach placed an emphasis on educating the public about the nature, extent and lay of the original town.

The simpler approach was advocated in 1923 by Thomas Adams, a British town planner who had come to Canada to work for the Commission of Conservation.[77] Following a visit to Louisbourg on behalf of the Parks Branch, Adams offered his thoughts on how best to develop the historical area. He wrote that the site was "an impressive one .... There is a certain grandeur and wildness ... that makes one feel in a mood to enjoy its romantic character and visualize the historic events." Adams regarded the existing structures as impediments to enjoyment of the site and recommended that they be removed. The 1895 monument he considered "harmless," but "it is the ruins, the earthworks and the barren burying ground that make the real memorials." He strongly urged the branch not to spend any money to reconstruct the fortifications, but to concentrate its efforts instead on making "the ruins endurable as 'ruins' ... to give the site the appearance of not having been tampered with by 'restorers' and only suffering from natural decay and the effect of time."[78] Before travelling to Cape Breton Adams had been told by F.H.H. Williamson of the Parks Branch to contact only Archdeacon Draper during his visit to Louisbourg.[79] Such an instruction is surprising considering that Senator McLennan, Walter Crowe and Dr. Webster were the most vocal and prominent of the site's boosters at the time. The explanation is likely that the branch feared the grandiose schemes these men might have proposed to

Adams, and that the planner might have agreed with them. It must have seemed safer to have him talk only to the knowledgeable but less "restoration"-oriented Archdeacon Draper.

And indeed, when McLennan, Crowe and Webster later formally submitted their schemes for the development of Louisbourg their recommendations were far more elaborate. This second approach was first worked out in detail by McLennan in 1928, following a visit to Valley Forge. The senator was extremely impressed by the American site and he drew up a development plan for Louisbourg using the same "underlying principles."[80] His ideas were endorsed by Webster and Crowe and formed the basis of the report the two HSMBC members submitted to the Parks Branch in 1930.[81] Their plan envisioned the reconstruction of selected areas of the original settlement so as to give the "ordinary visitor a vivid picture of the place where events of so great historical significance" had taken place. Secondary objectives included the collection and display of documents and artifacts in a permanent, fireproof museum and the provision of research material to interested archaeologists and historians. None of the proponents of this approach, including McLennan, had in mind anything as sweeping as the modern Fortress of Louisbourg reconstruction, but they did wish to see some of the fortifications, two gates, and a couple of the major buildings rebuilt, along with the marking of such things as streets and siege positions.[82] The call for such extensive development reflected the approaches McLennan, Webster and Crowe had seen in the United States at Valley Forge and Fort Ticonderoga, and echoed the ideas being put forth in post-World War I America where "for the first time, groups of people organized to reconstruct significant buildings that had ceased to exist."[83] Webster personally hoped to see France and Great Britain put up columns on the other heights of land similar to the Society of Colonial Wars monument. However, Senator McLennan was "steadfastly opposed" to this proposal, arguing that in a country "such as Canada is now, I think we want to avoid the suggestion that any work we do marks the victory of the British over the French" -- which he felt would be the case if the British monument were on a higher hill than the memorial to the French. Moreover, in McLennan's opinion, anything erected at Louisbourg should be "strictly in the spirit of the period, or exact replicas."[84]

Once the historic terrain at Louisbourg was finally in the

Parks Branch's control, how did it assess the development options and select the course of action to follow? To what principles or policy guidelines did it turn to decide whether it would have evocative ruins, reconstructed walls and buildings, commemorative markers or some other approach? Being much more preoccupied with its large western natural parks, the branch had not yet acquired much experience in historical matters and largely made up its policy as it went along. Some decisions were relatively easy, such as not allowing people to sell artificial flowers or open a tea room on the historic site.[85] But on the broader questions of development philosophy the branch was much less certain. Without much experience on its own small staff, it leaned heavily on the advice of the HSMBC members and knowledgeable citizens, such as Senator McLennan. But however impressed the staff of the Parks Branch may have been by the submissions of the Louisbourg enthusiasts,[86] there were certain budgetary realities they had to keep in mind. They simply did not have the funds to pay for all the projects urged by the site's boosters. They were constrained to begin modestly and spread the work over many years. Nevertheless, the plan they adopted incorporated most of the ideas put forth by McLennan, Webster, Crowe and others.

The Parks Branch programme began in 1929, and continued during the summer months over the next decade, with additional projects being undertaken in 1949, 1950 and 1955.[87] This work consisted primarily of doing further preservation work on the casemates of the King's Bastion, excavating selected building locations (barracks, hospital, convent, the De Mézy residence), reconstructing the walls of those structures to a height of several feet, and uncovering several of the streets of the original town. Progress was slow but the advancing work finally stopped the appeals for a special Louisbourg commission to take charge of the development of the site.[88] Instead, a group of interested and knowledgeable local people, including Senator McLennan, his daughter Katharine, Archdeacon Draper, and Mayor M.S. Huntington of Louisbourg were chosen to advise board members how best to proceed at the site.[89] The advisory committee's recommendations were numerous and well received, and the fact that they were made to feel a part of the process meant that there was largely an end to the earlier complaints concerning the Parks Branch's inaction or lack of expertise.[90] The branch also selected an Honorary Superintendent and a caretaker from the local population to look after the year-round maintenance and upkeep of the historic site. Those appointments, combined with the employment

Figure 2.Top: Unveiling of the Historic Sites and Monuments Board of Canada plaque commemorating the King's Bastion, 1926.(Courtesy of Parks Canada) Bottom:In the foreground, the excavated ruins of the King's Bastion barracks; in the background, the masonry museum completed in 1936, and beside it the former interim museum. (Courtesy Parks Canada).

generated by the projects carried out each summer, generally won the support of the nearby community for the work of the Parks Branch. The only contentious issue to surface between the branch and members of the community were charges that political affiliation was a factor in determining who was hired at various positions.[91]

To protect and display the artifacts recovered during the excavation, as well as other objects donated to the site, a masonry (that is, fireproof) museum was completed in 1936. Placed in charge of the collection, and given the title of Honorary Curator, was Katharine McLennan, who held the position for the next 25 years. Her contributions, all of which were made as a volunteer, included cataloguing the artifact collection, organizing the displays, writing the site's historical brochure, making two large models, and coordinating all special events. In many ways the opening of the museum represented the culmination of years of effort to preserve and develop Louisbourg as a historic site. Captain Kennelly had envisioned a museum within his proposed tower, and Senator McLennan, Dr. Webster and Walter Crowe had pushed for the construction of one throughout the 1920s and early 1930s to achieve the educational objectives they set for a properly developed historic site.[92]

In 1940, after additional land had been acquired in the area and following a campaign by another Cape Breton historical enthusiast, Albert Almon, an outsider to the McLennan, Webster and Crowe group,[93] the status of the site was raised so that it became the Fortress of Louisbourg National Historic Park. The inclusion of "fortress" in the official name was not welcomed by everyone because it did not reflect the 18th-century designation of the place, which had been as either "Ville de Louisbourg" or "Port de Louisbourg." Both Crowe and Webster had complained to Harkin in 1929 about the site being referred to by branch personnel as Fort Louisbourg, a name which they considered "unfortunate and inappropriate," apparently because it suggested that the original settlement had been little more than a military outpost. Their preference was for simply Louisbourg National Historic Park.[94] McLennan likely shared that view as he thought there should not be too much made of the military history at Louisbourg because "the two races who there competed ... are making Canada what it is" today.[95] Such views differed drastically from those expressed earlier in the 20th century and throughout the 19th century. Where Louisbourg had earlier been regarded almost exclusively as the site of one of the principal battles in the struggle for North America, McLennan and others were consciously attempting to minimize the military conflicts. It was the beginning of a trend that continues today in the modern reconstruction, with its emphasis on French civilian and garrison activities of 1744.

The story of the preservation of historic Louisbourg is largely one of a few dedicated individuals who believed, for a variety of reasons, that the site of the 18th-century French town deserved to be protected and commemorated. To that end, according to their perspective and means, they erected monuments and organized and prodded others into action. When the only private initiative, Kennelly's Louisburg Memorial Fund, failed, subsequent enthusiasts sought the blessing and financial assistance of the federal government. In that respect the situation was quite different from that which was occurring in the contemporary United States where wealthy philanthropists or groups of ordinary citizens were achieving similar results without government involvement. Most of the people involved in the preservation of Louisbourg considered government ownership of the site not only necessary but also desirable. Budget constraints and a general lack of familiarity with historical matters caused the government to react slowly, at Louisbourg and elsewhere. But in the end, through perseverance, the historical enthusiasts convinced the federal authorities to carry out a programme during the 1930s that achieved most of their development objectives.

And what was the overall goal of the effort? Why bother with the ruins of a settlement that had existed for less than five decades and then virtually disappeared from history? Obviously their purpose was not to foster ancestor worship as none of the individuals involved, except for a few of the New Englanders, could claim to be descended from people at all associated with 18th-century Louisbourg. Nor was it to preserve structures of architectural or aesthetic merit. Tourism was often cited as a likely side benefit, but never as a major goal. For Captain D.J. Kennelly, who seemed to feel an almost mystical bond with the past, the preservation of places like Louisbourg was the "sacred duty" of the 20th century. To most of the other enthusiasts, however, the project deserved to be undertaken for more commonplace, though no less worthy reasons. The most common argument was that a preserved Louisbourg would inspire Canadians. Henri Bourassa, for instance, stated that a trip to the site might be like "passing through the ruins of Pompeii," stimulating visitors to think of their nation's history. In particular, he mentioned that it might arouse in the "considerable foreign population" of industrial Cape Breton, "a desire to study the past of their adopted country."[96]

Dr. J.C. Webster was of a similar opinion, maintaining that historic sites like Louisbourg offer an "inspirational stimulus and foster an interest in the country." Webster contrasted historic sites, which he thought should be accessible to everyone, to the resort areas in natural parks which "cater to the rich" and which "the toiling masses will never see."[97] In a critical assessment of Canada's educational and cultural conditions, published in 1926, he lamented that the average Canadian "thinks of his land not as part of a mighty heritage which has been won through blood and sacrifice, and made sacred by the memories of the past, but merely of its value in dollars."[98] Webster saw historic site development as a way to counteract this deplorable situation. In the United States, he pointed out, citizens were taught to respect past achievements and heroes. He hoped that in Canada heritage preservation might encourage patriotism and a distinct identity.

Senator J.S. McLennan also seems to have believed that the preservation and development of historic Louisbourg might contribute to the creation of a distinctive national identity. More than any of the others involved in the project McLennan was sensitive to the bicultural reality of the country and the need to cultivate goodwill between French and English Canadians. Part of the explanation for this sensitivity seems to have been his Montreal upbringing,[99] for both he and his brother William, a well-known 19th-century novelist, were captivated by French-Canadian history. Yet nationalistic considerations only partly explain McLennan's passionate interest in preserving Louisbourg. The short, tumultuous history of the town fascinated him, and aware as he was from his years of research that "there is abundant material for an almost complete reconstruction of the town and its fortifications," he could never lose sight of that possibility. McLennan's proposals were always the most elaborate to be submitted, but more importantly, he placed the greatest emphasis on the need for professionalism in the treatment of the site, calling for thorough research and expert advice on specialty matters. It was McLennan's earnest hope that "in the fu-

PRESERVING HISTORY

ture those who see what has been done at this time, will recognize that the people in charge had high standards as to what their work should be" and that it will reflect "credit" on them.[100] He wished "to build up a monument - not only of the historic past - but to the intelligence and goodwill of all concerned in bringing it into existence."[101] One suspects that the preservation and development of historic Louisbourg was to McLennan above all else an intellectual challenge, a jigsaw puzzle of enormous proportions.

Ironically, most of the commemorative efforts of 1895-1940 did not have a long lifespan, at least in their original form. During the reconstruction project of the 1960s the Colonial Wars monument was relocated and damaged in the process. Two of the HSMBC cairns and plaques were simply removed. Most of the ruins excavated and stabilized during the 1930s were re-excavated, and then had buildings erected over them. Even the museum was not safe. Not only were its contents removed but there was also talk for a time that the structure itself might be torn down. Despite these changes, the early efforts must be judged a success, in that they had helped draw public and government attention to the 18th-century history of the site at Louisbourg. J.S. McLennan's dream of a reconstructed Louisbourg was not to be accomplished in his lifetime because he died in 1939, 22 years before that project began.[102] But the basic principles that he enunciated, first that preservation work must be undertaken only when it is based on research and directed by people with expertise, and second, that it is posterity and not just present-day concerns that will judge the merit of the work, have become the guiding rules at the best heritage projects across the country.[103]

Notes

1. The only detailed study of Louisbourg after the French departure in 1758 is Wayne Foster, "Post-Occupational History of the Old French Town of Louisbourg, 1760-1930" (manuscript on file, Fortress of Louisbourg, 1965).
2. CO 217, A82, Campbell to Secretary for the Council of Plantation Affairs, Memorial No. 1, 28 June 1768.
3. Quoted in Foster, "Post-Occupational History," pp. 63
4. See, for instance, the comments of Monseigneur Joseph-Octave Plessis, the Bishop of Quebec, cited in A.A. Johnston, *A History of the Catholic Church in Eastern Nova Scotia*, 2 Vols. (Antigonish: St. Francis Xavier University Press, 1960), Vol. 1, pp. 291, 282-83.
5. The phrase was used by John McGregor in *Historical and Descriptive Sketches of the Maritime Colonies of British America* (London: Longman, Rees, Orme, Brown,

and Green, 1828) and is quoted by Foster, "Post-Occupational History," p. 91.
6. This expression was used by the correspondent of the Toronto *Leader* who followed the Prince of Wales on his visit to Nova Scotia in 1860: P.B. Waite, "A Visit to Nova Scotia and to Louisbourg in 1860," *Nova Scotia Historical Quarterly* (2 June 1972), pp. 129-36.
7. John G. Bourinot, "Notes on a ramble through Cape Breton," *The New Dominion Monthly* (January 1868), p. 88.
8. Francis Parkman, *Montcalm and Wolfe* (New York: Collier Books, 1962), p. 388. First published in 1884.
9. This is what happened in Quebec City in 1872, which prompted Governor-General Dufferin to launch a campaign to preserve the historic character of the city. Dufferin's work at Quebec has been examined by Marc LaFrance, "Le projet Dufferin: la conservation d'un monument historique à Québec au XIXe siècle," in *Le Parc de l'Artillerie et les Fortifications de Québec: Études historiques présentées à l'occasion de la conférence des Sociétés Savantes*, Québec, 1970 (Québec, 1981), pp. 77-93.
10. A number of the memorials and monuments erected early in Canadian history are listed in M.H. Long, "The Historic Sites and Monuments Board of Canada," Canadian Historical Association, *Report* (1954), p. 2.
11. The following information is drawn from *Landmarks of Canada, A Guide to the J. Ross Robertson Canadian Historical Collection in the Toronto Public Library* (Toronto: Toronto Public Library, 1967), pp. 316-30: Monuments, Memorials, and Statues Raised in Canada: Pre-1800: 2; 1800-19: 1; 1820-39: 4; 1840-59: 6; 1860-79: 6; 1880-99: 50; 1900-19: 71. The list, which is undoubtedly incomplete, totals 174 memorials, all but a few of which were erected in Canada. The few exceptions were related to Canadian history but were put up in Great Britain, France or the United States. There are descriptions for each of the different monuments, but the year in which they were erected is given for only 140.
12. Rev. R. Murray and J. McLennan, "Cape Breton," in G.M. Grant, ed., *Picturesque Canada* (Toronto: Belden Bros., 1882), Vol. 2, pp. 841-52.
13. There developed in the United States during the 19th century a strong preservation and commemoration movement. Indeed, some Americans filled with patriotic fervour had begun to press for the preservation and marking of structures and places associated with the revolution soon after the end of the war with Great Britain. The movement gained momentum in the 19th century with numerous local and nation-wide campaigns to save or commemorate historic sites: Charles B. Hosmer, Jr., *Presence of the Past, A History of the Preservation Movement in the United States before Williamsburg* (New York: G. P. Putman's Sons, 1965). David Lowenthal discusses the ambivalence of Americans toward the past in "The Place of the Past in the American Landscape," in Lowenthal and Martyn J. Bowden, *Geographies of the Mind, Essays in Historical Geosophy in Honor of John Kirkland Wright* (New York: Oxford University Press, 1976), p. 90. Lowenthal is probably the most perceptive and provocative commentator on American attitudes toward the past. See also his "Past Time, Present Place: Landscape and Memory," *The Geographical Review*, Vol. 65 (January 1975), pp. 1-36, and "The American Way of History," *Columbia University Forum*, Vol. 9 (1966), pp. 27-32.
14. Gilbert Lewis Hall, *A Brief Historical Sketch of the Society of Colonial Wars in the District of Columbia on its Fiftieth Anniversary* (1944).
15. In a speech in the Red Chamber, Senator Pascal Poirier mentioned the newspapers that had protested the project of the Society of Colonial Wars. He also

quoted extracts from several of the journals. *Debates of the Senate of Canada*, 1895, pp. 136-39, Debate of 27 May 1895.

16. *Ibid.*, p. 139.

17. PAC, RG2 (Records of the Privy Council Office), Series 3, PC 1814, Two letters and motion of U.E. Loyalist Association, 4, 5, 7 June 1895.

18. The details of the 17 June 1895 unveiling, including the texts of the speeches, were published by the Society of Colonial Wars as "Report of the Committee on Louisbourg Memorial," an appendix to the *Annual Register of Officers and Members of the Society of Colonial Wars* (New York, 1896), pp. i-lxi. Comments concerning the French defeat included one by Frederic de Peyster, Governor-General of the Society of Colonial Wars, that "Few laurels can be won by defeating the horde of Asiatic slaves, but to tear the lilies from this citadel was, indeed, a splendid achievement," p. xii.

19. "Report of the Committee on Louisburg Memorial," pp. lv, xxiv-xv.

20. *Debates of the Senate*, 19 June 1895, pp. 332-38.

21. Benjamin Rand to Sir John Bourinot, Royal Society of Canada *Transactions*, Vol. 6 (1900), p. ix; Pascal Poirier, "Historic Sites of Acadia," *Acadiensis* (October 1902), pp. 229-37, and "Louisbourg en 1902," *Mémoires de la Société Royale du Canada*, 2e Série, Tome VIII, Section 1, (1902-03), pp. 97-126.

22. Poirier, "Historic Sites of Acadia."

23. Biographical information on Kennelly's early years is given in his obituaries (*Sydney Record*, 28 August 1907), *Sydney Daily Post*, 28 August 1907) and in an article entitled "Reminiscences about Late Capt. Kennelly," *Sydney Post-Record*, 3 July 1939. See also C.C. Gillispie, ed., *Dictionary of Scientific Biography*, (New York: Charles Scribner, 1973), Vol. 7, pp. 288-89. The Louisbourg to Milford Haven project is described by Kennelly himself in his booklet *The Atlantic Ferry. Louisburg and Milford Haven* (London, 1901).

24. The story of the ill-fated Cape Breton Coal, Iron and Railway Company and its plans for Broughton, C.B., are outlined in *The Montreal Daily Star*, 25 May 1907. Kennelly held $88,000 worth of bonds in the company at the time of his death. His will, dated 23 August 1907, and other documents pertaining to his estate are located in the Probate Office for the County of Cape Breton, Sydney.

25. "Reminiscences about Late Capt. Kennelly."

26. In his will Kennelly listed 12 pieces of property at Louisbourg which belonged to his "general estate" and referred to others which were to go to a specific trustee. Probate Office, County of Cape Breton.

27. [D.J. Kennelly], *Louisburg Memorial Fund* (Louisbourg, 1904).

28. PCO, FLO 2, Vol. 2, Central Registry, Report of F.H.H. Williamson on a visit to Historic Sites of the Maritimes, no date. The idea about future heroes being buried at Louisbourg was not mentioned in the promotional literature.

29. The patrons, committee members, etc., of the fund are listed in *Louisburg Memorial Fund*. President Roosevelt's letter to Kennelly, dated 7 July 1905, is transcribed on the sheet "Louisburg Memorial" enclosed within the above brochure.

30. Kennelly expressed this hope in his will. Probate Office, County of Cape Breton.

31. "Louisburg Memorial," *Louisburg Memorial Fund*.

32. The legislation was introduced by Cape Breton MLA Neil J. Gillis on 3 April, and it received third reading on 10 April. There is no record of any debate, though it was listed among the bills which were amended in committee: *Debates and Proceedings of the Nova Scotia House of Assembly 1906*, pp. 128, 144, 147, 157, 160. The act itself is located in *Statutes of Nova Scotia, 1906*, Chapter 56, pp. 80-82.

33. Louisburg Memorial," *Louisburg Memorial Fund*.
34. AFL, W. Crowe to Hon. R.E. Harris, Chief Justice of Nova Scotia, 18 May 1925.
35. AFL, Crowe to J.P. Edwards, 4 May 1923.
36. AFL, Letters to and from H.C. Burchell and Walter Crowe concerning the proposed meeting of the Trustees for 8 January 1913.
37. Kennelly will, Probate Office, County of Cape Breton.
38."Valuation of Real Estate, Mortgages, Bonds ... Capt. D.J. Kennelly," Probate Office, County of Cape Breton. The total value of Kennelly's estate was placed at $70,085, with the bonds being described as of "unknown value."
39. Vincent Mullins, Executor of D.J. Kennelly, Plaintiff, Versus The Trustees of the French Fortress, Supreme Court of Nova Scotia, B-3016 (1917), Probate Office, County of Cape Breton. The decision was handed down on 9 March 1919.
40. PCO, FLO 2, Vol. 2, Report of F.H.H. Williamson ..., n.d.
41. *Ibid.*, Vol. 14, S.O. Roberts to T.S. Mills, 19 December 1930.
42. *Ibid.*, Vol. 14, S.O. Roberts to T.S. Mills, 19 December 1930.
43. J.S. McLennan, *A Notable Ruin*, Louisbourg [Paper read before the Nova Scotia Historical Society, 10 November 1908], (1909), n.p.
44. Louis Bancroft Runk, "Fort Louisbourg: Its Two Sieges and Site To-Day," [Address before the Society of Colonial Wars in the Commonwealth of Pennsylvania, 9 March 1922], (Philadelphia, 1911); and Beckles Willson, "Louisbourg To-Morrow," *The Canadian Magazine* (February 1914), pp. 349-61.
45. McLennan wrote a chapter in Adam Shortt and Arthur Doughty, eds., *Canada and Its Provinces* (Toronto: T. & A. Constable at the Edinburgh University Press, 1917 [1914]), Vol. 1, "Louisbourg: an outpost of empire," pp. 201-27. He completed the manuscript of *Louisbourg from its foundation to its fall* in late 1913 and submitted it to the Champlain Society for publication. Since it was not simply a collection of documents the Society was not interested in publishing it. The outbreak of the First World War delayed publication until 1918, when Macmillan of London brought it out. Reviews of the study appeared in the *English Historical Review* (July 1919), *Canadian Historical Review* (March 1920), and Royal Society of Canada *Transactions*, (1922).
46. McLennan, *A Notable Ruin, Louisbourg*.
47. W.F. Lothian, *A History of Canada's National Parks*, Vol. 2, (Ottawa: Parks Canada, 1977). The first distinctive piece of national park legislation was passed in 1887, the Rocky Mountains Act. See also Robert Craig Brown, "The Doctrine of Usefulness: Natural Resource and National Park Policy in Canada, 1887-1914," in J.G. Nelson, ed., *Canadian Parks in Perspective* (Montreal, Harvest House, 1970), pp. 46-62.
48. The quote was made about Fort Anne: *Annual Report of the Department of the Interior (1916-1917)*, Part V, p. 60.
49. Long, "The Historic Sites and Monuments Board," pp. 3-4. The first members of the Board were Brigadier-General E.A. Cruikshank, Dr. James H. Coyne, Dr. Benjamin Sulte, W.C. Milner, Archdeacon W.O. Raymond, J.B. Harkin, and F.H.H. Williamson. For a biography of Harkin see William Russel, "James Bernard Harkin (1875-1955)," in "Miscellaneous Research Papers," *Manuscript Report Series*, Vol. 216 (Ottawa: Parks Canada, 1975-77).
50. FLO 2, Vol. 2, W.W. Cory to G.J. Desbarats, 4 November 1919; Desbarats to Cory, 26 November 1919; and G.A.R. Rowlings to W. Stuart Edwards, 8 January 1921.
51. *Ibid.*, Extract from minutes of HSMBC meeting of 21 May 1921.

PRESERVING HISTORY

52. *Ibid.*, G.A. Bell to W.W. Cory, 23 June 1921.
53. Known today as Fort Beauséjour National Historic Park at Aulac, N.B.
54. PCO, FLO 2, Vol. 3, Harkin to Cory, 22 November 1922, and Charles Stewart to J.S. McLennan, 28 December 1922; NBM, J.C. Webster Correspondence, McLennan to J.C. Webster, 23 November 1922, and McLennan to Harkin, 1 December 1922. McLennan first suggested the formation of a commission to take charge of Louisbourg's development in 1908. McLennan, *A Notable Ruin, Louisbourg*, p. 23.
55. See Ernest R. Forbes, *The Maritime Rights Movement, 1919-1927, A Study in Canadian Regionalism* (Montreal: McGill-Queen's University Press, 1979).
56. Beckles Willson suggested this approach in 1914 in "Louisbourg To-Morrow," p. 361.
57. W.C. Milner, later a member of the HSMBC, discussed the subject with Sam Hughes in 1916, and was told that the government intended to put the development of Louisbourg and other historic sites under the Québec Battlefields Commission. PCO, FLO 2, Vol. 2, Milner to Commissioner, Dominion Parks, 29 May 1916.
58. Harkin's thoughts on this matter were most clearly expressed in a 1929 memorandum, though he obviously held the sentiment years before. *Ibid.*, Vol. 10, [J.B. Harkin] to R.A. Gibson, 11 April 1929.
59. *Ibid.*, Vol. 4, extract from minutes of HSMBC meeting of 25 May 1923; AFL, Harkin to Crowe, 25 June 1923, Webster to McLennan, 9 January 1923.
60. Even before his July or August visit to Louisbourg, Edwards had said Louisbourg's "present condition was a disgrace." *Ibid.*, extract from minutes of HSMBC of 25 May 1923.
61. *Ibid.*, Edwards to Harkin, 15 August 1923.
62. *Ibid.*, E.A. Cruikshank to Harkin, 27 August 1923.
63. The five per cent figure comes from the projected expenditures for 1929. In that year the total amount to be spent by the Parks Branch was to be $1,358,000. Of that total, $42,000 was to be spent on historic sites across the country, $4,500 on Fort Anne and $10,000 on Fort Howe. In 1928 $23,000 had been spent at Louisbourg. *Debates of the House of Commons, 1929*, 12 June 1929, pp. 3547-48. Most of the money was earmarked for the western parks. Similarly, most of the Branch's attention was focused on those same parks, as a review of the *Annual Report of the Department of the Interior* for the 1920s and 1930s clearly indicates.
64. PCO, FLO 2, Vol. 5, Webster to Harkin, 11 October 1924.
65. PCO, File FB 2, Vol. 2, Webster to Harkin, 7 August 1923. The figure Webster mentioned that should be raised was $50,000.
66. PCO, FLO 2, Vol. 5, Draper to Harkin, 25 January 1924.
67. *Ibid.*, Webster to Harkin, 11 February 1924.
68. *Ibid.*, Vol. 4, Cory to E. Hawken, 12 October 1923. Equally damaging over the long run was the unchecked ransacking of ruins by residents and tourists in quest of unusual curios and souvenirs. As long as most of the site lay in private hands nothing would be done to prevent it, but even after the area was acquired by the Parks Branch the view that artifacts were simply trivial curios persisted in some circles. One Louisbourg town official wrote Ottawa that during the stabilization work "we are digging up all kinds of old French bottles, broken, the bottoms would make dandy ink bottles ... or ash trays." AFL, Louis Cann to T.W. Fuller, 16 July 1935.
69. Copies of Crowe's many letters concerning the legislation are located in AFL, dated February through May 1924. See also, PCO, FLO 2, Vol. 5, Crowe to Harkin, 5 April 1924. The bill submitted to the government by Crowe's firm for the legal

work was for $22.47. *Ibid.*, Edwards to Deputy Minister of Interior, 26 June 1924.
70. *Ibid.*, Vol. 6, Webster to Harkin, 1 December 1924; Crowe to Harkin, 26 December 1925; Harkin to Crowe, 22 January 1926; and Crowe to Harkin, 30 January 1926; NBM, Webster Correspondence, Crowe to Webster, 18 December 1925.
71. PCO, FLO 2, Vol. 7. A report on the day's activities is located in Crowe to Harkin, 21 August 1926.
72. All four texts were written in English, jointly or with input from J.P. Edwards, Senator McLennan, J.C. Webster and Walter Crowe. *Ibid.*, Vol. 4. Edwards to Martin, 25 September 1923. It was E.A. Cruikshank, chairman of the HSMBC, who raised the question of how many of them should be translated into French. He believed that at least one of them, the one which emphasized the valour of the French, should appear in both languages. J. Plimsoll Edwards opined that while it "might be a good thing" to have the one plaque in French and English, it would be "unnecessary" to have the other three translated. He felt it would make the lettering too small. *Ibid.*, Cruikshank to Harkin, 5 October 1923; *ibid.*, Vol. 5, Edwards to Harkin, 6 November 1923.
73. *Ibid.*, Vol. 5, handwritten note from F.H.H. Williamson to J.B. Harkin, with Harkin's concurrence indicated in the margin, n.d.
74. NBM, Webster Correspondence, Crowe to Webster, 18 December 1925.
75. *Toronto Star*, 13 August 1927; *Debates of the House of Commons, 1928*, pp. 2652-54.
76. The details of property acquisition, including photographs of the buildings then on the site, and the early plans for development are in PCO, FLO 2, Vols. 8 and 9.
77. Thomas Adams, *A Study of Rural Conditions and Problems in Canada* (Ottawa: Commission of Conservation, 1917).
78. PCO, FLO 2, Vol. 4, Thomas Adams to Harkin, 11 June 1923.
79. *Ibid.*; Adams mentions this at the start of his memo.
80. NBM, Webster Correspondence, McLennan to Webster, 28 November 1928.
81. PCO, FLO 2, Vol. 13, Webster and Crowe to Harkin, 29 November 1930, with attached report.
82. Both approaches, Adams's and that of McLennan, Webster and Crowe, considered as essential the removal of the dozen or so "modern" houses on the site. The fact that this small community had lived in the area for a century and a half, far longer than the 45-year lifespan of Louisbourg, was of no apparent concern. As a result, the buildings were removed soon after being acquired, with the exception of two houses that served as interim museum and caretaker's residence. They would later be demolished during the mid-1930s. See *Landmarks of Canada*, p. 323, for the adoption of a similar policy at Quebec City in 1908.
83. Hosmer, *Presence of the Past*, p. 146. Both Crowe and Webster were enthusiastic about the work being done at Fort Ticonderoga, while McLennan's respect for the treatment at Valley Forge has already been mentioned. Webster called his visit to Ticonderoga "one of the happiest experiences" of his life. PCO, FLO 2, Vol. 5, Webster to Harkin, 20 July 1923; *ibid*, Vol. 10, Crowe to Harkin, 14 July 1929; AFL, Report appended to Crowe's letter of 23 March 1929 to McLennan; NBM, Webster Correspondence, McLennan to Webster, 28 November 1928.
84. Webster proposed the two additional monuments on several occasions, beginning in 1924. PCO, FLO 2, Vol. 5, A. A. Pinard's memo of 5 January 1924; *ibid.*, Vol. 6, Webster to Harkin, 1 December 1924. McLennan spelled out his opposition to the idea most clearly in 1935. AFL, McLennan to G.W. Bryan, 17 May 1935; and NBM, Webster Correspondence, McLennan to Webster, 28 March 1935.

85. PCO, FLO 2, Vol. 19, Harkin to Miss Minnie Mosher, 10 June 1936, Harkin to D.R. Ingraham, 21 October 1936.
86. The enthusiasts' proposals were generally grounded in their knowledge of the history of Louisbourg. For McLennan, and to a lesser extent Webster, the familiarity had been gained through original research using 18th-century documents. For Crowe and others, their perspectives on the French regime in Cape Breton were likely shaped by conversations with McLennan and Webster, reading their books, and the books and articles of Francis Parkman, J.C. Bourinot and Richard Brown.
87. AFL, F.J. Thorpe to R.L. Way, 4 June 1962, "Louisbourg 'Restoration' 1930-60." That the work began in 1929, not 1930, was reported in PCO, FLO 2, Vol. 14, S.O. Roberts to T.S. Mills, 19 December 1930.
88. Discussion of a commission continued into 1930, then stopped. NBM, Webster Correspondence, Crowe to Webster, 26 December 1928, 27 March 1929; PCO, FLO 2, Vol. 10, [Harkin] to R.A. Gibson, 11 April 1929; *ibid.*, Vol. 11, Crowe to Harkin, 17 October 1929; Harkin to Crowe, 11 January 1930; and Crowe to Harkin, 26 February 1930. Instead of a separate commission, the HSMBC named Webster and Crowe as a special sub-committee to advise the Parks Branch on Louisbourg's development. *Ibid.*, Vol. 12, extract from minutes of HSMBC, 16 May 1930.
89. An advisory committee of non-government and non-HSMBC members was first suggested in 1928 (*ibid.*, Vol. 9, Crowe to Harkin, November 1928) then recommended again in 1931 (*ibid.*, Vol. 13, Webster and Crowe to Pinard, 10 March 1931). The board expressed its appreciation to the committee in May 1931, (*ibid.*, Vol. 14, extract from minutes of HSMBC, 29 May 1931). See also, *ibid.*, Vol. 15, Harkin to D.C. Harvey, 20 October 1932.
90. For a sampling of criticisms of the Branch see AFL, McLennan to Webster, 17 December 1928; and Webster to McLennan, 21 December 1928; PCO, FLO 2, Vol. 10, Webster and Crowe to Charles Stewart, 16 January 1929; AFL, Crowe to McLennan, 23 March 1929; NBM, Webster Correspondence, Crowe to Webster, 8 January 1934 and 8 November 1933.
91. Charles Shaw of Louisbourg, who worked at the site during the 1930s, recalled that Liberals got the jobs when the Liberals were in power and Conservatives when the Conservatives were in office. He stated that it was a fact of life and no one minded much. Interview by A.J.B. Johnston, 10 December 1981. However, there were some people who were not quite so philosophical about losing their jobs with changes in government. The first Honorary Superintendent, A.A. Martell, protested bitterly about being removed from his position in 1931; Lawrence Price, the first caretaker, was dismissed at the same time, but complained less strenuously. PCO, FLO 2, Vol. 14, Martell to Harkin, 30 November 1931; Martell to Harkin, 24 December 1931; and Price to Harkin, 4 November 1931.
92. At one point Webster, with the blessing of the federal government, even pursued the matter with the Carnegie Foundation. The hope was that the American philanthropic institution would put up the $40,000 required for the construction of suitable museums at Louisbourg and Beauséjour. When the idea fell through the government funded the projects on its own. Senator McLennan had hoped the De Mézy residence might be reconstructed to serve as a museum, but in the end the government decided to build a larger structure on land opposite where the King's Garden had been. *Ibid.*, Vol. 15, Harkin to H.H. Rowatt, 9 July 1932; and Webster to Harkin, 26 October 1932; *ibid.*, Vol. 16, G.W. Bryan for J.B. Harkin to Webster, 12 August 1933; PCO, FB 2, Vol. 9, Harkin to Dr. F.P. Keppel, President, Carnegie Corporation, 2 August 1932.

93. Almon was a Glace Bay plumber and amateur historian. Despite a lack of higher education and leisure time he worked throughout the 1930s and 1940s to promote Louisbourg and its history. Notwithstanding his efforts, Almon was not held in high regard by at least some of the other Louisbourg enthusiasts. But in 1949 St. Francis Xavier University awarded Almon an honorary M.A. for his historical work. Examples of negative remarks about Almon may be found in Sydney, J.M. McConnell Library, Louisbourg Museum File, Webster to K. McLennan, 1 August 1935, 20 August 1936; NBM, Webster Correspondence, K. McLennan to J.C. Webster, 8 December 1940. Almon's papers are located in the Beaton Institute of the University College of Cape Breton.
94. PCO, FLO 2, Vol. 10, Webster to Harkin, 14 February 1929, Crowe to Harkin, 16 February 1929.
95. *Ibid.*, Vol. 19, McLennan, "Memorandum on Louisbourg," October 1936.
96. *Debates of the House of Commons, 1928*, p. 2653, 3 May 1928.
97. McConnell Library, Louisbourg Museum File, Webster to K. McLennan, 28 March 1938.
98. John Clarence Webster, *The Distressed Maritimes. A Study of Educational and Cultural Conditions in Canada* (Toronto: The Ryerson Press, 1926), pp. 15, 16.
99. Roldolphe Lemieux comments on the "bicultural" sympathies of McLennan and his family in his review of McLennan's book on Louisbourg. Royal Society of Canada *Transactions*, Sect. I, (1922) pp. 121-27.
100. NBM, Webster Correspondence, McLennan to Webster, 28 November 1928; AFL, McLennan to Bryan, 17 May 1935.
101. PCO, FLO 2, Vol. 17, McLennan to A.G.L. McNaughton, 21 March 1934. McLennan wrote McNaughton because there was talk that an extensive "make-work" project might be carried out at Louisbourg to alleviate unemployment, and he spelled out his ideas on the development of the site in his memorandum.
102. Following the recommendations of I.C. Rand's *Report of the Royal Commission on Coal* (Ottawa, 1960), the federal government began the reconstruction of one-quarter of the original 18th-century town. That project, which began in 1961 as a make-work programme for unemployed coal miners, ultimately exceeded the most grandiose plans of the early enthusiasts.
103. It is difficult to say how typical were the early commemoration and preservation efforts at Louisbourg because there has been so little research on the topic elsewhere in Canada. Was there a national pattern of failed private initiatives followed by appeals for government action? And in those cases where government involvement was sought, were the inevitable delays perceived as proof that Ottawa was neglecting that region's history? One assumes it was fairly common to have a small group of professionals or socially prominent individuals acting as a pressure group, but was it? And where did the enthusiasts in other areas get their ideas for their projects? For Crowe, Webster and McLennan the inspiration clearly came from heritage projects in the United States, but were American examples followed elsewhere in Canada, or were British or French approaches adopted more often? And did distinctively Canadian programmes emerge in some areas? How many sites were "bicultural" and how did Canadians view that issue? The evolution in commemorative approaches adopted at Louisbourg, from monument-raising to preservation of extant ruins to the excavation and interpretation of archaeological features to the establishment of a museum, seems in retrospect to have been a natural, almost inevitable, progression. But there were definite obstacles and options along the way and the development of the site could have turned out quite

differently. How common the Louisbourg experience was will only be demonstrated by other case studies and further research.

Commemorating Louisbourg, c.1767

A.J.B. Johnston

In my recent article on the preservation of Louisbourg I stated that the first step to mark the 18th-century history of the French town occurred in 1895.[1] It turns out that I was mistaken. There had been a monument, so to speak, erected on the historic site around 1767,[2] 128 years before the American Society of Colonial Wars raised what I thought was the first memorial. All trace and memory of that early commemorative effort apparently vanished over the next few decades, or at least none of the 19th-century visitors to Louisbourg mentioned it. Despite its disappearance the 1767 monument was important, both for what it indicates about the people who raised it and because it may have been the first such commemoration in what is now Canada.

The man behind the 1767 memorial seems to have been Captain Samuel Holland (1728-1801), the Dutch-born British officer who was at the time Surveyor-General of the Province of Quebec and of the Northern District of North America. A veteran of the military campaigns of the Seven Years War (among other things he was beside Wolfe when the latter died on the Plains of Abraham in 1759),[3] Holland had been at Louisbourg in 1758 and travelled to Cape Breton on several occasions between 1764 and 1767 to carry out a detailed survey of the island.[4] In addition to his surveying Holland was an enthusiastic astronomer, keeping a detailed record of the observations he made on both St. John's Island (Prince Edward Island) and Cape Breton to ascertain the longitude and latitude of those places.[5] At Louisbourg, he even established an observatory in a building beyond the ruined fortifications, the second astronomical observatory to be erected in the town in 15 years.[6]

Before Holland left Louisbourg in 1767 -- never to return, for the garrison withdrew the following year -- he felt the need to somehow mark the British capture of the fortified town nine years earlier. He himself had participated in the 1758 siege as "General Wolfe's Engineer,"[7] so his desire to commemorate the military victory was that of someone who had lived through an event and looked back on it with a sense of pride and achievement. In that respect the 1767 monument was quite different from the later memorials, which would be erected by people whose appreciation for the importance of Louisbourg in history was strictly learned. Holland evidently had a reflective, sensitive side, which inclined him toward the commemoration of bygone events. In the same letter in which he described the monument, addressed to Sir Frederick Haldimand, brigadier of the Southern Department, Holland offered a few words of consolation concerning the death of Haldimand's nephew, who had drowned at Louisbourg in December 1765. Holland added: "Tho' we cannot help reflecting on these events, our remembering them, makes us more Sencible of their lose, then we where sencible of their friendship & assistance when living."[8] If that were true for people, then it might be equally true for events of importance. Hence, Holland and his colleagues erected their memorial at Louisbourg, and the surveyor talked of raising another to Wolfe at Quebec and the need for a third to General Henry Bouquet in Pensacola. Holland's account of the Louisbourg memorial is as follows:

> The Monument we have erected at Louisbourg, on the Ruins of the Citadel, is made with the Hewen Stones of the Ruinous Fortifications, the Inscription and Polishing the large Stones by young Grant & me, & the rest by the surveying party, & for Corring the materials together the officers & soldiers of the Garrison brought us more than we wanted, so there have been no expenses -- and as there were no work men to be had to Execute it as I could have wished it to be, it is in the Rustick taste, that the Injurys of Time can make but little impression on it. We are now making a project to erect a Monument on the Heights of Abraham in memory of Gel. Wolfe for which we will open a subscription. I hope there is something of this kind to be Don at Pensacola in memory of Gel. Bouquet -- I am convinced you will do your endeavour towards its.

Brief though it is, Holland's account offers some insight into the nature of the Louisbourg monument. The monument consisted of a selection of cut stones of the ruined French fortifications, material that was in plentiful supply, durable and symbolized the British conquest of the French. Both larger and smaller stones were used, and one assumes these were arranged vertically, as in a column, but that may not have been so. At least some of the stones were polished in an attempt to render the memorial more aesthetically pleasing. An inscription was added so that there would be no doubt in the future to whom or to what the stones were dedicated. Holland showed the same naive faith in his monument that all generations demonstrate; namely, a belief that their commemoration would stand forever. How long the memorial did stand is not known. It may have been dismantled soon after the British left, by people anxious to re-use the French cut stone on other building projects, in a nearby community, elsewhere on the island, or as far away as Halifax. Then again, perhaps only the inscription was vandalized, or worn away over time by the elements. The monument might have remained, but shorn of its identifying label it would have had no meaning for those who saw it. Indeed, could one or more of the piles of stones depicted by J.E. Woolford in 1818 -- for the illustration see *Acadiensis*, Volume 12, Number 2 (Spring 1983), page 59 -- be Holland's lost memorial?

Notes

1. A.J.B. Johnston, "Preserving History: The Commemoration of 18th Century Louisbourg, 1895-1940," *Acadiensis*, Vol. 12, No. 2 (Spring 1983), pp. 53-80.
2. I came across a reference to this early memorial by accident, while reading through Dilys Francis, "The Mines and Quarries of Cape Breton Island during the French Period, 1713-1760" (manuscript on file, Fortress of Louisbourg, 1965).
3. Holland's career is traced in Willis Chipman, "The Life and Times of Major Samuel Holland, Surveyor-General, 1764-1801," *Ontario Historical Society Papers and Records*, Vol. 21 (1924), pp. 11-90.
4. D.C. Harvey, ed., *Holland's Description of Cape Breton Island and Other Documents* (Halifax, 1935).
5. *Ibid.*, pp. 50-54.
6. The location of Holland's observatory is marked on plan 1767-1 in the Archives of the Fortress of Louisbourg. For an account of the earlier observatory see Kenneth Donovan, "Canada's First Astronomical Observatory," *Canadian Geographic*, Vol. 100, No. 6 (December 1980-January 1981), pp. 36-43.
7. Chipman, "Life and Times of Major Samuel Holland," p. 19.
8. PAC, Frederick Haldimand Papers, Add. Mss 21728 (B-68), Holland to Haldimand, 20 January 1768, pp. 255-57.

The Concept of the Louisbourg Underwater Museum[1]

Robert Grenier

Introduction

P arks Canada, part of the federal Department of Canadian Heritage, has been involved in managing the country's submerged marine heritage for more than thirty years. Its role expanded in 1961 when, in an effort to protect a number of historic wrecks of French navy vessels in Louisbourg harbour from the eighteenth-century wars between France and Britain, it claimed ownership. With the co-operation of the harbour authorities (under another federal department), Parks Canada prohibited unauthorized diving. For the next three decades these wrecks remained intact and became the jewels of national submerged heritage management and protection efforts. As successful as this approach has been, however, it is just one of five concepts used by Parks Canada to manage historic wrecks.

Management Concept 1: No Intervention

In this scenario, sites are left alone and no inventory or archaeological work is undertaken. Access may be either allowed or prohibited.

Management Concept 2: Minimal Intervention and Assessment of Potential

This option involves non-intrusive surveys or limited test excavations. A detailed plan of surface deposits is generally prepared; to ensure its protection, the site is sealed with sandbags or by other means. No immediate interpretation is planned. An example is the site of the *Saphire*, a British frigate that sank in 1696 in Bay Bulls, near St. John's.[2]

Management Concept 3: Maximum Intervention

This option consists of systematic on-site research, complete excavation (including total or partial recovery of the structure and its conservation), and detailed analysis and interpretation. Typical examples are the *Wasa* and *Mary Rose*. Parks Canada has applied this scenario to a gunboat sunk during the War of 1812 and to the *Machault*, a French frigate that sank in 1760 in the Baie de Chaleur.[3] Although more appealing to the general public, this approach entails exorbitant conservation and interpretation costs.

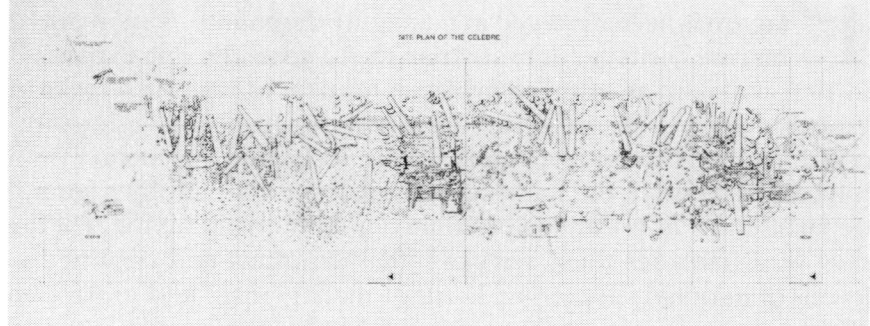

Figure 1. Site plan of the Célèbre provided as a road map for the divers. Source: Carol Piper. Parks Canada.

Management Concept 4: Comprehensive Recovery

This was the option used at the site of the sixteenth-century Basque whaling galleons discovered at Red Bay, Labrador.[4] After the discovery of the first galleon in 1978, it was decided to avoid the colossal cost of treating the ship's timbers, which often produces inadequate results (as with the *Wasa*). Instead, Parks Canada chose to expose the hull, disassemble it, bring it to the surface to record all data, and then rebury the sections under controlled conditions in an anaerobic environment. Through this excavation program we were able not only to save millions of dollars but also to collect a considerable amount of data inaccessible to *Wasa* or *Mary Rose* researchers. The interpretation of the Red Bay wreck will be carried out through reports, drawings, archaeological models, and audio-visual means, making it possible to bring to light much new information on sixteenth-century naval construction on the Iberian peninsula.

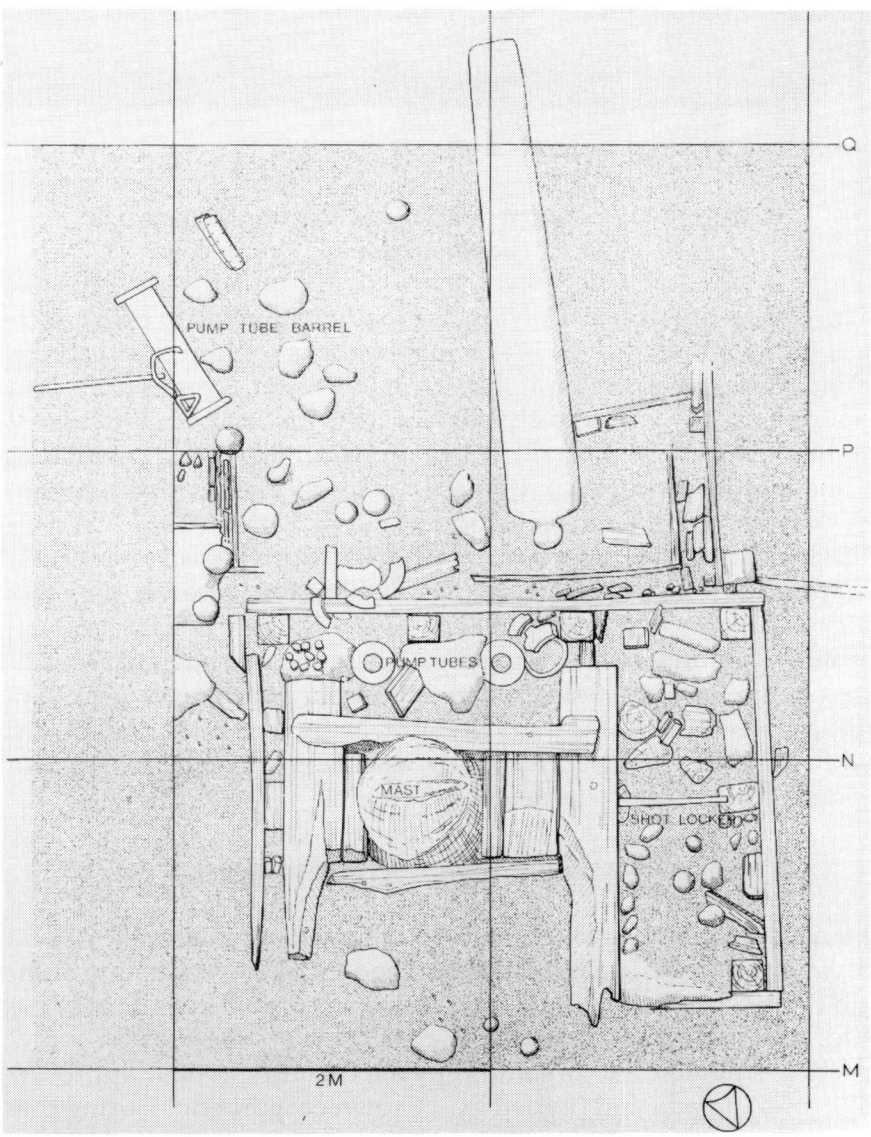

Figure 2. Detail of the central area of the Célèbre. Source: See Figure 1.

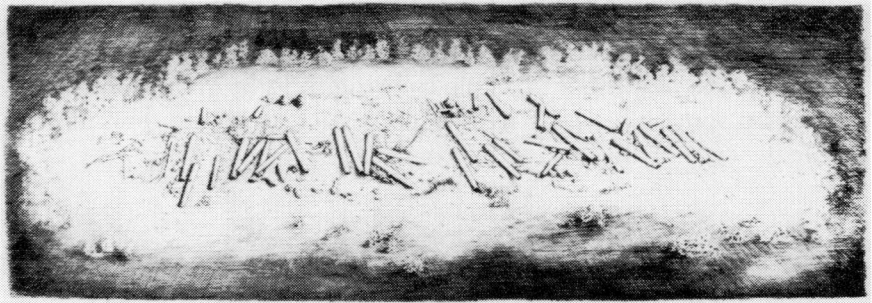

Figure 3. Site drawing of the Célèbre. Source: See Figure 1.

Management Concept 5: The Underwater Museum or Ecomuseum

The popularity of scuba diving has made it possible to bring tourists to the site of one wreck or more wrecks under certain conditions, thus transforming it into an underwater ecomuseum. This option not only is less costly but also is consistent with the current trend of enjoying cultural heritage in its original environment. In Canada, this concept is partially in place in Pacific Rim National Park Reserve on Vancouver Island and in Fathom Five National Marine Park in Georgian Bay, Ontario; two dozen wrecks have been made accessible to visitors in each. Fathom Five receives the most visitors, with more than 50,000 dives every year. But the best example of an underwater ecomuseum is found at a site not actually part of the Parks Canada system. Louisbourg harbour is just a few hundred metres outside the boundaries of the Fortress of Louisbourg National Historic Site. Louisbourg was a major commercial centre founded in the early eighteenth century.

Louisbourg Underwater Museum

Management of the historic wrecks in Louisbourg harbour may be divided into two separate stages. The first stage, stretching from 1961 to 1985, followed the second concept: a partial inventory of the sites and the establishment of a protection system that for a few years permitted dives organized by a local entrepreneur approved by Parks Canada and funded by a Crown corporation. During this period several relatively informal inspections were carried out by Parks Canada's Marine Archaeology Section. The concept of underwater museum management was further developed and translated into practice in 1986, following a request from the Fortress of Louisbourg superintendent. The aim was to allow divers access to Canada's submerged marine heritage in a manner consistent with Parks Canada's principles of cultural resource management, which include recognition of historic value, protection for present and future generations, promotion of real understanding of the resource, respect for its historic character, and respect for the integrity of the site.

This latter concept led to a partnership between two federal departments and the private sector. The Department of Transport, responsible for the Canadian Coast Guard, has jurisdiction over nautical activities in the harbour. At the request of Parks Canada, the wrecks' custodian on behalf of the Crown, it has controlled diving since 1961. Transport Canada now grants operating permits to local entrepreneurs who, provided they comply with park directives, receive permission to take paying divers to authorized sites. Parks Canada, the manager of the wrecks, has inventoried the sites, assessed their significance and capacity to withstand the effects of multiple visits, and drafted recommendations and directives.[5] Parks Canada also developed an annual site inspection program to assess any damage or signs of deterioration, and is responsible for advising the harbour master on the selection and qualifications of prospective entrepreneurs and on granting or revoking permits.

Louisbourg Sites

In the harbour and surrounding areas are at least twenty-six documented wrecks from the period 1713-1758. The most famous, the seventy-four gun *Prudent* and *Entreprenant*, and the sixty-four gun *Capricieux* and *Célèbre* were sunk during the siege of 1758. Because the remains of *Célèbre*, built in Brest in 1755, are better preserved and have greater visual impact, its site was chosen as a case study in implementing the concept. A detailed archaeological plan, produced in 1986-1987 under the direction of Willis Stevens, was used as a benchmark for the annual inspections required to assess the impact of visits to the site. The archaeological plan thus became a management tool, and it was subsequently modified slightly for use as an interpretation tool as well. Once the site's significant features were identified, the plan was printed on water-resistant paper for use as a diver's guide. In 1986 and 1987 we also made casts to better detect changes to the wreck. These became benchmarks to monitor minute changes on key timbers. We also developed techniques for removing kelp without damaging the wreck; if this were not done, divers would be unable to see it. Finally, we plan to install a system of anodes on the cannons to provide cathodic protection to slow their natural deterioration, visible through the oxygen bubbles escaping from them.

Guidelines

Eleven guidelines were issued for dive tour operators. The most important make the operator responsible for installing a permanent mooring system that will not threaten the security of the wreck or the divers; for accompanying the divers (never more than four); for providing the names and addresses of all divers to park authorities; for clearing the site (if necessary) of excess kelp; and for any accidental or intentional damage to the wreck or the site, which must be reported to the chief park warden. Divers, on the other hand, are required to stay at least three metres above the site; to maintain visual contact with the operator at all times; and to refrain from grabbing or pulling out kelp attached to the wreck and to avoid touching or otherwise disturbing any object at the site.

Interpretation Tools

To enable divers to make the most of their visits, the Marine Archaeology Section has produced two documents. The first, a twelve-minute videocassette, provides information on the site's historic context and fragility; on how divers can help to preserve the wreck for future generations; and on the key features that will help to understand the site better. The videocassette is also used to introduce the site to non-diving visitors. The second is a guide printed on water-resistant paper that identifies the important features. Divers can make their own notes on this map and can keep it as a souvenir.

Conclusion

Over thirty years of protecting *Célèbre* and other nearby wrecks have provided irrefutable evidence that only sound management can ensure the longevity of these irreplaceable and non-renewable marine heritage resources. The pillaging of dozens of important wrecks not far from Louisbourg further underscores this lesson and testifies to its success. The Louisbourg ecomuseum allows Canadians, heirs to this heritage, to become partners both in fighting for its survival and in understanding and disseminating this living chapter of history at minimal cost to taxpayers. The concept of an underwater museum has many possibilities, but unfortunately cannot be applied everywhere. At Louisbourg all the circumstances have come together to promote success.

Notes

1. An earlier version of this paper appeared under the title "Le concept du musée sous le mer de Louisbourg," *Actes des Colloques de la Direction du Patrimoine: Le patrimoine maritime et fluvial* (Paris, 1993), pp. 397-401.

      Robert Grenier is Chief, Marine Archaeology, Archaeological Research Branch, Parks Canada. A member of the Editorial Board of *The Northern Mariner/Le Marin du nord*, he is perhaps best known for his work on the wreck of a sixteenth-century basque whaler at Red Bay, Labrador.

2. V. Myles, "Artifacts from the 17th-Century Wreck of the *Saphire*, Bay Bulls, Newfoundland" (manuscript on file, Parks Canada, 1992).

3. Walter Zacharchuk and Peter J.A. Waddell, "The Excavation of the Machault: An 18th-Century French Frigate," *Studies in Archaeology, Architecture and History* (Ottawa: Parks Canada, 1986); and Douglas Bryce, "Weaponry from the Machault: An 18th-Century French Frigate." *Studies in Archaeology, Architecture and History* (Ottawa: Parks Canada, 1984).

4. R. Grenier and J. Tuck, *Red Bay, Labrador: World Whaling Capital A.D. 1550-1600* (St. John's: Atlantic Archaeology Ltd., 1988); Grenier, "Basque Whalers in the New World: The Red Bay Wrecks," in George Bass (ed.), *Ships and Shipwrecks of the Americas* (London: Thames and Hudson, 1988), pp. 69-84; P.J.A. Waddell, "The Disassembly of a 16th-Century Galleon," *International Journal of Nautical Archaeology*, Vol. 15, No. 2 (1986), pp. 137-148; and Waddell, "Reburial of a 16th-Century Galleon," in Oceans '88, *Proceedings* (Washington, D.C., 1988), pp. 833-36.

5. W. Stevens, "1986 Underwater Survey at Louisbourg" (manuscript on file, Parks Canada, 1987); H. Unglik, "Corrosion and Preservation of Metal Artifacts from a French Shipwreck Sunk at Louisbourg Harbour before 1758" (manuscript on file, Parks Canada, 1988); L.D.M. Murdock and T.W. Daley, "Conservation Environment and Preservation Assessment of the Louisbourg Wreck Site" (manuscript on file, Parks Canada, 1989); and L. Laflèche, "Wood Degradation Study from the New Wreck, Louisbourg" (manuscript on file, Parks Canada, 1990).

The Fortress of Louisbourg Archives: The First Twenty-Five Years

Eric Krause

In the late 1950s, unemployment in the mines of Cape Breton rose dramatically as coal sales throughout Canada plummeted. The federal government therefore appointed the Honourable Ivan C. Rand as a one-man Royal Commission to produce specific measures for alleviating the crisis. One of Judge Rand's requests was that the Historic Sites Division of the National Parks Branch of the Department of Northern Affairs and Natural Resources prepare a feasibility study for the restoration of historic Louisbourg, once the largest French fortress and naval base in North America, and a major focus for trade and the cod fishery.[1]

Construction of the fortified town of Louisbourg began in 1719 and continued until its capture by New Englanders and British forces in 1745. Returned to the French in 1748 by the Treaty of Aix-la-Chapelle, the fortress was recaptured by the British army under the command of Brigadier General James Wolfe and Major General Jeffrey Amherst in 1758 and systematically demolished in 1760 to prevent a French return.

In February 1960, the Engineering Services Division of the Department of Northern Affairs and Natural Resources issued a detailed report recommending that the restoration of the Fortress of Louisbourg and surrounding historically significant areas should be phased in over a twenty-year period at a cost of $40 million, of which $2 million was to be earmarked for archaeological and historical research by an information-gathering research team.[2] In August 1960, not long after receiving the Department of Northern Affairs' submission, Judge Rand issued his diagnosis of the plight of Cape Breton: the island's dependency upon coal mining was the reason for the region's unique socio-financial problems.[3] To correct this, Rand urged the introduction to the island of new wealth and a new intellectual and spiritual awareness through a variety of "alternative and supporting economic and cultural activities."[4] "What," he asked, "could be more stimulating to the imagination or instructive to the mind, not only for the people of Cape Breton and Nova Scotia, but of Canada and the Eastern portions of the United States," than a partial reconstruction of the fortress as "a revelation of European life and ... of the vicissitudes of North America's development?"[5]

Rand's vision of a symbolic or partial reconstruction was a far cry from the complete restoration which the Department of Northern Affairs had recommended just six months earlier. Nevertheless, his suggestion to expend no less than $1.5 million during each of the following 15 to 20 years was still imposing.[6] On 3 March 1961, the federal cabinet directed that the Department of Northern Affairs expend $1.1 million before 31 March 1962 on a "crash" programme to begin the process of tooling up and stockpiling materials.[7] Shortly thereafter, on 17 June 1961, Prime Minister John G. Diefenbaker rose in the House of Commons to announce the massive undertaking.[8] Finally, on 20 March 1962, the Cabinet decided that Louisbourg was to be a twelve-year, $12 million project that was to produce a substantial showing for Centennial year, 1967.[9]

On 9 November 1961, the Department signed a contract with Mr. and Mrs. Ronald Way as General Consultants to "advise the Director as to the overall and detailed means to be taken for a partial restoration of the Fortress of Louisbourg, ... as accurate as possible from an archaeological and historical viewpoint."[10] An Ottawa-based Research Director was to make available all historical and archaeological data and reports required to meet this goal.[11] From the inception of the project, therefore, authenticity was clearly to be the engine for driving the rebuilding programme at Louisbourg, and primary evidence, both archaeological and documentary, the fuel. The appointments of F.J. Thorpe as Research Director and of B.C. Bickerton as Senior Historian were evidence of a firm commitment to "identify and collect as soon as possible all manuscript materials required for the restoration."[12]

The final scope and magnitude of the Louisbourg project was without precedent in Canada. Ultimately, sixteen acres or one-quarter of the original townsite would be developed. Included in the undertaking would be the reconstruction of 2.72 kilometers of perimeter fortification walls, 50 buildings, 2 bastions, 2 town gates, several wharfs, and the landscaping of 5 town blocks.

It is puzzling that despite the very substantial commitment of the Canadian nation to a large-scale project that was to be unique in the annals of reconstruction, and despite the very commendable commitment to authenticity, based in large measure on historical research, no consideration was given to the immediate creation of an archives for the secure storage, organization, and retrieval of vital documentary information. Apart from a strong lobby for a "librarian-cum-file clerk" by Ronald Way, the General Consultant, all reports of the period ignored the need to provide suitable arrangement for the proper care and dissemination of project research documentation.[13] Strong evolutionary forces were nevertheless present to ensure the growth of a project archives. Researchers on the project immediately initiated the process of identifying and acquiring relevant historical documentation. Its rapidly accumulating bulk impelled them to analyze, describe, and classify their holdings and forced them to begin to think in terms of providing reference service for project historians and others. The need for archival staff gradually came to be accepted; holdings were centralized and consolidated; reference systems were constructed. As the project began to generate its own documentation -- research reports, plans, administrative files -- the archives increasingly assumed the function of institutional archives as well as research centre. Thus changing needs and perceptions led to an evolution from the simple notion of documentation as historians' research notes to the creation of a fully operational project archives. This transformation, however, would require time, and the initial focus was almost entirely upon the task of acquiring relevant historical documentation.

Until May 1966, the Historical Unit, including the Research Director, the Senior Historian, and the project documentation researchers, would remain in Ottawa, to be as close as possible to major libraries and in particular to its prime source of information, the Public (now National) Archives of Canada.[14] The understanding was that the work of the Historical Research group might eventually move to Louisbourg.[15] From its headquarters location the unit concentrated on "the gathering of material on all subjects related to the History of Louisbourg for later analysis," including the reproduction of all the relevant documents in the Public Archives of Canada.

A 1960 departmental report lamented the fact that although there already existed a considerable number of original eighteenth-century Louisbourg sources providing general information on "the main character of most of the public buildings and their interior divisions," many details were missing. Nonetheless, the report went on to speculate about new sources which might yet provide the building, landscaping, furnishing, shipbuilding, and socio-political-military details needed to produce an authentic representation of Louisbourg. Among these potential sources, archaeological findings and the observable features of extant buildings figured as the most promising, together with eighteenth-century manuscript materials dealing directly with Louisbourg, such as the French government's records in the *Archives des Colonies*, Series E, G^2 and G^3.[16] The report also recognizes both the value of "not yet seen" documents supposedly in the *Archives des Colonies*, Series $C^{11}B$, as well as the potential of "partly known sources" in Europe and in New England.[17]

In September 1961, prior to signing his contract as General Consultant to the restoration programme, Ronald Way submitted an initial report urging that "manuscript research ... [should] begin as soon as personnel [were] acquired" with the "assembling and co-relating [sic] [of] all manuscript material available in Canada," then move on to an "investigation of all available material in England, France and New England."[18] Foreign research was necessary, according to Way, because it was his experience that the Public Archives of Canada rarely transcribed all the "relevant plans for a particular project," since that institution was, understandably, less concerned with minute details than was a project devoted to authentic restoration.[19] Furthermore, such documentary research should continue over the years, its emphases being controlled by the stages of work in hand and its pace sufficiently in advance of construction to avoid difficulties, errors, and unnecessary expense.[20]

The primary records in the archives of France, Great Britain, and the United States which required long-term original research in the earliest days of the Louisbourg project fell into two broad categories: administrative, touching directly upon Louisbourg affairs for the period 1713-1758, and military, resulting from the successful New England Expedition of 1745. Way provided the names of researchers already stationed in Ottawa for a proposed fast survey of available primary manuscript sources known to exist in the various archives of Paris and London. In addition, they were to delve into published, secondary sources whenever possible.[21]

In the spring of 1962, the first survey team, consisting of F.J. Thorpe and J.R. McCartney, travelled to Paris and London, where they quickly confirmed Way's assertion that the transcription and microfilming programmes of the Public Archives of Canada had indeed missed a rich harvest of Louisbourg materials, particularly in the area of maps and plans. Thorpe initiated the photographic duplication of urgently required documents. The archives of the newly formed Historical Research Section at Ottawa was not only to maintain the accumulated resources for research purposes but also to send copies to Louisbourg for the Project Manager in charge of construction.[22]

Soon after his appointment in July 1962 as Research Director of both historical and archaeological research, Thorpe began the process of presenting the findings to Way. Not surprisingly, the Historical Research Section had initiated its programme by examining the existing French series at the Public Archives of Canada.[23] Then, in order "to reconcile historical research with the projected archaeological and reconstruction projects," Thorpe, along with Bickerton, the newly-appointed Senior Historian, decided to tie the examination of this French series (*Archives des Colonies* B, $C^{11}B$, $C^{11}C$, etc.), along with its English counterpart, to the pace of the project by grouping the sources in broad categories and then studying them in a predetermined sequence.[24] The Research Section then searched a variety of published guides and bibliographies of Louisbourg manuscripts existing in the United States, and in January 1963 signed a contract with Dr. M.C. Rosenfield for a survey of New England archives, libraries, and society repositories.[25] Together with Bickerton, Rosenfield examined material in Massachusetts, Rhode Island, Connecticut, Maine, New Hampshire, and the Library of Congress, looking for documents which should be microfilmed.[26] Although this new material contributed little to the project's knowledge of construction history, it was nevertheless invaluable, providing many new insights into the 1745 campaign, its supply, organization, and political background.[27]

Thorpe realized that the large amount of data being gathered was beginning to create a "serious problem of classification, recording, filing and retrieval" which threatened to slow down the pace of report production for the project.[28] No doubt too, he recognized that the results of his forthcoming survey/research trip to France, Belgium, and the United Kingdom, as well as that of Research Officer B.A. Pothier, who was about to spend nine months on documentary research in Paris and the French provinces, might serve only to intensify the problem.[29] Thorpe maximized the potential of these trips to add new knowledge while reducing the danger of information overload by restricting the search to manuscript materials not already at the Public Archives of Canada and by selecting for microfilming only those documents which met current research goals.[30]

By 1963, the Research Section was actually engaged in two distinct types of research activities, each making a major contribution to the evolution of a Louisbourg archives.[31] The first was the activity of "search," involving the identification, collection, usually by a photographic process, and the general indexing of relevant documents.[32] The second was the process of "analysis," the indexing of accumulated material point by point and its classification by subject according to the broad categories and order of importance enunciated in 1962.[33] While the immensity of the task ultimately postponed the completion of classification, the final analytical step remained the work of producing a report in a form useful to the project.[34] By 1963, the Ottawa research staff began to refer to its acquired documentation as forming an archives.[35]

Although the Section had now admitted to the existence of a project archives, it did not immediately appoint personnel from its own research staff to operate it. No doubt this lack of direct action resulted from the difficult deadlines and heavy work loads the staff were encountering in the process of collection and analysis. Instead, Thorpe decided to advertise for an "archivist-librarian ... to work initially in Ottawa and then to move to Louisbourg when the whole research section is combined there."[36] The strategy was that the "historical unit under Mr. B.C. Bickerton ... [would remain] responsible for the collection of copies of manuscript material, chiefly on microfilm ... [but these copies will come into the librarian's] general custody eventually."[37]

The possibility of an immediate move to Louisbourg also prompted some discussion about the size of the archival collection, its nature, and its storage. For example, "with instructions [in 1962] to move to Louisbourg, it became necessary to organize a vast copying operation which would permit us to have in our Louisbourg archives all the documents we would require for future use."[38] By August 1963, that meant 32,000 pages of documents on microfilm, another 2,000 in larger photocopied format, and numerous cards containing extracted information.[39]

On 12 November 1963, E.M.A. Riley became archivist-librarian. Shortly thereafter, Thorpe proposed the creation of the position of research clerk "to draw and put away research documents, maps and plans, and reports, being used by research director, historians, archaeologists, conservator, etc."[40] However, as late as September of 1964, Thorpe had not yet filled the position.[41] Early in 1964, there was "a fair amount of discussion on the subject of the development of an historical and archaeological research centre at the Fortress of Louisbourg after the main construction work ha[d] been completed ... because there ... [would] be in the Louisbourg Library a vast amount of research material collected from Canada, the United States, England and France."[42] Asked for his views, Way reported that "divorcing the library and archival material from the archaeological findings would do much to destroy the effectiveness of the Louisbourg research centre .... I doubt there would be much point to the research centre *without* the library."[43]

It was inevitable that the House of Commons would discuss the restoration work on several occasions. For example, on 13 October 1964, M.P. Douglas Fisher asked:

> What are the plans for the establishment of an archives and library at Louisbourg, Nova Scotia, including an estimated cost, the estimated space proposed, the number of books and documents to be housed, the scale and qualifications of the staff, the number of exhibition cases and tables, the kind of provisions made for the use of scholars and the structure of the management in relation to other Government departments?

The government's reply was as follows:

> There are no definite plans for the establishment of an archives and library for the use of scholars at Louisbourg during the restoration phase, although such a project has been suggested as a possible desirable development subsequent to reconstruction. Any eventual implementation of this proposal is so far in the future that no detailed estimates of cost, space required, staff, etc. have yet been considered. What books, plans and documents have already been acquired

were secured solely to assist in the production of a valid restoration.[44]

This answer might appear evasive in light of the longstanding intention to move the Historical Section to Louisbourg. Meanwhile, in 1964, rumours had begun to circulate in Ottawa that if the Section remained yet another year in the capital city, the research library, archives, and map collection would be in danger of transfer to a central branch library because of space problems.[45] Estimates were that the growing archival research collection would require 600 square feet of floor space.[46] Late in 1963, Thorpe and Bickerton argued most convincingly that the restoration could not progress unless archival research was accelerated by means of a substantial staff increase.[47] In January 1964, Wayne Foster and Chris E. Thomas surveyed the holdings of the Nova Scotia Archives; in June, Pothier went to New Hampshire and Vermont; then, beginning in July and October respectively, Julian Gwyn in England and Louise Miville-Dechêne in France embarked upon fresh collection sorties into the archives of Europe.[48]

It was also in 1964 that C.G. Lucas was appointed as Archivist and Acting Collections Historian in the Research Section, marking the assignment of archival duties to the full-time attention of a single individual.[49] Subsequently, in 1965 Lucas undertook a fresh American collection trip to the William Clements Library in Michigan, the City of New York, and a number of New England societies and libraries.[50] In September 1965, he issued the project's first comprehensive inventory of its archival holdings, a forty-two page report which provided brief descriptions of the collections and also noted the policies that had been followed in gathering and reproducing material.[51]

Some time in late 1965 or early 1966, the department finally set the spring of 1966 as the date for the transfer of the Research Section.[52] Unfortunately, only one staff member in Ottawa, Blaine Adams, decided to move to Louisbourg, while the others sought employment elsewhere. Adams arrived in Louisbourg as "Custodian of the archives and maps" on 16 May 1966. His immediate work was to reconstitute the archival and library collections from Ottawa and to organize the books and periodicals that were already in Louisbourg.[53] In addition to his duties as Administrative Historian, he was to be responsible for the security, operation, and supervision of the library and its staff, the purchase of books and archival materials, the proper deposition of reports in the project's vault, and the "manuscript and cartographic holdings and other historic material" of the archives.[54]

The material from Ottawa that Adams was to sort and organize consisted of 250 reels of microfilm and 43 boxes of photocopied documents from the archives of France, England, the United States, and Canada.[55] Another 181 reels of negative microfilm still at headquarters would be transferred to the Public Archives Records Centre in Ottawa, and would not be sent to Louisbourg until 1968.[56] In addition, he received a number of bound guides as well as 36 drawers of index cards required for locating information and 527 maps and plans relating to Louisbourg.[57] So extensive was this collection that, according to Lucas, failure to read his inventory would result in a researcher becoming "quite lost in a maze of drawers, boxes and cabinets whose contents ... [would] remain a mystery to him."[58]

In the summer of 1967, Adams left his dual administrative-archivist position.[59] He emphasized on his departure that there should be an evaluation of the archives, keeping in mind the possibilities of reorganization, systemization and additional indexing in order to lead researchers to possible sources of information.[60] Making the matter even more urgent were two factors indicating that the collection had still considerable potential for growth. First, Dilys Francis, a researcher, had, during 1965 and 1966, conducted a survey of remaining sources in England, and had enumerated a wide variety of manuscript documents which the Research Section should acquire.[61] Second, sections such as Engineering or Interpretation were producing a growing body of research-like data, including architectural drawings, background studies and photographs designed to meet their own particular in-house project requirements.[62] Circulation controls were loose, however, and some began to express concern that there would be a loss of important data unless there was a tightening up of procedures.[63]

There being no immediate replacement of Adams as archivist, once again there was "no one who ... [was] sufficiently familiar with the archives ... able to direct the others to possible sources of information."[64] Yet the necessity for proper archival control was becoming increasingly critical in view of the collection's obvious potential for growth. A report by Adams himself in 1967 stressed that there was still plenty of Louisbourg material in the provinces of France.⁶⁵ In the same year, too, Superintendent John Lunn pointed out that keen appreciation of the holdings of the archives would be essential to produce the historical reports necessary to Louisbourg's interpretive programme.⁶⁶ Meanwhile, the research staff continued to amass numerous copies of documents.⁶⁷

Shortly after his arrival in 1968, the project's new Research Director, John Fortier, addressed the problem directly:

> One of the two positions urgently required by Research is that of Archivist. It is inconceivable that a Project of our magnitude should not have someone to organize our archives and continue to search for source material in other repositories. This position was filled while the History Unit was in Ottawa, but it has been vacant since early 1966 [actually 1967]. The understandable inability of our present staff to organize our archival holdings at the same time as they use them is a serious liability to our operations and a cause of much duplicated effort.⁶⁸

As a result of Fortier's lobbying, Paul Rose began work as contract archivist on 25 November 1968.⁶⁹ His *Guide to the Louisbourg Archives: A Preliminary Inventory of Holdings*, published in February 1970, included all the previously mentioned records copied from the archives and/or historical societies of France, Great Britain, the United States, and Canada; information found in both contemporary and modern periodicals, newspapers, pamphlets, maps and photographs; additional material produced by the work of follow-up research trips such as that of Peter Bower to Massachusetts in 1967-68 and fresh documentation resulting from new discovery trips such as those of Nicole Durand and H. Paul Thibault to the Province of Quebec in 1969.⁷⁰ Rose also included inventories of the map collection and a number of original compilations in reader-printed, bound, and file box formats.

When Rose conducted his survey of the holdings at the Fortress, the Louisbourg Archives was responsible only for the deposits made by the Research Section. As a result, most of the material it was protecting consisted of eighteenth-century manuscripts reproduced on microfilm, a medium which reflected the Research Section's pioneering use of film in the 1960s as a relatively inexpensive and rapid means of copying selected documentation.⁷¹ Microfilming was also a procedure that did not require large teams of researchers abroad as would have been the case with the more traditional time-consuming method of manual recording and indexing of material.[72]

After Rose left the project, his replacement, Gilles Proulx, undertook to produce an enhanced, descriptive inventory of the map collection and to create a new architectural reference collection by assimilating non-Louisbourg plans, photos, and drawings which staff had been hoarding in their offices as a result of confusing "organization with physical location."[73] As Fortier pointed out, the archivist, rather than individuals exercising rights of possession, was the appropriate person to organize architectural drawings as a normal part of his job function.[74] His comments, however, reveal that project personnel did not yet regard the archives as the proper deposit and retrieval agency for all of the Louisbourg research materials.

The next people from the project to examine European holdings were researchers John and Brenda Dunn, who went to England in 1970, and graphics supervisor Paul Jeddrie, sent to France in 1972.[75] The purpose of Dunns' trip was to review newly discovered material at the Public Record Office. The result of Jeddrie's expedition was to update substantially the project's historical Map and Plan Collection, and to confirm that between 30 and 40 per cent "of the relevant maps and plans, and doubtless a similar proportion of the documents, have never been seen on this side of the Atlantic ... missed in the [major] copying efforts that were suspended in 1966."[76] As a result of Jeddrie's work and of a service contract with Raymonde Litalien, Proulx flew to France in 1974 to extend the project's archival holdings.[77]

Up to this time, the Fortress had emphasized "research, Reconstruction and the Administration of the Project."[78] However, the Fortress was beginning to move from a reconstruction project to the status of an operational park of National Historic Site significance. This future role was particularly apparent in light of plans for an accelerated park interpretive programme.[79] As this changed purpose gained momentum, support grew for an operational organization that included a permanent archival component. In 1973, a Louisbourg Task Force recognized that the size of both the documentary and artefactual collections made them "the most important repository of 18th century culture outside France itself," and concluded that "a continued small archaeological/historical establishment" at Louisbourg was virtually inevitable.[80] As a result, the

Task Force recommended the creation of one permanent archivist/librarian position.[81]

Proulx left the project in 1975, and Eric Krause unofficially assumed responsibility for the day-to-day operation of the archives in addition to his regular duties as historian.[82] Later, in February 1977, one result of the "growing awareness of the conservation maintenance requirements of the project" and future operational park was the proposal to create the permanent position of Historical Records Supervisor, with a support staff consisting of one librarian/archives technician and, later, one part-time archives clerk to deal exclusively with the extensive photo collection.[83] Appointed in an acting capacity in 1977, Krause became Historical Records Supervisor on 6 June 1978.[84]

In 1982, the Fortress of Louisbourg became a fully operational National Historic Park. Final development costs has escalated from the original allotment of $12 million in 1962 to $26 million in 1982. The estimated book value of the reconstruction was $45 million.[85] This change from fortress reconstruction project to National Historic Sites park enhanced the value and image of the Louisbourg archives for a number of reasons. The early 1980s witnessed a tremendous expansion of the programme of interpreted authenticity, as well as a recognition of the financial and ethical obligations inherent in the faithful maintenance of reconstructed buildings, properties, streets, and military features. As a result, such programmes increasingly began to turn to the archives for information, and in return, the archives came to be more generally regarded as the safe place where sections like Exhibits, Engineering and Works, and a revamped multi-disciplinary Historical Resources Section could store their valuable documents for future recall. Beginning in 1983, a five-year programme of acquisition, description, and conservation intensified the movement of this type of documentation from all sections to the archives.[86]

By 1984, the archives was directly responsible for a collection estimated at 3,000 cubic feet.[87] Because of the limited space available, additional deposits were accepted on an as-needed basis rather than according to any predetermined systematic schedule. As a result, an even larger physical collection, including the extensive reconstruction drawings collection, remained outside archival protection, conservation, or control. In 1988, the state of this outside material remains much the same as it did in 1984, although a recent increase in the physical size of the archives has allowed for some major new deposits from sections other than Research.[88] So large and so important was the Historical Records Collection to the various park programmes that the archives was able to convince the department of the need to purchase a computer for the creation of "an archival/library catalogue data base to meet operational maintenance, research and interpretive demands from within and without the park, including other National Parks and Historic Sites."[89] The extent of the collection which will ultimately form this data bank is indicated by the archives' manually produced descriptive entries which, in 1984, inventoried some 54,000 negatives and transparencies, 6,100 photoprints, a variety of documents including an approximate 750,000 pages on microfilm, 150,000 genealogical name cards, and 4,900 picture file cards.[90]

Since 1961, the archives has followed a shifting path in its growth to meet the changing goals, first of a reconstruction project and now of an operational historic park. The research sortie which Proulx had undertaken in 1974 was to be followed by others, including those of A.J.B. Johnston to Montreal and Quebec in 1979; of Ken Donovan to Massachusetts and Montreal in 1980; and of Johnston to France in 1985.[91] Given the range of unexplored documentation, the future will undoubtedly witness yet further trips. Just as certainly, the archives will continue to accept important new depositions of internally-generated records, such as the central registry files and structural design team minutes of the Fortress, both of which contain historical information critical to the success of Louisbourg's authenticity-oriented interpretive and maintenance programmes. The archives serves not only as a repository of the memory of those who originally built and inhabited Louisbourg, but also as guardian of the records which document an endeavour unique in the annals of historical reconstruction.

Notes

1. I.C. Rand, *Report of Royal Commission on Coal* (Ottawa, 1960), pp. ix, 74, Appendix G.
2. G.L. Scott *et al*, "A Plan for the Restoration of the Fortress of Louisbourg and the Area Surrounding the Fortress which has Historical Significance," unpublished report PD-34 (Ottawa, 1960), pp. 2, 33-34. See also, FL, Record Box 6/7, Anon., "Material in Ottawa Relating to the Fortress and Town of Louisbourg, Preliminary Inventory -- April 1961," n.d.

LOUISBOURG ARCHIVES

3. Rand, *Report*, p. 46.
4. *Ibid.*, pp. 46-47.
5. *Ibid.*, p. 47.
6. *Ibid.*, p. 53.
7. R.G. Glencross, September 1963, quoted in "Interpreting 18th Century Louisbourg: A Compilation," unpublished report PD-34 (FL, 1985-86), n.p.
8. *Hansard*, 17 June 1961, p. 6481.
9. Glencross, September 1963, in "Interpreting."
10. FL, Central Registry, File 50, E.A. Côté, 27 October 1961.
11. *Ibid.*
12. B.C. Bickerton to Research Director, 13 May 1963, quoted in "Progress Reports," unpublished report PD-7 (FL, n.d.).
13. Ronald L. Way to J.R. Coleman, 10 August 1961, quoted in "Recommendations Concerning the Louisbourg Restoration Project," unpublished report R-6 (FL, 1961), p. 4; R.G. Glencross, "Fortress of Louisbourg Restoration Project Documentation," unpublished report R-6 (FL, 1961), p. 16.
14. FL, Central Registry, file 36, Blaine Adams, 2 June 1966; Way to Coleman, 7 May 1964.
15. FL, Work/Research Files, John Lunn Files, file R-2, Competition Posters, 61-2428, 61-499, and 61-500, n.d.
16. Department of Northern Affairs and Natural Resources, National Parks Branch, "Fortress of Louisbourg: Historical Background," unpublished report R-17 (Ottawa, 1960), pp. i-iii.
17. *Ibid.*, p. iv.
18. Way, "Recommendations," p. 22.
19. *Ibid.*, Ronald L. Way, "Research -- Fortress of Louisbourg Restoration," unpublished report H-H1 (FL, 1962), p. 3.
20. Way, "Recommendations," pp. 27-29, 31, Appendix A, p. 2; Way, "Research," p. 5.
21. Way, "Research," pp. 3, 5, 7.
22. FL, Central Registry, file 22/3-M1, A.D. Perry to the Director, August 1962; *ibid.*, file 325-5, A.D. Perry to F.J. Thorpe, 24 September 1962.
23. FL, Work/Research files, History files, David Perry to F.J. Thorpe, 13 July 1962; FL, Central Registry, file 288, F.J. Thorpe to A.D. Perry, 1 October 1962; F.J. Thorpe, 31 October 1962, quoted in "Progress Reports."
24. *Ibid.*, F.J. Thorpe to A.D. Perry, 7 December 1962; *ibid.*, B.C. Bickerton to Research Director, 13 May 1963.
25. James R. McCartney, "Reports on Manuscripts Pertaining to Louisbourg in the United States," unpublished report H-H49 (FL, 1963), pp. 1-21; F.J. Thorpe, 4 February 1963, quoted in "Progress Reports."
26. F.J. Thorpe, 25 October 1963, quoted in "Progress Reports"; F.J. Thorpe, "Research Report for July, 1963," n.d.
27. FL, Record Box 6/24, M.C. Rosenfield, "Research Report of New England Archives," ca. January 1964.
28. F.J. Thorpe, 4 February 1963, quoted in "Progress Reports."
29. R.G. Robertson to N.A. Robertson, 4 March 1963, quoted in "Interpreting"; FL, Record Box 5/14, Bernard Pothier to B.C. Bickerton, 9 January 1964.
30. FL, Central Registry, file France: Correspondence on Trip; F.J. Thorpe to Director, 5 March 1963; Bickerton to same, 13 May 1963; Pothier to same, 9 January 1964.
31. FL, Central Registry, file 36, F.J. Thorpe to A.D. Perry, 11 June 1963; see also

B.C. Bickerton to A.D. Perry, 3 June 1963, quoted in "Progress Reports."
32. Central Registry, Thorpe to Perry, 11 June 1963.
33. *Ibid.*
34. Bickerton, 3 June 1963 in "Progress Reports."
35. FL, Central Registry, file 36, F.J. Thorpe to A.D. Perry, 24 June 1963.
36. FL, Record Box 8/73, F.J. Thorpe to William H. Whitely, 11 January 1963; *ibid.*, F.J. Thorpe to Alberta Letts, 28 January 1963.
37. *Ibid.*, F.J. Thorpe to Miss A. Riley, 12 November 1963.
38. FL, Record Box 10/30, F.J. Thorpe to A.J. Reeve, 26 August 1963.
39. *Ibid.*
40. FL, Central Registry, file 36, F.J. Thorpe to A.D. Perry, 29 November 1963.
41. FL, Record Box 8/77, A.D. Perry to the Senior Historian, 25 August 1964; FL, Record Box 9/47, B.C. Bickerton to B. Payette, 10 June 1964.
42. FL, Record Box 10/30, J.R. Coleman to A.D. Perry, 24 June 1964.
43. *Ibid.*, Ronald L. Way to A.D. Perry, 8 October 1964.
44. FL, Central Registry, file 36, A.D. Perry to the Director, 16 October 1964.
45. *Ibid.*, A.D. Perry to Acting Research Director, 29 October 1964.
46. *Ibid.*, B.C. Bickerton to Mr. Nicol, 30 October 1964.
47. FL, Central Registry, file 36, F.J. Thorpe to A.D. Perry, 29 November 1963; B.C. Bickerton to Research Director, "Overseas Collection Program," unpublished report H-H4 (FL, 1965), p. 6.
48. FL, Record Box 6/6, Wendy Stevenson, 16 December 1963; *ibid.*, 6/7, Chris E. Thomas to Mr. Bickerton, 10 January 1964; *ibid.*, 6/24, B.A. Pothier to B.C. Bickerton, 22 June 1964; FL, Central Registry, file 32-51, B.C. Bickerton to Mr. Perry, 13 January 1965; FL, Ottawa Files, file Progress Report, Ronald L. Way to Project Manager, 23 June 1964; FL, Central Registry, file 51 (sub), Ronald L. Way to Project Manager, 14 April 1965; FL, Record Box 5/14, Louise Dechêne, 25 July 1965.
49. Perry, 16 October 1964 and 27 October 1964; FL, Record Box 8/77, "Regulations" [6 November 1964].
50. FL, Record Box 8/77, Glen Lucas, July-August 1965; B.C. Bickerton to Ronald L. Way, 4 May 1965, quoted in "Interpreting."
51. G. Lucas, "Preliminary Inventory of Holdings - Archives Louisbourg," unpublished report H-H5 (FL, 1965), pp. [1-42].
52. FL, Work/Research Files, History Unit Files, R.P. Malis to Director, 5 January 1966; *ibid.*, B.C. Bickerton to Staff, 24 January 1966.
53. Adams, 2 June 1966.
54. FL, Work/Research Files, History Unit files, Ronald L. Way to Blaine Adams, 27 June 1966; see also *ibid.*, Ronald L. Way to Blaine Adams, 7 October 1966; *ibid.*, Blaine Adams to Park Superintendent, 4 April 1967.
55. FL, Central Registry, file 5 (sub) programming, John Lunn to Director, 14 October 1966.
56. FL, Work/Research Files, History Unit files, L. LaClare to Blaine Adams, 25 October 1966; *ibid.*, Peter Bureau to R.S. Gordon, 4 April 1968 and 24 May 1968.
57. Lunn, 14 October 1966.
58. Lucas, "Preliminary Inventory," foreword.
59. FL, Work/Research Files, History Unit files, Blaine Adams to Park Superintendent, 4 April 1967.
60. *Ibid.*, FL, Work/Research Files, History Unit files, Linda Hoad to Park Superintendent, 16 August 1967; *ibid.*, Peter Bower to John Lunn, [1967].

61. FL, Record Box 6/26, Dilys Francis, 29 September 1966.
62. FL, Work/Research Files, History Unit files, Blaine Adams to File, 8 July 1966.
63. *Ibid.*, John Lunn to Section Heads, 17 November 1966; FL, Central Registry, file 22/3-M1, 19 September 1966.
64. FL, Work/Research Files, History Unit files, Linda Hoad to Park Superintendent, 16 August 1967.
65. FL, Work/Research Files, History Unit files, file Research Abroad, Blaine Adams to Research Director, 21 August 1967.
66. FL, Central Registry, file 28-5, John Lunn to Regional Director, 16 August 1967.
67. *Ibid.*, file 22/1-A, Peter Bureau to Park Superintendent, 26 July 1968; *ibid.*, Peter Bureau to Research Director, 22 August 1968.
68. John Fortier, 16 September 1968.
69. FL, Central Registry, file 22/1-A1, John Fortier to Park Superintendent, 25 November 1968; *ibid.*, John Fortier to Park Superintendent, 13 May 1969; file 22/6-1, Anon., "Fortress of Louisbourg National Historic Park -- Organization Chart," 19 June 1969; FL, Work/Research Files, History Unit files, John Fortier to Park Superintendent, 23 June 1969.
70. Paul Rose, "Guide to the Louisbourg Archives: A Preliminary Inventory of Holdings," unpublished report H-H8 (FL, 1970), pp. [1-77]; FL, Central Registry, file 22/1-P13, Peter Bower to Park Superintendent, 19 January 1968.
71. FL, Ottawa Files, file Archaeology, Edward McM. Larrabee to B.C. Bickerton, 14 November 1964; B.C. Bickerton to Ronald L. Way, 4 May 1965, quoted in "Interpreting"; Lunn, 17 April 1967.
72. Bickerton, "Overseas Collection Program," p. 3.
73. FL, Central Registry, file 22/1-S4.2, John Fortier to Park Superintendent, 14 October 1970; see also Gilles Proulx, "Archives de la Forteresse de Louisbourg/Collection Cartographic/Map Collection," unpublished report H-H9, 3 vols (FL, 1970); FL, Central Registry, file 22/3-M1, Gilles Proulx to Section Heads, 4 February 1971.
74. *Ibid.*, file 22/1-S4.2, Fortier to Superintendent, 14 October 1970.
75. FL, Central Registry, file 22/7-R1, L.H. Robinson to Superintendent, 24 August 1970; *ibid.*, file 22/7-A1, John Fortier to Park Superintendent, 3 August 1972; FL, Work/Research Files, History Unit files, Paul Jeddrie to Head of Research, 8 December 1972.
76. *Ibid.*, file Research Abroad, John Fortier to Park Superintendent, 27 February 1973; FL, Central Registry, file 22/1-78, John Fortier to Park Superintendent, 16 March 1973.
77. *Ibid.*, John Fortier to Senior Historian, 19 February 1974; *ibid.*, file 22/4-C2, Raymonde Litalien to Robert J. Morgan, 22 September 1972; Gilles Proulx, 8 August 1974, in "Historical Records Series," unpublished report H-H15 (FL, 1978), item 11.
78. Department of Indian and Northern Affairs, "Management Improvement Study for National and Historic Park Branch: Fortress of Louisbourg," unpublished report PD-10-S ([Ottawa], 1969), p. 4; see also the "Preliminary Report," PD-10.
79. FL, Work/Research Files, History Unit files, John Fortier to Park Superintendent, 2 July 1969.
80. Louisbourg Task Force, "Recommended and Reduced Postures Development and O & M (Plus Long-Range Development Costs)," unpublished report I-25 (FL, 1973).
81. *Ibid.*

82. FL, Work/Research, History Unit files, file Personnel Records -- Proulx, n.d.
83. Bill O'Shea, "Park Organization, Operational Period," unpublished report PD-53 (FL, 1979); see also Anon., February 1977, quoted in "Interpreting."
84. FL, Work/Research Files, History Unit files, P.A. Thompson to E. Krause, 22 August 1978.
85. Susan Cann et al., "The Fortress of Louisbourg: A Development Project," unpublished report PD-64 (Halifax, 1983), pp. 12-14.
86. FL, Central Registry, file 1730-1 (84/89), Parks Canada, "Multi-Year Operational Plan (MYOP), F.Y. 1984-1989, Capital, Fortress of Louisbourg," 12 November 1982.
87. *Ibid.*, file 1730-1-1, Eric Krause, 19 November 1984.
88. *Ibid.*, file 1732-1, Eric Krause to John Johnston, 15 February 1985.
89. *Ibid.*, file 1730-1-1, attachment to Eric Krause, 19 November 1984.
90. *Ibid.*
91. *Ibid.*, file 8440-1, A.J.B. Johnston to Franciscan Fathers, 18 December 1978; *ibid.*, Ken Donovan to Terry MacLean et al., 15 September 1980; *ibid.*, Ken Donovan to Bill O'Shea et al., 14 October 1980; *ibid.*, A.J.B. Johnston to Valerie Hunt, 10 May 1984.

Louisbourg, the nascent fishing port, circa 1716-17. The peninsular town is established. Wharves, ships, and flakes for the drying of fish are in abundance. Fishermen and merchants have grabbed the prime waterfront land. Poles have been set on four hills to mark the trace for the future landward-facing fortifications. The scrub forest, once reaching almost to the shoreline, has begun to recede.[1]

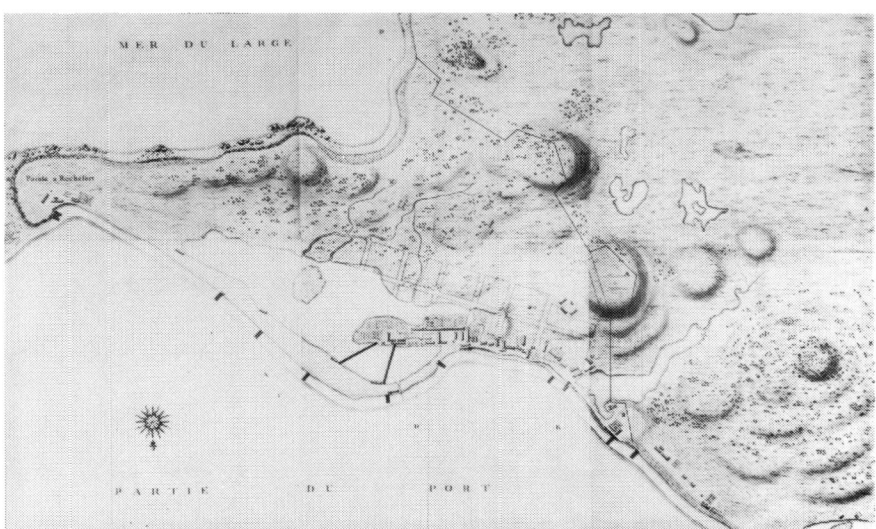

Conceptual development scheme for **le poste le plus important**, *1717. The fortifications, a classic bastioned trace, and the townsite take precedence over existing buildings. Standing buildings "out of alignment" with the grid were soon to be ordered "into alignment." The Fauxbourg, Louisbourg's suburb to the north, was tolerated, though not on a grid.*[2]

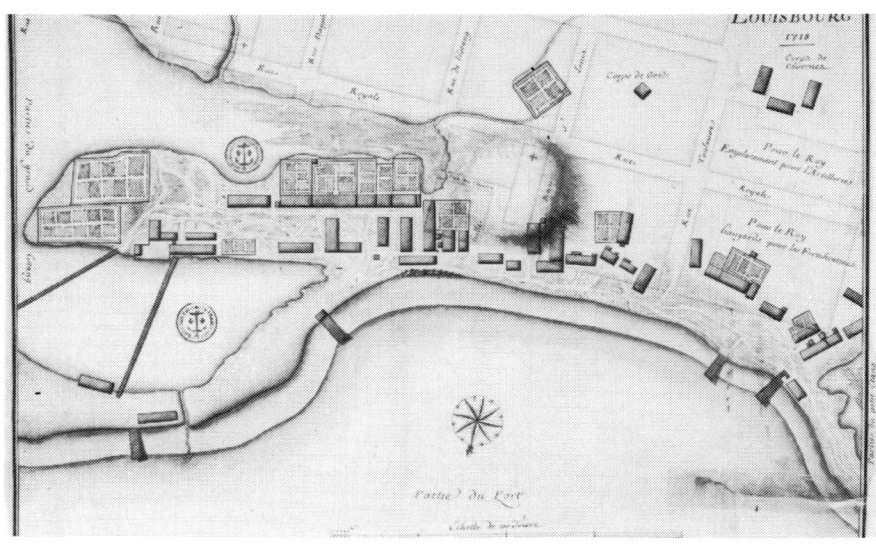

Waterfront development, 1718. A scattering of buildings and garden plots on land that was to serve a particular purpose: be it as a king's building, quay, market, fortification, cemetery, or simply open terrain. [3]

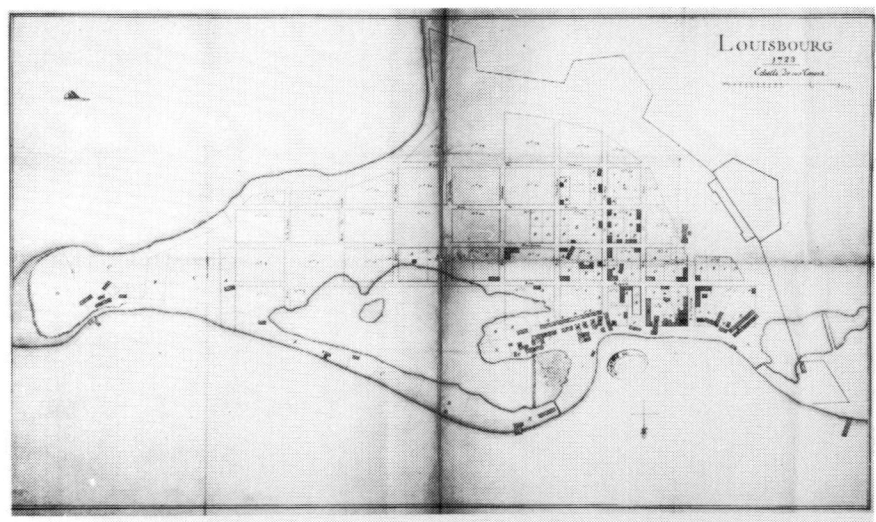

A symmetrical dream, 1723. On paper, more than a dozen intersecting streets, more than forty town blocks. In truth, many buildings were still "out of alignment," standing among meandering streets. [4]

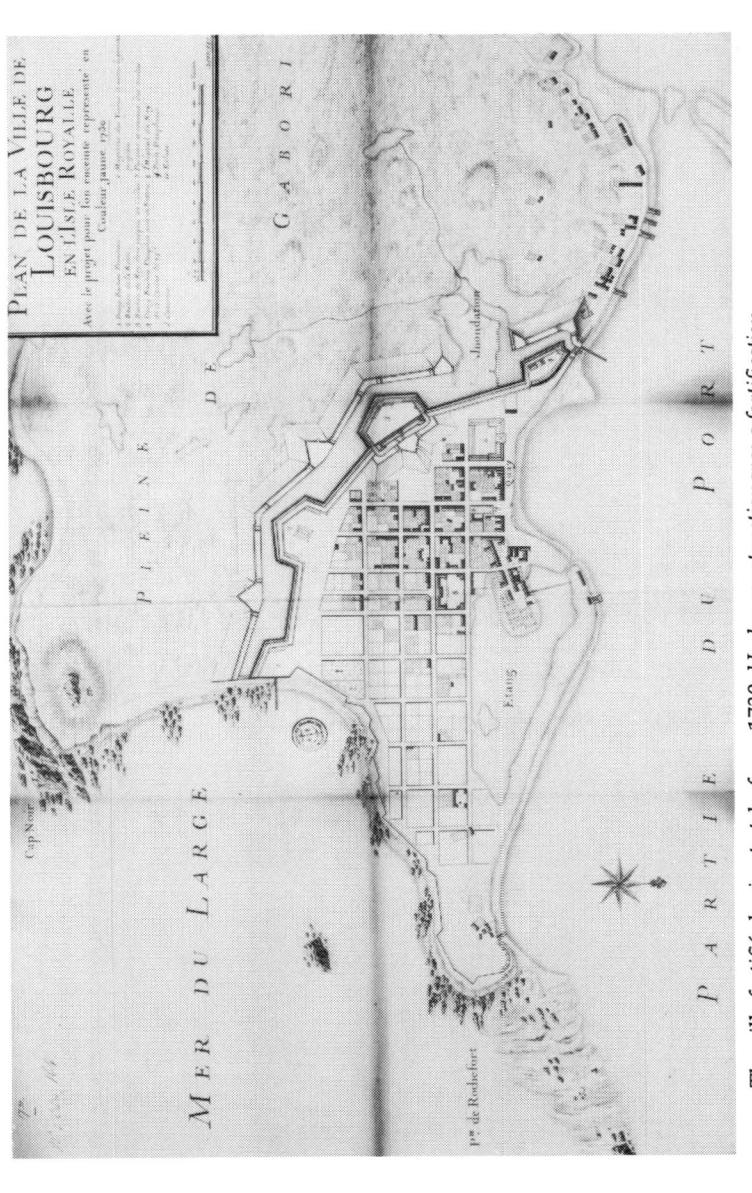

The *ville fortifiée* begins to take form, 1730. Under construction was a fortification line to form a double-crown work, a partial enceinte consisting of two full bastions occupying the centre, a half bastion on the harbour shore, and a half-bastion on the open coast. Within the fortifications was urban renewal: new construction replacing first construction, and on the approved grid.[5]

A proud Verrier fils, son of the chief engineer of Louisbourg, paints his town, 1731. Rising upwards are solid-looking buildings. The tallest of all are the King's Bastion Barracks and the King's Hospital, both topped by spires. Less formidable, but as appreciated, in between, the spire of the home of the Sisters of the Congregation of Notre-Dame.[6]

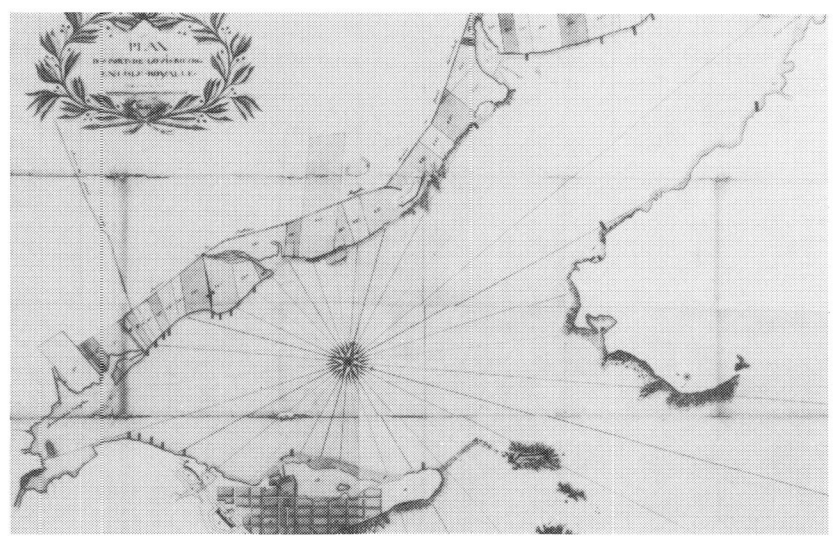

Not just an enclosed town, circa 1734. Ringing the harbour were fishing properties which held as many as twenty to thirty percent of total population prior to the first siege. After 1745, their share of the population lowered to just thirteen percent.[7]

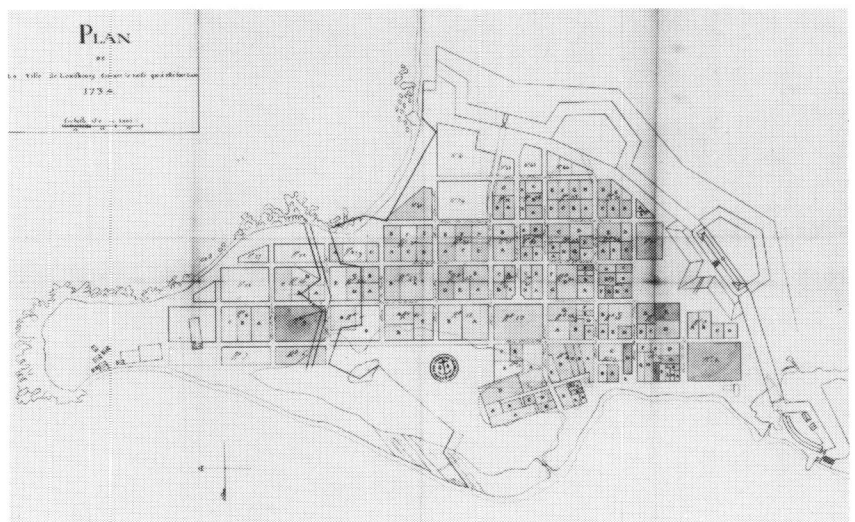

The official survey, 1734. By order of his Most Christian Majesty, King Louis XV himself, a proper survey of Louisbourg was undertaken to protect his interests, lest he continue his greater than decade long refusal to confirm property ownership. A proposed extension of the town's defences across the tip of the peninsula will result in expropriations.[8]

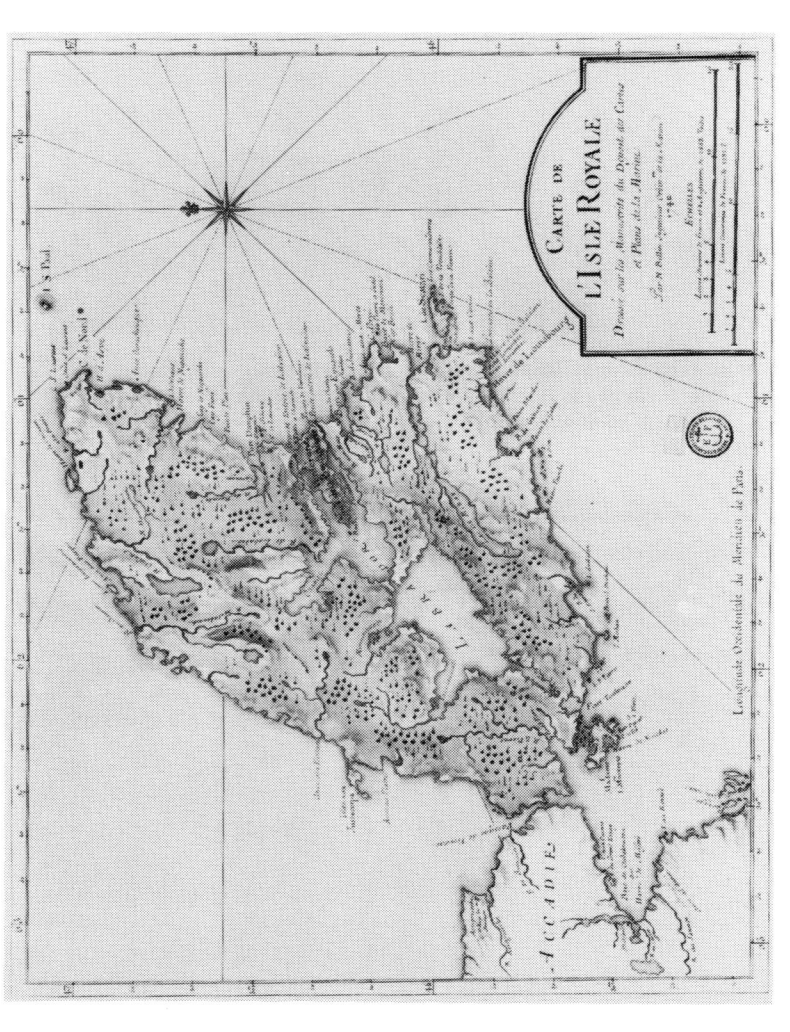

The Royal Island, mostly Atlantic coast settled, 1742. The dispersed pattern of coastal fishing settlements, where nearly all derived their living from the fishery, destined Louisbourg for entrepôt status.

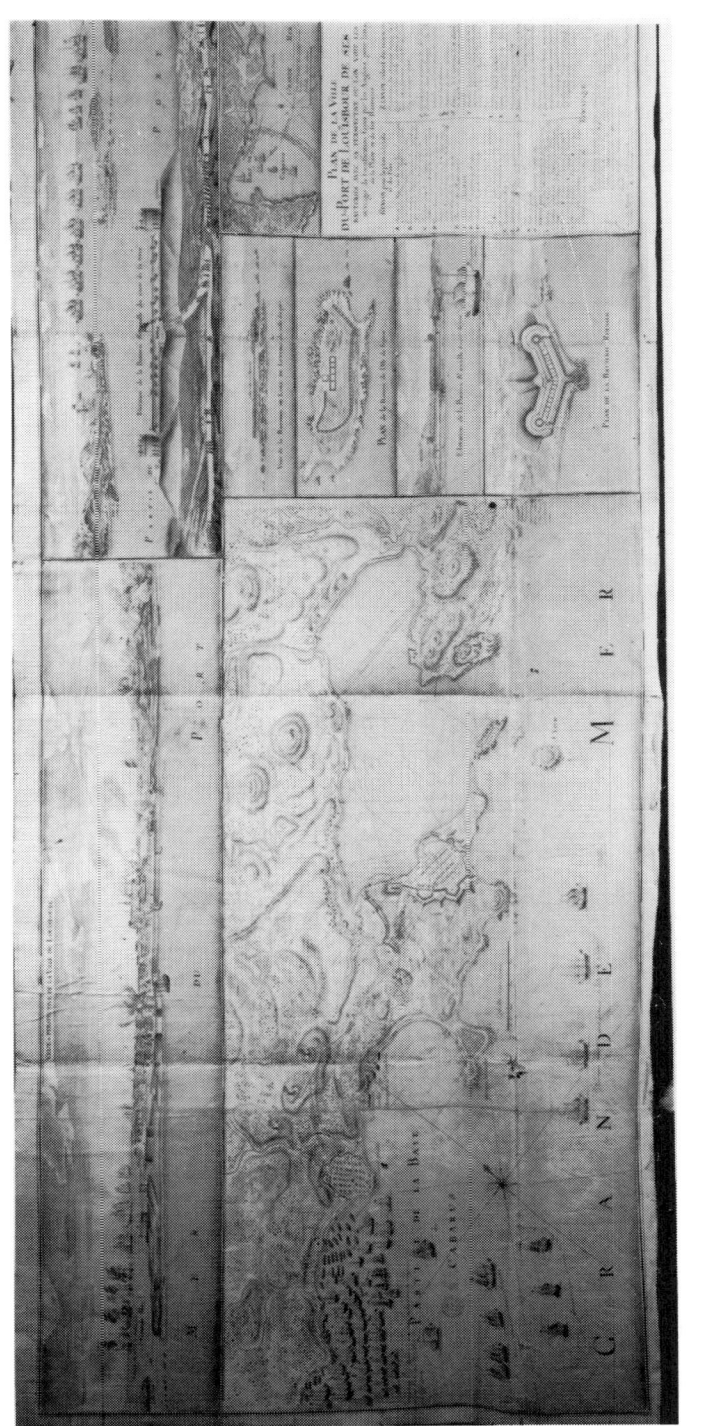

Ordeal, 1745. A six-week siege, complete with all the features of a swashbuckling epic, concludes with a systematic pounding of the town, placing its very being in serious doubt. No one is safe in a place shaped like an amphitheatre, open to the raking fire of cannonballs and musketry from surrounding heights.

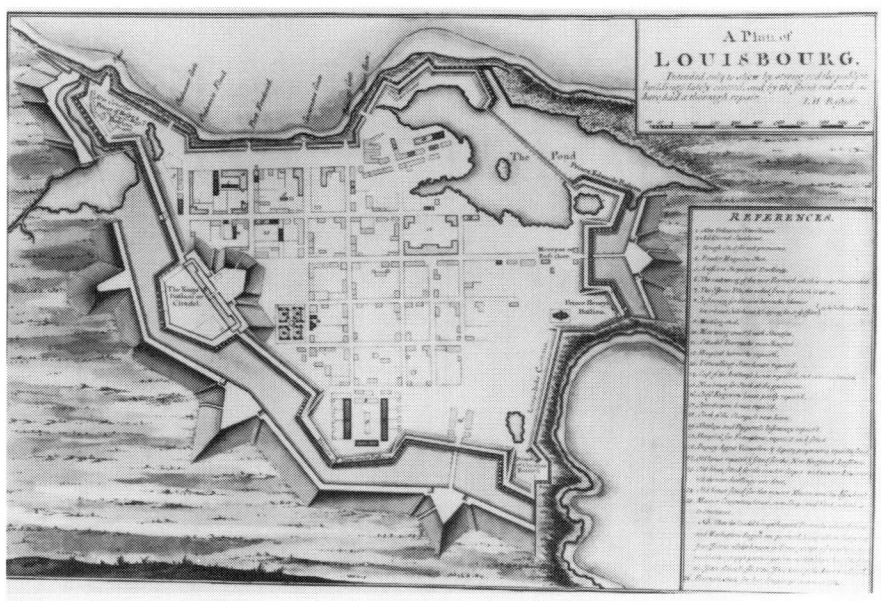

The fully enclosed fortified French town under New England and British rule, 1746. The occupying forces repair, construct, and neglect Louisbourg as they so choose. Some new work includes prefabricated buildings brought up from New England, re-assembled in Louisbourg, and abandoned, in 1748-9, for the use of the returning French.[11]

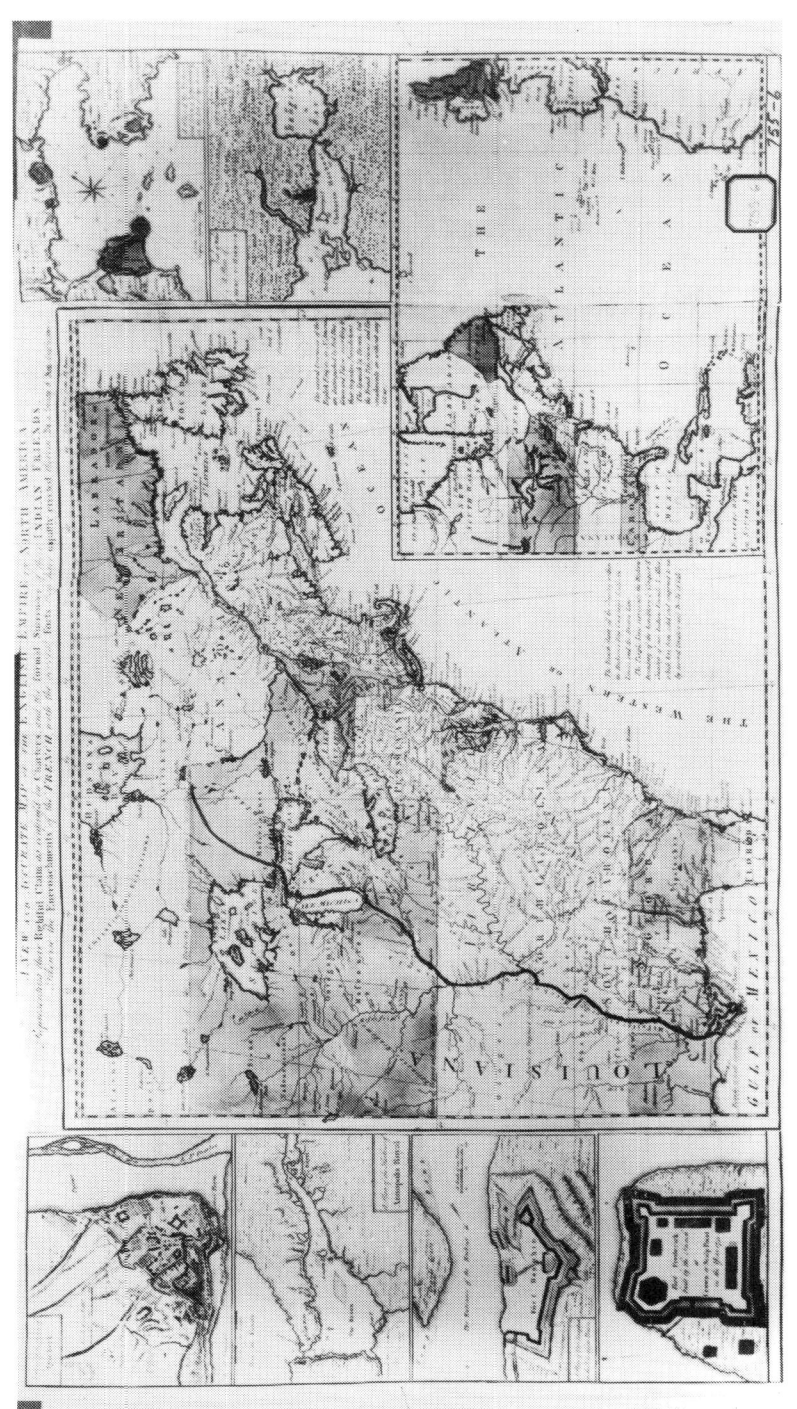

The world of Isle Royale, 1755. Its trading partners were France, the French West Indies, New England, Canada, and Acadia; its life line —the North American and European cod fishing grounds.[12]

Notes

1. Photo courtesy of the Edward E. Ayer Collection, The Newberry Library, Ayer MS Map 118, c. 1716-17. *Veüe du Port de Louisbourg dans L'Isle Royalle.*
2. Photo courtesy of the AN, Outre-Mer, DFC, IV-145, 1717. *PLAN DE LA GRANDE GRAUE DE LOUISBOURG Avec le Principal trait des fortifications & les lignes des profils Marquées.*
3. Photo courtesy of the AN, Outre-Mer, DFC, IV-146, 1718. *HABITATIONS DE LOUISBOURG 1718.*
4. Photo courtesy of the AN, Col., C^{11}A, Vol. 126, fol. 212, 1723. *LOUISBOURG 1723.*
5. Photo courtesy of the AN, Outre-Mer, DFC, IV-164, 1730. *PLAN DE LA VILLE DE LOUISBOURG EN L'ISLE ROYALLE Avec le projet pour fon enceinte representé en Couleur jaune 1730.*
6. Photo courtesy of Bibliothèque Nationale de France, Paris, Cartes & Plans, GeC. 5019, 1731. *VEüE DE LA VILLE DE LOUISBOURG PRISE EN DEDANS DU PORT 1731.*
7. Photo courtesy of AN, Col., C^{11}A, Vol. 126, ff. 263-266, c. 1730-1735. *PLAN.DV.PORT.DE.LOVISBOVRG.ENLISLE.ROYALLE.*
8. Photo courtesy of AN, Outre-Mer, DFC, IV-183, 1734. *PLAN DE LA ville de Louisbourg suivant le toisé quiá esté fait LAN. 173.4.*
9. Photo courtesy of Bibliothèque Nationale de France, Paris, Cartes & Plans, Service Historique, 131-2-6, 1742. *CARTE DE L'ISLE ROYALE Dressée sur les Manuscrits du Depost des Cartes et Plans dela Marine Par N. Bellin Ingenieur Ordin.^{re} dela Marine 1742.*
10. Photo courtesy of Bibliothèque Nationale de France, Paris, Cartes & Plans, Service Historique, 131-2-6, 1745. *PLAN DE LA VILLE et DU PORT DE LOUISBOURG DE SES BATTERIES AVEC SA PERSPECTIVE OU L'ON VOIT LES ouvrages de fortifications faites par les Anglois pour lattaque de la Place et de ses Batteries.*
11. Photo courtesy of Beinecke Rare Book and Manuscript Library, Yale University Library, New Haven, CT., ca. 1746. *A Plan of Louisbourg. Intended only to shew by strong red the publick buildings lately erected, and by faint red such as have had a thorough repair.*
12. Photo courtesy of the William L. Clements Library, University of Michigan, 1755. *A NEW AND ACCURATE MAP OF THE ENGLISH EMPIRE IN NORTH AMERICA Representing their Rightful Claim as confirm'd by Charters, and the formal Surrender of their INDIAN FRIENDS, Likewise the Encroachments of the FRENCH, with the several Forts they have unjustly erected therein ....*